Innovation Ecosystems in the New Economic Era

PETER LANG

Brussels • Berlin • Lausanne • New York • Oxford

Business & Innovation

Vol. 31

The creation of new activities, of news production and consumption modes, of new goods and services, of new markets and new jobs (etc.) depends as much on the heroic action of entrepreneurs as on the strategies of big corporations which develop their activities at a global scale. Innovation and business are interlinked. The main themes of the books published in this series are: Entrepreneurship, enterprise and innovation; Innovation strategies in a global context; Innovation policies and business climate; Innovation, business dynamics and socio-economic change. The synergies between innovative entrepreneurship, firms' strategies and innovation policies is of major importance in the explanation of technological paradigms change and of the transformations in economic and social structures of wealthy and less wealthy countries. In this series are published books in English or in French specialized in economics, management and sociology of innovation and also dealing with change and entrepreneurship in a local, national or international perspective.

This series is supported by the Research Network on Innovation.

Laurent Adatto, Camille Aouinaït,
Son Thi Kim Le and Michelle Mongo (Eds.)

Innovation Ecosystems in the New Economic Era

Digital Revolution and Ecological Transition

Business and Innovation
Vol. 31

Bibliographic information published by "Die Deutsche Nationalbibliothek".
"Die Deutsche National Bibliothek" lists this publication in the "Deutsche Nationalbibliografie"; detailed bibliographic data is available on the Internet at <http://dnb.de>.

Publié avec le soutien du Réseau de Recherche sur l'Innovation (RRI) et de l'Université du Littoral Côte d'Opale (ULCO)

ISBN 978-2-87574-524-8 • ISSN 2034-5402
E-ISBN 978-2-87574-525-5 (ePDF) • E-ISBN 978-2-87574-526-2 (ePUB)
• DOI 10.3726/b20656
D/2023/5678/05

International Academic Publishers
Bruxelles, 2023
1 avenue Maurice, B-1050 Brussels, Belgium
brussels@peterlang.com

This publication has been peer reviewed.

www.peterlang.com

Table of Contents

List of Contributors

Laurent ADATTO, Researcher, Research centre on Innovation and Industrial Strategies (ISI/Lab.RII), University of Littoral Côte d'Opale, Research Network on Innovation, France.
Email: lradatto@yahoo.com

Raffaele ANEDDA, Researcher, Applied Economics Department, ENSTA Paris - Institut Polytechnique de Paris, France.
Email: raffa.anedda@gmail.com

Camille AOUINAÏT, Researcher in Economics and Management of Innovation at AGROSCOPE, Switzerland and Research Network on Innovation, France.
Email: camille.aouinait@gmail.com

Sophie BOUTILLIER, Professor of Innovation and Entrepreneur Economics, University of Littoral Côte d'Opale, Research Network of Innovation, France.
Email: sophie.boutillier@univ-littoral.fr

Jean-Michel DEGEORGE, Lecturer and Research Director, Mines Saint-Etienne, MRI Department, Institut Henri Fayol - Coactis Laboratory EA 4161, France.
Email: jean-michel.degeorge@emse.fr

Abdelaziz ELABJANI, Professor of Entrepreneurship and Business Creation, Research Director, FSJES Marrakesh, Department of Law, Economics and Social Sciences, Cadi Ayyad University, Morocco.
Email: aelabjani@gmail.com

Valérie LAFOREST, Professor and Research Director, Mines Saint-Etienne, Université Lyon, Université Jean Moulin, Université Lumière,

Université Jean Monnet, ENTPE, INSA Lyon, ENS Lyon, CNRS, UMR 5600 EVS, Institut Henri Fayol, Département GEO, France.
Email: valerie.laforest@mines-stetienne.fr

Stephanie LANG, Research Associate, Department of Innovation Economics, University of Hohenheim, Stuttgart, Germany.
Email: stephanie_lang@uni-hohenheim.de

Blandine LAPERCHE, Professor of Innovation Economics, Research centre on Innovation and Industrial Strategies (ISI/Lab.RII), University of Littoral Côte d'Opale, President of Research Network on Innovation (http://2ri.eu), France.
Email: blandine.laperche@univ-littoral.fr

Son Thi Kim LE, Lecturer-Researcher, Research centre on Innovation and Industrial Strategies (ISI/Lab.RII), ISCID-CO Business School, University of Littoral Côte d'Opale (ISI/Lab.RII), Research Network on Innovation, France.
Email: sontk.le@univ-littoral.fr

Didier LEBERT, Associate Professor and Associate Director, Applied Economics Department, ENSTA Paris - Institut Polytechnique de Paris and i3-CRG Ecole Polytechnique - CNRS (UMR 9217), France.
Email: didier.lebert@ensta-paris.fr

Yassine MEHROS, PhD Student in Management Science, LIRE-MD and COACTIS Laboratory EA 4161, Jean Monnet University, France.
Email: mehros.yassine@gmail.com

Michelle MONGO, Lecturer-Researcher, Mines Saint-Etienne, Institut Henri Fayol - Coactis Laboratory EA 4161, France.
Email: michelle.mongo@emse.fr

Florin PAUN, PhD, Economist, Scientific Collaboration Director, ARESIA, France.
Email: info@florin-paun.com

Eric PIATYSZEK, Lecturer, Mines Saint-Etienne, Université Lyon, Université Jean Moulin, Université Lumière, Université Jean Monnet,

ENTPE, INSA Lyon, ENS Lyon, CNRS, UMR 5600 EVS, Institut Henri Fayol, Département GEO, France.
Email: eric.piatyszek@mines-stetienne.fr

Andreas PYKA, Professor of Innovation Economics, Chair for Innovation Economics, University of Hohenheim, Stuttgart, Germany.
Email: a.pyka@uni-hohenheim.de

Jean-Claude RUANO-BORBALAN, Professor, Conservatoire National des Arts et Métiers (CNAM Paris), Chair of Mediation of Technology and Science in Society, France.
Email: jean-claude.ruano-borbalan@lecnam.net

Lea F. STÖBER, Researcher, Innovation Economics (520i), University of Hohenheim, Stuttgart, Germany.
Email: lea.stoeber@uni-hohenheim.de

Audrey TANGUY, Lecturer-Researcher, Mines Saint-Etienne, Université Lyon, Université Jean Moulin, Université Lumière, Université Jean Monnet, ENTPE, INSA Lyon, ENS Lyon, CNRS, UMR 5600 EVS, Institut Henri Fayol, Département GEO, France.
Email: audrey.tanguy@emse.fr

Cheikh Abdou Lahad THIAW, Researcher, Polytechnic School (ESP) / Cheikh Anta Diop University (UCAD), Senegal.
Email: cheikh.thiaw@esp.sn

Dimitri UZUNIDIS, Professor of Innovation Economics and of Political Economy, Research Network on Innovation, France.
Email: dimitri.uzunidis@univ-littoral.fr

Ingrid VAILEANU, Economist, Co-founder and President of Xvaluator, France.
Email: news@interviewfrancophone.net

General Presentation: Innovation Ecosystems in a Changing World: Concepts, Contexts, and Perspectives

1. Definition of innovation ecosystems

The modern era is marked by a decrease in the share of tangible capital in favor of intangible capital. This evolution is mainly stimulated by investments in training, R&D, and dissemination of knowledge (David & Foray, 2002; Laperche & Uzunidis, 2007). The research field of the knowledge economy is particularly well suited to the analysis of this dynamic. Indeed, the knowledge economy emphasizes intangible elements related to the production of knowledge, scientific contributions, technical skills, and "human capital" (Foray, 2013). Moreover, information as an intangible asset has also been at the center of the digital revolution, shaping much of economic evolution for several decades. This informational and digital revolution involves a restructuring of economic actors around the generation, storage, processing, and transfer of information (Grange & Sponem, 2021). With its roots in the industrial boom of the 1960s, during the 1980s the informational and digital revolution allowed the introduction of new technologies that support or replace activities that had previously been performed solely by humans (Boccara, 2016; Grange & Sponem, 2021). Thus, the information and communication technologies arising from the digital revolution are laying the foundations of a new network economy (Muet, 2006), the knowledge economy being correlated with these innovative processes.

Indeed, innovation is the key factor in this new context, conditioning the prospects for economic growth (Uzunidis, 2008a), and this at the macro, meso, and micro-economic levels. In its organizational and service forms, it also contributes to the social dynamics of innovative territories (Mongo, 2021).

Relating to the Oslo Manual (2018), "Innovation refers to a new or improved product or business process (or combination thereof) that differs significantly from the unit's previous products or processes and that has been commercialized or implemented by the firm" (OECD, 2018).

From a theoretical point of view, the problem of innovation has been the subject of an abundant literature aimed in particular at characterizing its conditions of emergence. Initially developed by Schumpeter (1939), the analysis of innovation processes has gradually evolved from an individualistic and linear vision to a more systemic one. Indeed, innovation process is now mainly expressed in terms of a "system", characterized in particular by its capacity for change, especially technical, managerial, and organizational. It is connected to a complex set of innovation actors constituting an innovation ecosystem (Laperche et al., 2019). There is no single definition of innovation ecosystems. In a recent review of nearly 120 publications on innovation ecosystems, Granstrand & Holgersson (2020) identify 21 definitions of innovation ecosystems. Based on these definitions, the authors conclude that: "An innovation ecosystem is the evolving set of actors, activities, and artifacts, and the institutions and relations, including complementary and substitute relations that are important for the innovative performance of an actor or a population of actors".

In addition, innovation ecosystems can be generated at different scales.

At the macro-economic level, it is the National Innovation System (NIS) that forms the innovation ecosystem (Laperche et al., 2019). In this framework, innovation results from the connection and interactions between different actors (notably institutional, political, research, and economic) in the same country (Bengt-Åke, 2007) and for which innovation dynamics are at work (Laperche & Uzunidis, 2007). The meso-economic level is characterized by a Local Innovation System (including regional innovation systems, industrial districts, and innovative environments) in which the relationships that link the different actors of the system have a very strong operational dimension (Uzunidis, 2008b). Sectoral systems can be added that link the institutional representatives of a profession (in particular professional unions) with public authorities and companies. These interconnections between actors contribute to the territorial dynamics of innovation (Breschi & Malerba, 1998). Finally, the micro-economic level refers to an innovation system centered on the firm. In this system, companies form a coalition around the pivotal actor who has succeeded in imposing his standard, while at the same time creating value for his partners through processes of coopetition (which combine both competition and cooperation, in particular through sub-contracting and co-contracting activities). In this context, we speak of a business ecosystem (Moore, 1993; Boutillier et al., 2015).

These different innovation systems can be interconnected and lead to the formation of innovation networks in which actors interact through processes of "translation" referring to the sociology of innovation (Callon, 1986).

2. Definition of the digital age in relation to the challenge of planet protection

Innovations linked to the digital sector are notably the vector of the Fourth Industrial Revolution. This digital revolution is notably allowed by the new steps of: the processing power of computer chips, IT devices progress, Artificial Intelligence, 3D printing, quantum computing, and an always greater interconnection of vast and faster networks, from Internet to 5G and the Internet of Things. In relation to this, the Fourth Industrial Revolution generates a whole multitude of innovative applications, transforming everyday life, and which is notably related to an almost unlimited economic potential.

These innovative applications building on IT contain major assets to provide solutions to planetary, environmental, and care issues that include global warming, a shortage of non-renewable resources, a better consideration of social and geographical inequities, and better access to health care. Regarding e-health and bio-medical progress driven by digital technologies, Artificial Intelligence is already interpreting MRI with a previously unknown precision. This innovation permits the preventive detection of infinitesimal signs of diseases, such as tumors in their first stages, which could not be detected by MRI human interpretation. In addition, innovations of robotics and Augmented Reality applied to the medical sector are already improving the efficiency of surgery tasks.

Among the innovative applications of the Fourth Industrial Revolution are those related to computer processing of the increasingly massive digital information deposits of Big Data. Advances in digital data treatments generate huge ranges of new services. These include smart-city and transport, to optimize the fluidity of travel, and thus to combat

CO2 emissions. Artificial Intelligence is a key for enabling autonomous transport and cars. Also e-agriculture, which builds on the robotization of agricultural machinery and drones to manage agricultural fields with less water and resources. Multiple agricultural devices can be linked together with the Internet of Things and satellites. There is a need for a rationalized consumption, which is less polluting, being processed by Big Data, as well as short circuits that are compatible with the conservation of the Earth's resources. Innovative smart sensors also contribute to the optimization of resources. Smart factories linked to digital applications will also provide better production management, in a more ecological and less resource-intensive way. The innovative concept of a digital twin allows us to simulate, in the virtual world, production requirements and impacts, for their optimization in the real world. The related flexibility of production will allow consumers to become end-user organizers for more sustainable on demand products. Furthermore, smart factories, through digital technology and 3D printing, will be integrated locally, with a view to establishing short circuits, and reducing the transport of goods and therefore of the linked pollution. Cloud Computing, which also allows on demand access to computing resources, has already generated a reduction in resources compared to a sector that would have produced additional occurrences of similar treatment, and therefore pollution. Thus, the current innovations of Green Computing aim to make this Fourth Industrial Revolution even more resource-efficient. In that way, IT devices can become less and less energy consuming and have a lower carbon footprint. This affects even the new cryptocurrencies, and related blockchain processes using planet-friendly technologies and resources.

Thus, this digital revolution will improve an efficient and ecological way to preserve the planet. And as we will see, related innovation ecosystems have a key role to contribute and accelerate this progress.

3. Importance of ecosystems in the era of digital and ecological transition and their particularities

The current era of digital – as in the age of the new scientific and technological revolution – has changed the way knowledge is explored and produced. The increasing connectedness and interdependence in the digital era has impacted on how knowledge is produced: the creation and dissemination of new knowledge happens in a much more distributed manner. It is not only more collaborative, but also more oriented toward transdisciplinary and interdisciplinary knowledge production (Gibbs, 2015). Given the importance of knowledge in the digital era, the majority of business has recognized that they must invest all their efforts and resources in developing new and innovative ideas. To be successful, the knowledge creation process, as well as innovation activities, thanks to the digital revolution, should be more "open". This reality, in turn, raises the importance of the ecosystem, especially business ecosystems.

The concept of the ecosystem, borrowed from biology, refers to "a group of interacting companies that depend on each other's activities" (Jacobides et al., 2018, p. 2256). Assessing an ecosystem at the level of companies, the development of a business ecosystem is more likely to depend on "open" and "collective" innovation (Chesbrough, 2003; Uzunidis, 2018). Digital transformations underway in our societies have largely disrupted the conditions of formation, organization, and deployment of innovation systems. Innovation can emerge and be marketed inside and outside the boundaries of the company through outside-in and inside-out strategies of open innovation and coupled with open innovation. In the age of digital technologies, innovation should be nurtured within an ecosystem meant for the co-creation of value through collaboration. The novelty-generating interactions and collaborations in a business ecosystem all aim at reinforcing the knowledge capital of companies (Laperche, 2017).

In addition, the climate crisis and its sometimes-irreversible effects on ecosystems (IPCC, 2018) warn about the end of a linear growth model that is aimed at "produce, consume and throw away" in order to move toward the model of circular economy that tends to minimize resource waste and environmental impact while improving efficiency at all stages of the production process (Gallaud & Laperche, 2016). This is the principle of the circular economy and industrial ecology strategies (Boldrini, 2018; Gallaud & Laperche, 2016). Here again, the circular economy raises the question of responsibility and ownership of climate issues for all actors in an ecosystem (Asayehegn et al., 2017). This responsibility raises more general questions about the modalities of governing common resources (Holland & Sene, 2010). In this context, innovation must be responsible and at the service of a more sustainable development (Mobhe Bokoko, 2020). In this context of resource constraints and pressures over our territories, resource-constrained innovations emerged as reshaping innovation toward reducing material and immaterial resources consumption. Several new forms of innovation toward sustainability and frugality are explored: eco-innovation (Arundel & Kemp, 2009); social innovation (Dandurand, 2005; Richez-Battesti et al., 2012); frugal innovation (Radjou & Prabhu, 2015; Le Bas, 2016; Haudeville & Le Bas, 2016) and reverse innovation (Hussler & Burger-Helmchen, 2016; Laperche & Lefebvre, 2012) and develop more or less strongly depending on the geographical context (developed and developing countries (Le, 2020)) and the resource constraint of the ecosystem (Semaan, 2020). The re-designing of innovation models aims at repositioning them to be more resilient to progressive changes affecting territories such as climate change and resource scarcity.

4. Are ecosystems at the root of a general disruption of innovation at the company/ sector/global level?

Innovation ecosystems can be defined as an intersection of actors, activities, and artifacts together with different entities like institutions to collaboratively achieve innovation. The interactions that emerge within an innovation ecosystem are the drivers of the innovative performance that these actors can realize. These ecosystems are not new in the 21st century. They appear in the 1990s, related to the biology field with James Moore (1993) and his publication entitled "Predators and Prey: a new ecology of competition". Following this foundation article, the innovation ecosystem evolved by including managerial involvements.

The creation of a concrete network of actors, sharing resources, whether human, financial, informational, or material, impacts the internal organization of firms. Activities divided in different services or departments within a firm should work together to reach independent goals that concern specific actions. Also, common goals can be fulfilled by a collaborative effort. Transdisciplinarity and interdisciplinarity can be seen as by-products of innovation ecosystem, in which many disciplines, know-how and knowledge intervene in one project.

Furthermore, the external organization of the firms is also concerned. As a result, the sectors' level is impacted by the use and the expansion of innovation ecosystems. As the non-linearity of innovation that led to the open innovation concept, well documented by Henri Chesbrough, taken up and studied by other scholars and authors, the innovation ecosystem concept implies permanent interactions and numerous feedback loops between the stakeholders. One main disruption for the sectors concerns the emergence of new structures organized around major themes, as is the case for competitiveness clusters, technology parks, and regional or national innovation systems, amongst others.

In the energy, agri-food, health, service, environment sector, for instance, various institutions have been created and organized to be able to collaborate, while being in competition. These institutions, private or public firms, research institutions, associations, public institutions, deploy various activities. The latter include Research and Development activities in collaboration with technological platforms when needed, in line with firms' needs and market needs (Paun, 2011). Further examples comprise territorial activities in order to implement tailor-made solutions completing customers' expectations.

Finally, digital innovation that has been developed and implemented in many sectors represents one tool that is used efficiently in these ecosystems to reduce barriers to collaboration, like geographical distance and temporal boundaries for knowledge diffusion. Moreover, facilitating open innovation and the multiple collaboration activities (e.g. crowdsourcing, licensing, open software use) is therefore possible (Lima & Seulliet, 2019).

This also concerns the global level, in which actors around the globe are allowing cooperation within diverse projects, sharing commonalities through the structure of an ecosystem. Finally, innovation ecosystems are at the root of a general disruption of innovation at the company level, the sector level, and the global level.

5. Presentation and prospective of the book, sections, and chapters

The current situation of our planet is disturbing. The consumption of natural resources, the organization and functioning of many industries, the way of life of many populations, are highlighted in different reports and research activities conducted by experts and scientists at a global level. Sustainability is not a new topic in the 21st century. However, it has been raised at the core of many discourses, whether it concerns environment, health, finance, agriculture, clothing, transportation, or building sector.

The existing socio-economic systems could be redesigned toward diverse potential orientations. Increasingly popular, innovation is almost always used as a core driver of this redesign. The non-linearity nature of the innovation process mainly used by actors in different sectors is a strength. This strength serves several objectives: income growth, employment, reduced environmental impacts, competitiveness on national or international scales for example. Furthermore, knowledge is the other immaterial assets developed and used in a knowledge-based economy. This knowledge can flow between the actors of the innovation ecosystem, with tacit or codified vectors to perform innovative activities. Mutual learning and knowledge creation are by-products in this setting. It can take many forms. Techno-industrial innovation took place within a linear process with scientific discoveries transferred to development protocols for a final economic and marketable product. However, social innovation, which is progressively implemented in firms, focuses on individuals as part of a group, being proactive in the organizational or social changes in their environment. Active players providing solutions directly implemented in specific situations is one power of participatory actions in social innovations. The ecosystem can act here as a catalyst for the emergence of solutions.

In this frame one can, interestingly, question the origin of innovation ecosystem. The economic theory was linked to the theory of natural ecosystems. Different participants in these ecosystems evolve together while at the same time being in competition. One product of this organization is innovation, and knowledge as a by-product, which can be beneficial to everyone in the ecosystem. The challenging component of an innovation ecosystem is also an evolving component, as the actors confront their cognitive frames to reach a common frame, crucial for ecosystem efficiency.

On an ecological level, the components and especially the actors that make up the innovation ecosystems will interact, as sustainability embraces a lot of patterns. Moreover, sustainability can be interpreted differently by the actors. Therefore, the innovation ecosystem design should be clear, with procedures and interactive flows to ensure understandable achievements to target and foster cross fertilization with cooperation between the actors.

A transition that is in progress with a digital revolution and an ecological transition would be a success through the inclusion of all possible stakeholders. The adoption of innovations is linked to customers' acceptance and to matching their needs and expectations. Nevertheless, these topics are not straightforward in an exploration of solutions. Sustainable innovations that must be transposed from niche to mass markets can produce interesting spillovers. Many actors can introduce innovations and results in the long run. An example of a transition at stake in the agri-food sector concerns an increase in short food supply chains. Consumers are demonstrating an increasingly powerful motivation for healthier food consumption, more connection to the roots of agri-food production and a simpler lifestyle.

However, some characteristics can outline the orientations of short food supply chains in terms of structural organizations and consumer targets. Geographical and organizational proximity rate highly in the functioning of this sector and the existing territorial ecosystem. In addition, logistics issues related to the critical size of firms evolving in the sector, low visibility of products, and a lack of human resources, are serious for the rise of these food chains. The latter are located between the innovation approach and the transition approach, with local actors working at their level to go beyond this scale to achieve a greater impact.

Besides the ecological focus that short food supply chains wish to make, the digital revolution exemplifies innovation that is spreading among many sectors. Digitization is a great opportunity to overcome the traditional obstacles with which firms must cope. It represents one tool for consumers to regain the opportunity to improve their food consumption. Consumers can be directly involved in their food choices. Many innovations were developed in the health crisis context, such as e-shop, managed by producers or their partners to provide and deliver fresh, local, and seasonal food items. Moreover, alternative food chains or niches like SFSCs could be described; ecological transition is one major feature included in consumers' motivations to purchase food from them.

Besides, diverse stakeholders are bringing their support and expertise to the innovation ecosystem. Nevertheless, to succeed in this gamble, collaborations should take different forms to contain the variety of actors, potential partnerships, and individual interests. In addition to this, new knowledge should be created for the transition from a socio-economic system to a more sustainable system with a systemic approach, which is possible in an ecosystem perspective.

Regarding all the developed issues, the book is divided into three sections.

Section 1: Economic issues of knowledge, innovation, and sustainable development

The chapter "Innovation ecosystems in core digital technologies" starts from the idea of interactions between business ecosystems and innovation ecosystems and the development of entreprises' knowledge capital due to these interaction modalities. The chapter, written by Blandine Laperche and Dimitri Uzunidis, analyzes the main characteristics of the semiconductor industry in Europe – a core technology in the backbone of our digital economies and, then, provides an overview of the global semiconductor value chain and the business model and firms' strategy in the business ecosystem of the semiconductor industry. It highlights vertical cooperation and networks in the semiconductor business ecosystem and the co-evolution of companies' business ecosystems and national or regional innovation ecosystems. Multiple stakeholders within semiconductor value chains in different ways, maintain exchange relationships in a coevolution process. Strong business ecosystems around large corporations in turn contribute to the growth of industry or regional innovation ecosystems. This chapter also provides a summary on national policies of the main regions in the global semiconductor value chain (including the US, China, Taiwan, South Korea) in order to boost domestic semiconductor manufacturing, especially in the international context marked by Covid-19 and a troubled geopolitical situation. Such nations adopted quite similar policies, which are aimed at increasing their domestic production and moving up the value chain in order to produce the most advanced types of semiconductors. Finally, the authors analyze the semiconductor innovation ecosystem in Europe and assess the impacts of European plans which aim to strengthen the microelectronics innovation ecosystem at European level, foremost among which is the European Chips Act of 2022. The results show that, instead of building strong business ecosystems around European competitive advantages and leading companies to enrich their knowledge capital by tapping into the resources of a larger European innovation ecosystem, European policies currently aim to develop various projects in different European Member States, to attract production capacities from other countries, and to try to develop some of the most advanced semiconductors. This policy direction seems highly risky, especially in an unstable economic environment.

The chapter "The entrepreneurial function in digital ecosystems", written by Sophie Boutillier and Dimitri Uzunidis, firstly outlines a theoretical framework of the evolutionary theory of the entrepreneur that explains how new organizations are created and how entrepreneurs transform their organizations and mobilize resources (human, financial, material, etc.) in doing business. The authors then apply this theoretical framework to study the socio-economic trajectory of the eight entrepreneurs in the digital social networking industry in building digital innovation ecosystems. The results show that these entrepreneurs have built a digital innovation ecosystem based on the knowledge, financial, and social resources they have extracted from the institutional context of the United States where they are placed. The emergence and development of these digital innovation ecosystems is based on the combination of resources of other actors, of universities and research centers, of other digital companies in the market, and public policy measures. More precisely, the social origin (parents' occupations), education framework, and professional experience of entrepreneurs provide them with not only tacit knowledge and codified knowledge, managerial and technical experience, but also, in some cases, financial support which is from investment fund companies in the college and university campus, or by leaving the company where they were employed. The acquisition of knowledge in the academic and professional framework also offers individuals the opportunity to create and to develop a network of social relations. These social relations, in turn, due to relations of proximity, support entrepreneurs to acquire and mobilize other resources in the institutional context in which they are inserted. Finally, the development of digital innovation ecosystems has also benefited from public policy measures in the United States aimed at supporting innovation in digital technologies.

The chapter "A sustainable knowledge-based economy analysis" written by Andreas Pyka, Stephanie Lang and Lea F. Stöber analyzes in the context of current global societal challenges, that economic systems need to transform toward sustainable, knowledge-based economies. For that purpose, knowledge represents the key matrix for economic development. However, the nexus between a knowledge-based economy and sustainability has not yet received the necessary attention. Knowledge-based economies have the power to contribute to sustainability transitions without fundamentally reducing the prospects of growing welfare. Considering the innovation ecosystem perspective, this chapter addresses the question of how existing systems can be redesigned to overcome their exclusive focus on international competitiveness, income growth and employment, and instead support the transformation toward a sustainable economy. In that perspective, a focus is made on innovation ecosystems at the macro level to elaborate how dedicated innovation ecosystems need to be developed from national innovation systems in order to initiate sustainability transitions. This qualitative shift of innovation systems requires overcoming lock-ins, adopting a normative perspective, and integrating stakeholders, as consumer lifestyles have to change alongside production paradigms. The recognition of normative aspects and the decisive role of transformative knowledge enable the creation of a virtuous circle between demand, supply, and policy interventions on the path to a sustainability paradigm.

The chapter "Digital ecosystems for agilizing innovation", written by Florin Paun and Ingrid Vaileanu, extends the field of digital ecosystems building on the dynamics of agile innovation. Academic research on collaborative and open innovation is highlighted. On this basis, the authors of the chapter refine the concept of the digital ecosystem using successful illustration projects. They link the potential for cooperation within digital ecosystems to the vectors, tools, and methods that can boost the level and the efficiency of interactions. In that perspective, there is an emphasis on the agile paradigm. The self evolution of this agile paradigm is detailed, so that even readers not familiar with this field could benefit efficiently from the knowledge of the chapter. The cooperative methods of open innovation are analyzed. The authors show how digital ecosystems can benefit from agile dynamics. A typology of the different types of stakeholders related to open digital ecosystems is incorporated. The in situ studies are an important asset for the shaping of the work and are related to successful European, North American, and Asian digital ecosystems. The impacts of the stakeholders of digital ecosystems are shown at different levels of interpretation: micro, meso, and macro-economic. The authors analyze the fact that agile innovation vectors are able to boost the field of cooperation in digital ecosystems, and so their success with elements of detail that contribute to the great interest in this chapter.

Section 2: Key role of innovation ecosystems in mechanisms of generation, adoption, and diffusion of innovation

The chapter "The emergence of the blockchain technosystem", written by Raffaele Anedda and Didier Lebert, extends the field of the mapping methodology of innovation ecosystems building on patent data. For that purpose, their work takes into consideration emerging technologies and networks. These highlight the temporal evolutionary line of the "blockchain technosystem" and the effects of these advances for the purpose of their analysis. Their high-level work is written in a way that allows non-engineers or people not familiar with these technologies to clearly understand the issues.

The steps that have built the patent field of the blockchain, including the role played by the European Patent Office (EPO), are clearly outlined. That of Marku et al. (2020) is linked mainly to patent texts and to the lexical scope of the blockchain, as well as the movement that distances itself from this vision and reverses it. First, that of Clarke et al. (2020), which emphasizes the technological nomenclature. The chapter combines these two approaches to efficiently detect patent portfolios around the blockchain.

Networks and technosystems are fully integrated into the approach. Thus, in a second step, the authors can analyze the evolution of the blockchain innovation technosystem in a precise way. The fields of application are covered, including the domain of financial cryptography. In particular, they show that the blockchain technosystem has largely evolved toward a structuring around the security of communications. Furthermore, the blockchain technosystem has acquired properties of a singular universe, the sophistication of which is demonstrated.

The chapter "Innovation ecosystems and entrepreneurial opportunity", presented by Yassine Mehros, Jean-Michel Degeorge, and Abdelaziz Elabjani, focuses on innovation ecosystems and entrepreneurial opportunities. The authors seek to understand the interactions between the actors of an innovation ecosystem, which allow the entrepreneur to recognize, evaluate, and seize entrepreneurial opportunities. This work also allows the authors to identify the key players within an innovation ecosystem who promote entrepreneurial opportunity. To do this, the authors carry out an exploratory qualitative study of the key players in the innovation ecosystem of the Loire department (in France), in particular its institutions, support networks, and clusters. The study takes, as its analytical framework, the theoretical foundations that result from work on innovation ecosystems, in particular open innovation strategies, and shows to what extent these contribute to the recognition of entrepreneurial opportunity. The results of the study, conducted by interviews with different actors in the Loire ecosystem, reveal the existence of strong links between the different actors that make up this ecosystem. The study also reveals that the creation of strong bonds of trust between these actors is facilitated by their geographical and relational proximity. Actors collaborate on projects involving companies, and in particular start-ups. All these elements combine to enable companies to recognize and capture entrepreneurial opportunities.

To cope with resource-constrained contexts, about which there are global warnings, the concept of the circular economy has been attracting the attention of business and government leaders. Among the potential solutions to support the emergence and development of the circular economy, reshaping innovation toward reducing resource consumption highlights the importance of resource-constrained innovations. The chapter “From bricolage to ecosystems of resource-poor firms”, written by Son Thi Kim Le, provides an overview about bricolage, which is known as an innovation pathway induced by a resource-constrained environment. The author presents a summary about the emergence, determinants, and importance of bricolage for the innovation ecosystem and, then, for the emergence of a new socio-economic paradigm: the circular economy. Further, bricolage capabilities were analyzed by exploring some specific firms' capabilities such as making do, improvisation, and networking. Through this brief presentation, several advantages of bricolage are explored. For instance, bricolage behavior enables resource-poor enterprises to overcome scarcity and introduce affordable and good-enough products for the scarcity environment, to seek innovative solutions for social needs by making do with any resources at hand, to reduce resource and raw materials consumption, as well as waste and dangerous emissions. By doing so, bricolage and entrepreneurial bricolage drive innovation toward frugality and sustainability. Further, this process also, in turn, requires the building of collaborations and partnerships with various stakeholders and, thus, enables the establishment of a collaborative ecosystem, known as an innovation ecosystem.

The chapter “Medical devices building on open paradigm”, written by Laurent Adatto, analyzes how, in relation to the necessity to face up to the pandemic emergency, cooperations have been set up to shape innovation ecosystems that build on the open paradigm of the digital era, including open innovation, open source, 3D printing, and open digital specifications. The aim was to design and produce medical components and devices up to the most critical and sophisticated equipments to save lives during the pandemic: medical ventilators.

For that purpose, the chapter builds on multiple case studies to detail the structuring and synergies driven by these ecosystems, and the induced innovations, at the level of organization, product manufacturing, open circulation of created knowledge for an optimal diffusion via digital networks, and cooperation combining public and private organizations, universities, research laboratories and hospitals, engineers, and medical practitioners. The chapter is also written in a didactic way, with an analysis of supporting concepts, contextual background, and lessons learned from the case studies.

Beyond the pandemic crisis, such cooperative innovation ecosystems based on the open paradigm and the possibilities induced by the advent of the digital era highlight the path to progress, particularly in the areas of reindustrialization in local areas through IT, digital access, smart factories, 3D printing that relocates more and more production and thus limits freight pollution, the concept of the digital twin, and a better access to health care through new opportunities of e-health. This chapter is therefore in line with the potential of the Fourth Industrial Revolution.

Section 3: Evolution of innovation ecosystems facing new societal issues

The chapter "Innovation diversity in human societies", written by Jean Claude Ruano-Borbalan, considers the dual nature of innovation. It is related to multiple practices, from consumption and marketing to techno-scientific processes, from industrial production to public policies. In this perspective, the chapter analyzes and categorizes related elements, discourses of promotion and justification. Discourses are categorized in three key orientations: linear techno-scientific innovations; managerial and administrative innovations; social innovations. Those discourses have become the common credo of a world focused on techno-scientific engineering, industrial economic development, and economic growth. Such ideology and practices of innovation face a huge and almost insurmountable problem: it is powerless, at least, and surely more harmful, to resolve some of the main systemic challenges that are currently occurring (including global warming and persistence of inequalities). The chapter pledges to consider reinforcing regulation and public policies, but mainly proposes a bet on the relevance of humanist education and knowledge, that means an important transformation of higher education in order to develop new ways for new innovation.

The chapter "Evolution of the food sector in innovation ecosystems", written by Camille Aouinaït, considers the large changes of the food sector that are notably related to the environmental emergency, the economic problems and the social needs with stakeholders from society, corporate, and economic organizations. This evolution builds also on social ties and local food products. The chapter topics include the importance of short food supply chains, health, economic, ethical, environmental, and uncertain social context. Improvements related to pandemic recovery are treated, with a special issue about the agri-food sector and its digitization, and from an ecosystem innovation approach.

In the chapter "Territorial development in the face of climate change", Michelle Mongo, Audrey Tanguy, Valérie Laforest, and Eric Piatyszek provide a discussion around territorial development and its evolution with regard to climate and environmental challenges. To respond to these climate challenges, the resilience of territories, which is defined as "not only the ability to cope with major events and absorb crises. It is also the capacity (of the city) to constantly renew itself and to assimilate disturbances and recurring crises or those to come by adapting and anticipating these events" (Laganier & Serre, 2017), is posed as a necessary condition. In this context, the authors question organizational processes at the territorial level, which allow the achievement of greater resilience. To do this, the authors draw on the literature on territorial innovation systems to understand the local dynamics of innovation, which help to explain local development. They also show how the awareness of all the stakeholders in the face of climate and environmental issues has caused these territorial systems of innovation to evolve, which are too focused on economic objectives and the competitiveness of companies toward local processes which take into account socio-economic and environmental issues. Approaches such as the circular economy or industrial ecology are presented to illustrate this greening of practices within the territories. The authors nevertheless draw the limits of these approaches and show to what extent the scarcity of resources implies taking into account other innovations developed in a situation of resource constraints. Initiatives such as Low Tech or frugal innovations that consist in doing better with less are presented as examples of good practices to be taken into account in the territorial dynamics of innovation to allow greater resilience of the territories.

In the perspective of the advent of the digital age, the chapter "Clusters and the digital dependency", written by Cheikh Abdou Lahad Thiaw, is in line with the trend of innovations outside closed physical structures and which are based on external cooperation and networks. In this perspective, the author analyzes the emergence of "translocal" innovation networks. These new networks do not oppose the earlier models of clusters but complement them to enrich global innovation capacity. For that purpose, the chapter proposes an analysis of the conceptual background and refines the notion of innovation networks notably emphasized by Porter.

The author shows that the accessibility of digital vectors and support in most of the interstices of the economy constitutes an opportunity for the development of innovations. Moreover, this evolution is in phase with the globalization of the economy, exchanges, and markets. These opportunities offered by digital technologies can rely on local actors. The author extends this problematic by the notion of "translocal clusters" linked to nomadic elements whose level can change. This notion is efficient with regard to the different types of innovation networks. The local scale is a vector of opportunities for neighborhood networks, of high potentiality for common interest, of complementarity of implied value chains.

A detailed analysis is made of the innovation ecosystems and their dynamics based on technology and science, in the context of the knowledge economy. The author then shows the great interest of "nomadic" innovation networks based on ICT and the progress of digital materials and networks with increasingly widespread local access. It is shown that "nomadic" innovation networks are at the origin of translocal innovation spaces. These spaces include great opportunities, especially linked to local institutional, academic and research, industrial, and economic structures. The mutualization of linked dynamics by relying on digital tools generates innovations. This was the case during the pandemic when local activities were necessary and showed their qualities by building on opportunities of "nomadic" innovation networks, including the pooling of industrial forces, complementarity of practices for common needs, and virtualization and the creation of new relocalized value chains based on these ICT vectors. The nomadic clusters can also combine various innovation ecosystems on these criteria, which also include the reduction of costs due to transport, a greater flexibility linked to the work of local agents, and the use of virtual environments.

References

Arundel, A., & Kemp, R. (2009). Measuring eco-innovation. United Nations University. UNU-MERIT. *OECD Org*. 2009–2017. https://www.oecd.org/greengrowth/consumption-innovation/43960846.pdf

Asayehegn, K., Iglesias, A., Triomphe, B., Pédelahore, P., & Temple, L. (2017). The role of systems of innovation in adapting to climate change: The case of the Kenyan Coffee and Dairy Sectors. *Journal of Innovation Economics & Management, 3*(3), 127–149.

Bengt-Åke, L. (2007). National innovation systems – Analytical concept and development tool. *Industry and Innovation, 14*(1), 95–119. https://doi.org/10.1080/13662710601130863

Breschi, S. & Malerba, F. (1998). *Systems of innovation: Technologies, institutions and organizations*. In *Long range planning* (Vol. 31). https://doi.org/10.1016/s0024-6301(98)90244-8

Boccara, P. (2016). La révolution informationnelle, ses ambivalences, ses antagonismes, ses potentialités. *Economie et Politique*. Retrieved from http://66.pcf.fr/sites/default/files/eco_po_742_743_dossier_0.pdf

Boldrini, J. C. (2018). La co-création de valeur dans un projet d'innovation collaboratif: un cas de transition vers l'économie circulaire. *Innovations, 1*(55), 143–171.

Boutillier, S., Levratto, N., & Carré, D. (2015). *Les écosystèmes entrepreneuriaux: rencontre entre entreprise et territoire* (Vol. 2). ISTE Group.

Callon, M. (1986). Éléments pour une sociologie de la traduction: La domestication des coquilles Saint-Jacques et des marins-pêcheurs dans la baie de Saint-Brieuc. *L'Année Sociologique* (1940/1948-), 36(troisième série), 169–208. Retrieved from www.jstor.org/stable/27889913

Chesbrough, H. W. (2003). *Open innovation: The new imperative for creating and profiting from technology*. Harvard Business Press.

Dandurand, L. (2005). Réflexion autour du concept d'innovation sociale, approche historique et comparative. *Revue française d'administration publique, 3*(115), 377–382.

David, P. A., & Foray, D. (2002). Une introduction à l'économie et à la société du savoir. *Revue Internationale Des Sciences Sociales, 171*(1), 13–28.

Foray, D. (2013). L'industrie du luxe et l'économie de la connaissance. *Innovations, 2*(2), 71–90. https://doi.org/10.3917/inno.041.0071

Gallaud, D., & Laperche, B. (2016). *Circular economy, industrial ecology and short supply chain*. John Wiley & Sons.

Gibbs, P. (2015). *Transdisciplinary professional learning and practice*. New York: Springer

Grange, C., & Sponem, S. (2021). Les travailleurs du savoir face au bouleversement technologique. *Gestion, 1*(1), 42–49. https://doi.org/10.3917/riges.461.0042

Granstrand, O., & Holgersson, M. (2020). Innovation ecosystems: A conceptual review and a new definition. *Technovation*, 90–91(May 2019). https://doi.org/10.1016/j.technovation.2019.102098

Haudeville, B., & Le Bas, C. (2016). L'innovation frugale, paradigme technologique naissant ou nouveau modèle d'innovation ?. *Innovations, 3*(3), 9–25.

Holland, G., & Sene, O. (2010). Elinor Ostrom et la Gouvernance Economique. *Revue d'économie Politique, 120*(3), 441–452.

Hussler, C., & Burger-Helmchen, T. (2016). Inversée vous avez dit inversée ? – Une typologie stratégique de l'innovation inversée. *Revue Française de Gestion, 42*(255), 105–119.

IPCC. (2018). *Global warming of 1.5 Degrees*. Retrieved from https://report.ipcc.ch/sr15/pdf/sr15_spm_final.pdf

Jacobides, M. G., Cennamo, C., & Gawer, A. (2018). Towards a theory of ecosystems. *Strategic Management Journal, 39*(8), 2255–2276.

Laganier, R., & Serre, D. (2017). Les conditions et la mise en oeuvre de la résilience urbaine. In Thomas, I. & Da Cunha, A. (Eds.), *La ville résiliente, comment la construire ?* (Collection, p. 322). Montréal.

Laperche, B. (2017). *Entreprise Knowledge Capital*. London: ISTE/Wiley.

Laperche, B., & Uzunidis, D. (2007). Le Système national d'innovation russe en restructuration: Réformes institutionnelles et politique industrielle. *Innovations, 2*(2), 69–94. https://doi.org/10.3917/inno.026.0069

Laperche, B., & Lefebvre, G. (2012). The globalization of Research & Development in industrial corporations: Towards "reverse innovation": The cases of General Electric and Renault. *Journal of Innovation Economics & Management, 2*(2), 53–79.

Laperche, B., Lima, M., Seuillet, E., & Trousse, B. (2019). *Ecosystèmes d'innovation: Regards croisés des acteurs clés* (No. hal-02418541).

Le, S. T. K. (2020). Measuring innovation efforts of developing countries: Empirical evidence from Vietnam. *Journal of Innovation Economics Management*, (3), 163–194.

Le Bas, C. (2016). The importance and relevance of frugal innovation to developed markets: milestones towards the economics of frugal innovation. *Journal of Innovation Economics & Management, 3*(21), 3–8.

Lima, M., & Seulliet, E., (2019), Chapitre 1. Évolution des écosystèmes d'innovation : des origines de la métaphore écologique à une nouvelle génération, in *Les écosystèmes d'innovation*, 35–46. Paris: L'Harmattan. https://doi.org/10.3917/har.laper.2019.01.0035

Mobhe Bokoko, D. (2020). Responsible innovation and social innovation. *Journal of Innovation Economics & Management, 32*(2), 229.

Mongo, M. (2021). Services innovants et action publique pour dynamiser les économies territoriales: éléments d'analyse. *Technologie et Innovation, 6*(1), 1–11.

Moore, J. F. (1993). A new ecology of competition. *Harvard Business Review, 71*(3), 75–86. Retrieved from http://blogs.law.harvard.edu/jim/files/2010/04/Predators-and-Prey.pdf

Muet, P. (2006). Impacts économiques de la révolution numérique. *Revue économique, 3*(3), 347–375. https://doi.org/10.3917/reco.573.0347

OCDE. (2018). *Manuel d'Oslo 2018 : lignes directrices pour le recueil, la communication et l'utilisation des données sur l'innovation*, 4ème édition.

Paun, F. (2011). 'Demand Readiness Level' (DRL): A New Tool to Hybridize Market Pull and Technology Push Approaches - Introspective Analysis of the New Trends in Technology Transfer Practices (February 18, 2011). *Springer Encyclopedia*, Forthcoming, Available at SSRN: https://ssrn.com/abstract=1763679

Radjou, N., & Prabhu, J. (2015). Frugal Innovation: How to do more with less. *The Economist.*

Richez-Battesti, N., Petrella, F., & Vallade, D. (2012). L'innovation sociale, une notion aux usages pluriels : Quels enjeux et défis pour l'analyse ?. *Innovations, 2*(2), 15–36.

Schumpeter, J. (1939). *Business cycles: A theoretical, historical, and statistical analysis of the Capitalist process* (Vol. 2). New York.

Semaan, M. (2020). Effectuation and innovation in resource constrained contexts: A literature review. *Innovations, 63*(3), 153–178

Uzunidis, D. (2008a). The logic of the innovative milieu. In Laperche, B., Uzunidis, D., & Von Tunzelmann, G. N. (Eds.). (2008), *The genesis of innovation, systemic linkages between knowledge and the market* (pp. 187–207). Cheltenham: E. Elgar.

Uzunidis, D. (2008b). Milieux innovateur et gestation d'un entrepreneuriat innovant. *Marché et organisations, 1*(1), 119–145. https://doi.org/10.3917/maorg.006.0119

Uzunidis, D. (2018). *Collective innovation processes: Principles and practices.* London: ISTE/Wiley.

Part 1:

Economic Issues of Knowledge, Innovation and Sustainable Development

Presentation

This current era of digital highlights the importance of knowledge, especially the manner of exploring, producing and transferring knowledge. Knowledge is studied as the vital production factor of knowledge-based economies and thus is a key component for supporting economic development. Knowledge, regardless under the form of tacit or codified, considerably enables the emergence of innovation activities. These roles of knowledge become more prominent in the context of digital era which has witnessed a strongly emergence of innovation networks across numerous sectors and industries.

Overtime, the management of innovation activities, thus, has been changed towards open innovation in which enterprises collaborate with multiple partners at all stages of innovation process, from design to development of new products and services (Laperche, 2017). The analysis of collaborative innovation with an 'open' approach identifies three open innovation processes: (1) *outside-in* innovation; (2) *inside-out* innovation; (3) coupled process of innovation (Chesbrough, 2006). The collaborative process in open innovation process enables turn the "knowledge" of several actors in innovation ecosystems into "value" for all of them. This process allows the actors engaging open innovation process to accumulate knowledge-capital which is defined as the set of scientific and technical knowledge and information produced, acquired, combined and systematized by one or several firms for productive purposes (Laperche, 2017). Beyond an open innovation among only businesses, the collective process of constituting knowledge capital is the result of cooperating process among multiple actors from enterprises in different industries, sectors, sizes to universities and research institutions as well as users of innovation, etc. (Laperche, Uzunidis, 2019).

As an obvious result of "openness", innovation ecosystems emerge overtime and enable the production and dissemination of knowledge to become more open and collective (Uzunidis, 2018). In current era, the circulation of knowledge among the actors of innovation ecosystem is facilitated thanks to the digital revolution. It, thus, highlights the importance and development of the connectivity and interdependence among actors in the network under the digital age. As a result, some research issues that are frequently examined in a variety of contexts are: Which type of stakeholders, collaboration modalities, communication channels for knowledge exchange and circulation, etc. are chosen and undertaken in innovation ecosystems in order to promote innovation processes, especially in digital age? What are the following impacts at the micro, meso and macro-economic level? Part 1, including fours chapters, will answer above wondering and then provide an overview about such economic issues of knowledge and innovation in the context of health crisis and the societal transformations induced by ecological transition and digital revolution.

Firstly, the pandemic crisis caused shortages of certain products, especially in high-tech industries. However, the evolution of digitalization has supported for the way innovation ecosystems operate and develop in such industries. The close linkages and co-evolution of business ecosystems and national or regional innovation ecosystems in these industries has changed the manner in which the transdisciplinary and interdisciplinary knowledge production takes place. A chapter analyses these interaction modalities in semi-conductor industry – a core technology at the backbone of our digital economies – to explore in detail how knowledge capital is accumulated and the evolution of industrial policies to support the development of this sector.

The literature on innovation shows that the emergence and development of innovation ecosystems is mainly based on the interaction and combination of knowledge, information and resources among multiple stakeholders, including other enterprises, users, universities and research institutions, governments, etc. These interaction modalities and the combination manners may be different among sectors, industries, countries due to the differences in the nature and characteristics of industries, institutional contexts of countries, user's behaviours, etc. In recent times, the growth of digital technologies results in the strongly development of several digital enterprises as well as digital innovation ecosystems. A chapter of the part 1 analyses the resource mobilization and combination of innovative entrepreneurs in the world of digital social network enterprises to build their digital innovation ecosystems.

Regarding the impact of innovation paradigms at the macroeconomic level, sustainability has been identified by several governments as an important goal in dealing with current global societal challenges. Knowledge and innovation play a critical role in the process of transforming our socio-economic systems towards this sustainability. At the same time, digitalization contributes considerably on the generation, application, and diffusion of transformative knowledge. Another chapter of the part 1 explains the reason and manner that innovation ecosystems should be designed and organized towards dedicated innovation ecosystems in order to achieve higher degrees of sustainability.

Continuing these issues, the importance of collaborative innovation and open innovation is emphasized more in the context of digital ecosystems. Hight intensity of collaboration within digital ecosystem has proven to be a critical trigger for facilitating innovation process. To what extent and how do multiple stakeholders in the digital ecosystem interact and collaborate? The last chapter of part 1 opens a new nuance on agile innovation and explains the pattern of high collaborative intensity in digital ecosystem along with potential impacts at the micro, meso and macro-economic level.

References

Chesbrough, H. (2006). *Open innovation: The new imperative for creating and profiting from technology* (Harvard Bu).

Laperche, B. (2017). *Enterprise knowledge capital.* London, John Wiley & Sons.

Laperche B., & Uzunidis D. (2019). The knowledge capital and the network firm: Socialization versus business appropriation of scientific work. In Blast, G., Carayannis, E. G., & Campbell, D. (Eds.), *The future of education and labor.* Springer, pp. 57–75.

Uzunidis, D. (2018). *Collective innovation processes: Principles and practices.* London: ISTE/Wiley.

Innovation ecosystems in core digital technologies

Blandine Laperche, Dimitri Uzunidis[1]

Abstract: Faced with a shortage of electronic components in an international context marked by Covid- 19 and a troubled geopolitical situation, national and European policies are planning to strengthen the microelectronics innovation ecosystem. Given the characteristics of this industry (high investment expenditure and R&D costs, global value chain, where each country or region specializes in a specific segment), is the scientific and technical potential of European countries sufficiently rich for the production of a wide range of electronic components in the medium term? In this paper, we propose to analyze the semiconductor innovation ecosystem in Europe, to assess its strengths and limitations in comparison with the main competitors, and to study the impacts of the proposed plans at European level, foremost among which is the European Chips Act of 2022.

Keywords: Semi-conductor, Innovation ecosystem, Global value chain, Public policy, Europe

Introduction

Semi-conductors can be considered as core technologies at the heart of our digital economies. They are present in all our current products (smartphones, computers, cloud etc.) and at the origin of many major and minor innovations in many industries. European countries, like all other consumer countries, are facing a shortage of electronic components,

[1] University of Littoral Côte d'Opale, Research Network on Innovation, France.

which takes place in an international context marked by Covid-19 and a troubled geopolitical situation, characterized by the war in Ukraine and the increasing tensions between China and Taiwan. The shortages already led many industries (especially automakers) to halt production (Ramani et al., 2022). Tensions are increasing between China and Taiwan, and they show the world's reliance on Taiwan for semiconductors, where the company TSMC is considered to be the world's largest chip foundry and Apple's main producer of chips (Young, 2022).

In reaction, many countries and regions are investing in the semiconductor sector. In this article, we particularly focus on European policies to strengthen the microelectronics innovation ecosystem in Europe. How is Europe trying to cope with this context of shortage in the semiconductor industry? What are the positive aspects and limitations of European policy in the semi-conductor industry, in the light of other leading countries' experience?

To answer these questions, we develop an analysis based on the characteristics of the value chains and of the strategies of companies in the semi-conductor industry. The concept of the ecosystem provides a relevant framework for understanding corporate strategies and value chains in a given context. Systems or ecosystems can be studied at the level of companies (Moore, 1996; Grandstrand, 2000; Lundvall & Rikap, 2022), or at the level of sectors and territories (regional, national) (Freeman, 1987; Grandstrand, 2020). At the level of companies, fostering the development of a business ecosystem is in fact a matter of "open" and "collective" innovation (Chesbrough, 2003; Uzunidis, 2018): the dialogue between actors makes it possible to anticipate developments in the field and to mobilize more intelligence in understanding emerging issues. It aims to reinforce the knowledge capital of companies (Laperche, 2017). However, we consider that there is a continuum – or an interaction – between ecosystems built at the level of companies and innovation ecosystems, especially in high tech sectors where core technologies such as semi-conductors are produced. In other words, multiple stakeholders within these value chains, in different ways, maintain exchange relationships in a coevolution process. The building of strong business ecosystems around large corporations contributes to the development of an innovation ecosystem at the sectoral or regional level.

Our analysis is based on secondary data and aims at building a framework of analysis for an empirical analysis of European corporate strategies in the European context. The paper is organized as follows. We first develop the idea of a continuum, or interaction, between business or corporate ecosystems and innovation ecosystems (Part 1). In the second part, we present the characteristics of the semi-conductor industry (Part 2). We then develop the positive aspects and limitations of the European policy in the light of other industrial policies implemented in other countries and we put forward some possible alternative solutions based on the strengthening of its innovation ecosystem (Part 4). The conclusion sums up the main findings and gives insights for further work.

1- The interaction between business ecosystems and innovation ecosystems

Innovation is becoming increasingly open, collaborative, and transdisciplinary (Uzunidis, 2018). In order to emerge, innovation therefore needs a "protective cocoon" that is able to initiate and nourish all of these novelty-generating interactions. The concept of the system and now the more popular "ecosystem", borrowed from biology, translates these interactions (what the concept of system already did) while insisting on the fragility of these interactions and on the need for protection.

Ecosystems take many different forms. They can be organized around companies (business ecosystems) or on the scale of territories (innovation ecosystems comprising the triple helix business – university/research centers – government/support agencies), or even take more virtual forms (open innovation platforms). They are also differentiated by the forms of organization that are more or less formal (competitiveness clusters or more informal forms of organization such as innovation communities (Laperche et al., 2019)).

1-1 Developing enterprise knowledge capital through business ecosystems

The ability to innovate depends on the constitution and constant reinforcement of knowledge capital defined "as all the scientific and technical information and knowledge produced, acquired, combined and systematized by one or more firms for productive purposes and, more globally, for value production" (Laperche, 2017). Knowledge capital refers to the knowledge accumulated by one or more firms. It is integrated into the individuals (know-how), machines, technologies, and routines of the firm. It is constantly enriched by information flows. Knowledge capital is more than the sum of its parts: a process of cross-fertilization between all these sources of information and knowledge means that the return from the use of this combined set of information and knowledge is higher than the return from the use of each of these pieces of knowledge and information taken separately. Knowledge capital is therefore a dynamic concept – a process – that defines the knowledge accumulated by one or more firms and which is continuously enriched or combined in different ways. This productive objective – the creation of value – is the main characteristic that turns knowledge into "capital".

The constitution of knowledge capital is today a collective process, the fruit of the cooperation of multiple actors, companies of different sizes, competitors or complementary companies, universities and research centers, users.... The boundaries of companies are becoming porous and are expanding (Uzunidis, 2018; Laperche & Uzunidis, 2019).

The constitution of a business ecosystem can be considered as a strategy that is meant to reinforce the knowledge capital of enterprises. James Moore (1993), in "*Predators and Prey: a new ecology of competition*" proposed the term of business ecosystems to explain to managers how to develop their innovation. "In a business ecosystem, companies coevolve capabilities around a new innovation: they work cooperatively and competitively to support new products, satisfy customer needs, and eventually incorporate the next round of innovations" (Moore, 1993). In his article, he recognizes the existence of a large literature about networks and alliances but proposed this term that became very popular to demonstrate to managers the advantages of co-opetition over competition. We can also link it to "open innovation", developed by Chesbrough (2003), which goes into detail on the types of relationships that a company can develop with other enterprises and institutions in order to develop and commercialize innovation.

At the same time, the economics of innovation has for a long time demonstrated that innovation needs to be anchored in solid ground in close connection with the territories. Alfred Marshall (1890) was already talking about the positive effects of "agglomerations" at the end of the 19th century. A century later, Michael Porter (1990) drew on this to construct the concept of "clusters". The essential process that makes innovation emerge within these agglomerations is that of proximity, which takes various forms associating space (geographical proximity), but also social relations, a common knowledge base, organizational forms, and shared institutions (Torre & Zimmermann, 2015; Uzunidis, 2010; Boschma, 2005). Innovation also flourishes best when it is driven by communities of users who are co-creators. It is also essential – in an environment that is changing ever more rapidly – to be agile, to share risks, and to pool resources. This is how we can link business ecosystems with innovation ecosystems.

1-2 The interaction between business ecosystems and innovation (eco)systems

The concept of an innovation ecosystem is currently very popular. Granstrand and Holgersson's literature review leads them to define innovation ecosystems as "the evolving set of actors, activities, and artifacts, and the institutions and relations, including complementary and substitute relations, that are important for the innovative performance of an actor or a population of actors" (Granstrand & Holgersson, 2020, p. 3). This concept finds its roots in the previous definition by Moore of business ecosystems, but also draws from the systemic approach of innovation developed by evolutionist theory. Many innovation economists have indeed focused on the analysis of innovation systems at the national (initially developed by Freeman, 1987, and Lundvall, 1992) or sectoral level (Malerba, 2002). Their analysis makes it possible to identify the organizations and institutions involved in the innovation process, to compare the performance of these systems in different countries, regions, and sectors, and to assess their strengths and limitations in order to guide public policy. Some authors question the necessity to add the prefix (eco) to an analysis of "innovation systems" (Oh, 2016; Ritala & Almpanopoulou, 2017). As a matter of fact, according to them, the ecological metaphor is not really explained and, as such, is not very rigorous.

However, this ecological metaphor can be interpreted as a way to stress the fragility of the innovation process due to its more and more collective and socialized dimension (Uzunidis, 2018). In that sense, an innovation "ecosystem", defined as the set of organizations and institutions acting to develop innovation in a specific sector and place, can be considered as institutional arrangements that are meant to reduce the difficulties that arise in partnership relationships and provide a favorable framework for building and exploiting firms' knowledge capital. They increase trust and reduce information asymmetries, promote learning to work together, and accelerate the diffusion of innovation. They constitute a form of innovation incubator, protected by the network that each type of ecosystem constitutes (Laperche, 2019).

In this sense, the concept of an ecosystem provides a relevant framework for understanding corporate strategies and value chains in a given context. The Value Chain is viewed not only as a set of steps to produce a final good, but it also considers the technology that is at its origin and which gives birth to a variety of products (see Figure 1). It also takes account of the diversity of actors that are linked together and which form an ecosystem. As such, value chains, and also segments of these value chains, can be considered as innovation ecosystems. These are built by the common action of companies and public policies.

Within them, leader companies develop their own business ecosystems. Support from institutions and in particular public policies which will give incentives to capital investments and R&D are central to the development of business ecosystems. It is here where the interaction between business ecosystems and innovation ecosystems lies: the strength of leaders' business ecosystems depends on the resources available in the innovation ecosystem and vice versa.

The concept of a "corporate innovation system" proposed by Lundvall and Rikap (2022) and applied to the case of China also shows the interaction between systems created at the level of companies and larger, place-based, or virtual ones. It aims to show the "co-evolution of national and corporate innovation systems, where the latter is controlled by a dominant firm and constituted by a multitude of more or less subordinate firms and knowledge institutions" (Lundvall & Rikap, p. 1). In the field of Artificial Intelligence, Lundvall and Rikap show how Alibaba's and Tencent's innovation activities rely on knowledge sources within China's national innovation systems, combined with diverse international collaborations, organizing research and development (R&D) that is developed beyond China.

Analysis of the semiconductor industry will give us the opportunity to illustrate this fundamental interaction and to show the role of the semiconductor, considered as a core technology, in the emergence of systemic innovations.

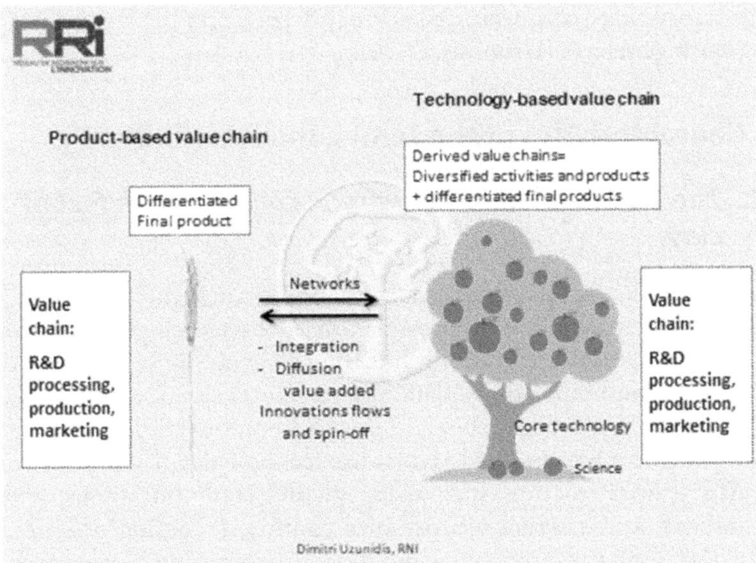

Figure 1: Value chains and core technologies
Source: Uzunidis (2022)

As a matter of fact, the core technology can be defined as the technology from which (a) a set of major or minor innovations are introduced into the economy that modify the structures of the markets; (b) new technological and organizational models on different levels are installed that modify in depth or marginally the structures of the economic actors, whether they are private (companies) or public and parapublic (administrations, associations, etc.). The main result of the valorization of the core technology is the realization of the process of systemic innovation in a broad technological, economic, and social space. Thus, the systemic innovation emerges and spreads from a core technology (in this case the semi-conductor) resulting from the sociotechnical system of innovation, itself "naturally" unstable. This innovation is diffused, captured, and adapted through the interactions of the actors, thanks to incremental innovations within and between sectors, and also via complementary disruptive innovations. This process leads to the realization of new combinations of innovations, called "systemic innovations". In turn, systemic innovations (sets of innovations resulting from new combinations made possible by the diffusion/adaptation of a core technology) destabilize the socio-technical system, whose robustness depends on the strength of the routines it generates (Uzunidis, 2020).

2- Characteristics of the semi-conductor industry

2-1. The semiconductor industry: A colossus with feet of clay

Semiconductors, also known as integrated circuits, microchips, or just "chips", are key enabling technologies, or core technologies, for emerging mission-critical applications and thus systemic innovations in data processing, communications, data infrastructure, cloud, advanced computing, and AI. As such, they are the backbone of digital economies. Semiconductors are classified as dual-use technologies. They are essential for critical infrastructure, such as energy and communications, and to the internal and external security of a country, including defense and space. According to a study by the Boston Consulting Group and the Semiconductor Industry Association (BCG & SIA, 2021), semiconductors are the world's fourth-most-traded product after only crude oil, refined oil, and cars.

Over the next ten years, the industry will need to invest about $3 trillion in R&D and capital expenditure globally across the value chain in order to meet the increasing demand for semiconductors, required by our digital economies. The global semiconductor industry, which includes all firms involved in the design or manufacture of integrated circuits, is worth $439 billion in 2020. It is a fast-growing industry ($314 billion in 2010).

Semiconductors are very complex products requiring high R&D and capital investments. There are more than 30 types of semiconductor product categories, each optimized for a particular function in an electronic subsystem. However, they can be classified in three main categories (see Table 1)

Table 1: Categories of semiconductors

Category	Definition	Share of industry revenue/ production capacity
Logic	Integrated circuits functioning on binary codes (0–1), Building block of computing: microprocessors, general purpose logic, microcontrollers MCUs, connectivity	42 % of industry revenues 39 % of global capacity of production
Memory	Semiconductors used for storing the information necessary to perform computation: DRAM, NAND	26 % of industry revenues 32 % of global capacity of production
Discrete, Analog and others (DAO)	Semiconductors that transmit, receive, and transform information dealing with continuous parameters such as temperature and voltage	32 % of industry revenues 29 % of global capacity of production

Source: based on BCG & SIA (2021)

These three categories of semiconductors are used in all types of electronic devices, from smartphones, consumer electronics, computers, ICT infrastructure, automobiles, and other industrial devices. Only 2 % of the semiconductors produced are on nodes[2] below 10 nm, and 37 % are between 10 and 20 nm. These smallest semiconductors are mainly used for the "Logic" and "Memory" categories, while the biggest ones (above 100 nm) are mainly used for the DAO category.

As a consequence, the global value chain is very specialized and regions perform different roles ensuing from comparative advantages (see Figure 2). According to the BCG & SIA (2021), the US leads in the most R&D-intensive activities—electronic design automation (EDA), core intellectual property (IP), chip design, and advanced manufacturing equipment. This is explained by the presence of world-class universities, of a vast pool of engineering talent, and a market-driven innovation ecosystem. East Asia (including South Korea, Japan, and Taiwan) is at the forefront in wafer fabrication, which requires massive capital investments supported by government incentives as well as access to a robust infrastructure and skilled workforce. China is a leader in assembly, packaging, and testing, which is relatively less skill- and capital-intensive, and is investing aggressively to expand throughout the value chain.

---

[2] The term node is meant to refer to the size in nanometers of the transistor gates in the electronic circuits.

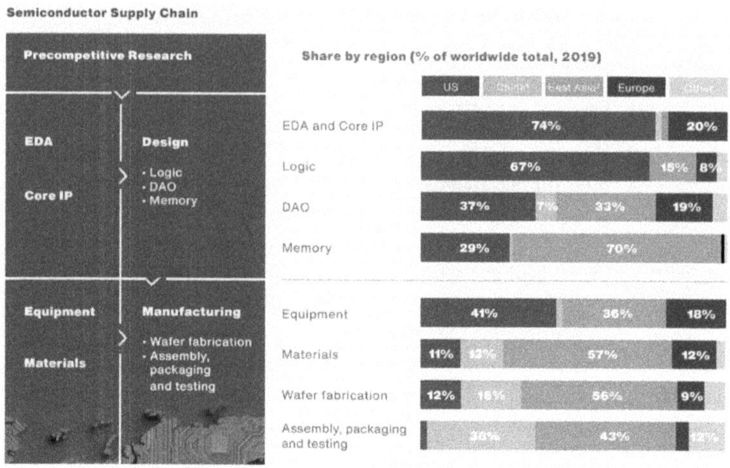

Figure 2: A specialized global value chain
Note: DAO = discrete, analog, and other (including optoelectronics and sensors); EDA = electronic design automation; OSAT = outsourced assembly and test
1. Mainland China 2. East Asia includes South Korea, Japan, and Taiwan
Source: BCG & SIA (2021).

Some elements of the supply chain are concentrated in some regions. This is the case with manufacturing capacity, since 75 % is located in China and East Asia. Most important, all of the world's most advanced semiconductor manufacturing capacity—in nodes below 10 nanometers—is currently located in South Korea (8 %) and Taiwan (92 %).

This global structuration of the supply chain has fueled the development of our knowledge-based and digital economies and its structure has made it possible to supply new technology features at lower prices. However, this structure involves increasing risks of dependence and largely contributes to explaining the shortage in the context of the Covid-19 pandemic.

In their study, based on an analysis of 209 press articles from June 2019 to June 2021, Ramani et al. (2022) present the main causes and consequences of the shortage of semiconductors in the automobile industry. From this analysis, six main causes, leading to production disruptions, inflationary pressures (in the semiconductor and the automobile sector), labor issues, and reductions in stocks and sales, are identified. First, the global pandemic provoked lockdowns and consumer demand variations.

Second, supply disruptions have been marked by production or plant disruptions, logistical delays, and other disruptions. Third, the auto supply chain complexity, characterized by multi-tiered supply chains, manufacturing concentration, and problems of supply chain coordination, aggravated the shortages. A fourth reason lies in chip manufacturing realignment strategies based on the reallocation of production toward producing chips for consumer electronics manufacturers where they could make higher margins compared to chips produced for auto manufacturers. Then, the post-pandemic recovery increased demand but the production capacity of chips was not able to respond to it. Finally, geopolitical risks, mainly characterized at this date by the trade war between the USA and China, have impacted the sector.

If many of the reasons invoked to explain the shortages in the semiconductor industry in recent years are due to external shocks, the difficulties encountered find explanations in the structural characteristics of the sector.

Over the last twenty years, the market has expanded further thanks to exploration of new application areas in key sectors of contemporary society such as medicine and the environment. This diversity of uses and outlets has been stimulated by the miniaturization of components, which increases the performance of this intermediate product while reducing production costs and consequently the selling price (Jorgenson & Vu, 2005).

If the microelectronics industry is both a powerful economic engine and the origin of the new socio-technological system, it nevertheless remains structurally fragile for two major reasons: the first concerns the product itself; the second is related to the market and the evolution of sales.

- Semiconductors are high-tech products with a short lifespan because innovation is central to this industry. Products replace each other rapidly and market players are constantly seeing new product families appear and old ones disappear.
- The market is very cyclical and unstable (IC insight[3], Liu, 2005, Aubry & Renou Messan, 2014), alternating periods when companies' production capacities increase while prices and investments

[3] https://www.icinsights.com/news/bulletins/Top-10-Companies-Hold-57-Of-Global-Semi-Marketshare/

decrease, and periods when these variables move in the opposite direction.

These characteristics largely impact the evolution of firms' business models, as developed below.

2-2. Business models and firms' strategies: From vertical integration to vertical cooperation and networks

Due to the technological complexity of semiconductors, no company or region in the world can master the complete value chain of semiconductors, as was the case in the 1960s where firms were fully integrated. Nowadays, most companies specialize in specific segments of the value chain. Due to high investment expenditure and the cost of R&D, each segment is dominated by the top three players, which represent between 50% and 90 % of segment revenues.

Four main categories of companies are usually identified (Figure 3)

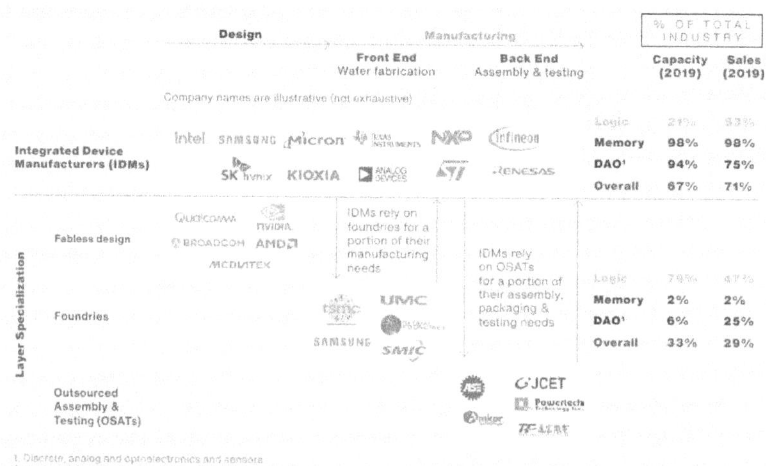

Figure 3: Main categories of companies in the semiconductor supply chain
Source: BCG & SIA (2021)

Integrated device manufacturers (IDM) correspond to semiconductor companies which design, manufacture, and sell integrated circuit (IC) products. Examples are Intel, Samsung, and STMicroelectronics. This model predominated at the beginning of this industry but was questioned by the size of the investment in R&D and in capital expenditure. These account for 67 % of global production and 71 % of total sales in 2019.

Fabless industries are focused on the conception of IC products. They outsource production to foundries and OSATs. They are mainly present in the USA and in Europe.

Foundries focus on the production of IC products, for Fabless companies and also for IDMs which do not always have sufficient production capacities. They are mainly located in Asia.

Outsourced Assembly and Testing companies (OSATs) are companies contracting with IDMs and Fabless companies. This part of the value chain is the result of the offshoring strategies of US IDMs in the 1960s. The Fabless-foundry business model also contributed to the emergence of other OSATs companies.

The existence of these categories of companies lead to the existence of various business models in the semiconductor industry: the first is the business model of IDMs which are present on the whole value chain, and the second one is the Fabless & Foundry business model, characterized by alliances between fabless industries and foundries. The Fabless-Foundry model allows each company to specialize in a core business. While owning a foundry for a chip design company can be seen as a competitive advantage, given the high capital cost, the fabless-foundry model tends to dominate.

The reasons are first the high capital costs of foundries (semiconductor manufacturing plants). For example, TSMC's (Taiwan) latest plant, capable of manufacturing 3nm semiconductors and completed in 2020, cost $19.5 billion. Intel, which also is an IDM, is however considering outsourcing some of its production to TSMC.

The second reason is that most of the players in this industry have specialized in one part of the production chain and not all of them produce the same type of component. For example, the French-Italian STMicroelectronics specializes in chips for the automotive sector or Qualcomm in 5G chips.

The third reason is the high R&D investments that are needed to develop the next generation of semiconductors. For example, the top five fabless firms invested $68 billion in R&D between 2015 and 2019.

Companies have to face two objectives: to meet demand (supplying producers of final goods: automotive, household appliances, smartphones, aerospace, etc.) and to innovate. These two imperatives imply the implementation of strategies to lower costs, increase quality, reduce lead times, and increase flexibility. These firms are thus obliged to look for new organizational structures: to build networks or to position themselves in a specific production sector. Firms are confronted with a double uncertainty which concerns, on the one hand, the outcome of R&D and, on the other hand, the commercial success of the introduction of the product on the market. The innovation process requires heavy and long-term investments, while the expected profit can be difficult to predict. Hence the often observed Fabless-Foundry Model strategy.

The uncertainty associated with the cost/benefit differential can be seen in the cyclical nature of the evolution of the microelectronics industry, already mentioned above. Two economic cycles appear: long-term cycles (about five years) linked to macroeconomic cycles and shorter-term cycles (about every two years) linked to the fact that production capacities are difficult to adjust.

One of the solutions is cooperation, and more specifically vertical cooperation (which replaces vertical integration), which seems to be a way of limiting uncertainty regarding supply and the reception of end markets. The coordination of investments in R&D and marketing of the final product increases the probability of success for their innovation, not only technologically but also commercially.

A good example is given by Intel with the development of the **Intel Foundry Services (IFS)** Accelerator (Figure 4), which consists of the building and constant reinforcement of its business Ecosystem around Electronic Design Automation (EDA), Silicon IP, and Design Service providers

17 companies are already cooperating in this ecosystem which allows an adaptation to clients' need in the diversified semi-conductor markets

> "*IFS Accelerator, an alliance designed to help Intel's foundry customers bring their silicon products from idea to implementation. The alliance enables an ecosystem of best-in-class Electronic Design Automation (EDA), Silicon IP, and Design Service providers to deliver a seamless interface with Intel's process technologies. Through deep collaboration, the Intel Foundry Services (IFS) Accelerator taps the best capabilities available in the industry to accelerate customer innovation on IFS manufacturing platforms.*" Intel's website

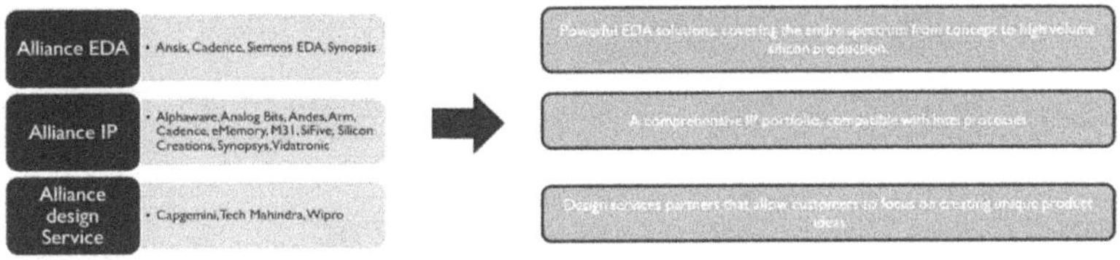

Figure 4: Intel Foundry Services Accelerator – An example of a business ecosystem
Sources: Intel's website

Intel is following a value chain strategy that has as its asset the mastery and increase of its knowledge capital related to the core technology (Laperche, 2017): semiconductors, integrated circuits, software, applications. The strategy is based on co-creation (interactive – user innovation) and open innovation strategy. The construction of this business ecosystem is strongly related to US innovation policies, as shown in Part 3.1.

According to us, this example is illustrative of the co-evolution of companies' business ecosystems and a national innovation ecosystem. Can we make the same statement in the case of Europe? The following part aims to give answers to this question.

3- European policy: Building an innovation ecosystem in the microprocessor industry

3.1. Europe's position among competitors in the semiconductor sector and support policies

Among the six regions of the world that participate in the global Value Chain of the semiconductor industry (US, China, Taiwan, Korea, Europe, and "Others"), Europe is lagging behind the main competitors. It represents 10 % of global output and 20 % of the consumption of semiconductors (Figure 5).

Figure 5: Share of the main countries/regions in global output and the consumption of semiconductors
Source: BCG & SIA (2021)

Europe, and France by extension, has chosen to focus on R&D and design (Fabless) in this sector of activity. Between 2010 and 2019, the US and Europe each contributed 30 % of the total patents filed (converted into triadic patents) which demonstrates this specialization in semiconductor R&D. Europe hosts one of the leading semiconductor institutions, located in France (CEA-Leti). It is specialized in applied research in microelectronics and nanotechnology

The current European policy in the field of semiconductors, just like other countries' policies such as those of America or China, aims to address the weaknesses associated with the global specialized supply chain. Many countries are using industrial policy tools (e.g. government subsidies, business incentives, R&D funding, etc.) to boost domestic semiconductor manufacturing. One of the main goals of recent national or regional programs (see Table 2) is to increase domestic production. However, the objective to achieve self-sufficiency does not seem realistic. According to BCG & SIA, for the US, for example, such an objective "would require over $400 billion in government incentives and cost more than one trillion dollars over ten years" (BCG & SIA, 2021, p. 6).

Table 2: Recent national and regional strategies toward the semi-conductor industry in the main countries/regions

Country/ region	Recent policies for semiconductor industry	Source
USA	CHIPS Act July 2022 $52 billion in manufacturing grants and research investments 25 % investment tax credit (ITC) to incentivize semiconductor manufacturing in the U.S	SIA, Semiconductor Industry Association
China	Five-Year Plan (2021–2025) Technology development considered as a national security issue. Increase in R&D spending of 7 % per year. Semiconductor identified as a key technology	Center for Strategic and International Studies (Feng, 2022)
South Korea	Road Map July 2022 Investment infrastructures Tax credit Development of clusters Support for R&D	https://koreajoongangdaily.joins.com
Taiwan	Began to invest in 1974 Creation of TSMC in 1987 – origin of the Fabless-Foundry model Incentives for new fabs corresponding to 25 to 35 % of the total cost of ownership during the 2010 decade International development of TSMC, the leader in the most advanced semiconductors.	BCG & Sia 2021 Center for Strategic and International Studies (Arcuri, 2022) Reuters.com
Japan	The Strategy for Semiconductors and the Digital Industry – June 2021 (1) Invitation to foreign companies to build their semiconductor foundries in Japan together with Japanese companies and institutions. (2) Acceleration of digital-related investments and strengthening the design and development of cutting-edge logic semiconductors. (3) Promotion of green innovation. (4) Strengthening of the portfolio of the domestic semiconductor industry and enhancing its resilience.	https://accesspartnership.com/strategy-for-revival-of-the-japanese-semiconductor-industry/#_ftn3
Europe	Industrial Alliance on Processors and Semiconductor Technologies (2021) European Chips Act – February 2022 €43 billion public and private investment	European Commission

Source: Authors from diverse sources

Making the statement that the share of modern semiconductor manufacturing capacity located in the U.S. has eroded from 37 % in 1990 to 12 % today, the American Congress passed the CHIPS Act in July 2022, which includes semiconductor manufacturing grants, research investments, and an investment tax credit for chip manufacturing (SIA, consulted on 4 August 2022). This tax credit will be offered to national companies like Intel, but also foreign ones like Samsung or TSMC, which is already investing to build a plant in Arizona (see below).

China is also trying to increase its self-sufficiency. This began with the definition in 2014 of the Guidelines to Promote the National Integrated Circuit Industry, which called for a $150 billion investment in semiconductors. In 2015, The National Semiconductor Fund was set up by the Ministry of Finance and the China Development Bank Capital to facilitate state investment. It allocated around two-thirds of its investments in chip manufacturing and maintained minority stakes in over 70 companies. In May 2015, Beijing announced its Made in China 2025 initiative, which—among other objectives—aimed to raise the local content of semiconductor chips to 40 % by 2020 and 70 % by 2025. The 14th Five Year Plan elevated technological development to a national security issue, increased R&D spending by 7 % over the next five years, and identified semiconductors as a critical technology (Feng, 2022).

South Korea has recently defined a road map for the next few years aimed at increasing Korea's global chip market share to 10 % from the current 3 % and increasing material, parts, and equipment independence to 50 % from 30 %. This policy is oriented toward infrastructure development, tax credit for large companies, and support for R&D. Infrastructure development will be centered on two main companies, SK Hynix and Samsung electronics, and aims to develop their clusters (the Yongin Cluster for SK Hynix and the Pyeontaek semiconductor campus for Samsung electronics) and the size of their plants. Tax credits for large companies investing in chips are to be increased by 2 % from the current 6-to-10 %. The credit will also be available for a wider range of activities, including research and development, chip design, and verification equipment. Moreover, administrative requirements will be eased as well as feasibility studies. The plan includes 450 billion won of projects related to high-energy efficiency and environment-friendly semiconductors, 500 billion won of auto semiconductor projects, and 1.25 trillion won of AI semiconductor developments. 1.5 trillion won will be allocated to fund research and development, product testing, and overseas expansion.

Employees recruited from overseas will get a 50 % tax break for ten years, up from the current five years.

Taiwan has become a critical node in the semiconductor supply chain since the 1980s when Taiwan Semiconductor Manufacturing Co Ltd (TSMC) was created (1987). It was the first "contract" company on which engineering semiconductor companies could rely for the production of the chips they designed. This business model contributed to the emergence of the Fabless-Foundry model and also to the erosion of American production capacity. Similar firms emerged in Japan, Korea and China and these four countries accounted for nearly 80 % of production capacity in 2019 (Arcuri & Lu, 2022). TSMC is the global leader in the production of the most advanced chips (see Figure 6) and attracts the attention of the main competitor countries.

For example, the US succeeded in attracting TSMC, which has started the construction of a site in Arizona where it plans to spend $12 billion to build a computer chip factory in June 2022. The factory plans to produce the company's five-nanometer production technology starting in 2024 (https://www.reuters.com/technology/tsmc-says-construction-has-started-arizona-chip-factory-2021-06-01/).

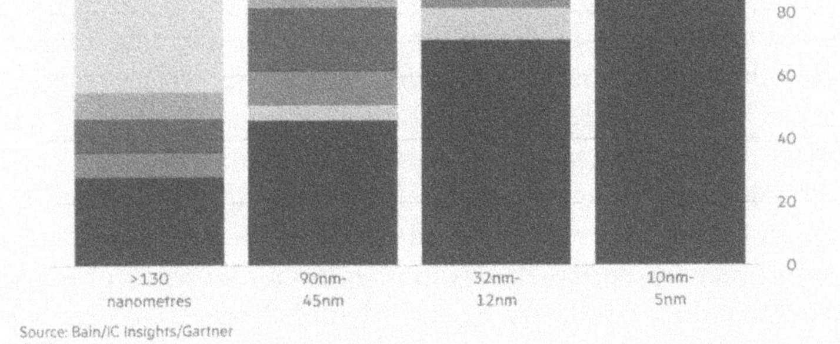

Figure 6: TSMC: the leader in advanced chips.
Source: https://www.ft.com/content/05206915-fd73-4a3a-92a5-6760ce965bd9

In Japan, the Strategy for Semiconductors and the Digital Industry was announced in June 2021. As with other big players in the semiconductor industry, Japan's position declined in the 1990s after being the leader with a market share of more than 50 % in the late 1980s. It represents 14 % of global output and 6 % of global consumption. The new policy announced in 2021 aims at (1) Inviting foreign companies to build their semiconductor foundries in Japan together with Japanese companies and institutions; (2) Accelerating digital-related investments and strengthening the design and development of cutting-edge logic semiconductors; (3) Promoting green innovation; (4) Strengthening the portfolio of the domestic semiconductor industry and enhancing its resilience. Japan also convinced Taiwan Semiconductor Manufacturing Co. (TSMC), the world's biggest contract chipmaker, to invest in Japan: on 14 October 2021, TSMC announced the construction of its first-ever chipmaking plant in Japan, with the aim of strengthening the local semiconductor supply chain. The foundry will be specialized in 22-nanometer and 28-nanometer chip production. This project is supported by large subsidies and fiscal advantages offered by the Japanese government. The plan is also developed in partnership with the domestic global player Sony. Sony will invest some $500 million in the TSMC subsidiary, which will be called Japan Advanced Semiconductor Manufacturing Inc. (JASM), representing an equity stake of less than 20 %. Moreover, Denso (auto part maker) will also invest in the project, leading to an increase in TSMC's investment. "Denso will provide $350 million in equity for JASM, taking a stake of over 10 %. The expected increase in funding will help TSMC build a production line for 12-to-16-nm chips in Kumamoto, in addition to the 22-to-28-nm chip production line envisaged in the original plan" (https://accesspartnership.com/strategy-for-revival-of-the-japanese-semiconductor-industry/#_ftn2).

Europe has for years developed support for the semiconductor industry, especially through programs supporting public and private collaboration such as the Key Digital Technologies Joint Undertaking, aimed at reinforcing Europe's innovation potential, boosting its competitiveness, and ensuring technological sovereignty in the field of electronics[4]. The European Innovation Council also supports equity investment in breakthrough innovation, in order to support the creation and reinforcement of ecosystems in the semiconductor industry. Several Member States have already joined the Project of Common European Interest (IPCEI) on Microelectronics

4 (https://www.kdt-ju.europa.eu/what-we-do)

and Communication Technologies launched in 2018. This State aid tool for Member States allows "public co-financing under the condition that it concerns large integrated cross-border projects to overcome market failures and enable breakthrough innovation in key sectors and technologies, up to first industrial deployment, as well as important infrastructure investments, with positive spill-over effects for the EU economy at large"[5]. The Alliance on Processors and Semiconductor Technologies was established in 2021. It brings together businesses, Member State representatives, academia, users, as well as research and technology organizations, with the objective to identify current gaps in the production of microchips and the technology developments needed for companies and organizations.

The most recent plan is the European Chips Act (2022) which contains a Communication, two proposals for a Regulation (that has to be adopted by the European Parliament and by Member States) and a Recommendation. The two main lines of action are: (1) Strengthening the European electronics design ecosystem; (2) Establishing the necessary manufacturing capacity. The aim is to support the emergence of networks of European and global players to produce the next generation of processors, electronic components, and technologies: moving Europe toward the production of technologies from 16 nanometers (nm) to 10 nm, as well as from 5 nm to 2 nm and beyond. These are the most advanced types of semiconductors that, in addition to increasing performance, have the potential to massively reduce the energy used by any activity, from phones to data centers.

The overall Chips Act funding package pools together €43 billion of public and private investment and measures to prepare for, respond rapidly to, and anticipate and prevent future supply chain disruption, in collaboration with Member States and international (especially North American) partners. It will enable the EU to achieve its ambition of doubling its current market share to 20 % by 2030. Among this, €11 billion will be made available to strengthen existing research, development, and innovation, and more than €30 billion of investments by Member States to support the development of its industry.

In sum, we can observe that all countries involved in the global semiconductor value chain develop quite similar policies, aimed at increasing their domestic production and moving up the value chain in order to

---

5 (https://www.ipcei-me.eu/what-is/)

produce the most advanced types of semiconductors. However, not all of them have the same strengths and do not consider in the same way the role of their domestic leaders and the competitive advantage that they already have. This particularly concerns the European policy, which could reduce the impacts of the new policy orientations.

3.2. Limitations of the European policy in the semiconductor industry

The European strategy, which consists of relocating production to Europe, suffers from a number of imprecisions.

One of the major issues is about the concentration or dispersion of R&D, design, and manufacturing units in Europe. This is a longstanding characteristic of the European semiconductor industry (Martin, 1996). At the beginning of this industry, the leaders were first the USA and then, by the late 1970s, Japanese industry had matched US technology in most areas and surpassed it in some. On the contrary, the European industry has always been lagging behind the leaders. Among the factors behind this European lag is "(…) the fragmentation of the European Market into a set of national submarkets, no one of which is able to provide a base for a world class semiconductor operation" (Martin, 1996, p. 726).

On the other hand, building new factories will not solve the problem of the current shortage, since it can take up to five years to get them up and running. The processes of setting up new production capacity (very long), design (long), and innovation (immediate) in the semiconductor industry are asynchronous.

The alternative would be to strengthen the existing ecosystem that has made innovation and design its strengths, especially in e-health, AI and data security, defense, or even aerospace and to verticalize the sector by linking European semiconductor players more closely to user sectors where Europe already has a competitive advantage. European market leaders such as Germany's Infineon, NXP in the Netherlands, and the French-Italian STMicroelectronics focus on supplying devices to the automotive, aerospace, and industrial automation industries, among others. These are not the most advanced micro-processors, but as shown above (see Section 2.1), all kinds of microprocessors are today needed in current digital products. Building strong business ecosystems around the European leaders that could enrich their knowledge capital by tapping into the resources of a larger European innovation ecosystem, just like the example of Intel developed above (see Section 2.2) would certainly help to strengthen the European position.

However, the choice that seems to be made by Europe is at the same time to develop various projects in different European Member States, to attract production capacities from other countries, and to try to develop some of the most advanced semiconductors, which is considered by some players as a dangerous strategy[6]. The projects of investments (production and R&D) by Intel in Europe announced in March 2022 (€80 billon in the next 10 years) – which will benefit from the European Chips Act – recognize this (see Figure 7). A first wave of investments, worth €33 billion, will concern Germany, France, Italy, Spain, Ireland, and Poland. Magdeburg, Germany, will host two chip production plants.

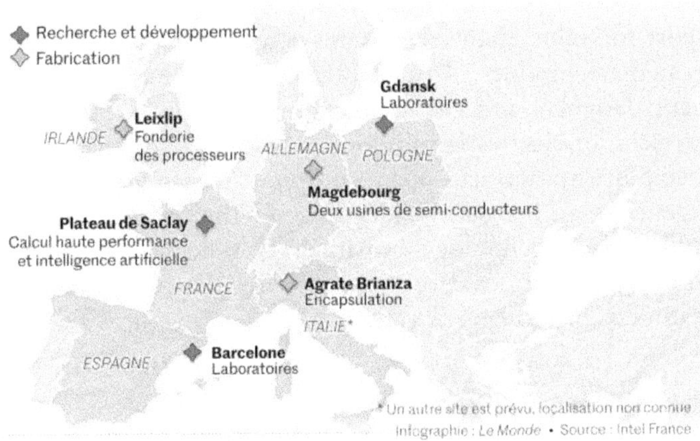

Figure 7: Intel's investment projects in Europe
Source: Le Monde, https://www.lemonde.fr/economie/article/2022/03/16/semi-conducteurs-intel-va-investir-massivement-en-europe_6117715_3234.html

6 A senior executive interviewed by the Financial Times considers that the willingness to develop the most advanced chips in Europe is a dangerous strategy: "We are at 22 nm now. Going from 22 to 2 nm is like jumping to the top of the Taipei 101 skyscraper — if you fail, you crash," "In addition, our need for cutting-edge capacity in Europe is really not that convincing. We specialize in semiconductors that are different from the chips for mass market consumer devices that dominate US chip demand, and therefore the cost gains from cutting-edge production technology are not as crucial for us as for TSMC's American customers.", https://www.ft.com/content/05206915-fd73-4a3a-92a5-6760ce965bd9, March 24 2021.

Another problem is the dependence on rare earths – 80 % of which are found in China. To get out of this situation, the United States re-launched the Mountain Pass mine in California at the beginning of the year, which had been closed in 2002 (when it will be operating at full capacity it will provide 16 % of the world's supply of rare earths). The European Alliance for Raw Materials (Erma[7]), launched by the Commission in 2020, has identified 14 extraction or recycling projects in Europe to ensure 20 % of European needs in the medium term. Several European countries, including France, the world's second largest maritime area, are also interested in the seabed, which could supply them with rare metals.

There is a need to broaden the framework of analysis to understand the relationships that firms can create with external actors, whether they are companies or public institutions: the latter must take into account the change in the boundaries of companies and promote dynamic ecosystems around products. The work can, in fact, be done through clear support for value chain ecosystems adapted to the introduction of the intermediate product. This involves bringing together not only component designers and end-product manufacturers, but also developers of services, or electronic solutions, as well as research laboratories. This strategic orientation can open up opportunities for differentiation and can generate an increase in added value. The company thus ensures the visibility of its technology and its development. This strategy provides clear support to innovative and small user companies while prioritizing investments in strategic sectors.

Conclusion

The semiconductor industry is at the heart of the industrial policy strategies of all countries involved in the globalized value chain. The context of shortage experienced since the beginning of the Covid-19 pandemic has highlighted the fragility of this highly specialized value chain. Moreover, international geopolitical tensions, and in particular those between the United States and China, are exacerbated by Taiwan's position, whose company TSMC is at the heart of the production of the most innovative semiconductors, those that will be the engine of the digital economy under construction.

---

7 https://erma.eu/

All the countries concerned are seeking to increase their independence in these core technologies at the heart of digitized economic sectors, as diverse as automotive, consumer electronics, telephony, and communications, but also infrastructure management and national defense. Our study develops the hypothesis that there is a close link between the business ecosystem built by leaders to enrich their knowledge capital and the national or regional innovation ecosystems from which they can draw. This hypothesis is the one adopted by the main countries present in the value chain, the United States with Intel, Japan around Sony, South Korea with Samsung, and of course Taiwan around TSMC. Of course, these policies also rely on the international partnerships that the State-Industry alliance can build (for example, the cooperation between Sony and TSMC for Japan, or Intel and TSMC for the United States). The European policy seeks on the contrary to strengthen its innovation ecosystem by investing in all directions and without building this strategy around its competitive advantages and its leading companies in certain market segments. Given the costs associated with moving up the value chain and the desire to produce the most advanced semiconductors, this policy direction seems highly risky, especially in an unstable economic environment.

This article provides a better understanding of the recent evolution of industrial policies in the semiconductor field. It can be the basis for empirical studies on the strategies developed by the European leaders in the semiconductor sector.

References

Arcuri, G., & Lu, S. (2022). Taiwan's semiconductor dominance: Implications for cross-strait relations and the prospect of forceful unification. Center for Strategic and International Studies, March 22. https://www.csis.org/blogs/perspectives-innovation/taiwans-semiconductor-dominance-implications-cross-strait-relations

Aubry, M., & Renou-Messant, P. (2014), Semiconductor industry cycles: Explanatory factors and forecasting. *Economic Modelling, 39*, 221–231

Boschma, R. (2005). Proximity and innovation: A critical assessment. *Regional Studies, 39*(1), 91–74.

BCG and SIA. (2021). Strengthening the global semiconductor value chain in an uncertain era, Report.

Chesbrough, H. W. (2003). *Open innovation*. Boston, MA: Harvard Business School Press.

Feng, J. (2022). How are Washington and Beijing utilizing Industrial Policy to Bolster domestic semiconductor manufacturing?. *Center for Strategic and International Studies*, https://www.csis.org/blogs/new-perspectives-asia/how-are-washington-and-beijing-utilizing-industrial-policy-bolster

Freeman, C. (1987). *Technology policy and economic performance*. London: Printer.

Granstrand, O. (2000). Corporate innovation systems. A comparative study of multi-technology corporations in Japan, Sweden and the USA, report submitted to the EU Dynacom project, CIM report 2000:01, Dept. of Industrial Management and Economics, Chalmers University of Technology. https://citeseerx.ist.psu.edu/document?repid=rep1&type=pdf&doi=c8e36b93ba064cd5fffc7527d4a579d9230d008e

Granstrand, O., & Holgensson, M. (2020). Innovation ecosystems: A conceptual review and a new definition. *Technovation, 90–91*, 102098.

Jorgenson, D. W., & Vu, K. (2005). Information technology and the world economy. *The Scandinavian Journal of Economics, 107*(4), 631–650.

Laperche, B. (2017). *Entreprise knowledge capital*. London: ISTE/Wiley.

Laperche, B. (2019). Les écosystèmes d'innovation au service du capital savoir des entreprises. In Laperche, B., Lima, M., Seulliet, E., & Trousse, B. (Eds.), *Les écosystèmes d'innovation. Regards croisés des acteurs clés*. Paris: L'harmattan, pp. 97–118.

Laperche B., & Uzunidis D. (2019). The knowledge capital and the network firm: Socialization versus business appropriation of scientific work. In Blast, G., Carayannis, E. G., & Campbell, D. (Eds.), *The future of education and labor*. Switzerland: Springer, pp. 57–75.

Laperche B., Lima M., Seulliet E., & Trousse, B. (2019). Les écosystèmes. Espaces d'émergence d'innovation (Introduction). In Laperche, B., Lima, M., Seulliet, E., & Trousse, B. (Eds.), *Les écosystèmes d'innovation. Regards croisés des acteurs clés*. Paris: L'harmattan, pp. 17–27.

Liu, W. H. (2005). Determinants of the semiconductor industry cycles. *Journal of Policy Model, 27*, 853–866.

Lundvall, B.-Å. (Ed.). (1992). *National innovation systems: Towards a theory of innovation and interactive learning*. London: Pinter.

Lundvall, B.-Å., & Rikap, C. (2022). China's catching-up in artificial intelligence seen as a co-evolution of corporate and national innovation systems. *Research Policy, 51*, 104395.

Malerba, F. (2002). Sectoral systems of innovation and production. *Research Policy, 31*(2), 247–264.

Marshall, A. (1890). *Principles of economics*. London: Macmillan.

Martin, S. (1996). Protection, promotion and cooperation in the European Semiconductor Industry. *Review of Industrial Organization, 11*, 721–735.

Moore, J. F. (1993). *Predators and prey: A new ecology of competition. Harvard Business Review, 71*(3), 75–86.

Moore, J. (1996). *The death of competition, leadership and strategy in the age of business ecosystems*. Harper Business.

Oh, D. S., Phillips, F., Park, S., & Lee, E. (2016). Innovation ecosystems: A critical examination. *Technovation, 54*, 1–6.

Porter, M. (1990). *The competitive advantage of nations*. New York: Free Press.

Ramani, V., Ghosh, D., & Sodhi, M. S. (2022). Understanding systemic disruption from the Covid-19-induced semiconductor shortage for the auto industry. *Omega, 113*. https://doi.org/10.1016/j.omega.2022.102720.

Ritala, P., & Almpanopoulou, A. (2017). In defense of 'eco'in innovation ecosystem. *Technovation, 60*, 39–42.

Torre, A., & Zimmermann, J. B. (2015). Des clusters aux écosystèmes industriels locaux. *Revue d'Economie Industrielle, 52*, 13–38.

Uzunidis, D. (2010). Innovation et proximité. Entreprises, entrepreneurs et milieux innovateurs. *Revue des sciences de gestion, 241*, 13–22.

Uzunidis, D. (2018). *Collective innovation processes: Principles and practices*. London: ISTE/Wiley.

Uzunidis, D. (Ed.). (2020). *Systemic innovation: Entrepreneurial strategies and market dynamics*. London: ISTE/Wiley.

Uzunidis, D. (2022). Overview of the systemic of value chains, Spring of Innovation 2022, Research Network on Innovation, Online.

Young, C. (2022). A China-Taiwan conflict could lead to a catastrophic semiconductor shortage in the world, Interesting Engineering. https://interestingengineering.com/culture/a-china-taiwan-conflict-could-lead-to-a-catastrophic-semiconductor-shortage-in-the-world

The entrepreneurial function in digital ecosystems

Sophie Boutillier, Dimitri Uzunidis[1]

Abstract : The objective of this chapter is on the one hand, to outline a holistic theory of the entrepreneur that combines economics, sociology, political science, psychology, and history and, on the other hand, to mobilize this theoretical framework to trace the socio-economic trajectory of entrepreneurs who have created major digital social network companies (Facebook, YouTube, WhatsApp, Messenger and Instagram). We will thus show how these entrepreneurs created their businesses in a given institutional context (United States), from which they extracted and appropriated the resources necessary to carry out their project and constitute their resources potential. How did these entrepreneurs in the digital social networking industry identify business opportunities and extract the tangible and intangible resources through which they were able to combine them, and then how did they build digital innovation ecosystems that helped to transform the institutional framework in which they are embedded?

Keywords : Entrepreneur, Innovation, Tangible and intangible resources, Resources potential, Digital social network, Digital innovation ecosystem.

1. Introduction

Since the beginning of the 21st century, a number of digital social networks have been created to exchange information of all kinds between individuals and/or companies around the world. This evolution has been made possible by the development of digital technologies and the

[1] University of Littoral-Côte d'Opale, Research Network on Innovation, France

Internet, which began at the end of the Second World War in the context of the Cold War. The emergence, dissemination, and development of these technologies are essentially due to the military (Isaacson, 2015). However, they have found civilian applications thanks to the creativity of a few enterprising individuals with fertile imaginations and appropriate public policy measures. To understand these transformations, we cannot rely on a simple analysis centered on the individual to identify his resources, his motivations, how he identified a need not met by existing entrepreneurs, and the result he achieved. The entrepreneur, like any economic agent, is socially embedded in a given institutional context, in the sense given to it by institutionalist economists (Veblen, 1899). It is therefore by following this logic that we have constructed our analysis. We have thus sought to identify a dialectical relationship between the entrepreneur and the institutional context in which he is embedded.

The economic theory of the innovative entrepreneur as initiated by Schumpeter (1911, 1942) at the beginning of the 20th century placed great emphasis on the institutional context in which the entrepreneur acts. The entrepreneur whose behavior and decisions Schumpeter analyses, whether European or American, lives in a capitalist economy driven by the second industrial revolution. Before this period, according to Schumpeter, men of action had other means to rise in the social hierarchy, generally through war and feats of arms. His analysis is not about a 15th century merchant who had to circumvent the power of the guilds. It is therefore well dated and anchored in a specific institutional context. This is what we have tended to forget when we talk about the Schumpeterian entrepreneur in a very general way, and we ignore the institutional context in which the entrepreneur is a stakeholder and in which his innovation ecosystem is formed. It is true that since these pioneering works, many researchers have been interested in the institutional context in which the individual becomes an entrepreneur (Granovetter, 1985; Baumol, 1993; Boutillier et al., 1999, 2014).

Since the beginning of the 20th century, researchers have focused on non-economic variables to understand the behavior of entrepreneurs by placing them in their institutional contexts. Weber's (1905) analysis of Protestant and Catholic entrepreneurs constitutes a significant advance in this respect. More broadly, the German Historical School (Sombart, 1913) had developed a very relevant analysis by combining the contributions of economics, sociology, political science, and of course history (Boutillier & Tiran, 2016). The German Historical School, such as Schumpeter (1911, 1942), challenges the microeconomic theory (Walras, 1874), according to which the entrepreneur is a rational economic agent who makes decisions with the objective of maximizing his profit according to the price of the factors of production. The context in which the entrepreneur makes his decisions is understood only on the basis of economic considerations (nature of the market and the product, circulation of information, flexibility of production factors, etc.). All non-economic criteria are excluded from the analysis, in particular all social and political considerations. This gap had been partly filled by the institutionalist theory, initiated by Veblen (1899) at the end of the 19th century, which also condemned the Walrasian theory.

The economic theory of the entrepreneur has evolved considerably since the second half of the 20th century and has become more complex, taking for granted the principle of the contextualization of entrepreneurial action at the economic, sociological, managerial, political, and historical levels, with particular reference to the evolutionary theory of the entrepreneur. We thus place ourselves within the framework of the evolutionary theory of the entrepreneur, whose main representative Aldrich (2012) explains how new organizations are created, how entrepreneurs transform the organizations they create and mobilize resources (human, financial, material, etc.) to cope with changes in competition, how they overcome or fail to overcome the problems they face, thus creating new routines, and finally, how the routines they have created are imitated and perpetuated by other entrepreneurs.

Within this institutional framework, entrepreneurial ecosystems (Scaringella & Radziwon, 2018; Boutillier, 2021; Spigel, 2020) develop, usually in given territories, which unite economic actors who share common values, a common vision of business and innovation. In these ecosystems, entrepreneurs develop cooperative or competitive relationships. They can also benefit from business creation and innovation support organizations, financing through investment funds or cooperation with research centers, universities and private or public companies. Businesses are set up supported by relations of proximity, which can be spatial, organizational, or cognitive. Proximity considered a priori is linked to the existence of externalities that produce spatial agglomeration effects and innovation dynamics based on the organization and circulation/capture of knowledge. The role of the State is fundamental. It intervenes through public policy measures, with the objective of supporting business creation and innovation in sectors considered to be priorities in the light of the evolution of the international economic context.

Our main objective in this chapter is twofold. On the one hand, it is to outline a holistic theory of the entrepreneur that combines economics, sociology, political science, psychology, and history and, on the other hand, to mobilize this theoretical framework to trace the socio-economic trajectory of eight entrepreneurs who have created major digital social network companies (Facebook, YouTube, WhatsApp, Messenger and Instagram). We will thus show how these entrepreneurs created their businesses in a given institutional context, that of the United States, from which they extracted and appropriated the resources necessary to carry out their project. We hypothesize that their success lies in their ability to create what we call a digital innovation ecosystem, the definition of which will be partly the subject of this chapter.

The selection criterion is essentially the notoriety of the social networks they have created and the number of monthly active users in the world. We selected the first five companies because they were all created in the United States, i.e. in the same institutional context. Moreover, it is in the United States that these technologies emerged at the end of the 1970s with the creation of Apple by Steve Jobs and Microsoft by Bill Gates for microelectronics, then at the end of the 1990s with the creation of Google by Larry Page and Sergey Brin. These three companies, Apple, Microsoft, and Google, were in our view at the center of the technological revolution that took place at the end of the 20th century, which led to the development of the laptop industry and then mobile phones and the development of the Internet, through which the digital social network companies could be created, according to the principle of innovation clusters (Schumpeter, 1939; Uzunidis, 2020).

Our research question is: how did these eight entrepreneurs in the digital social networking industry identify business opportunities and extract the tangible and intangible resources through which they were able to combine them, and then how did they build digital innovation ecosystems that helped to transform the institutional framework in which they are embedded? To answer this question, we will start with a review of the literature, followed by a presentation of our methodology and results, then a discussion and a conclusion.

2. Innovation ecosystem of the entrepreneur

2.1. The entrepreneur embedded in a given institutional context

From a theoretical point of view, we do not rely on an exhaustive review of the literature on the capacity of the entrepreneur to generate innovations in a given institutional context, in the image of the Schumpeterian theory of the entrepreneur, according to which the entrepreneur is the economic agent who creates new combinations of production factors. We have built our theoretical framework on the basis of some pioneering research on the theory of the entrepreneur. We start from the evolutionary theory as initiated by the Sussex school (notably Freeman and Perez) during the 1970s–1980s, which we link to Schumpeter's (1942) theory of the entrepreneur, and then to Audretsch's (1995) theory of knowledge spillovers, at the contextual level. At the individual level, to analyze the behavior of the entrepreneur, we mobilize (again) Schumpeter (1942) with Penrose's (1959) theory of resources and Granovetter's (1985) theory of social embeddedness. Entrepreneurs' resources are both material and immaterial. These considerations lead us to mobilize the theory of social capital (Bourdieu, 1980; Granovetter, 1973; Boutillier & Uzunidis, 2017), and consequently to question the capacity of individuals to mobilize networks of social relations. The entrepreneur is indeed socially embedded. They mobilize resources in the institutional context in which they are inserted. This leads us to mobilize the evolutionary theory of the entrepreneur, as developed by Aldrich (2012), which emphasizes the entrepreneur's capacity to create organizations and transform them according to the opportunities he has identified.

The literature review on which we rely is part of the evolutionary theory of the entrepreneur and entrepreneurial ecosystems (Spigel, 2020). As mentioned above, the evolutionary theory of the entrepreneur was essentially initiated by Aldrich (2010). It is more broadly based on the pioneering work of Freeman and Perez (1988) on the theory of techno-economic paradigms, on the one hand, and Nelson and Winter's (1982) theory of the evolutionary theory of the firm, on the other. According to the former, economic and social history is punctuated by a succession of long waves which are at the origin of the formation of techno-economic paradigms. Each phase of evolution is characterized by the appearance of driving activities that develop in clusters. This can easily be identified from the first industrial revolution with the development of the iron and steel industry, the steam engine, and the textile industry, to the end of the 20th century with the development of the microelectronics industry and the Internet. Each technological revolution is characterized by an explosion of new products, industries, and infrastructures, which gradually give rise to a new techno-economic paradigm. This paradigm guides entrepreneurs, researchers, innovators, managers, investors and consumers in their individual decisions and interactions (competition or cooperation) during the propagation of this set of technologies. Each wave brings its own transformations in social, political, technical, and economic organization (Freeman & Perez, 1988). The basis of each wave is characterized by a particular form of social, political, technical, and economic organization (Freeman & Perez, 1988), which gives rise to a new technological style, a radical transformation in the organization of production (business) and society (consumer). These technical developments are largely generated outside the entrepreneurial framework, since they were first developed in a military research framework (Isaacson, 2015). Knowledge is thus produced in company research centers, university laboratories, and other institutions. There is then a phenomenon of 'knowledge spillover' or a kind of positive externalities of knowledge that will not immediately be transformed into innovations. According to Audrestch (1995), knowledge does not exist as such. It is embodied in the individuals who possess it. It is therefore through the intermediary of entrepreneurs, the bearers of knowledge, that knowledge circulates to give rise to innovations and enterprises.

These transformations are accompanied by political, institutional, and cultural changes. In the course of these different transformations, the competitive relationships between companies are changing. The role of the State in its capacity to define a coherent scientific and technical policy is preponderant. Under these conditions, the entrepreneur is indeed the product of economic, social, technical, and scientific transformations from which he is able to benefit (Boutillier et al., 2014). The institutional framework in which the entrepreneur is embedded thus consists of four poles:

- **Education and Sciences**: The educational, scientific, and technical pole made up of universities, public and private research centers, etc.,

- **Finance**: The financial sector made up of banks, investment funds, crowdfunding platforms, etc.,
- **Market**: The market formed by the companies in place which structure the offer of products and services that new entrants can disrupt,
- **The State and public policy**: which through public policies supports the development of a particular sector of activity to support existing companies, create jobs, increase the supply of companies, and support economic growth.

Entrepreneurs are the vectors of these transformations. They occupy functions that have been defined by the institutional context in which they are inserted. Social relations are formed and dissolved according to their objectives and resources. These social relations do not take place in a vacuum, they develop physically in a given territory/environment. In the context of our study, university campuses and the incubators they house play a decisive role in the success of an entrepreneurial project by bringing together individuals with different resources: for some, knowledge and ideas; for others, material resources; and for others, financial resources to be developed, hence the importance of proximity relationships. They all communicate with each other. They exchange ideas, knowledge, techniques, etc. These relationships are generally based on a given geographical framework. All the universities from which the entrepreneurs we studied come have long-standing relationships with companies (Etzkowitz, 2022). Students are in constant contact with companies. They have the opportunity to undertake internships in innovative start-ups or large companies. This spatial proximity is also organizational and cognitive. As a whole, proximity produces localized externalities that generate agglomeration effects and territorial dynamics. Spatial proximity reduces the distances (and the time) that physically separate individuals, a necessary condition for the development of recognition and inter-recognition relationships between them. Organizational proximity resides in belonging to the same organization (company, R&D laboratory, university, department within the same company or administration, etc.), to the same "community of destiny". Cognitive proximity refers to the adherence by different individuals to the same conception of innovation, to the same routines, to the same heuristics, to the same thinking algorithms, to the same conventions, to the same traditions, to the same beliefs, to the same internal codes, to the same languages and/or to the same procedures of learning, deliberation, decision making, and governance (Uzunidis, 2021). It is located within organizations, networks, and communities. Managers may sit on the board of universities, or conversely researchers may sit on the board of companies. Managers or engineers may also teach at universities.

This model is also that of the entrepreneurial university which developed in industrial countries at the end of the 20th century, but which developed much earlier in the United States than in Europe.

To summarize, the relationships of spatial, organizational, and cognitive proximity contribute greatly to the formation by (and for) the entrepreneur of his innovation ecosystem. The diagram below (Figure 1) represents the basic inputs and interactions necessary for the formation of this ecosystem.

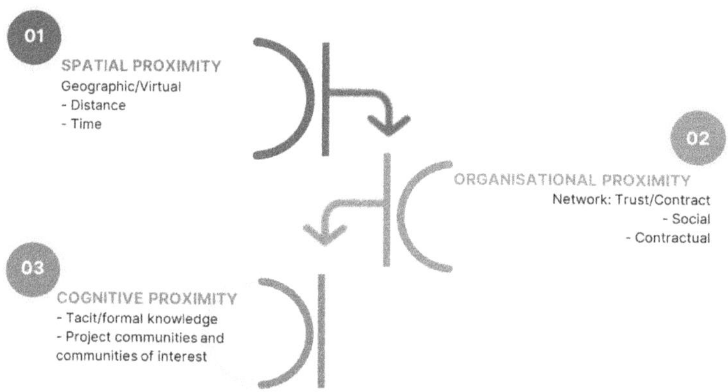

Figure 1: Proximity and the innovation ecosystem
Source: authors.

2.2. *The resource potential of the embedded innovative entrepreneur*

At this stage of our analysis, the question arises as to how the entrepreneur identifies investment opportunities. Is he in a state of alertness (Kirzner, 1973) and thus able to transform consumer expectations into innovation? Does the entrepreneur create new combinations of factors of production in a process of creative destruction, in a spirit of challenge, in a game against the established companies that structure the market (Schumpeter, 1942)? But whatever the answer to the question of the entrepreneur's capacity to innovate, the fundamental question is the resources that the entrepreneur mobilizes. To answer this question, we rely on the theory of resources (Penrose, 1959), which does not focus on the entrepreneur, but on the firm. However, it provides relevant elements of analysis. Penrose distinguishes between the services that a firm can obtain from the material and human resources at its disposal. Each firm, thanks to the distinction between resources and services rendered, is unique, depending precisely on the resources it mobilizes. This goes far beyond the definition of the firm as a production function as defined by neoclassical economists. By applying this reasoning to the entrepreneur, the latter also appears unique in terms of the resources he collects. It is thus possible to understand how entrepreneurs can have different trajectories.

The entrepreneur's resources are both material and immaterial. While it is fairly easy to identify material resources (production equipment, current materials, raw materials and intermediate products, etc.), the identification of immaterial resources presents some difficulties. These considerations lead us to mobilize the theory of social capital (Bourdieu, 1980; Granovetter, 1973), which allows us to understand how and why individuals build and mobilize networks of social relations. The type of resources mobilized by the entrepreneur is shaped by the institutional context in which he is inserted. This is what leads individuals to create organizations, in other words to become entrepreneurs, which they transform according to the profit opportunities identified.

The social dimension of the entrepreneur's behavior is obvious since, as he or she evolves in society, he or she is in constant interaction with other entrepreneurs, consumers, bankers, researchers, etc. To succeed in a market, the innovative entrepreneur must first master a complex body of knowledge (technological, commercial, managerial, legal, etc.). However, the resources at his disposal are partial by nature. Contrary to what neoclassical economists have claimed, the entrepreneur is not inserted in a market of pure and perfect competition where information is perfect. However, it is by living in society that he draws on resources to which he would not have had access if he had lived in isolation (Hayek, 1960). The entrepreneur thus learns from the market, from his mistakes and successes, and builds a strategy that enables him to seize profit opportunities (Kirzner, 1973). In this way, he draws on the resources with which he will give life to his idea in accordance with the objectives he has set (Simon, 1955; Uzunidis, 2021).

Based on the resource theory (Penrose, 1959), we therefore identify three types of resources, which form the resource potential of the entrepreneur and which develop in interaction:

- **Knowledge resources**: these are both tacit knowledge acquired through family and professional socialization, and codified knowledge acquired in the school setting, from primary school to university. In this context, it is easy to understand the importance of the entrepreneur's family and social background in understanding his or her trajectory.
- **Financial resources**: these are actual resources (own savings, personal and/or family assets) and potential resources (access to bank credit, grants, prizes and awards, crowdfunding, venture capital, etc.). The presence on a university campus of investment fund companies looking for new ideas is a determining factor for the launch of an entrepreneurial project, such as incubators.
- **Social resources**: this refers to the network of informal social relations (family relations, friends, neighbors, etc.) or formal social relations (networks of social relations formed in the school and university, professional and institutional framework). In the first case, we will speak of strong links and in the second of reliable links, but in both cases, the common denominator is the trust that can unite the entrepreneur with other stakeholders (other entrepreneurs, financiers, organizations supporting entrepreneurship, etc.). In this respect, the importance of family socialization is clear, as it is usually the families who place their children in a particular school (depending on their social background) and who will then pay more or less attention to their children's schooling.

To summarize our discussion:

We started from the institutional framework in which the entrepreneur is inserted, which is composed of four poles (educational, scientific and technical, financial, supply constituted by the companies present on the market and the state). The entrepreneur is the product of this context through the education he or she has received, the professional experience he or she has gained by working in different companies before launching his or her project (Casson, 1982), and the financial resources he or she will be able to access to carry out his or her project. This leads us to focus on the following proposals:

- Within this institutional framework, innovation ecosystems are formed, which entrepreneurs use to bring their project to life. Equipped with tacit and codified knowledge, entrepreneurs work on the technical and commercial feasibility of their project, how it differs from the products/services offered by existing companies.
- The success of the entrepreneurial project is fundamentally based on the development of relationships of trust that will be built with other entrepreneurs or companies, research centers, financiers, etc. Hence the entrepreneur's ability to take risks. These relationships of trust are the cement for the creation of innovation ecosystems, via the development of relationships of proximity (spatial, organizational and cognitive).
- Relationships of proximity with entrepreneurial resources and their human or technological vectors contribute directly to the formation of the innovation ecosystem which supports both the entrepreneur and his project.

We will apply this theoretical framework to study the trajectory of the eight entrepreneurs we have identified.

3. Entrepreneurs of giant digital companies

3.1. Presentation of the study

In order to carry out our research (Yin, 1994), we have chosen the top five digital social networking companies in the world by number of monthly users: Facebook, YouTube, WhatsApp, Messenger, and Instagram. Our objective is both to trace the professional trajectory of the founders of these companies, focusing in particular on the project formation phase: how they identified the business opportunity that drove their success, the material and immaterial resources they mobilized to achieve this goal, and then how they built an ecosystem of digital innovation. In some cases, the entrepreneurial success was so great that it attracted predators. The heroic company is then bought up by a more powerful one, in this case Facebook and Google. These two companies are particularly important because of their ability to identify and buy up innovative companies.

The identified entrepreneurs are presented in Table 1. We have selected the first five enterprises, because all these entrepreneurs started their businesses in the United States and are therefore embedded in the same institutional context. Moreover, as we will have the opportunity to show below, they come from a very small number of universities. Moreover, among those who have professional experience, they were employed by companies in the digital industry and services, or even pioneering companies in their field (PayPal and Yahoo, in particular).

Table 1: The top five social networks worldwide in 2022 by number of monthly active users

Entrepreneurs	Enterprise	Date of creation	Number of monthly active users (billon per month)
Mark Zuckerberg	Facebook (Meta)	2004	2,912
Steve Chen Chad Hurley Jawed Karim	YouTube Sold in 2006 to Google	2005	2,291
Jan Koum Brian Acton	WhatsApp Sold in 2014 to Facebook	2009	2
Mark Zuckerberg	Messenger	2011	1,3
Kevin Systrom Michel (Mike) Krieger	Instagram Sold in 2012 to Facebook	2010	1,287

Source: https://www.leptidigital.fr/reseaux-sociaux/liste-reseaux-sociaux-14846/

These entrepreneurs created digital social networking companies with billions of users worldwide in a relatively short period of time, between 2004 and 2011. What they all have in common is that they started their businesses in the United States, even if they were not all born there. They all went to university in the United States. They studied mainly computer science, but some studied finance and economics. Most of them did not have a long period of work experience and started their own business quite quickly after their studies. These eight founding entrepreneurs are at the head of a very large fortune in 2022, although not all of them are among the world's top 20 wealthiest, except for Mark Zuckerberg. Characteristically, they have accumulated this fortune in a very short period of time, less than ten years.

3.2. The trajectories of the major digital entrepreneurs

For each of the entrepreneurs surveyed, we identified information on: their social origin, their school and university career and their professional experience before creating their company. We based ourselves mainly on the economic press available on the Internet and on a few reference works (Ichbiah, 2011; Kirkpatrick, 2010; Battelle, 2006; Vise 2005). We also cross-checked the information for authenticity. We did not identify any contradictory information in the course of this investigation.

Thanks to the collection of this information, we traced the trajectory of these entrepreneurs based on their social origin (parents' occupations), their education and their professional experience. This was done in order to study the contribution of their proximity relationships to the conception and development of their projects. This information is presented in Table 2.

Mark Zuckerberg was born in 1984 in New York State, USA. He comes from an upper middle-class family. His father is a dentist and his mother a psychiatrist. At a very young age, he developed a passion for computers. He began by learning BASIC, and then created his first program, ZuckNet, which was a messaging system that allowed communication over a local area network between the family's computers and his father's dental surgery, located on the ground floor of the house. During his high school years, he created Synpse Media Player, a music player adapted to the tastes of its users thanks to artificial intelligence. AOL and Microsoft offered to buy it from him for a million dollars and to work for them. But he refused. He could have been a millionaire at the age of 17… In 2003, he developed FaceMash, a site to compare the physical assets of two students and vote for the most attractive. In 2004, he created Facebook with three colleagues from Harvard University, where they were studying: Eduardo Saverin, Dustin Moskovitz, and Chris Hughes. What started out as an exchange site for students at the university very quickly became a company. It was created with a small start-up capital of $1,000, which was financed by Eduardo Saverin, who had accumulated this sum through numerous stock exchange gains. But Zuckerberg left Harvard as a sophomore, without having finished his studies. From Harvard, the company moved to Silicon Valley where the venture capital fund Accel Partners invested $12.7 million in Facebook.

Steve Chen was born in 1978 in Taiwan. His family moved to the United States when he was eight years old. He showed an early interest in computers. He studied computer science at the University of Illinois. He began his professional career at PayPal where he met the two colleagues with whom he created YouTube. After PayPal, and before creating YouTube, he was hired by Facebook.

Chad Hurley was born in 1977 in Pennsylvania in United States. He graduated from Indiana University with a degree in Fine Arts. While in high school, he became interested in computers and electronic media. He was hired by PayPal and designed the logo that was used by the company for ten years. He left PayPal in 2002 when it was acquired by eBay. Like Steve Chen and Jawed Karim, he received a bonus to create a company. He also received financial support from PayPal's financial director.

Jawed Karim was born in 1979 in East Germany. In 1980, his family moved to West Germany, and in 1992 they immigrated to the United States. He studied computer science at the University of Illinois. However, he left the university before graduating. He comes from a cosmopolitan family. He was exposed to many cultures in his early years. His mother is a German scientist and was a professor of biology at the University of Minnesota in the United States. His father is an American from Bangladesh and a researcher at 3M. He was hired by PayPal where he worked for a few years. He was even one of its first employees. He created YouTube with Steve Chen and Chad Hurley in 2005. But the three founders sold YouTube to Google in 2006 for $1.6 billion. Jawed Karim shows his ability to take risks through his professional decisions by leaving university before graduation to work in a newly created and innovative company, PayPal.

Jan Koum was born in 1976 in Ukraine. His family emigrated to the United States when he was 16 years old. In the United States, he had a very difficult life. His father stayed behind in Ukraine because he could not afford to travel to the United States. He worked as a cleaner to support himself and his mother. He joined a hacker group called w00w00. There he met the future co-founder of the online music site Napster. He studied computer science at San Jose State University. In 1997, Brian Acton invited him to Yahoo for a job interview. He worked in Yahoo's advertising department until 2007. Koum and Acton don't like marketing and advertising. He quit with Brian Acton, who shared the same lack of interest in marketing. For a year they traveled around the world. When they returned, they applied for a job at Facebook, which turned them down. The idea for the creation of WhatsApp came from Jan Koum. He wanted to create an advertising-free messaging system where it is not possible to identify individuals. He was traumatized by the years he spent in Ukraine where the state controlled everyone's life. He joined forces with a Russian developer Igor Solomennikov in 2009. Former Yahoo employees are also investing in WhatsApp. In 2007, Apple created the IPhone, which brings new features to the mobile phone. Then Brian joined them in 2010 after turning down a job at Twitter and Facebook. In 2014, WhatsApp was bought by Facebook for $19.3 billion.

Brian Acton was born in 1972 into a wealthy American business family in Florida. He studied computer science at the University of Pennsylvania and then at Stanford University. He first worked for Rockwell International, then for Apple and Adobe Systems. He joined WhatsApp after its creation, which he left in 2017, a few years after the acquisition by Facebook, following a dispute with Mark Zuckerberg.

Kevin Systron was born in 1983 in Massachusetts in a family of entrepreneurs. His mother has had a great influence on him through her entrepreneurial spirit and interest in technology. She is a marketing manager for a car-sharing company. His father is vice-president of a retail chain. He is passionate about photography. He was president of his high school photography club. He studied computer science and he also studied finance and economics at Stanford University. During his studies, he worked in a vinyl shop in Boston. He also undertook an internship at the startup Odeo, a free podcasting website. There he met Jack Dosay, the co-founder of Twitter. In 2004, he turned down Mark Zuckerberg's job offer for Facebook to finish his studies. After graduation, he worked in management and marketing for Google, which he left in 2009 for the travel recommendation start-up Nextstop, founded by former Google employees. In this startup, he has more freedom to develop programs and improve his knowledge. While still working for Nextstop, he created an application (BURBN, named after his favorite drink bourbon) to search for places to go out and post photos. At an event for Silicon Valley start-ups, he convinced investors. He then left Nextstop to develop his project and offered co-founder status to a colleague from Stanford University, Mike Krieger, who had a background as a software engineer. Instagram was created in 2010, but was bought by Facebook in 2012 for $1 billion, with a promise from Mark Zuckerberg to let Instagram run itself in relation to Facebook. But in 2018, Kevin Systrom and Mike Krieger left Instagram following a dispute with Facebook.

Mike Krieger was born in 1986 in Brazil. He traveled a lot with his father during his childhood and mastered several languages. In 2004, he moved to the United States to study at Stanford University, where he deepened his knowledge of symbolic systems, computer science, psychology, philosophy, cognition, and artificial intelligence. He benefited from Stanford's Mayfield Technology Ventures Program, which offers 12 selected students the opportunity to develop skills to create and manage high-tech companies. As part of the program, he had the opportunity to intern at a Silicon Valley startup. When Kevin Systrom asked him to work with him for Instagram, he accepted, but his integration into the company was delayed for administrative reasons related to transforming his student residence permit into a work permit.

Table 2: Entrepreneurial trajectories of founders of digital social networking giants

Name	Social origin	Graduation	Professional background
Mark Zuckerberg with three students of Harvard university: Eduardo Saverin Dustin Moskovitz Chris Hughes	Mother: psychiatrist Father: dentist	Studied computer science at Harvard University but did not graduate	No professional experience before creating Facebook, but experience in family and university settings
Steve Chen	His family left Taiwan when he was eight years old	Computer science studies at the University of Illinois	Worked at PayPal where he met the colleagues with whom he created YouTube. After PayPal, he was hired by Facebook
Chad Hurley	No information	Studied Fine Arts at Indiana University	Worked at Paypal where he met the colleagues with whom he created YouTube
Jawed Karim	Mother: scientist and professor of biology at Minnesota University Father: American from Bangladesh, researcher at 3M	Studied computer science Illinois University but did not graduate	
Jan Koum	Mother: cleaning lady Father: manager of a government construction company	Studied computer science as a self-taught learner, then studied computer science at San José University	During his studies, he worked at Ernst&Young as a security consultant. This allowed him to work on the computer systems of Yahoo where he was hired. He created WhatsApp in 2009. Brian Acton joined him in 2010.

(*Continued*)

Table 2: Continued

Name	Social origin	Graduation	Professional background
Brian Acton	Family of wealthy American entrepreneurs Mother: entrepreneur in the transport of goods	Studied computer science at Stanford university	He has worked in a number of large companies: Rockwell International Apple Adobe Systems
Kevin Systron	Mother: marketing manager at Zipcar, a car-sharing company Father: Vice President of the TJX distribution chain	Studied computer science, finance and economics at Stanford University	He is passionate about computers and programming. He started out as an employee in a Boston vinyl store. He undertook an internship in the startup Odeo, a free podcasting site where he met Jack Dorsey, co-founder of Twitter. He worked for Google for Nextstop, a start-up created by ex-Google employee
Michel (Mike) Krieger	Not much information He traveled a lot with his father in Portugal, Argentina, and in the United States during his childhood	Studied symbolic systems at Stanford University, but also psychology, philosophy, cognition, and artificial intelligence	At 13 years old, he created an enterprise in web design with a friend He worked for the social network Meebo, then created Instagram with Kevin Systron

Sources :
https://www.futura-sciences.com/tech/personnalites/facebook-mark-zuckerberg-1684/
https://fr.wikipedia.org/wiki/Mark_Zuckerberg
https://fr.wikipedia.org/wiki/Steve_Chen
https://inspire-media.fr/youtube-comment-steve-chen-chad-hurley-et-karim-jawed-ont-battu-280-sites-concurrents-en-2005/
https://fr.celebs-networth.com/steve-chen-net-worth

https://fr.wikipedia.org/wiki/Chad_Hurley#Jeunesse
https://autourdelafrance.com/fortune-de-chad-hurley-2021-age-taille-poids-femme-enfants/
https://fr.wikipedia.org/wiki/Jawed_Karim
https://fr.wikipedia.org/wiki/Jan_Koum
https://www.challenges.fr/high-tech/qui-est-jan-koum-le-fondateur-ukrainien-de-whatsapp-l-application-rachetee-par-facebook_165790
https://www.latribune.fr/actualites/economie/international/20140220trib000816358/jan-koum-de-l-ukraine-communiste-aux-19-milliards-de-whatsapp.html
https://inspire-media.fr/comment-jan-koum-ukrainien-pauvre-et-parlant-mal-langlais-a-cree-whatsapp/
https://en.wikipedia.org/wiki/Brian_Acton
https://autourdelafrance.com/brian-acton-fortune-2020-age-taille-poids-femme-enfants/
https://fr.celeb-true.com/brian-acton-american-internet-entrepreneur-computer-programmer
https://startuppers.club/fr/startuppers/kevin-systrom-biographie-instagram/
https://www.parismatch.com/Vivre/High-Tech/Kevin-Systrom-e-milliardaire-523239
https://fr.wikipedia.org/wiki/Mike_Krieger
https://autourdelafrance.com/fortune-de-mike-krieger-2021-age-taille-poids-femme-enfants/

4. Institutional context and resource potential: Entrepreneurs innovation ecosystems

4.1. Analysis of the institutional context

4.1.1. Entrepreneurial universities

The performance of American entrepreneurs in the field of digital social networks, as in other high-tech sectors, lies mainly in the development of close relationships between universities and companies. Some universities, such as Harvard and Stanford, have played a pioneering role for several decades in developing entrepreneurial universities whose function is no longer limited to the production and transmission of knowledge, but also to its valorization and thus to the creation of companies

Introduced by Burton Clark in 1998, based on a study of five European universities, the entrepreneurial university model emerged to take stock of the breakthroughs of the transition and the anchoring of the university's missions, teaching, and research to that of economic development. According to Etzkowitz (2016, 2022), the entrepreneurial university came into being when the university's contribution to economic development was added to the university's two original missions. This opened the university to the economy and society, whereas it would have been walled up in its "ivory tower" (Etzkowitz, 2016) for several centuries. The entrepreneurial university is the product of the rapprochement between the university, the company, and the state, i.e. the three stakeholders of the Etzkowitz triple helix (2016). It must therefore play a major economic role and develop an increased capacity to interact and negotiate with businesses and public institutions. The university must clearly move toward activities to support economic development.

Calling the university entrepreneurial implies redefining the content of academic tasks according to the new socio-economic requirements. The university must therefore encourage the creation and development of companies, but also hybrid public-private organizations to support entrepreneurship and innovation, via research valorization units. In this context, universities in industrialized countries have sought since the 1980s to develop an entrepreneurial culture among both staff (teachers-researchers and administrators) and students. The scientific spin-offs of the entrepreneurial university are numerous. For the latter, the partnership with the company allows the development of scientific knowledge and reinforces fundamental research, while ensuring the transmission of university values to the company.

Researchers can enrich their teaching with concrete examples and open up new fields of research by having access to new means of funding. Students can then have access to more interesting job opportunities, while benefiting from richer training, because they are closer to the company. The latter can also recruit employees who correspond to its needs and who will more easily assimilate the company's values. Innovation is thus the result of strong interactions between the university, the company, and public administrations. The university thus forms a kind of "natural ecosystem" (Etzkowitz, 2022). In order to integrate into the knowledge economy, the university is thus resolutely turned toward business.

This evolution was accompanied in the United States in 1980 by the Doyle-Bah Act, which allowed American universities and non-profit organizations receiving public funds to patent their discoveries and inventions. This law provides a general framework for bringing universities and businesses closer together and, more specifically for digital social networks and the Internet, it is important to emphasize the so-called "information superhighway" program, which in the 1990s was at the origin of the development of the Internet in order to extend its use to civil applications.

American universities, first and foremost Harvard, played a fundamental role in the development of the Internet in connection with nuclear warfare as early as the 1960s (Ceruzzi, 2012). It is in this framework that the research that led to the creation of the current Internet began within the framework of the ARPA (Advanced Research Projects Agency) project of the U.S. Department of Defense, founded in 1958 following the placing of Sputnik into orbit by the Soviet Union. Subsequently, in 1981, the BITNET network was developed to link IBM mainframe computers on American campuses.

Three universities stand out, those of Stanford, Illinois, and Harvard, from which Mark Zuckerberg comes. The first one is very well known as the centerpiece of Silicon Valley.

The innovation ecosystems of the entrepreneurs studied in this chapter have taken shape thanks to the cognitive, then spatial, and finally organizational (design thinking, project conception, business…) proximity of these entrepreneurs to universities with a strategy deliberately oriented toward the valorization of research and ideas. The conclusion is this: American entrepreneurial universities (through their policy of openness to the business economy and the funds they mobilize) are at the center of the formation of entrepreneurial innovation ecosystems, fueled by the strategy of large companies, as we will see later in the analysis of our cases (Table 3).

Table 3 : Three major entrepreneurial universities

Universities	Date of creation	Shanghai ranking	Academic disciplines	Enterprises created by students of the university (selection)	Incubators (selection)
Harvard	1636	1st	Mathematics Engineering Art Medicine Law Management Economics Psychology etc.	Facebook	Harvard-Innovation Lab Startup Tribe
Stanford	1891	2nd	Computer science Mathematics, Economics, etc.	Hewlett-Packard Yahoo Google LinkedIn Instagram Snapchat Netflix	Stanford Technology Ventures Program
Illinois	1851	11th	Journalism Economics Theater, etc.	PayPal YouTube Tesla	Enterprise Works

4.1.2. The deliberate support of large companies

Four large companies have played a fundamental role, directly or indirectly, in the creation of the companies identified, as we have shown through the study of the trajectories of the entrepreneurs considered: Google, Yahoo, PayPal and Facebook. The latter company plays a particular role both as a result and as a driver of this dynamic (Table 4). These four companies were created by students, mainly from Stanford universities. These companies played a role or influenced the creation of the five digital social networking companies we studied in this chapter, either because some founders were employees in one of these four companies, because the several founders invested their severance in the creation of their new company, because former employees from one of these four companies invested in the new company, or because the company was bought out.

Table 4 : Companies looking for opportunities

Companies	Date of creation	Activities	Relations with universities	Role or influence in the creation of the five studied companies
Yahoo	1994	Web services: email, search engine, web hosting	Created by Stanford university	Brian Acton and Jan Koun worked for Yahoo Former Yahoo employees invested in Whatsapp
Google	1998	Internet search engine that has developed a variety of activities	Created by two Stanford students	Google bought YouTube Kevin Systron worked for Google
PayPal	1998	Online payment system	Founded by students at the University of Illinois and developed by Elon Musk, who studied in South Africa, Canada, and the United States. While a student at Stanford, he stopped his studies to start a business.	Steve Chen, Chad Hurley, and Jawaed Karim received a bonus from PayPal with which they created YouTube
Facebook	2004	Platform of exchange of information, photos, and video	Created by students of Harvard University	Facebook bought WhatsApp and Instagram

4.2. Analysis of the innovative entrepreneur's resource potential

4.2.1. Knowledge resources, the nerve of business?

The entrepreneur's potential is composed of three types of resources: knowledge, financial, and his or her network of social relations. The strength of the resource potential of the entrepreneurs studied lies in their academic studies in computer science at American universities, including those born outside the United States, in this case in Taiwan, East Germany, and Ukraine. Three universities stand out from the rest: Stanford, Illinois and Harvard. This taste for study and more particularly for the study of computer science was born very early, in the family. They all had a passion for computers and programming from childhood. They were born at the end of the 1970s or the beginning of the 1980s, a period during which microcomputing, via the microcomputer, progressively imposed itself in homes and businesses, as an essential consumer or production good. The 1990s were marked by the development of mobile telephony and the Internet, which gave rise to new technical and commercial opportunities, marked first by the creation of Google (in 1998), then by the creation by Apple of the IPhone (in 2007), which combines the potential of both the computer and the cell phone.

The knowledge acquired in the university setting was for most of these entrepreneurs enriched by a job in a company, usually a company in the industry and/or digital services, such as Yahoo (created in 1994) and PayPal (created in 1998), two pioneering companies in the digital sector. The former by creating one of the first online directories, the latter by creating a secure online payment system.

In addition, all these entrepreneurs come from upper middle class American families. Only Jan Koum's background was difficult in the Ukraine and the United States, but he was able to insert himself into the computer science community through his studies at the University of San Jose and by being part of a hacker group. Jan Koum has developed a particular aversion to any form of enquiry into the personal lives of individuals, whether through state surveillance apparatus, as he experienced in Ukraine, or through corporate advertising and marketing in the United States. The acquisition of knowledge in the academic and professional framework also offers individuals the opportunity to create and to develop a network of social relations, to which we will return.

4.2.2. Financial resources as a secondary issue?

Some of the entrepreneurs selected for this study have received funding from venture capitalists who, through information intelligence and a powerful social network, have been able to identify promising entrepreneurs. The existence of close spatial and cognitive relationships on the campuses of venture capital firms in the context of incubators facilitates this type of connection.

Later, however, the company is bought by a very powerful company. In our case, these buyouts, primarily Google and Facebook, have allowed the founders of these companies to pocket several million, even several billion dollars, to start new ventures.

4.2.3. The network of social relations, a very small world?

The network of social relations of individuals plays a role in the constitution of a network of social relations, whether in an academic or entrepreneurial context. Mark Zuckerberg created Facebook with three other Harvard University students, one of whom had accumulated stock market capital that helped to finance the creation of the company. Steven Chen, Chad Hurley, and Jawed Karim, the three founders of YouTube, met while working at PayPal. They left the company when it was acquired by Google and created YouTube with their severance pay.

Jan Koum is without question initially the least socially endowed. He worked as a cleaner. He worked at Ernst&Young as a security consultant. He had access to the security systems of Yahoo, where he was hired later. Brian Acton, who was then working at Yahoo, interviewed him and hired him. Brian Acton comes from a completely different background as he comes from a family of entrepreneurs. He studied at Stanford University. They became friends and resigned from Yahoo because marketing turned them off. Then they traveled for a year in different countries. Facebook refused to hire them. Jan Koum created WhatsApp, an application allowing people to communicate with friends for free thanks to Wifi. Brian Acton joined him a few months after the creation of the company. But Mark Zuckerberg bought WhatsApp in 2014, five years after its creation.

Kevin Systron and Mike Krieger met while attending Stanford University. They are united by the same passion for computer science. Kevin Systron is older and has more professional experience than Mike Krieger. He worked at the startup Odeo, a free podcasting site where he met Jack Dorsey, one of the founders of Twitter. He also worked for Google and for the startup Nextstop created by Google. For his part Mike Krieger worked for the social network Meebo.

Figure 2 summarizes the different elements of our scientific approach. We start from the left with the four poles of the institutional context in which the entrepreneur is embedded, which has been shaped by the techno-economic paradigm. From the institutional context, entrepreneurs have extracted three types of resources (knowledge, financial, and social). Thanks to their resource potential, itself shaped by the context, entrepreneurs have created their innovation ecosystem. This is how we can trace the entrepreneurial trajectories of the eight individuals selected in this study.

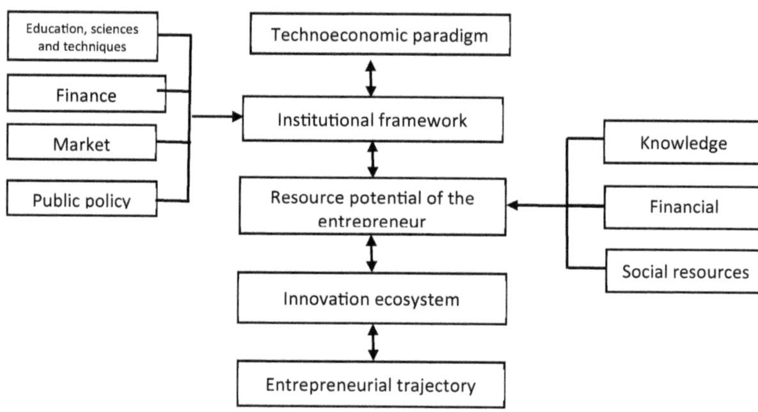

Figure 2: From the institutional context to the resource potential of the innovative entrepreneur
Source: authors.

5. Conclusion

Facebook, Instagram, YouTube, Messenger, WhatsApp… since the beginning of the 21st century, a large number of social networks have emerged on the Internet, punctuating the lives of millions of people around the world. Because of the importance they have acquired in economic and social life, we forget that they did not always exist and that they are the product of the fertile imagination of some creative entrepreneurs. We have presented the path taken to create these digital social networks and the economic and social circumstances of their "emancipation". We have drawn on the resource potential of the entrepreneurs who gave birth to them. The resource potential of the entrepreneur combines the contributions of resource theory (Penrose, 1959), social embeddedness (Granovetter, 1973), and the innovative entrepreneur (Schumpeter, 1911, 1942). The entrepreneurial project is by definition socially embedded: the entrepreneur as an economic and social agent draws his resources from the social environment in which he is embedded, at different levels (individual, family, social). These resources are varied (knowledge, financial, and social). The entrepreneur thus creates an innovation ecosystem that supports his project or is inserted into an innovation ecosystem in which he imposes his project; in doing so the entrepreneur asserts himself as a nodal function of the evolution of capitalism (Boutillier & Uzunidis, 2017).

This brief presentation highlighted two key theoretical elements: the importance of the institutional context in which entrepreneurs are embedded, and how this context shapes them, their project, and their innovation ecosystem. These entrepreneurs come from a small number of universities and have built professional experience in a small number of large companies.

All these companies were founded in the United States by entrepreneurs who were born in the country or abroad (primarily Ukraine, Taiwan, and East Germany). These entrepreneurs are united by their interest in computer science, a discipline they all studied at university. American universities, mainly Harvard, Stanford, and Illinois, have developed a culture of entrepreneurship over the past several decades, which is reflected in the presence on campus of incubators and venture capitalists looking for investment opportunities to grow their capital. The United States ranks third in the global innovation index[2].

In addition, public policy measures aim to develop research, but also the relationship between science and industry, especially since the end of the Second World War and the beginning of the Cold War. In this context, the emphasis has been placed particularly on nuclear energy and information technology, via the creation and development of the Internet since the 1960s. The entrepreneur, whatever his performance, is not a genius or a providential being for the market economy. He is the product

---

2 https://www.wipo.int/publications/fr/details.jsp?id=4560

of the institutional context in which he is inserted. The trajectory of each entrepreneur and the ecosystem that "produces" are part of this context. The family background and the profession of the parents, followed by a university education, play a fundamental role in the success of the project.

Thanks to the knowledge, financial, and social resources they have extracted from the institutional context in which they are inserted, they have built digital innovation ecosystems that have combined the resources of other actors, those of universities and research centers, digital companies present on the market, and public policy measures:

- These entrepreneurs all had a background in higher education, although some gave up their degree. On college campuses, some also received financial support from investment fund companies,
- These entrepreneurs have all benefited from work experience, usually in large companies. They have gained managerial and technical experience, but some have also benefited from financial support by leaving the company where they were employed.
- More generally, all these entrepreneurs have benefited from public policy measures in the United States aimed at supporting innovation in digital technologies.

References

Aldrich, H. E. (2010). Beam me up, Scott (ie)! Institutional theorists' struggles with the emergent nature of entrepreneurship. In *Institutions and entrepreneurship*. Bingley: Emerald Group Publishing Limited.

Aldrich, H. E. (2012). The emergence of entrepreneurship as an academic field: A personal essay on institutional entrepreneurship. *Research Policy, 41*(7), 1240–1248.

Audretsch, D. (1995). *Innovation and industry evolution*. MIT Press.

Battelle, J. (2006). *La révolution Google*. Eyrolles.

Baumol, W. (1990). Entrepreneurship: Productive and destructive. *Journal of Political Economy, 98*, 893–921.

Baumol, W. J. (1993). Formal entrepreneurship theory in economics: Existence and bounds. *Journal of Business Venturing, 8*(3), 197210

Bourdieu, P. (1980). Le capital social. *Actes de la recherche en sciences sociales, 31*, 2–3.

Boutillier, S., Laperche, B., & Uzunidis, D. (1999). *La légende de l'entrepreneur : Le capital social, comment vient l'esprit d'entreprise.* FeniXX.

Boutillier, S. (2021). Business – Business creation and innovative entrepreneurial ecosystems. In Uzunidis, D., Kasmi, F., & Adatto, L. (Eds.), *Innovation economics, engineering and management handbook 1.* ISTE-WILEY Editions, pp. 61–68.

Boutillier, S., & Tiran, A. (2016). La théorie de l'entrepreneur, son évolution et sa contextualisation. *Innovations, 50*, 211–234.

Boutillier, S., & Uzunidis, D. (2014). The theory of the entrepreneur from heroic to socialized entrepreneurship. *Journal of Innovation Economics & Management, 14*, 9–40.

Boutillier, S., & Uzunidis, D. (2017). *The entrepreneur.* ISTE Editions.

Casson, M. (1982). *The entrepreneur. An economic theory.* Barnes & Nobles Books.

Ceruzzi, P. E. (2012). Aux origines de l'Internet : projets militaires, intérêts commerciaux, désirs de communautés. *Le temps des médias, 18*, pp. 15–28.

Etzkowitz, H. (2016). The entrepreneurial university: Vision and metrics, industry and higher. *Education, 30*(2). https://doi.org/10.5367%2Fihe.2016.0303

Etzkowitz, H. (2022). Entrepreneurial university Icon, Stanford and Silicon Valley as innovation and natural ecosystem. *Industry and Higher Education, 36*(4), 361–380.

Freeman, C., & Perez C. (1988). Structural crises of adjustment, business cycles and investment behavior. In Dosi, G., Freeman, C., Nelson, R., Silverberg, G., & Soete, L. (Eds.), *Technical change and economic theory.* Pinter, pp. 39–62.

Granovetter, M. (1973). The strength of weak ties. *American Journal of Sociology, 78*(6), 1360–1380.

Granovetter, M. (1985). Economic action and social structure: The problem of embeddedness. *American Journal of Sociology, 91*(3), 481–510.

Hayek, F. (1960). *The constitution of liberty.* University of Chicago Press.

Ichbiah, D. (2011). *Les 4 vies de Steve Jobs.* Paris: Éditions Leduc.

Isaacson, W. (2015). *The innovators: How a group of inventors, hackers, geniuses, and geeks created the digital revolution.* Simon & Schuster.

Kirkpatrick, D. (2010). *The Facebook effect : The inside story of the company that is connecting the world.* Simon & Schuster.

Krizner, I. (1973). *Competition and entrepreneurship*. The University of Chicago Press.

Nelson, R., & Winter, S. (1982). *An evolutionary theory of economic change*. Harvard University Press.

Penrose, E. (1959, 1959/1995). *The theory of the growth of the firm*. Oxford University Press.

Scaringella, L., & Radziwon, A. (2018). Innovation, entrepreneurial, knowledge, and business ecosystems: Old wine in new bottles?. *Technological Forecasting & Social Change, 136*, 59–87.

Schumpeter, J. A. (1911/2021). *The theory of economic development*. Routledge.

Schumpeter, J. A. (1942/2018). *Capitalism, socialism and democracy*. Harper Perennial Modern Classics.

Schumpeter, J. A. (1939). *Business cycles*. McGraw-Hill Book.

Simon, H. (1955). A behavioral model of rational choice. *The Quarterly Journal of Economics, 69*(1), 99–118.

Sombart, W. (1913). Der Bourgeois. Zur Geistesgeschichte des modernen Kapitalismus [The Bourgeois: On the Intellectual History of Modern Capitalism]. Munich: Verlag von Duncker & Humblot.

Spigel, B. (2020). *Entrepreneurial ecosystems. Theory, practices and futures*. Edward Elgar.

Uzunidis, D. (2020). *Systemic innovation: Entrepreneurial strategies and market dynamics*. ISTE/Wiley.

Uzunidis, D. (2021). Personality – The deviant personality of the innovative actor, Dimitri Uzunidis. In Uzunidis, D., Kasmi, F., & Adatto, L. (Eds.), *Innovation economics, engineering and management handbook 2*. ISTE-WILEY Editions, pp. 225–232.

Uzunidis, D., Boutillier, S., & Laperche, B. (dir.), (2014). The entrepreneur's 'resource potential' and the organic square of entrepreneurship: Definition and application to the French case. *Journal of Innovation and Entrepreneurship, 3*(1). DOI: 10.1186/2192-5372-3-1.

Uzunidis, D., Kasmi, F., & Adatto, L. (Eds.). (2021). *Innovation economics, engineering and management handbook*. ISTE-WILEY Editions.

Veblen, T. (1899). The preconceptions of economic science. *Quaterly Journal of Ecoonomics, 13*(4), 396–426.

Weber, M. (1905). *L'éthique protestante et éthique du capitalisme*, French translation 1964. Paris: Plon.

Yin, R. (1994). *Case study research: Design and methods*. Sage Publications.

A sustainable knowledge-based economy analysis

ANDREAS PYKA, STEPHANIE LANG AND
LEA F. STÖBER[1]

Abstract: In the light of current global societal challenges, our economic systems need to transform toward sustainable, knowledge-based economies. In this regard, knowledge represents the key component for economic development. However, the nexus between a knowledge-based economy and sustainability has thus far not received the attention required. Only knowledge-based economies have the capability to contribute to sustainability transitions without fundamentally reducing the prospects of growing welfare. Considering the innovation ecosystem perspective, this chapter addresses the question of how existing systems can be redesigned to overcome their exclusive focus on international competitiveness, income growth and employment, and instead support the transformation toward a sustainable economy. We approach this question by focusing on innovation ecosystems at the macro level and elaborate how *dedicated innovation ecosystems* need to be developed from national innovation systems in order to initiate sustainability transitions. This qualitative shift of innovation systems requires overcoming lock-ins, adopting a normative perspective, and integrating all stakeholders, as consumer lifestyles have to change alongside production paradigms. The recognition of normative aspects and the decisive role of transformative knowledge enable the creation of a virtuous circle between demand, supply, and policy interventions on the path to a sustainability paradigm.

Keywords: Sustainability, Transformative knowledge, Path dependencies, Digitalization

1 University of Hohenheim, Innovation Economics (520i), D-70599 Stuttgart, Germany.

1 Introduction: The emergence of the knowledge-based economy

Over the past few decades, knowledge has been understood as one of the key drivers of economic development (Powell & Snellman, 2004; Pyka & Hanusch, 2006). Our economies develop from being agriculture- and manufacturing-based toward knowledge-based systems (Russell & Smorodinskaya, 2018). Knowledge fosters economic growth by being adopted, produced, and distributed throughout economies (Chen & Dahlman, 2005). The first reference to a knowledge economy concept was made in the 1960s in the context of new economic trends and new data. The revival of the concept took place in the 1990s, when knowledge was discussed as a central component of the modern economy (Godin, 2006). The knowledge-based economy comprises "production and services based on knowledge-intensive activities that contribute to an accelerated pace of technical and scientific advance, as well as rapid obsolescence." (Powell & Snellman, 2004). Unlike the agricultural and industrial economies, the knowledge-based economy relies not only on physical or natural inputs, but also on intellectual property and skills (Powell & Snellman, 2004). According to White et al. (2013), the main knowledge-based components are open innovation, education, knowledge management, and creativity. These components rely heavily on information and communication technology infrastructure (White et al., 2012). Hence, the rise of modern digital technologies, affecting both production and consumption systems, is closely related to the emergence of the knowledge-based economy. Indeed, knowledge-based economies seek to achieve economic growth through high-tech industries, implying investments in innovation and a highly skilled workforce (Birner, 2018).

As the concept's name indicates, knowledge is the most central aspect; the engine for long-term economic growth and the source of competitiveness across all sectors (Chen & Dahlman, 2005; Hadad, 2017).More specifically, innovation is the driver of long-term growth in a knowledge-based economy. Innovation is a non-linear process, resulting from the production of new knowledge or recombination of existing knowledge (Edquist, 2006). For successful innovation activities, "an efficient system of distribution and access to knowledge is a sine qua non condition [...]. Knowledge distribution is the crucial issue" (David & Foray, 1994). In fact, knowledge-based economies create innovation systems consisting of different actors that form a creative environment for mutual learning and knowledge creation (Pyka & Prettner, 2018).

The definition by Powell and Snellman (2004) indicates that today's society is confronted with a rapid dynamic of technological advances. Technologies that have just been brought to the market are shortly being replaced with newer versions. This, combined with our current consumer society where more is always better, poses major challenges as we consume more resources than we have available. To be precise, according to the Global Footprint Network's calculations, we need 1.75 Earths to meet the world's resource demands; and this is only the global average; several countries like the USA (5.1 Earths), Germany (3.0 Earths), or France (2.8 Earths) require even more if all other countries were to live like them (Global Footprint Network, 2022). For this reason, sustainability should be considered as an imperative in knowledge-based economies.

In this chapter, we examine the innovation ecosystems perspective against the background of transformations toward sustainability. For this purpose, we consider sustainability transformations and their systemic features from an evolutionary innovation economics perspective in Section 2. Section 3 introduces the innovation ecosystem perspective, which is essential for successful transformations of socio-economic systems toward sustainability. How this perspective can be adopted to initiate and steer sustainability transitions is elaborated in Section Four, before we summarize and conclude our arguments in Section Five with transitions in the mobility sector as a summarizing example.

2 Transformations toward Sustainability

The multitude of problems, such as climate change, environmental pollution, resource depletion, and an unequal distribution of income and food security, can be classified as wicked problems (Rittel & Webber, 1973). They are interrelated and systemic, their causes are emergent, complex, and deeply embedded in our socio-economic structures and their impact is uncertain. Therefore, they are extremely difficult to define, making them seem impossible to solve. As outlined by Schlaile et al. (2017), these challenges have also been referred to as persistent problems (Rotmans & Loorbach, 2009), complex challenges (Hassan, 2014), grand challenges (Cagnin et al., 2012; Kuhlmann & Rip, 2014; Von Schomberg, 2013), or super wicked problems (Levin et al., 2012). But no matter how they are framed, these problems threaten Planet Earth and thus the foundation of human existence. We are at a point where we face the threat of irreversible changes to our Earth's system (as Rockström et al. (2009) discovered in their research on planetary boundaries). There is no denying that since the industrial revolution human actions have become the main driver of global environmental change. Hence, one of the central questions of the 21st century is how we can restore the sustainability of our socio-economic systems. This topic has been in the public and political discourse since publication of the Brundtland report in 1987. Since then, sustainable development has become a guiding principle in politics, economics, and society. Sustainable development "meets the needs of the present without compromising the ability of future generations to meet their own needs" (World Commission on Environment and Development, 1987). To accomplish this change and to steer the process of growth toward a desired state of sustainability, one thing is certain: radical, multi-dimensional, long-term changes of prevailing socio-economic systems are inevitable.

Such major socio-economic changes are classified as transformations (Hölscher et al., 2018). As a response to the aforementioned grand sustainability challenges, sustainability transformations, shifting an unsustainable system state to a more sustainable system state (Markard et al., 2012; Rotmans et al., 2001), are initiated and discussed across various industries and sectors, such as, for example, renewable energy sources in the electricity sector (Verbong & Geels, 2010), transitions to sustainable agriculture and food systems (El Bilali & Allahyari, 2018; El Bilali et al., 2019), transitions in the mobility sector (Kemp & Rotmans, 2004) such as e-mobility or multimodal transportation, circularity in the clothing sector (Fischer & Pascucci, 2017; Niinimäki et al., 2020) or energy-efficient houses and sustainable practices in the building sector (Fastenrath & Braun, 2018; Gibbs & O'Neill, 2014). Geels (2018) defines sustainability transformations as "multidimensional and co-evolutionary processes that involve changes in technology, user practices, business models, policies and governance approaches, and cultural meanings" (p. 26). In economic literature, these massive system shifts have been termed techno-economic paradigm changes (Freeman, 1991; Dosi, 1982).

Evolutionary economists portray technological change in a cyclical model (Dosi, 1982; Nelson & Winter, 1982; Sahal, 1981). The cycle begins with a technological discontinuity followed by a period of economic expansion characterized by a high degree of technical variation until a dominant design prevails. This is followed by a phase of incremental developments, which is only disrupted by another technological breakthrough, causing the cycle to start again (Kaplan and Tripsas 2008). In this model, technological innovations, including those that lead to technological discontinuity, emerge along prevailing technological paradigms. The notion of technological paradigms implies that only a limited number of possible technological alternatives and hypothetical future developments are considered. Progress occurs along technological trajectories (Dosi, 1982), which means that problem-solving activities take place within pursued technology paths and not all possible technological paths are followed. Potential solutions are thus limited by technologies and processes used in the past (Pyka, 2019). Such path dependencies exist due to the cumulative character of technological advances, as described by Nelson (1995): "In a cumulative technology, today's technical advances build from and improve upon technology that was available at the start of the period, and tomorrow's in turn builds on today's" (p. 74). Path dependencies can lead to so-called lock-ins (Unruh, 2000, 2002), making it difficult to shift from one system state to another. This phenomenon is not caused by a single technology, but rather by a number of complementary and interdependent technological, infrastructural, behavioral, and institutional developments. Thus, it takes a change and interaction of all these elements to replace an old paradigm with a new one; in the case of sustainability transformation, the prevailing paradigm is replaced with a more sustainable one (Pyka & Prettner, 2018).

An example for path-dependent lock-ins is the dependency on fossil-based resources of contemporary economies (Unruh, 2000). In this context, the establishment of a knowledge-based bioeconomy is discussed as a solution to overcome carbon lock-ins and to shift economies from using fossil-based to bio-based resources (Lewandowski, 2018; Pyka & Prettner, 2018; Pyka, 2017). The European Commission defines bioeconomy as "using renewable biological resources from land and sea, like crops, forests, fish, animals and micro-organisms, to produce food, materials and energy" (European Commission, 2018). Since the bioeconomy is not automatically sustainable, resource-efficient use of renewable resources and their linkage with circular economy practices (e.g. recycle, reuse, reduce) is critical.

The transformation of prevailing socio-economic systems toward sustainability is not a straightforward process given path-dependent lock-ins (Unruh, 2000, 2002) and the complexity and dynamics of economic systems, meaning they do not follow a linear cause-and-effect mechanism (Nelson et al., 2018; Arthur, 2021). From a systemic and co-evolutionary perspective, there is no predefined transition path to an ultimate state of sustainability. Long-term fundamental changes in social systems – like a transformation toward sustainability – involve feedback effects and continuous change processes (Schlaile & Urmetzer, 2018). A successful transformation to a sustainable, knowledge-based economy, and a more sustainable system state, requires fundamental changes in existing production and consumption patterns (Pyka & Prettner, 2018). Thus, an exclusive supply-side perspective is not sufficient. In addition to technological innovations, also social, political, and ecological innovations are required (Pyka, 2017). These changes must be initiated and accompanied at all system levels.

3 The Innovation Ecosystem Perspective

In the OECD Oslo Manual 2018 innovation is defined as "a new or improved product or process (or combination thereof) that differs significantly from the unit's previous products or processes and that has been made available to potential users (product) or brought into use by the unit (process)" (OECD, 2018). In economics, Schumpeter (1939) resumed the research on innovation processes and the emergence of innovation after it was marginalized with the so-called neoclassical revolution at the beginning of the 20th century. It took more than half a century until the view on innovations had changed from being focused on a linear development of innovation to a systemic perspective on the complexity of innovation processes. This implies that for an innovation to be successful, it often depends on other successful innovations in its external environment (Adner & Kapoor, 2010). Hence, firms do not innovate on their own, but through interactions and interconnections with other actors and components within a system (Edquist, 2006). When analyzing the emergence of innovations and how they are developed, this can be differentiated between adaption and exploration. Already Schumpeter (1947, p. 150) explained that "[w]henever an economy or a sector of an economy adapts itself to a change in its data in the way that traditional theory describes [...] we may speak of the development as adaptive response. And whenever the economy or an industry or some firms in an industry do something else, something that is outside of the range of existing practice, we may speak of creative response."

The addition of the systemic perspective in the analysis of innovations was first developed in the late 1980s. Concepts such as national, regional, and sectoral innovation systems were introduced and since then systemic approaches have been developed further (Granstrand & Holgersson, 2020). According to Lundvall et al. (2009, p. 6) an innovation system is "an open, evolving and complex system that encompasses relationships within and between organizations, institutions and socio-economic structures which determine the rate and direction of innovation [...]". Innovation systems can be conceptualized as so-called complex adaptive systems, consisting of a multitude of different actors that learn and adapt to changing circumstances through interactions with others. Complex adaptive systems are not controlled by a central coordinating body but rely on their dynamic mechanisms for self-organization. Hence, the ecosystem of actors and their relationships within an innovation system evolves over time (Breslin et al., 2021).

The notion of innovation ecosystems is derived from natural ecosystems. The United Nations (1992, p. 3) defines natural ecosystems as a "dynamic complex of plant, animal and micro-organism communities and their non-living environment interacting as a functional unit". Natural ecosystems have the characteristic to regenerate themselves and generate new ecosystems. Nonetheless, these self-sustaining systems do not arise out of nowhere but require continuous and permanent work (Xu & Maas, 2019). The concept of business ecosystems developed by Moore (1993) was the first approach to link the theory of natural ecosystems with economic theory: Moore proposes to see a business not only as a participant in an industry or sector but as an actor within a business ecosystem where companies compete and at the same time co-evolve around an innovation to meet the demand of their customers. This co-evolution is built on both cooperative and competitive strategies of the companies. The difference between natural ecosystems and business ecosystems lies in the conscious decision-making of actors in business ecosystems. If one ecosystem is not able to regenerate itself, the actors of this ecosystem need to find ways to generate new business ecosystems or get into already existing but more promising ones. From a systemic perspective, it does not matter which business ecosystem survives (Moore, 1993).

In the early 2000s, the notion of innovation ecosystems emerged to analyze non-linear innovation processes (Smorodinskaya et al., 2017). The research in this field is diverse and there is neither only one type of innovation ecosystems nor a unique definition for innovation ecosystems.

Klimas and Czakon (2022) identified 50 different types of innovation ecosystems. Granstrand and Holgersson (2020) reviewed almost 120 definitions. They define innovation ecosystems as "the evolving set of actors, activities, and artifacts, and the institutions and relations, including complementary and substitute relations, that are important for the innovative performance of an actor or a population of actors" (Granstrand & Holgersson, 2020, p. 3). Innovation ecosystems promote innovation by creating an environment that supports collaboration, improves innovation capacity, and enhances the innovation performance of the entire system (Smorodinskaya et al., 2017; Klimas & Czakon, 2022). This system is not restricted to actors that are geographically close to each other, but they are independent of location, which allows for new ways of co-evolution and co-creation (Adner & Kapoor, 2010). Hence, it differs from the traditional cluster theory developed by Porter (1980) by considering more than one industry or sector and further recognizes not only organizations but also other actors within the innovation ecosystem that are interconnected (Klimas & Czakon, 2022; Teece, 2007). The main objective is co-innovating for value co-creation. Coopetition or even cooperation between direct competitors within an innovation ecosystem is necessary to develop innovations and create value for consumers in the system (Klimas & Czakon, 2022).

4 Innovation ecosystems dedicated toward sustainability transformation

In a knowledge-based economy, innovation is the driving force behind long-term economic growth and competitiveness across all sectors. The knowledge-based economy is seen as a complex adaptive system (Hadad, 2017). Likewise, innovation ecosystems are conceptualized as complex adaptive systems. Innovation in a national innovation ecosystem stems from the interaction and relations between different actors (Lundvall, 2007). Innovation is not only the result of these interactions but also the process that motivates actors to co-create value for consumers (Adner, 2006). Breslin et al. (2021, p. 65) indicate that ecosystems are "created, shaped, and maintained through innovation". They argue that innovations play a key role in changing rules of interactions and consequently shaping new patterns within the ecosystems. Innovation not only maintains already existing patterns in an innovation ecosystem but also pushes radical changes which can disrupt the entire system. In the sense of creative destruction (Schumpeter, 1939), radical changes can cause a paradigm shift and transform prevailing socio-economic systems toward higher degrees of sustainability (Pyka & Prettner, 2018).

4.1 Overcoming lock-ins

Paradigmatic changes transform our socio-economic systems by overcoming lock-ins (Pyka & Prettner, 2018). Lock-ins arise from technological, organizational, industrial, and societal co-evolution resulting in a techno-institutional complex system which creates an environment of predictability, reliability, and inertia to change (Unruh, 2002). This is problematic as public and private actors do not anticipate long-term future outcomes in their decision-making. This potentially leads to unintended consequences, the most prominent and threatening being the current global sustainability crisis. Hence, system interventions become necessary to overcome lock-ins and initiate a transformation.

Unruh (2002) names three general policy approaches to intervene in socio-technological systems: end of pipe (i.e. not changing the system but treating the apparent issues), continuity (i.e. amending selected system elements or dynamics but maintaining the overall system structure), and discontinuity (i.e. addressing root causes by replacing the entire system with a different, superior system). For a transformation toward higher degrees of sustainability, a discontinuity approach, in the sense of radical change (Dosi, 1982; Anderson & Tushman, 1990) across all system levels is necessary. However, the greater the desired change, the likelier and stronger the resistance in the system. Therefore, for radical change, in addition to technological forces, social and institutional forces play a key role in order to overcome lock-ins (Unruh, 2002). At this point, it should be noted that elements in a complex system interact and are interdependent, so that changes in one area may bring about changes in another. A paradigm shift is thus always the result of a number of interdependent changes in various system elements.

From a technological perspective, radical innovations in terms of superior technological breakthroughs cause paradigmatic change (Unruh, 2002). The principal source of such radical innovations is small and often new firms or creative entrepreneurs (Pyka & Nelson, 2018), operating exogenously to the dominant design (Unruh, 2002). Similarly, literature on sustainability transition adopts the multi-level perspective to describe transition processes. Here, radical socio-technical changes are understood as the result of pressures on the prevailing technological regime (i.e. the meso level). On the one hand, pressure is exerted from the landscape level (i.e. the macro level) due to profound structural changes and, on the other hand, by niche actors (i.e. the micro level) where new technologies are developed in a protected environment (Geels, 2002, 2005). In general, changes in socio-technical systems tend not to be limited by science and technological developments, but rather by organizational, social, and institutional changes needed for the diffusion of new technological solutions (Unruh, 2002) and by underpinning cognitive models (Kaplan & Tripsas, 2008).

A transition toward higher degrees of sustainability must be facilitated at the societal level by establishing a countervailing consensus for action. This can be achieved by increasing awareness at the political and social level of the severity of global sustainability challenges, such as environmental degradation caused by fossil fuel technologies. Recognizing the sustainability crisis as an actual crisis might be a focusing event that not only initiates change, but also creates acceptance for change (Unruh, 2002). Nevertheless, there is a time lag between public perception of the problem and taking actual actions to solve it. The reasons for this are threefold. First, the complexity of the grand challenges makes educating the public a lengthy process (Unruh, 2002), delaying the establishment of a countervailing consensus for action. Second, the absence of clear cause and effect mechanisms of wicked problems (Rittel & Webber, 1973) complicates the search process for potential solutions (Schlaile et al., 2017). Third, radical changes require the expansion of our cognition (Kaplan & Tripsas, 2008), challenging the way we think and act. Every actor in an innovation system has its own, often conflicting, cognitive frames of the problem and potential solutions. Producers, users, and institutions must interact to reach a collective cognitive frame for both. The necessity to challenge cognitive patterns of thinking highlights the central role of consumers and creative entrepreneurs in transformation processes, for they test new cognitive lenses (Kaplan & Tripsas, 2008). Alongside changes in normative patterns of thinking, the generation, application, and diffusion of transformative knowledge as well as attaining a critical mass for sustainable innovations are decisive factors in overcoming existing lock-ins and accomplishing a transformation toward higher degrees of sustainability. In the following sub-chapters, we take a closer look at these arguments, their interrelations, and we explore how these critical factors may be achieved.

4.2 Taking a Normative Perspective

Sustainability is a highly normative concept as it does not describe the current state of the system, but what it should look like (Blok et al., 2016; Schlaile et al., 2017). Sustainability serves as the desired goal for the future, while at the same time opinions on what the desired state should look like vary. Therefore, the measures and actions taken differ depending on the desired outcome they are intended to achieve (Blok et al., 2016). Exactly what the desired outcome looks like depends on the individual's ability to predict the consequences of the measures taken (Renn, 2007). Dealing with sustainability is therefore an extremely complex matter, as there is no single understanding of what sustainability should look like, but rather a collection of different norms, values, beliefs, and worldviews (Schlaile et al., 2017). The situation is similar with the transformation to sustainability. Finding a single correct definition of what the sustainability transformation actually means is difficult, if not impossible (Wijen, 2014). Theoretically, all relevant actors would have to agree on what is sustainable and which behaviors can be described as sustainable. But again, the problem of the high complexity of this normative concept arises, because sustainability can be defined in many different ways, based on individual decision criteria (Delmas et al., 2013; Wijen, 2014).

Due to the normative nature of the concept of sustainability, the transformation toward a knowledge-based economy needs an adaptive coordination of interactions and learning processes within the innovation ecosystem in order to foster cross fertilization and cooperation among the actors (Pyka, 2017). While the early literature on innovation (eco)systems focuses on economic development and competitiveness as desirable outcomes of innovation processes, an innovation ecosystem *dedicated* to sustainability emphasizes innovation processes that contribute to sustainability. This implies that dedicated innovation systems (DIS) are less oriented toward the predominant economic goals, such as economic growth and international competitiveness, but rather focus on transformative innovation, not only in technological but also in systemic terms (Urmetzer et al., 2020). It cannot be denied that dedicated innovators still focus on economic goals. However, there is a need for a holistic view on sustainability. Turning to sustainability requires consideration of the entangled nature of global problems and the complex normativity of the concept of sustainability (Schlaile et al., 2017; Pyka et al., 2022).

4.3 Strengthening transformative knowledge

Within (dedicated) innovation ecosystems knowledge is generated, diffused, and exploited. When it comes to knowledge, there are different opinions regarding the properties of knowledge. For instance, neoclassical economists describe knowledge as a public good. However, innovation economists define knowledge as a latent public good (Nelson, 1989), in that it combines public and non-public features. The non-public attributes impact central processes (i.e. the generation, diffusion, and application of knowledge) in innovation ecosystems. Due to its cumulative character, knowledge can only be generated if a certain level of know-how resides, so that new knowledge can be combined with existing knowledge. This implies that knowledge in itself has no value. The diffusion of knowledge requires absorptive capacities, which are skills to understand and utilize new knowledge (Galunic & Rodan, 1998; Cohen & Levinthal, 1989, 1990). Generally, learning and utilization of knowledge is easier if the new knowledge is similar to what is already known. If, in contrast, the knowledge base is different, a person needs higher absorptive capacities to integrate the new knowledge in its existing knowledge base.

In the light of the grand sustainability challenges, simply improving the exchange and transfer of economically relevant knowledge is insufficient (Schlaile et al., 2017). To broaden the perspective accordingly, transformation researchers propose the joint consideration of system, normative, and transformative knowledge (Wehrden et al., 2017; Wiek & Lang, 2016). While general economic relevant knowledge is mostly limited to the creation of economic value, the aforementioned knowledge types go a bit further, especially with regard to sustainability transformation (Urmetzer et al., 2018). Systems knowledge is necessary to understand the systemic context of the problems. It has cross-connections to other knowledge types, has cumulative properties, and is often difficult to codify. We need systems knowledge to understand in what systems we live, how these systems function, and how they interact with other systems or respond to interventions. Normative knowledge is necessary to have a vision of what should be and what should not be. Against the background of system knowledge, normative knowledge helps to define a desirable system state and evaluate normative goals. We need normative knowledge to identify what we want or where we want to go, and what price we are willing to pay to get there. Transformative knowledge is necessary to develop strategies based on systems and normative knowledge to induce a system transformation (Urmetzer et al., 2018; Abson et al., 2014). Due to the high location and context dependency of normative knowledge, the implementation of transformative knowledge can only be successful in a context-specific way. The development of absorptive capacities for the generation and diffusion of transformative knowledge is dependent on systemic and normative knowledge. Hence, for a successful diffusion of transformative knowledge, knowledge holders must be able not only to use their cognitive abilities, but also to access deeper cognitive levels in order to question prevailing values, assumptions, and paradigms (Urmetzer et al., 2020). Only in this way can existing lock-ins be overcome.

When generating and disseminating the knowledge required for a transformation, there must always be a comparison with current demands, societal developments, and economic feasibility. Necessary knowledge bases can never be static, as they are confronted with true uncertainty (Knight, 1921) and non-linear developments. The question is, what can be done to promote knowledge distribution. One approach is to question existing systems in terms of their ability to impart systemic knowledge and ways of thinking to face the global challenges. In this context, interdisciplinary and transdisciplinary research, and especially education, are most important, as the search for solutions to complex, global problems can no longer be left to politicians and scientists alone, but should involve all societal actors (Kubisch et al., 2021).

4.4 Integrating Civil Society

The sustainability challenges are global, societal problems. Therefore, the integration of civil society in search and problem-solving processes becomes crucial. The transformation of our socio-economic systems can only succeed through the integration of all stakeholders. This includes a public discourse on goals and pathways toward a more sustainable knowledge-based economy. Societal participation not only increases acceptance of innovations and demand for innovations, but also uncovers questions and conflicting goals (Albrecht et al., 2012; Urmetzer et al., 2018).

According to Jackson (2004) two aspects are crucial with regard to sustainability from a consumer perspective: First, people no longer buy goods just for the sake of consuming, but consumption represents a way of life. Second, consumers are influenced by their habits, cultural backgrounds, and traditions and their "everyday consumption is comprised of routines and habits" (Jaeger-Erben et al., 2015, p. 784). These changes in consumption are usually incremental changes in a consumer's individual habits (Lazaric & Oltra, 2012). Changes in consumer behavior affect the transformation toward a sustainable knowledge-based economy and thereby accelerate the shift from the current system state to a more sustainable one. Due to the dynamics in complex systems, behavioral changes in one sphere of life are likely to cause further changes in a virtuous cycle. A consumer starting to reduce his/her meat consumption by switching to bio-based meat substitutes is likely to make further changes in his/her lifestyle, such as, for example, buying sustainably sourced and fairly produced clothes, covering shorter distances by bike instead of using the car, and so forth. As more consumers choose to consume sustainable goods, there will also be a greater offer of sustainable alternatives in the future (Wilke et al., 2021). This is because creative entrepreneurs discover economic opportunities in the behavioral changes of consumers. The more consumers change their behavior, the higher the demand and thus the greater the supply. In this way, a tipping point can be reached at which not only consumer behavior but the entire system changes in the sense of creative destruction (Schumpeter, 1939). The old system is replaced from the bottom up by a new more sustainable system.

Burns (2012, p. 1127) compares this pattern change with "a new societal revolution comparable in scale and significance to the industrial revolution". New sustainable concepts, targets, production techniques, and process technologies are developed and adapted. This shift from the classic growth-oriented paradigm to a more sustainable-oriented paradigm involves not only the rethinking and reorganizing of producers but also of consumers (Burns, 2012). Changes do not take place independently on each side, but in collaboration between producers and consumers, for example through so-called open innovation processes or user innovations (Laperche, 2017).

4.5 Benefiting from digitalization

Digitalization not only impacts the rise of a knowledge-based economy, it can also accelerate transitions toward sustainability across various sectors. For a successful transformation toward sustainability, sustainable innovations need to be scaled up (Loorbach et al., 2020). In other words, these innovations must achieve a critical mass for their adoption rate to become self-sustaining (Rogers, 2003). Due to low diffusion rates of sustainable innovations, their environmental benefits may not be fully realized (Fichter & Clausen, 2021). The diffusion of sustainable innovations from niche to mass markets can, furthermore, create a virtuous cycle on the consumption and production side, as changes in one area may impact changes in another. Nevertheless, many sustainable innovations currently diffuse to mass markets at a low rate (Fichter & Clausen, 2021).

Green (digital) platforms may be able to create the necessary critical mass for the diffusion of sustainable innovation, and thus accelerate the transformation toward higher degrees of sustainability by enabling and connecting various actors in an innovation (eco-)system, reducing transaction costs, and providing essential services (Pyka & Stöber, 2023). Innovation networks or platforms enable actors to share ideas, knowledge, and resources as well as to develop interfaces and visibility. Kenney and Zysman (2016, p. 61) define platforms as "multisided digital frameworks that shape the terms on which participants interact with one another". From an innovation economics perspective, platforms result from creative destruction and the seizing of business opportunities in terms of business model innovation (Mathews, 2020).

Perren and Kozinets (2018) categorize platforms based on their degree of intermediation and social interaction into four types: forums, enablers, matchmakers, or hubs. Depending on their role in the exchange relation between supplier and consumer, these platform types decrease transaction costs in different ways. For example, forums bring actors together, which reduces their search costs, while hubs are the center of a transaction and mediate the flow of goods and services between the actors. Thereby a standardization of transaction is achieved which lowers its search, decision, monitoring, and enforcement costs (Perren & Kozinets, 2018). This may result in low market entry barriers for consumers and producers. Pyka and Stöber (2023) outline various opportunities for how the four platform types can support the transformation toward sustainability on both the consumption and production side by creating more sustainable markets and entrepreneurial opportunities as well as by accelerating the diffusion of sustainable products. Platforms connect actors in innovative ecosystems and allow a critical mass to emerge, which can empower these actors. If an actor or a group of actors has a dominant role in a system, they are capable of driving radical change to solve problems, compensate for policy failures, tackle threats, or seize opportunities. At the same time, a shift in power can lead to similar outcomes, when the new dominant group pushes a new paradigm (Burns, 2012). However, platforms are not automatically sustainable, as shown by various real-life examples that favor developments in the opposite direction. Platform providers and their users may use the power gained through platforms to promote unsustainable paradigms. Hence, platforms only become truly 'green' (i.e. sustainable) if its operators and users consider sustainability in all its dimensions in their decisions and actions, and thus become dedicated agents. Infobox 1 outlines some examples of how the four platform types outlined by Perren and Kozinets (2018) offer opportunities for the sustainability transformation in the business-to-consumer market context (the examples are taken from Pyka and Stöber (2023)).

Box 1: How digital platforms support the sustainability transformation

Forums promote different forms of sharing models by providing a platform for dedicated agents to connect so that providers and demanders of certain products or services offered for sharing are paired. Forums thus lower the search costs of dedicated agents. The *food sharing* platform, for example, connects its users so that they can share their surplus food with the *food sharing* community or rescue food from businesses. This helps to reduce food waste.

Enablers equip dedicated agents with the necessary means to provide a service or good to another user. The platform coordinates the transaction between seller and buyer and minimizes their interaction, reducing the agents' search and decision-making costs. Examples include online marketplaces such as *Vinted* and *Shpock* for second-hand clothes. These platforms facilitate the buying and selling of used goods, which contributes to the conservation of resources.

Matchmakers match dedicated agents and mediate service flows between providers and consumers. The high degree of intermediation through the platform reduces search, decision, and control costs of the dedicated agents. One example is *BlaBlaCar,* an international online ride-sharing service where users can offer a ride to other members or search for a ride themselves. The platform provides services such as payment processing, cancellation and quality assessments. Sharing rides can reduce the number of vehicles on the roads and thus associated negative environmental impact.

Hubs are at the center of a transaction between dedicated agents, with supp*ly and demand flowing directly through the platform. In addition to a high degree of intermediation, service flows are highly standardized, reducing search, decision-making, monitoring and enforcement costs of the transaction for dedicated agents. Similar to enablers, hubs reduce barriers for individuals or small organizations to offer their (sustainable) products and services because of the low transaction costs. For example, the Avocado Store* offers a platform for different suppliers of green products. In this online store, customers can find a sustainable alternative for almost all conventional products, such as fashion, household, cosmetics, technology, and office products. The business concept of such sustainable online shops is based on sustainability criteria, such as resource-conserving, low-emission production and the reduction of waste and CO2 emissions, and thus reduces the negative impact of e-commerce.

5 Conclusion

In an increasingly globalized and digitalized world, economies and innovation activities within economies become more and more knowledge-intensive. Knowledge is a key resource for economic development and growth through the acquisition, development, and sharing of knowledge. Likewise, for the transformation of our socio-economic systems toward a more sustainable economy, new knowledge is required, because the current problems cannot be solved by existing knowledge that created these problems in the first place. Transformative knowledge (e.g. Abson et al., 2014; Wiek & Lang, 2016; Urmetzer et al., 2018) which relies on systemic and normative knowledge is particularly relevant in this context. Thus, a knowledge-based economy is the core of economic and sustainable development.

To solve the man-made global sustainability challenges (i.e. wicked problems, see Rittel and Webber (1973)), that we face today, prevailing socio-economic systems need to change radically. However, this transformation cannot be easily initiated and steered as our socio-economic systems are locked-in (Unruh, 2000, 2002) due to path dependencies and the cumulative nature of technological developments (Nelson, 1995). Root causes need to be addressed and prevailing systems replaced in the sense of a discontinuity approach (Unruh, 2002) to overcome lock-ins and truly transform our socio-economic systems toward higher degrees of sustainability. Hence, changes in our economic system will go beyond simple substitutions of technologies with more environmentally-friendly innovations. Complementary and interdependent infrastructural, behavioral, and institutional innovations at both the production and consumption level, as well as the interaction of these system elements, are required to cause old paradigms to shift toward new, more sustainable ones. However, as our economic systems are highly dynamic and complex with no clear cause-effect mechanisms (Arthur, 2021; Nelson et al., 2018), there is no optimal, predefined transition path. Beyond that, the normative character of the sustainability concept leads to a multitude of possible, imagined transition paths. Therefore, adaptive learning processes in innovation ecosystems are required to create collaborative and interactive environments that promote knowledge creation and diffusion in socio-economic systems.

In this chapter, we adopted an evolutionary economics perspective with regard to innovation ecosystems and argued that the perspective of innovation ecosystems needs to be revisited toward dedicated innovation ecosystems. This perspective provides the possibility to cease thinking in terms of pure substitution patterns and instead address a holistic system transformation. The mobility sector can serve as an example to illustrate this argument. To begin with, past developments in the automotive sector demonstrate a high degree of path dependency and lock-in. Technological developments in the past few decades have built on those of the combustion engine. Instead of developing more sustainable alternatives, attempts were made merely to make the existing technology more efficient, despite the fact that the first patent for an electric motor was registered as early as 1837. In the face of global sustainability challenges, electric vehicles are currently gaining momentum. This shift is not only based on the emergence of the technology. Certain infrastructures (e.g. charging stations) are required for the differentiation to the mass market and the political influence on producers and consumers also plays a decisive role, which underpins the relevance of an innovation ecosystems perspective. However, switching from combustion engines to electric motors and building the relevant infrastructure (i.e. the simple substitution of an old with a new technology) does not imply a holistic view on the innovation ecosystem as embraced in a dedicated innovation ecosystem perspective. Besides technological innovation, social innovation such as modal transportation, car sharing, or car-free cities should be discussed as viable options. Such potential changes illustrate the magnitude of the reshaping of our existing systems in terms of consumer lifestyle, production, and business opportunities. The example of the mobility sector shows that the transformation toward sustainability requires more than just new technologies. We also need to think about how we want to move in the future (e.g. shared or (inter)modal mobility) and how we can reduce our daily commutes and overall travel distances (e.g. through home offices or video conferencing). Furthermore, we need to be cautious that by focusing on certain technologies we do not create new technological lock-ins by not pursuing or considering other promising and novel technologies (e.g. autonomous driving or fuel cell engines). From a normative standpoint, what society and each individual is willing to contribute to a more sustainable socio-economic system is to be clarified.

Various implications for future research emerge from our arguments. First, the normativity of the sustainability concept should be reflected. Researchers and practitioners should clearly present their definition and relevant sustainability aspects to enrich the public discourse on the matter. Second, how different actors in the innovation ecosystem work together to shape a more sustainable future should be explored in more detail. For example, it is not clear which forms of collaboration are particularly promising. Considerations on the contribution of digitalization trends, such as green platforms, to this should also be further explored and validated. Third, transformative knowledge needs transformative research and education for its creation, adoption, and diffusion. This implies systems thinking (i.e. systems knowledge) and discussing various normative standpoints (i.e. normative knowledge), for example with respect to creating a sustainable and just future. And, last but not least, following participatory research approaches can encourage the sharing of knowledge and different normative perspectives across diverse social groups. In this way, different stakeholders embark on the search for solutions and create knowledge jointly. Considering normativity, strengthening transformative knowledge, integrating civil society, and embracing digitalization trends, create opportunities to overcome existing lock-ins and transform our current socio-economic systems toward sustainability.

References

Abson, D. J., Wehrden, H. von, Baumgärtner, S., Fischer, J., Hanspach, J., Härdtle, W. et al. (2014). Ecosystem services as a boundary object for sustainability. In *Ecological Economics, 103*, pp. 29–37. DOI: 10.1016/j.ecolecon.2014.04.012.

Adner, R. (2006). Match your innovation strategy to your innovation ecosystem. *Harvard Business Review, 84*(4), 98. Available online at https://www.researchgate.net/profile/jorge-gomes-4/post/can_anyone_recommend_studies_about_innovation_strategies_in_companies/attachment/59d61f5179197b807797dc47/as%3a283732029263872%401444658395617/download/adner_2006_hbr.pdf.

Adner, R., & Kapoor, R. (2010). Value creation in innovation ecosystems: How the structure of technological interdependence affects firm performance in new technology generations. *Strategic Management Journal, 31*(3), 306–333. DOI: 10.1002/smj.821.

Albrecht, S., Gottschick, M., Schorling, M., & Stirn, S. (2012). Bio-Ökonomie – gesellschaftliche Transformation ohne Verständigung über Ziele und Wege? Hamburg: Universität Hamburg (BIOGUM research paper, 26).

Anderson, P., & Tushman, M. L. (1990). Reproduced with permission of the copyright owner. Further reproduction prohibited without permission. Technological discontinuities and dominant designs: A cyclical model of technological change. *Administrative Science Quarterly, 35*(4), 604–633.

Arthur, W. B. (2021). Foundations of complexity economics. In *Nature reviews. Physics, 3*(2), 136–145. DOI: 10.1038/s42254-020-00273-3.

Blok, V., Gremmen, B., & Wesselink, R. (2016). Dealing with the wicked problem of sustainability in advance. *Business and Professional Ethics Journal.* DOI: 10.5840/bpej201621737.

Breslin, D., Kask, J., Schlaile, M., & Abatecola, G. (2021). Developing a coevolutionary account of innovation ecosystems. *Industrial Marketing Management, 98*, 59–68. DOI: 10.1016/j.indmarman.2021.07.016.

Burns, T. R. (2012). The sustainability revolution: A societal paradigm shift. *Sustainability, 4*(6), 1118–1134. DOI: 10.3390/su4061118.

Cagnin, C., Amanatidou, E., & Keenan, M. (2012). Orienting European innovation systems towards grand challenges and the roles that FTA can play. In *0302-3427 39*(2), 140–152. DOI: 10.1093/scipol/scs014.

Chen, D. H. C., & Dahlman, C. J. (2005). The knowledge economy, the Kam Methodology and World Bank Operations. World Bank Institute. Washington, D.C., U.S.A. (37256). Available online at https://ssrn.com/abstract=841625, checked on 12/5/2021.

Cohen, W. M., & Levinthal, D. A. (1989). Innovation and learning: The two faces of R & D. *The Economic Journal, 99*(397), 569–596. Available online at https://www.jstor.org/stable/2233763.

Cohen, W. M., & Levinthal, D. A. (1990). Absorptive capacity: A new perspective on learning and innovation. *Administrative Science Quarterly, 35*(1), 128. DOI: 10.2307/2393553.

David, P. A., & Foray, D. (1994). Dynamics of competitive technology diffusion through local network structures. In Leidersdorff, L. & van den

Besselaar, P. (Eds.), *Evolutionary economics and Chaos Theory: New developments in technology studies*. London: Pinter.

Delmas, M. A., Etzion, D., Nairn-Birch, N. (2013). Triangulating environmental performance: What do corporate social responsibility ratings really capture? *AMP,* 27(3), 255–267. DOI: 10.5465/amp. 2012.0123.

Dosi, G. (1982). Technological paradigms and technological trajectories. *Research Policy, 11*(3), 147–162. DOI: 10.1016/0048-7333(82)90016-6.

Edquist, C. (2006). Systems of innovation: Perspectives and challenges. Oxford University Press.

El Bilali, H., & Allahyari, M. Sadegh. (2018). Transition towards sustainability in agriculture and food systems: Role of information and communication technologies. *Information Processing in Agriculture, 5*(4), 456–464. DOI: 10.1016/j.inpa.2018.06.006.

El Bilali, H., Callenius, C., Strassner, C., & Probst, L. (2019). Food and nutrition security and sustainability transitions in food systems. *Food and Energy Security, 8*(2), e00154. DOI: 10.1002/fes3.154.

European Commission. (2018). A sustainable bioeconomy for Europe: Strengthening the connection between economy, society and the environment: Updated bioeconomy strategy | Knowledge for policy. Available online at https://data.europa.eu/doi/10.2777/478385, checked on 3/21/2022.

Fastenrath, S., & Braun, B. (2018). Sustainability transition pathways in the building sector: Energy-efficient building in Freiburg (Germany). *Applied Geography, 90*, 339–349. DOI: 10.1016/j.apgeog.2016.09.004.

Fichter, K., & Clausen, J. (2021). Diffusion of environmental innovations: Sector differences and explanation range of factors. *Environmental Innovation and Societal Transitions, 38*, 34–51. DOI: 10.1016/j.eist.2020.10.005.

Fischer, A., & Pascucci, S. (2017). Institutional incentives in circular economy transition: The case of material use in the Dutch textile industry. *Journal of Cleaner Production, 155*, 17–32. DOI: 10.1016/j.jclepro.2016.12.038.

Freeman, C. (1991). Networks of innovators: A synthesis of research issues. *Research Policy, 20*(5), 499–514. Available online at https://econpapers.repec.org/article/eeerespol/v_3a20_3ay_3a1991_3ai_3a5_3ap_3a499-514.htm.

Galunic, D. C., & Rodan, S. (1998). Resource recombinations in the firm: Knowledge structures and the potential for schumpeterian innovation.

Strategic Management Journal, 19(12), 1193–1201. DOI: 10.1002/(SICI)1097-0266(1998120)19:12<1193::AID-SMJ5>3.0.CO;2-F.

Geels, F. W. (2005). The dynamics of transitions in socio-technical systems: A multi-level analysis of the transition pathway from horse-drawn carriages to automobiles (1860–1930). *Technology Analysis & Strategic Management, 17*(4), 445–476. DOI: 10.1080/09537320500357319.

Geels, F. W. (2002). Technological transitions as evolutionary reconfiguration processes: A multi-level perspective and a case-study. *Research Policy, 31*(8–9), 1257–1274. DOI: 10.1016/S0048-7333(02)00062-8.

Geels, F. W. (Ed.). (2018). *Oxford research encyclopedia of environmental science*. Oxford University Press.

Gibbs, D., & O'Neill, K. (2014). Rethinking sociotechnical transitions and green entrepreneurship: The potential for transformative change in the green building sector. *Environment and Planning A, 46*(5), 1088–1107. DOI: 10.1068/a46259.

Global Footprint Network. (2022). How many Earths? How many countries? – Earth Overshoot Day. Available online at https://www.overshootday.org/how-many-earths-or-countries-do-we-need/, updated on 3/9/2022, checked on 3/20/2022.

Granstrand, O., & Holgersson, M. (2020). Innovation ecosystems: A conceptual review and a new definition. *Technovation, 90–91*, 102098. DOI: 10.1016/j.technovation.2019.102098.

Hadad, S. (2017). Knowledge economy: Characteristics and dimensions. *MDKE, 5*(2), 203–225. DOI: 10.25019/MDKE/5.2.03.

Hassan, Z. (2014). *The social labs revolution. A new approach to solving our most complex challenges. With assistance of Joi Ito* (1st ed.). Oakland: Berrett-Koehler Publishers Incorporated. Available online at https://ebookcentral.proquest.com/lib/kxp/detail.action?docID=1407853.

Hölscher, K., Wittmayer, J. M., & Loorbach, D. (2018). Transition versus transformation: What's the difference? *Environmental Innovation and Societal Transitions, 27*, 1–3. DOI: 10.1016/j.eist.2017.10.007.

Jackson, T. (2004). Negotiating sustainable consumption: A review of the consumption debate and its policy implications. *Energy & Environment, 15*(6), 1027–1051. DOI: 10.1260/0958305043026573.

Jaeger-Erben, M., Rückert-John, J., & Schäfer, M. (2015). Sustainable consumption through social innovation: A typology of innovations for sustainable consumption practices. *Journal of Cleaner Production, 108*, 784–798. DOI: 10.1016/j.jclepro.2015.07.042.

Kaplan, S., & Tripsas, M. (2008). Thinking about technology: Applying a cognitive lens to technical change. *Research Policy, 37*(5), 790–805. DOI: 10.1016/j.respol.2008.02.002.

Kemp, R., & Rotmans, J. (2004). Managing the transition to sustainable mobility. In Elzen, B., Geels, F., & Green, K. (Eds.), *System innovation and the transition to sustainability*. Edward Elgar Publishing.

Kenney, M., & Zysman, J. (2016). The rise of the platform economy. *Issues in Science and Technology, 32*(3), 61. Available online at https://www.nbp.pl/badania/seminaria/25x2016_2.pdf.

Klimas, P., & Czakon, W. (2022). Species in the wild: A typology of innovation ecosystems. *Review of Managerial Science, 16*(1), 249–282. DOI: 10.1007/s11846-020-00439-4.

Knight, F. (1921). *Risk, uncertainty and profit*. Houghton Mifflin.

Kubisch, S., Parth, S., Deisenrieder, V., Oberauer, K., Stötter, J., & Keller, L. (2021). From transdisciplinary research to transdisciplinary education—The role of schools in contributing to community well-being and Sustainable Development. *Sustainability, 13*(1), 306. DOI: 10.3390/su13010306.

Kuhlmann, S., & Rip, A. (2014). The challenge of addressing Grand Challenges A think piece on how innovation can be driven towards the "Grand Challenges" as defined under the prospective European Union Framework Programme Horizon 2020.

Laperche, B. (2017). *Enterprise knowledge capital* (1st ed.). London: Wiley-ISTE.

Lazaric, N., & Oltra, V. (2012). Sustainable consumption in an evolutionary framework: How to Foster behavioural change? In Laperche, B., Levratto, N., & Uzunidis, U. (Eds.), *Crisis, innovation and sustainable development. The ecological opportunity*. Online-ausg. Cheltenham: Edward Elgar (Science, innovation, technology and entrepreneurship), checked on 6/9/2022.

Levin, K., Cashore, B., Bernstein, S., & Auld, G. (2012). Overcoming the tragedy of super wicked problems: Constraining our future selves to ameliorate global climate change. *Policy Sciences, 45*(2), 123–152. DOI: 10.1007/s11077-012-9151-0.

Lewandowski, I. (Ed.). (2018). *Bioeconomy. Shaping the transition to a sustainable, biobased economy*. Cham: Springer International Publishing.

Loorbach, D., Wittmayer, J., Avelino, F., Wirth, T. von, & Frantzeskaki, N. (2020). Transformative innovation and translocal diffusion. *Environmental Innovation and Societal Transitions, 35*, 251–260. DOI: 10.1016/j.eist.2020.01.009.

Lundvall, B.-Å., Vang, J., & Joseph, K. J. (2009). Innovation system research and developing countries. In *Handbook of innovation systems and developing countries*. Edward Elgar Publishing. Available online at https://www.elgaronline.com/downloadpdf/edcoll/9781847206091/9781847206091.00006.xml.

Markard, J., Raven, R., & Truffer, B. (2012) Sustainability transitions: An emerging field of research and its prospects. *Research Policy, 41*(6), 955–967. DOI: 10.1016/j.respol.2012.02.013.

Mathews, J. A. (2020). Schumpeterian economic dynamics of greening: Propagation of green eco-platforms. *Journal of Evolutionary Economics, 30*(4), 929–948. DOI: 10.1007/s00191-020-00669-5.

Moore, J. F. (1993). Predators and prey: A new ecology of competition. *Harvard Business Review, 71*(3), 75–86. Available online at http://blogs.harvard.edu/jim/files/2010/04/predators-and-prey.pdf.

Nelson, R., Dosi, G., Helfat, C., Pyka, A., Saviotti, P.-P., Lee, K. et al. (Eds.). (2018). *Modern evolutionary economics: An overview*. Cambridge, UK: Cambridge University Press. Available online at https://ideas.repec.org/p/hal/journl/hal-02097506.html.

Nelson, R. R. (1989). What is private and what is public about technology? *Science, Technology, & Human Values, 14*(3), 229–241. DOI: 10.1177/016224398901400302.

Nelson, R. R. (1995). Recent evolutionary theorizing about economic change. *Journal of Economic Literature, 33*(1), 48–90. Available online at http://www.jstor.org/stable/2728910.

Nelson, R. R., Winter, S. (1982). The Schumpeterian tradeoff revisited. *The American Economic Review, 72*(1), 114–132. Available online at https://www.jstor.org/stable/1808579.

Niinimäki, K., Peters, G., Dahlbo, H., Perry, P., Rissanen, T., & Gwilt, A. (2020). The environmental price of fast fashion. *Nature Reviews Earth & Environment, 1*(4), 189–200. DOI: 10.1038/s43017-020-0039-9.

OECD. (2018). Oslo Manual 2018: Guidelines for collecting, reporting and using data on innovation. Available online at https://www.oecd.org/sti/inno/oslo-manual-2018-info.pdf, checked on 1/19/2022.

Perren, R., & Kozinets, R. V. (2018). Lateral exchange markets: How social platforms operate in a networked economy. *Journal of Marketing, 82*(1), 20–36. DOI: 10.1509/jm.14.0250.

Porter, M. E. (1980). Industry structure and competitive strategy: Keys to profitability. *Financial Analysts Journal, 36*(4), 30–41.

Powell, W. W., & Snellman, K. (2004). The knowledge economy. *Annual Review of Sociology, 30*(1), 199–220. DOI: 10.1146/annurev.soc.29.010202.100037.

Pyka, A. (2017). Dedicated innovation systems to support the transformation towards sustainability: Creating income opportunities and employment in the knowledge-based digital bioeconomy. *Journal of Open Innovation, 3*(1). DOI: 10.1186/s40852-017-0079-7.

Pyka, A., & Nelson, R. R. (2018). Schumpeterian competition and industrial dynamics. In Nelson, R., Dosi, G., Helfat, C, Pyka, A., Saviotti, P.-P., Lee, K. et al. (Eds.), *Modern evolutionary economics: An overview.* Cambridge, UK: Cambridge University Press.

Pyka, A., & Prettner, K. (2018). Economic growth, development, and innovation: The transformation towards a knowledge-based bioeconomy. In Lewandowski, I., Lask, J., Maier, J., Tchouga, B., &Vargas-Carpintero, R. (Eds.), *Bioeconomy. Shaping the transition to a sustainable, biobased economy. With assistance of Nicole Gaudet* (1st ed.) 2018. Cham, Switzerland, Hohenheim: Springer Open; University of Hohenheim, pp. 331–342.

Pyka, A., & Stöber, L. F. (2023). Services of green platforms for the sustainability transformation from an evolutionary economics perspective. In Gallouj, F., Gallouj, C., Monnoyer, M.-C., & Rubalcada, L. (Eds.), *Elgar encyclopedia of services.* Edward Elgar Publishing.

Pyka, A., Ari, E., Alva-Ferrari, A., & Urmetzer, S. (2022). The bioeconomy transition process: Sailing through storms and Doldrums in unknown waters. *Journal of Innovation Economics & Management, 38*(2), 35–61. DOI: 10.3917/jie.pr1.0110.

Renn, O. (2007). The role of social science in environmental policy making: Experiences and outlook. *Science and Public Policy, 28*(6), 427–437. DOI: 10.3152/147154301781781192.

Rittel, H. W. J., & Webber, M. M. (1973). Dilemmas in a general theory of planning. *Policy Sciences, 4*(2), 155–169. DOI: 10.1007/BF01405730.

Rockström, J., Steffen, W., Noone, K., Persson, Å., Chapin, F.S., III, Lambin, E. F. et al. (2009). A safe operating space for humanity. *Nature* (461), 472–475.

Rogers, E. M. (2003). *Diffusion of innovations* (5th ed.). New York: Free Press.

Rotmans, J., Kemp, R., van Asselt, M. (2001). More evolution than revolution: Transition management in public policy. *Foresight* (3), pp. 15–31.

Rotmans, J., & Loorbach, D. (2009). Complexity and transition management. *Journal of Industrial Ecology, 13*(2), 184–196. DOI: 10.1111/j.1530-9290.2009.00116.x.

Sahal, D. (1981). Patterns of technological innovation. *Reading, MA: Addison-Wesley, 198*(1). Available online at https://www.oeaw.ac.at/resources/record/990000495490504498.

Schlaile, M., Urmetzer, S., Blok, V., Andersen, A., Timmermans, J., Mueller, M. et al. (2017). Innovation systems for transformations towards sustainability? Taking the normative dimension seriously. *Sustainability, 9*(12), 2253. DOI: 10.3390/su9122253.

Schlaile, M. P., & Urmetzer, S. (2018). Transitions to Sustainable Development. In Leal Filho, W., Wall, T., Azeiteiro, U., Anabela Marisa, A., Brandli, L., Gökcin Özuyar, P. (Eds.), *Good health and well-being.* (Encyclopedia of the UN Sustainable Development Goals, pp. 1–16). Cham: Springer International Publishing.

Schumpeter, J. A. (1939). *Business cycles.* New York: Mcgraw-Hill. Available online at https://www.mises.at/static/literatur/buch/schumpeter-business-cycles-a-theoretical-historical-and-statistical-analysis-of-the-capitalist-process.pdf.

Schumpeter, J. A. (1947). The creative response in economic history. *Journal of Economic History, 7*(2), 149–159. DOI: 10.1017/s0022050700054279.

Smorodinskaya, N., Russell, M., Katukov, D., & Still, K. (2017). Innovation ecosystems vs. innovation systems in terms of collaboration and co-creation of value. Available online at https://scholarspace.manoa.hawaii.edu/handle/10125/41798.

Teece, D. J. (2007). Explicating dynamic capabilities: The nature and microfoundations of (sustainable) enterprise performance. *Strategic Management Journal, 28*(13), 1319–1350. DOI: 10.1002/smj.640.

United Nations. (1992). Convention on biological diversity. Available online at https://www.cbd.int/doc/legal/cbd-en.pdf, checked on 3/21/2022.

Unruh, G. C. (2000). Understanding carbon lock-in. *Energy Policy, 28*(12), 817–830. DOI: 10.1016/S0301-4215(00)00070-7.

Unruh, G. C. (2002). Escaping carbon lock-in. *Energy Policy, 30*(4), 317–325. DOI: 10.1016/S0301-4215(01)00098-2.

Urmetzer, S., Lask, J., Vargas-Carpintero, R., & Pyka, A. (2020). Learning to change: Transformative knowledge for building a sustainable bioeconomy. *Ecological Economics, 167*, 106435. DOI: 10.1016/j.ecolecon.2019.106435.

Urmetzer, S., Schlaile, M., Bogner, K., Mueller, M., & Pyka, A. (2018). Exploring the dedicated knowledge base of a transformation towards a sustainable bioeconomy. *Sustainability, 10*(6), 1694. DOI: 10.3390/su10061694.

Verbong, G. P. J., & Geels, F. W. (2010). Exploring sustainability transitions in the electricity sector with socio-technical pathways. *Technological Forecasting and Social Change, 77*(8), 1214–1221. DOI: 10.1016/j.techfore.2010.04.008.

Von Schomberg, R. (2013). A vision of responsible research and innovation. In Owen, R., Bessant, J., & Heintz, M. (Eds.), *Responsible innovation.* Chichester, UK: John Wiley & Sons, Ltd, pp. 51–74.

Wehrden, H. von, Luederitz, C., Leventon, J., & Russell, S. (2017). Methodological challenges in sustainability science: A call for method plurality, procedural rigor and longitudinal research. *Challenges in Sustainability, 5*(1). DOI: 10.12924/cis2017.05010035.

Wiek, A., & Lang, D. J. (2016). Transformational sustainability research methodology. In: Sustainability Science. Dordrecht: Springer, pp. 31–41. Available online at https://link.springer.com/chapter/10.1007/978-94-017-7242-6_3.

Wijen, F. (2014). Means versus ends in opaque institutional fields: Trading off compliance and achievement in sustainability standard adoption. *AMR, 39*(3), 302–323. DOI: 10.5465/amr.2012.0218.

Wilke, U., Schlaile, M. P., Urmetzer, S., Mueller, M., Bogner, K., & Pyka, A. (2021). Time to say 'Good Buy' to the passive consumer? A conceptual review of the consumer in the bioeconomy. *Journal of Agricultural and Environmental Ethics, 34*(4). DOI: 10.1007/s10806-021-09861-4.

World Commission on Environment and Development. (1987). Our common future: Report of the World Commission on Environment and Development.

Xu, Z., & Maas, G. (2019). Innovation and entrepreneurial ecosystems as important building blocks. In *Transformational Entrepreneurship Practices*. Cham: Palgrave Pivot, pp. 15–32. Available online at https://link.springer.com/chapter/10.1007/978-3-030-11524-1_2.

Digital ecosystems for agilizing innovation

Florin Paun, Ingrid Vaileanu[1]

Abstract: Collaborative innovation has been the subject of numerous scientific works (Laperche & Uzunidis, 2012), especially on open innovation (Chesbrough et al., 2018), as a highly collaborative process (Paun, 2012), highlighted in particular by innovative digital ecosystems in the last twenty years. In the first part, we will define and present a digital ecosystem with reference to concrete cases and examples in Europe, the USA, and Asia. Then we will define and discuss the high collaborative intensity based on dense and multiple interactions between the actors of a digital ecosystem and the importance of tools for facilitating innovation processes (Typologies of innovative actors in digital ecosystems, the tools of the DRL-TRL tool, Agile Demo-Tech for the agilization of innovation processes and organizations, and the "Contract of sharing risk and benefits"). In a third part, we will present the actors of the relevant digital ecosystems and their functions and potential impacts at the micro, meso, and macro-economic level.

Keywords: Agility, "Agilization innovation", Agile organizations, Agile demo-tech, Human factors, Open innovation, Digital ecosystems, "Open qualification"

I. Definition and presentation of open digital ecosystems with reference to concrete cases in Europe, the USA, Asia

First, we will explain the concepts to make the understanding of the chapter more accessible for a wider readership. Through four articles illustrating the diversity of areas of expertise in which agility can be studied,

[1] ARESIA, Xvaluator, France.

this special issue of RRI *Innovations, Journal of Innovation Economics & Management* provides a subtle and complementary insight into the principles presented above.

Christian Dianoux, Sandrine Heitz-Spahn, Béatrice Siadou-Martin, Géraldine Thevenot, and Hélène Yildiz describe how the flexibility, adaptability and low cost of nudges strengthen the ability of the organizations that use them to improve their agility. Stéphane Goria explores the relationship between creativity and economic monitoring. He suggests using an OODA loop (Observation, Orientation, Decision, Action) to estimate its agility. Using a multiple-case-study analysis of co-design in the field of energy, Laurent Dupont, Joëlle Mastelic, Nathalie Nyffeler, Sophie Latrille, and Éric Seulliet identify the agile levers in the Living Lab that favor trust between stakeholders. Finally, on the basis of the illustrated case of the Swatch watch, Brunelle Marche, Vincent Boly, Laure Morel, Frédérique Mayer, and Roland Ortt, focusing on the innovative supply chain, highlight the fact that both concepts of the agile supply chain and the agility of the supply chain support innovation.

Agility has been defined by researchers (Dumont, 2019) as the ability of an organization to effectively immerse itself in its ecosystem, understood as all the entities that interact in a technological, economic, societal, and cultural environment. The structures concerned therefore systematically involve all stakeholders in the development of new products and/or services, in order to accelerate understanding of the various needs.

The term "agile" is now commonly used to describe organizations that are able to adapt and function well in rapidly changing environments (Overby et al., 2006). "*Flexibility*" or "*lean*" are other terms (Edin Grimheden, 2013) to describe similar approaches. In fact, since the early 2000s, agile methods have popularized the concept of agility, in particular through the dissemination of the *Agile Manifesto*, designed for software development and which advocates three fundamental principles (http://www.agilealliance.org) (Highsmith et al., 2001).

By adapting the principles of the Agile Manifesto, it is possible to go beyond strict technological developments and disseminate the following three agile innovation practices within organizations: (1) Foster interactions between individuals supported by agile processes and tools. Indeed, from an agile perspective, the team is much more important than the tools (structuring or control) or the operating procedures. It is preferable to have a united team that communicates rather than a team of experts working in isolation. (2) Encourage collaboration with customers in the form of flexible contracting. The client must be involved throughout the development. It makes no sense to negotiate and freeze a contract at the beginning of the project, while the client's demands can evolve with understanding of his needs and the framework of possibilities. In this context, the very notion of a customer can undoubtedly be rethought. Customers are actors in the project and must be considered as stakeholders to be satisfied. Including them in the process is one of the pillars of a "*robust agility*". (3) Focus on adapting to change, or even embodying change, rather than monitoring a plan. In a changing context, where the "ecosystem" can inhibit leads or offer new opportunities in a short time, the initial planning and structure of the product or service must be flexible to allow the adaptation of customer demand (or market demand). It is necessary to be pro-active together.

The aim of agility is therefore to enable organizations to create value by making their operation more flexible by developing a culture of change and collaboration.

The importance of highly collaborative practices and tools for open innovation

Presented Shkarupeta, Savon, and Avlasenko (2020) as a model of the active interaction of companies with the external environment in the process of innovation with the aim of exchanging technologies, knowledge, and competencies, which is realized through the use of the following tools: innovation project competitions, financing of external innovation projects to finalize proposals, corporate accelerators, corporate business incubators, corporate technology parks, corporate venture funds, spin-offs of internal developments, acquisition of companies and others. Thus, scientists observed how Airbus makes intersections between great ideas, people, and challenges happen by partnering with the outside world to translate innovative ideas into aerospace breakthroughs more quickly than ever before. The way Airbus works with partners is open and agile. This is the Airbus approach to accelerating innovation.

The importance of the agile innovation processes is even more relevant in the Frugal Innovation ecosystems (Ahuja & Chan, 2016) mainly practiced in developing countries such as India, China, Brazil, and Kenya (Radjou & Prabhu, 2015). In emerging economies, firms that practice frugal innovation are better able to successfully overcome infrastructure, financial, social, and technological constraints. They achieve this by focusing on products and services that are centered on affordability, simplicity, and sustainability. Researchers define a frugal ecosystem as one that is characterized by significant institutional voids and resource constraints, but where the collective relational connections of the ecosystem participants are channelled toward developing affordable and sustainable solutions to fill institutional voids and overcome constraints (Costello, Donnellan, & Curley, 2013). It is important to note that firms do not operate in isolation and several other entities participate in a frugal ecosystem. These may include the focal firm, its suppliers, its extended network of customers and vendors, government agencies, business support services, logistics and delivery providers, alliance partners, and often even rival firms.

Analyzed thanks to their success in the United States, Europe, and Asia, innovative digital ecosystems are in particular a highly collaborative, firstly organizational innovation process that integrates a wide variety of public and private actors, sometimes in the form of communities of thought and action that create, share, and disseminate different knowledge aimed at collectively and individually creating shared value through innovation (incremental, radical, or disruptive) in a wide variety of sectors and markets (Paun, 2014). In the light of observations and analyses of concrete experiments, sharing of good practices and tools for accelerating innovation in Europe, the United States and Asia, this article also reveals the impacts of digital ecosystems on the shortening of cycles of innovation, and consequently of accelerating the processes of creation of value shared by Major Groups, SMEs, ETIs, laboratories and acceleration structures, territories, etc.

The methodology based on both successful pioneering and inspiring experiments in Europe (IoT Tribe Space Endeavour, Paris Saclay, SATT, Competitiveness clusters in France, Cluj IT Cluster in Romania) in the United States (Orlando University), and in Asia (Singapore but also Indonesia), corroborated with the identification of new tools and strategies for capturing increased value through agile processes of collaborative, open innovation, reveal innovative pedagogical concepts and tools.

Thus some examples in France are of public renown. For Airbus, there is the innovative approach of Bizlab, the A3 accelerator, as well as the use of the "HYPE" platform for collaborative innovation within Airbus. New practices such as "awakening" seminars to "open innovation", provided voluntarily by the author of Programme/Project managers for groups such as EDF, Valeo, are now followed by groups such as

Stelia. Mechanisms at work to be able to inject start-ups into the research and innovation programs of large groups are springing up everywhere, such as l'Accélerateur Deep-Tech de Incub-Alliance, Starbust, the Pegase Growth Accelerator, the Aerospace Business Nursery Valley, or the Joint Accelerator of the BPI with the GIFAS with the objective of accelerating around sixty SMEs in order to better implement them in the programs of the Major Groups and their networks such as MEDEF. To these examples we can in particular add the new Mission Innovation service desired, built, and made operational within Inter-company Mediation by the Mediator Pierre Pelouzet.

In Asia, we notice the same dynamic of hybridization of the Tech-Push and Market-Pull approaches (Paun, 2021) in the emerging digital ecosystems in Indonesia with the BIC Indonesia digital ecosystem of Kristanto Santosa, or the new collaborative innovation tools created in Europe (the French DRL-TRL which completes the American tool TRL), which are at the heart of changes for the evolution of the national innovation system for more agility and efficiency and the democratization of innovation processes, especially in the digital sector.

Specificities and tools for agilization innovation processes and organizations: DRL-TRL, Typologies of innovative actors in digital ecosystems, Agile Demo-Tech, Agilization of innovation processes, Contract at Risk and shared benefits

Digital ecosystems require a great diversity of sectors and innovation players. This represents an asset if the collaborative relationships are facilitated by tools for "compensating asymmetries" and if the management methodologies are in favor of and capable of capturing and valuing the direct and indirect, socio-economic, and ecological impacts at all levels and stages of agile innovation processes. The development potential of a digital ecosystem of collaborative innovation depends on the number and diversity of the actors who are members of the ecosystem, their capacity for collaboration and exchanges, the quality of the tools, and the methodology for capturing the impacts and valuation of each person's inputs (Paun, 2018).

The concept of open innovation and the role of open innovation backed by digital ecosystems will be highlighted as a "highly collaborative process".

Collaborative innovation and especially "open innovation" (Chesbrough & Van Haverbeke, 2008; Paun, von Tunzelmann, &

Richard, 2011) is perceived as an essential process for creation and valorization, thus integrating a greater number of diversity of actors and "observers' perspectives" (as the innovative start-up Xvaluator in 2016) , representing not a threat (as in the Fordian segmentation approach) but a strength as important inputs if "the diversity of the asymmetries" (Paun et al., 2011) (culture asymmetries, risk asymmetries, temporality asymmetries, etc.) between the innovation actors are compensated by innovative tools (Paun & Richard, 2009) in order to facilitate collaborations and "shared augmented value creation". The result of these highly collaborative interactions and tools are the "agilizing innovation processes" (Paun, 2018) aiming to reinforce the capacities and capabilities (Paun, 2011) of actors to perform by integrating *ex ante* the direct and indirect impacts at social, ecological, economical levels.

I.1. Highly collaborative ecosystems

The **valorization potential of a highly collaborative innovation ecosystem** depends, at the same time, on the number and the diversity of the actors involved in interactions, of their collaboration capacities and "capabilities" (Paun et al., 2011), as well as of the quality of the adaptive tools (including digital tools and new approaches) and methodologies supporting them to perceive, qualify, share, and valorise the inputs of each of the actors.

The quality of a highly collaborative innovation ecosystem is:

- directly proportional to the square of the number of the ecosystem actors,
- directly proportional to the actors integrating the ecosystem with the intention to OFFER (respond to demands) (Tech-Push),
- indirectly proportional to those expressing a DEMAND and the intention of the ecosystem to benefit (Market-Pull),
- directly proportional to the specific characteristics (asymmetries) of the direct members of the ecosystem and
- indirectly to their own external potential networks (especially their diversity and complementarity) and directly proportional to the "capabilities" (Paun et al., 2011) of action and success of each of the innovation actors involved. (Paun, 2018)

These "capabilities" depend on the quality and efficiency of dynamic tools and collaborative strategies (DRL-TRL, IRL, Shared Risks and

Benefits Contracts, etc.) (Paun & Richard, 2009), as well as of the capacity of the actors to use these and evaluate innovation on long trajectories, not only on a "one shot" innovation project or product.

The Value of a Collaborative Innovation Ecosystem = N square – N / 2 x N offer / N benefx As (Div, Compl.) x Cap (Tools, Action) Source: (Paun & Vaileanu, 2018) **Valorization of the collaborative innovation ecosystems**

N = Number of innovation actors in a collaborative innovation ecosystem

NV offer = Number of innovation actors with the intention and resources to OFFER solutions to the other ecosystem members

NV benef = Number of innovation actors with the intention to benefit from the ecosystem solutions for their DEMAND

As = Specific Characteristics – asymmetries identified within the ecosystem members

Div = The degree of diversity of the ecosystem members

Compl = The degree of complementarity of the ecosystem members

Cap = Capabilities of the ecosystem

Tools = Collaboration and exchange tools, aiming to compensate asymmetries in order to facilitate highly collaborative agile innovation processes

Act = Capability of members to be dynamic and engage RESOURCES and ACTIONS

The integration of the diversity of impacts in collaborative innovation practices is co-substantial to the agile and highly collaborative process as the more we integrate diversity at all levels (subjects of interest, topics, localizations and temporalities that are different in accordance with each specific context of each member of the ecosystem), the more we increase the perimeters of competences and capabilities of all actors and thus the more chances to create shared value for all the ecosystem members and even for their external, indirectly impacted, networks of stakeholders.

Even if, at the beginning of the collaborative innovation process, the impacts seem to be observed more internally to the firms (in terms of an increase in competences of the human resources, new approaches, new ideas, etc.) the longer we persist in "agilizing the innovation ecosystems" (Paun, 2018), the more we impact stakeholders directly or indirectly, even in totally different sectors to the initial collaborations, and thus contribute to scaling-up the evolution of economic models in all sectors and territories (impacts registered at macro-economic level).

"Agilising innovation process"
Long-term Collaborative innovation process
"Agile Demo-Tech Thinking"
Direct and Indirect impact, external and internal to the firm and to the sectors;
Integration of social and environmental impact
"Monetary Value-Capitalistic Value"
"Impacts Augmented Value"

In recent years, digital technology, social networks, and the impact

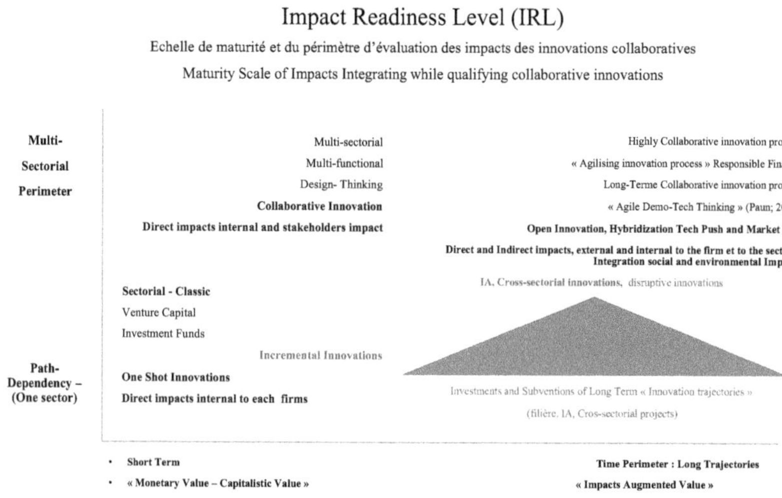

Figure 1: Impacts Readiness Level (IRL) measuring the degree of maturity and intensity of the highly collaborative process of innovation
Source: Paun and Vaileanu (2018)

of AI have changed the centers of creation and development. The value of innovations is increasingly based on the ability to integrate new and evolving services (with a very short "time to market" and which is often uncoupled from the sectoral subject such as GPS, a digital innovation which has grafted onto mobility features and can no longer be lacking in a new car). Digital solutions, 3D printers, AI, all call into question a number of foundations in traditional valuation, including exclusivity, social status, authenticity.

I.2. Typologies of actors in innovative and open digital ecosystems

Due to the fact that the innovation process is mainly expressed in terms of a "system" characterized in particular by its aptitude for change, in particular technical, managerial, and organizational, and that it is connected to a complex set of actors which are bearers of innovation constituting an innovation ecosystem (Laperche & Uzunidis, 2012) we analyse the evolving set of actors, activities and artefacts, as well as the evolutions of their strategies, institutions, and their relationships, including complementarity and substitution relationships, which are important for the innovative performance of an actor or a population of actors.

Three major typologies of innovation-ready innovators identified in digital ecosystems in Europe (Paun, 2020) connecting actors in European digital ecosystems linking Space Tech and IoT Tribe and in particular using Space Tech in the European acceleration program, have been identified for the first time with a specificity: having already integrated aerospace technologies or having identified the need to integrate these technologies which are consistent with the devices and tools of innovation.

One of the methodologies used is a diagnosis that is both scientific and participatory thanks to a process of co-evaluation together with large groups, SMEs, start-ups, detailed exchanges during meetings, videoconferences to understand business models, markets already identified, barriers to developing innovation, and open innovation capabilities.

(a) "Early stage" Start-Up (start-ups in this typology are generally in the incubation process but do not yet have a clear Go to Market Strategy)

(b) Start-Ups "Crossing the chasm" in the process of their transition to a phase of rapid growth "crossing the chasm". In this typology there are start-ups that have successfully launched their product/service (or Product plus service functionality) on a well-identified market, they have a base of committed customers and co-development partners. They have already launched their S-Curve sales and they are in the middle of the process of starting larger sales (derivative expansion) with the potential for positive impacts and externalities: reducing risk, diversifying the portfolio, and increasing the intensification of uses of its production.

(c) "Mature Booming" Start-Ups. Start-ups that have already been successful and are already growing are also interested in high-performance accelerators like the IoT Tribe Acceleration Program with the aim of creating new Business Units based on Products/Services (or functionalities), new and diverse.

Digital ecosystems have this specificity of positioning themselves on multi-actor, multi-sector, multi-market and even "out of the traditional market" approaches, the more we develop capabilities to "make innovation processes more agile" the more therefore we develop the context for "human capital" to create "shared value without dividing" through serendipity and, above all, aimed at disruptive innovation.

I.3. The shared risk and benefit contract

This is the "Shared Risk Development Contract" developed by the PhD Florin Paun at Onera and then taken over by the networks of large groups, the SATTs, the competitiveness clusters, which was developed and signed, for the first time in France, between an EPIC (ONERA) and a commercial company.

Indeed, in this technology maturation phase between TRL 2 and TRL ¾, the risk is still too great to be assumed by the SME alone as long as the technological proof, as well as the complete understanding of the technology, are not carried out. This type of contract is therefore a very good tool, both financial and technical, for collaboration in a logic of co-design for the development of a new product. This tool allows the two parties to together cross, in the sense of Aoki's theory based on Nash's equilibrium (Aoki, 2000), a possible financial barrier that could induce a blockage. In addition to compensating for the risk and technological asymmetry between the two parties, this contract subsequently proved to be a good tool for reducing the (transactional) information asymmetry (Stiglitz, 1992) between the start-up and its investors, to which are added other asymmetries (of risk, temporality, cultural, etc.) in the collaborative processes discovered in open innovation processes (Paun, 2012). This is due to the fact that during the "due diligence" phase between the creators of the start-ups and the Business Angels, the Shared Risk Development Contract provides substantial information as much on the product and the target market as on the development's technologies and their costs.

I.4. The European DRL-TRL tool for agilizing innovation processes and organizations

Since 1985 innovation practitioners and theorists have ignored the importance of the degree of maturity of demand and expression of needs, and followed the only scale of technology maturity, Technology Readiness Level – TRL (Mankins, 1995). Tech-Push Approaches are often opposed to Market-Pull Approaches. With the DRL-Demand Readiness Level tool (Paun, 2009) the bases of innovative approaches to the management of collaborative innovation processes propose the acceleration of innovations thanks in particular to the tools of "compensation for the asymmetries of the actors" and of hybridization of Tech (TRL) and Market Pull (DRL) methodologies to support national innovation strategies (Paun, 2018). The more we integrate (during all stages of the "DRL-TRL" innovation process) the impacts perceived by a greater number of stakeholders, the more we increase the capacities and capabilities "to make the innovation process more agile" (Paun, 2018).

Among the pioneers in the experimentation and adaptation of these DRL tools, DRL-TRL, were research institutions (ONERA – Office National d'Etudes et Recherche Aerospatiale), innovation support networks such as the Conference of Parliamentarians for the national innovation strategy, or the SATTs (Technology Transfer Acceleration Structures) of business networks (MEDEF, PACTE PME), but also of schools (among the first was the ANRT School of Innovation, MBAs from Toulouse Business School, Paris School of Business), trainers such as EUROSAE, DENT Associates, Marcus Evans, Innovation Johnson, members of research and innovation networks such as Réseau CURIE and even government support structures for innovation like the (BIC – Business Innovation Center), a visionary structure that is supporting the emergence of a new national open innovation strategy in Indonesia, to democratize the use of collaborative tools like DRL-TRL.

Then DRL (Paun et al., 2011) was quickly disseminated and used by communities of scientists and practitioners (including, among the first in France, the SATT, MEDEF-Commission Open Innovation, PACTE PME-Guide Open Innovation, École de l'innovation de ANRT, more than 500 students and doctoral students from the Air School, Toulouse Business School MBA, EUROSAE training and expertise, major groups such as Siemens, and other participants in the Marcus Evans conferences, etc.) (see figures 2 and 3).

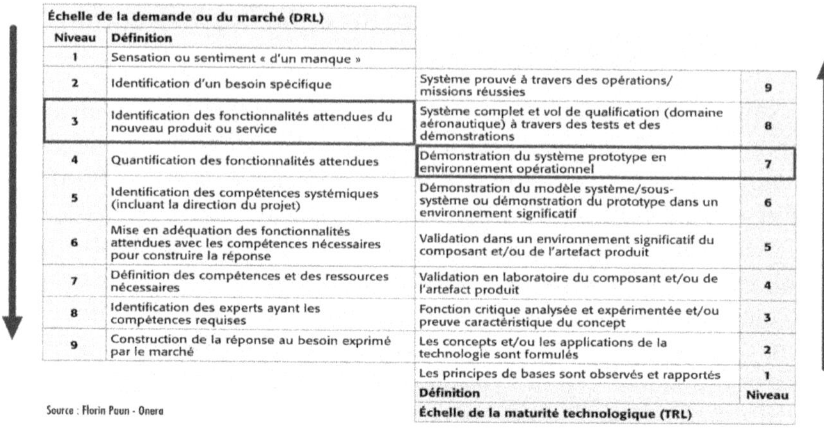

Échelle de la demande ou du marché (DRL)	
Niveau	**Définition**
1	Sensation ou sentiment « d'un manque »
2	Identification d'un besoin spécifique
3	Identification des fonctionnalités attendues du nouveau produit ou service
4	Quantification des fonctionnalités attendues
5	Identification des compétences systémiques (incluant la direction du projet)
6	Mise en adéquation des fonctionnalités attendues avec les compétences nécessaires pour construire la réponse
7	Définition des compétences et des ressources nécessaires
8	Identification des experts ayant les compétences requises
9	Construction de la réponse au besoin exprimé par le marché

Définition	Niveau
Système prouvé à travers des opérations/missions réussies	9
Système complet et vol de qualification (domaine aéronautique) à travers des tests et des démonstrations	8
Démonstration du système prototype en environnement opérationnel	7
Démonstration du modèle système/sous-système ou démonstration du prototype dans un environnement significatif	6
Validation dans un environnement significatif du composant et/ou de l'artefact produit	5
Validation en laboratoire du composant et/ou de l'artefact produit	4
Fonction critique analysée et expérimentée et/ou preuve caractéristique du concept	3
Les concepts et/ou les applications de la technologie sont formulés	2
Les principes de bases sont observés et rapportés	1
Définition	**Niveau**
Échelle de la maturité technologique (TRL)	

Source : Florin Paun - Onera

Figure 2: "DRL-TRL" – the (patented) tool for agilizing innovation processes through Tech Push (TRL) and Market Pull (DRL) hybridization strategies
Source: Paun, 2011

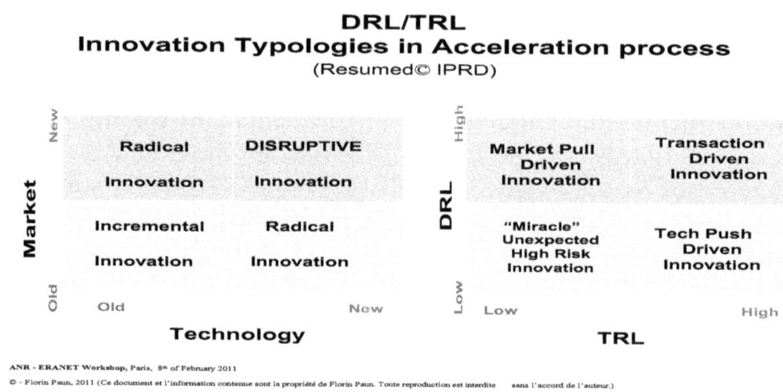

Figure 3: Various uses and adaptations in France of the DRL-TRL tool for accelerating disruptive innovation
Source: Paun, 2011

It can be emphasized that the different levels can only be partially achieved and this is often insufficient to guarantee the success of an innovation project.

To overcome the various existing asymmetries, in recent years the French State has implemented instruments such as Technology Transfer Acceleration Companies (SATT) and Research and Technology Institutes (IRT), two mechanisms generically positioned in the graph between the levels of technological maturity corresponding to Proofs of Concept and Technology Demonstrators. The difference between these two instruments is significant. SATTs are supposed to operate in a Technology Push approach, to mature emerging technologies developed by public laboratories in order to offer licenses on the market, but their strategies have evolved toward a hybridization of Tech-Push and Market-Pull for more efficiency. The IRTs are used in a Market-Pull approach to define the strategic roadmaps between the major integrator groups and their Tier 1 equipment manufacturers, also using the skills of the research laboratories in a campus spirit and bringing all participants up to speed.

Economists thus believe that we are witnessing a "disintegration" of the company but also of the coordination of the value chain, which tends to be centralized around companies that are "system integrators" and projects (upstream and downstream) with a capacity investment in innovation. The intensity of the systems integrator's relationship with its first-tier suppliers tends to become so strong that the supplier develops its detailed R&D, production, and distribution plans in direct consultation with the integrator's needs and objectives, its development becoming dependent on the direct control of the integrator. Downstream, the relationship with customers and partners is nowadays more supervised in order to consider optimal adaptations thanks to constant feedback. These systems integrators (capable of migrating to this augmented form of business) with knowledge of technological needs will be able to ensure the lion's share in the sharing of value resulting from transactions between the actors of these new innovation ecosystems prepared for new cycles of innovation (Schumpeter, 1939) or adapted to the future context resulting from the impact of artificial intelligence.

II. Presentation of the actors of the relevant digital ecosystems and their functions and potential impacts at the micro, meso, and macro-economic level

Integrated into new forms of innovation (open innovation), these tools and innovation agilization processes (Paun et al., 2022) provide new solutions for innovative digital ecosystems given the need for the pooling and sharing of key resources, on the one hand, while ensuring the protection (aimed at the appropriation, the valorisation) of the resources generated following the collaborative processes of innovation, such as, for example, the Intellectual Property Rights (henceforth IPR), on the other hand.

One of the essential players in the collaborative innovation of digital ecosystems remains the University, which could acquire an important role in local economic development, in particular thanks to the positive impacts of collaborative and entrepreneurial innovation strategies. The example of the University of Central Florida (UCF) is significant for the collaborative innovation methodology used which has enabled the University, thanks to its approaches that are always of the "shared risks and benefits" type, to become a lever for the diversification of the local economy, which is also highly dependent on the tourism and hotel sectors, sectors known for their relatively low wage levels. Since its creation in 1999, the UCF Business Incubation Program (UCFBIP) has become the catalyst for entrepreneurial initiatives through agile approaches to collaborative innovation offering incubation and acceleration functionalities through training, business centers, innovation competition, etc. The entrepreneurial and innovation ecosystem created is based on pillars that allow economic development through complete processes from the idea, to research, to patent registration, to commercialization. It contributes to the creation of both direct and indirect jobs and it generates taxes that replenish the state budget: for each dollar invested, four other dollars are returned to the state through the taxes generated. Thus, public money allows new funds to be invested and to support this virtuous circle.

It is within the framework of research and innovation work at ONERA that the tools for agilizing innovation processes have been discovered and developed (Paun, 2012) by highlighting the Dynamic Capabilities (SEN, 1985) of research collaborators and their partners and by transforming the culture of research solely into a culture of research and innovation, which translates to a particular example on the development of the capacities of innovative structures and of these SME partners absorbing the technology developed by ONERA at the following technology transfer trial (Paun, 2012). The Alumni Onera network led by Bruno Sainjon and Bruno Chanetz continues today to disseminate collaborative innovation approaches by sharing its innovative tools with generations and communities of innovation.

Among these major players in France are also Technology Transfer Acceleration Structures, the Paris-Saclay Plateau, a real French and international success in terms of innovation with its three stages of the innovation agilization rocket: first the SATT Paris Saclay, directed by Xavier Apolinarski, which extracts the technology from research laboratories such as ONERA and their multidisciplinary teams, then the incubation activity with IncubeAlliance which completes the team and defines the business model of the innovative players, and finally Deeptech Acceleration where we accelerate development and commercial deployment to create innovative solutions that are marketed and marketable. All of this dynamic is territorialized on the Paris Saclay Plateau in the middle of the ecosystem between research laboratories, SMEs, and large groups practicing open innovation.

Starbust, created by François Chopard, is another model of French success present in the United States, which also energizes business networks which are added to the success of networks such as MEDEF, Le Mouvement des Entreprises de France, Pacte PME (Pacte PME, 2016), but also those of schools, doctoral students, and visionary leaders such as Carole Miranda and Alain Quevreux from the School of Innovation of the Association for Research and Technology, expert training institutions such as EUROSAE led by Éric Maini, Toulouse Business School, Paris School of Business, and Day One created by writer and entrepreneur Denis Jacquet in Monaco, who signs agreements in Africa and Brazil, to ensure that this European digital ecosystem becomes a network of ecosystems global.

Other successful SATTs (Technology Transfer Acceleration Structures) are those of Toulouse, built by Pierre Dufresne and Christophe Haunold, and Brittany and Pays de Loire, by Vincent Lamande, whose success is added to the network of competitiveness headed by Jean Luc Beylat, President of the Federation of Poles and Pole Sistematic in Ile de France.

The SAFE Pole at PACA and Pegasse Croissance have become a success thanks to leaders such as André Soulage, Géraud Parjadis, Philippe Richard, but also thanks to collaborative innovation tools and strategies with high territorial value, including the first Territorial Open Innovation Charter (Paun, 2018) signed with more than 10 Major Groups committing to partnership practices with SMEs (in particular on IP), three other Competitiveness Clusters (Optitech, Pole Mer and Eurobiomed), the DGA and the PACA region with the participation of its Vice-President, Renaud Muselier in September 2016.

With the European partnership projects of the digital, IoT and aerospace ecosystems represented by the flagships of French aerospace research such as ONERA, ESA, CNES, CNRS, SATTs, competitiveness clusters are today successful experiments with new tools and strategies for creating shared value.

Innovative digital ecosystems based on complementary and interdependent territorial, sectoral, and functional divisions are also the Toulouse Aerospace Valley, led by Yann Barbaux, the Bic Montpellier Cluster, led by Isabelle Prévôt, Romain Latoux, Data Science Montpellier ISDM, led by Anne Laurent, and above all the Adocc Région Occitanie, directed by Nicolas Shaeffer, Fréderic Faivre, and Gilles Lucato.

In Montpellier, there are success stories of great start-ups that have experienced strong growth (often helped by the Region), which have been bought out by French or foreign companies, and whose takeover helps to accelerate growth, such as in the case of Teads by Altice (FR), Techsia, acquired by Schlumberger, Medtech by Zimmer Biomet (US), Bime by Zendesk (US), Septeo, taken over by the Hg Capital fund (UK), Matooma by Wireless Logic (UK).

In Romania, the Cluj IT Cluster, led by Stelian Brad, is the digital ecosystem that has given the city in Transylvania the reputation of being the Silicon Valley of Eastern Europe and is formed by organizations active in the field of IT information: service providers and software solutions, universities and research institutes, public bodies and other catalyst organizations: more than 70 companies, 14 universities and research centers, 11 public institutions.

In Europe, the future of space is digital and vice versa: space technologies are no longer aimed at a niche market limited to defense and communications, but are relevant in all sectors of the economy, which has been shown by digital ecosystems like IoT Tribe, founded in Spain by Tania Suarez, the BluSpecs CEO and co-initiator with the French PhD Florin Paun, from the European project "Space Endeavour", bringing together more than 60 European start-ups and innovation experts to select and coach European IoT and Space innovators: Quant Cube, Safetyn, Ajuma, Geofem, Growdspace, Action Tracker, Orbital Eos, Alphablock, Lanu, Morphee, Quantum South, Alenspace, Bubbl, Hopu. In the bottom-up analyses of weak signals and qualified information, several criteria are taken into account: the degree of maturity and the sources of the innovation, the motivation and stimulation levers for identifying new needs to specify the demand in several sectors, and the stage of maturity of this multi-sector demand, the dynamics of new capabilities, etc.

In Asia, the number of Indonesian publications indexed globally during the years 1996–2016 reached 54,146 articles/reviews. Compared to Singapore, Thailand, or Malaysia, Indonesia's ranking is still well below these three ASEAN countries. In Asia, Indonesia's position ranks 11th, while in ASEAN, it ranks fourth. The current discourse within the Indonesian government is the urgency to integrate the results of research and development (R&D), not just respecting budgetary responsibility (85–90 % of R&D funding comes from the government). The efforts of the Indonesian government for downstream innovations and technology transfers have encouraged the emergence of business incubators for start-up companies, whether it is business incubators or technology incubators. However, the lack of market or demand orientation of R&D activities is often used to explain poor performance. The Business Innovation Center (BIC) and the CIS School of Innovation are relevant digital and innovation ecosystems that have been trying since 2018 to implement French tools and strategies (DRL-TRL) to "hybridize" national innovation strategies by integrating together the Technology Readiness Level (TRL) and the Demand/Market Readiness Level (DRL), in order to bring together the actors of innovation on the technology side (input side, supplier side or upstream side) and the actors on the demand side (the market or customer), to make the innovation process and organizations more agile. This in turn has increased the need for a new way of managing technology transfer processes through and beyond the realm of R&D to the commercial world; and moreover, to contribute to the competitiveness of the industry.

III. Potential impacts of highly collaborative digital ecosystems and their agilizing innovation tools

Researchers consider (Kolloch & Dellermann, 2017) that the high level of openness in innovation makes firms more dependent on each other, as well as dynamics within the firm's environment (Adner & Kapoor, 2010). Therefore, innovation ecosystems are an ensemble of interdependent and heterogeneous actors (e.g. suppliers, distributors, competitors, customers, government, and other institutions) (Moore, 1993; Teece, 2007) that emerge around an innovation (i.e. a technological network)

The modularity of digital innovation is therefore changing the traditional value chain into value networks and fundamentally reshaping the traditional innovation logic (Garud & Kumaraswamy, 1993). In particular, the combinable developmental process of novel digital technology explains how components interact with other components and reshape an ecosystem of human and non-human actors.

The concept of such an ecosystem helps to analyze interdependencies more explicitly (Adner & Kapoor, 2010; Moore, 1993). Innovation ecosystems are defined as a [...] loosely interconnected network of companies and other entities that coevolve capabilities around a shared set of technologies, knowledge, or skills, and work cooperatively and competitively to develop new products and services.

One of the potential impacts of innovation agilization tools of digital ecosystems is to democratically qualify value based on digital highly collaborative tools like Xvaluator French innovation in order to better guide citizens based on qualified opinions.

In fact, humans have only a 57 % accuracy of detection, even when a deception mindset is activated with information on cues of fake online reviews. Therefore, micro-linguistic automated detection solutions could be used to democratically qualify and organize the content of reviewing websites to protect online users of the fake news.

Previous research (Plotkinaa, Munzel, & Palluf, 2020) shows that online reviews affect sales (Fan, Che, & Chen, 2017; Liu, Huang, & Zhang, 2016), purchase intentions (Park, Lee, & Han, 2007), and product choices (Fagerstrøm, Ghinea, & Sydnes, 2016). Because of their growing influence, online reviews are becoming increasingly relevant to marketers (Chen & Xie, 2008; Chong, Li, Ngai, Ch'ng, & Lee, 2016). The empirically supported effects of reviews on consumers and the difficulty in obtaining reviews have led companies to engage in malicious practices to manage their online reputations (Munzel, 2016). These corporate practices to manipulate opinions by posting deceptive content are referred to as deceptive online communication, or "fake reviews" (Mayzlin, Dover, & Chevalier, 2014). Although fake online reviews are illegal in many countries, they still exist, with companies ready to take risks to deceive their customers. For instance, in 2017, nine California car dealerships paid $3.6 million to settle charges brought by the Federal Trade Commission (FTC) for posting fake online reviews (Davis, 2017). Deception poses a problem for both society and the marketplace. It undermines trust, and the consequences are costly (e.g. Keep & Schneider, 2010). Previous studies have shown that consumers evaluate not only textual (e.g. Ketron, 2017), but also contextual indicators to determine the trustworthiness of online reviews (Munzel, 2016). Therefore, future studies should account for the effects of context (e.g. the platform and product (Park & Lee, 2009)) on humans' capacity to detect deceptive content.

The example of the innovation Xvaluator as a universal tool of democratically qualifying relevant data in the numerical innovative ecosystems can be an important breakthrough in the democratically qualifying opinions based on a highly collaborative process and algorithm, inclusive, inspired by Share Secret Theory and by the functional economy model. As the Xvaluator is an example of innovation in the evaluation and qualifying sectors it could impact all industries, services, decision processes and innovation choices if integrated in the collaborative qualification and valorisation. Such innovative tools are based on different cognitive related concepts like "tiers inclus", cross-fertilization in the highly collaborative process of open innovations "mangrove forest", replacing the simple "value chain", or the "recursive causality" (Morin, 2011), as well as the AI strategies of "open valorization" and "open qualification" of data "like" in real time (see the start-up Xvaluator in 2016) supports the increase in capacities of observations and the collaborative valorization process. Thus, new high-quality values could emerge unexpectedly further to the observations, qualification, and connectivity of different brands with their stakeholders. There is this probability of the creation of new centers of high-quality value (initially "not-quality" previous to observations), so initially undetermined yet potentially determinable as "high quality augmented value".

The old philosophical problem of the objective existence of phenomena independently of our observations is now revisited in the specific context of high-quality products, services, and quality experiences. Based on the quantic approach (including Bohr's Copenhagen interpretation) we could envisage the question of if the observation is producing the observed attributes, in our case if the open valorization ("like") by multiple "observers" is in fact producing the "high quality" attributes of new forms of quality value which are not predestined initially, which are beginning (before the observation – valorisation) to become of quality value.

The more different actors become "observers" of subjects "potentially having high value" the more the process of observation-evaluation (for example, giving "likes" opinions on different digital platforms) could have a bigger probability to allow the emergence of "high quality values" of the products and integrated services under the observation process ("open valorization") made possible by the digital innovative tools (see the start-up Xvaluator in 2016)(Xvaluator, 2016).

This research approach of the "subject high value" reminds us of the analogy with the experiment "the cat or the paradox of Schrödinger" (Goswami, 2001) which provides new ways to foresee the existence of high value or of a potential high quality functionality or a center of augmented value creation, depending on the observation conditions (emerging high quality value corresponds to the observation that the cat as alive and the lack of quality value during the observation corresponds to the observation of the cat as dead).

Conclusion

We see the impact at the micro-meso and macro-economic level of collaborative tools such as DRL-TRL, the Contract at Risk, and Shared Benefits, in particular on the capacity building of actors and digital innovation ecosystems to "shorten the cycles of innovation" and agility of innovation processes and organizations (Paun, 2018), which is part of a new innovation paradigm. The quality in terms of the efficiency and agility of innovative ecosystems thus depends on the quality of the collaboration tools put in place, as well as the ability of the members of the digital ecosystems to use them, to act, and to evolve on long innovation trajectories. The evolution of innovation models is permanent, as well as their practices and new tools associated with collaborative innovation starting from C&D type models ("connect & develop"), "lead user method" (Hippel, 1988), "Open Innovation" (Chesbrough et al., 2018), to arrive at the "Total Innovation Model" (Xu, 2007), "Hybridization Tech Push and Market Pull" – "TRL-DRL" (Paun, 2011), or "liberated and augmented enterprise".

References

Adner, R., & Kapoor, R. (2010). Value creation in innovation ecosystems: How the structure of technological interdependence affects firm performance in new technology generations. *Strategic Management Journal, 31*(3), 306–333.

Ahuja, S., & Chan, Y. (2016). Digital innovation: A frugal ecosystem perspective., Thirty Seventh International Conference on Information Systems, Dublin.

Aoki, M. (2000). "*Information, corporate governance and institutional diversity: Competitiveness in Japan, the USA, and the transition economics*". Oxford: Oxford University Press.

Chen, Y., & Xie, J. (2008). Online consumer review: Word-of-mouth as a new element of marketing communication mix. *Management Science, 54*(3), 477–491.

Chesbrough, H., Lettl, C., Ritter, T. (2018). Value Creation and Value Capture in Open Innovation, *Journal of Product Innovation Management*, 35(6), 930–938.

Chesbrough, H., Vanhaverbeke, W., & West, J. (2008). "*Open innovation: Researching a new paradigm*". OUP Oxford, p. 400.

Chong, A. Y. L., Li, B., Ngai, E. W., Ch'ng, E., & Lee, F. (2016). Predicting online product sales via online reviews, sentiments, and promotion strategies: A big data architecture and neural network approach. *International Journal of Operations & Production Management, 36*(4), 358–383.

Costello, G., Donnellan, B., & Curley, M. (2013). "A theoretical framework to develop a research agenda for information systems innovation." *Communications of the AIS, 33*(1), pp. 26.

Davis, W. (2017). MediaPost. https://www.mediapost.com/publications/article/297107/ car-dealerships-settle-with-ftc-over-misleading-ad.html.

Dumont, L. (2019). Agile innovation: Creating value in uncertain environments.

Edin Grimheden, M. (2013). Can agile methods enhance mechatronics design education? *Mechatronics, 23*(8), 967–973. https://doi.org/10.1016/j.mechatronics.2013.01.003

Fagerstrøm, A., Ghinea, G., & Sydnes, L. (2016). Understanding the impact of online reviews on customer choice: A probability discounting approach. *Psychology and Marketing, 33*(2), 125–134.

Fan, Z. P., Che, Y.-J., & Chen, Z.-U. (2017). Product sales forecasting using online reviews and historical sales data: A method combining the bass model and sentiment analysis. *Journal of Business Research, 74*, 90–100.

Garud, R., Kumaraswamy, A. (1993). Changing competitive dynamics in network industries: An exploration of sun microsystems' open systems strategy, *Strategic Management Journal, 14*(5),351–369.

Goswami, A. (2001). *The Paradox of Schrödinger's Cat, The Physicists' View of Nature Part 2, The Quantum Revolution*, Springer Science+Business Media New York, 139–146.

Highsmith, J., & Fowler, M. (2001). The agile manifesto. *Software Development Magazine, 9*(8), 29–30.

Hippel, E. (von). (1988). *"The sources of innovation"*. New York: Oxford University Press.

Iansiti, M., & Levien, R. (2004). Strategy as ecology. *Harvard Business Review, 82*(3), 68–81.

Keep, W. W., & Schneider, G. P. (2010). Deception and defection from ethical norms in market relationships: A general analytic framework. *Business Ethics—A European Review, 19*(1), 64–80.

Ketron, S. (2017). Investigating the effect of quality of grammar and mechanics (QGAM) in online reviews: The mediating role of reviewer credibility. *Journal of Business Research, 81*, 51–59.

Laperche, B., & Uzunidis, D. (2012). "Eco-Innovation, knowledge capital and the evolution of the firm". *The IUP Journal of Knowledge Management, X(3),* July 2012, 14–34.

Liu, Q., Huang, S., & Zhang, L. (2016). The influence of information cascades on online purchase behaviors of search and experience products. *Electronic Commerce Research, 16*(4), 553–580.

Mankins, J. C. (1995). "Technology readiness levels, A white paper", April 6, Advanced Concepts Office, Office of Space Access and Technology, NASA.

Mayzlin, D., Dover, Y., & Chevalier, J. (2014). Promotional reviews: An empirical investigation of online review manipulation. *American Economic Review, 104*(8), 2421–2455.

Moore, J. F. (1993). "Predators and prey: A new ecology of competition." *Harvard Business Review, 71*(3), 75–83.

Munzel, A. (2016). Assisting consumers in detecting fake reviews: The role of identity information disclosure and consensus. *Journal of Retailing and Consumer Services, 32*, 96–108.

Overby, E., Sambamurthy, A., & Bharadwaj, V. (2006). Enterprise agility and the enabling role of information technology. *European Journal of Information Systems, 15*(2), 120–131.

Park, D., Lee, J., & Han, I. (2007). The effect of on-line consumer reviews on consumer purchasing intention: The moderating role of involvement. *International Journal of Electronic Commerce, 11*(4), 125–148.

Paun, F. (2011). 'Demand Readiness Level' (DRL): A New Tool to Hybridize Market Pull and Technology Push Approaches - Introspective Analysis of the New Trends in Technology Transfer Practices (February 18, 2011). *Springer Encyclopedia*, Forthcoming, Available at SSRN: https://ssrn.com/abstract=1763679

Paun, F. (2012). "The demand readiness level scale as new proposed tool to hybridize market pull with technology push approaches in technology transfer practices". In *Technology transfer in a global economy.* Springer series: International studies in entrepreneurship, Vol. 28, 397.

Paun, F. (2014). "J'innove, donc je suis! Visionnaires du XXIe siècle", Editions L'Harmattan, pp. 27–92. http://www.ubifrance.fr/001978234 3020051+j-innove-donc-je-suis-.html.

Paun, F. (2018). "Raccourcir les cycles d'innovation, dans TECHNOLOGIE ET INNOVATION, Nr. Dynamiques d'innovation dans les industries aérospatiale et de défense", Vol. 3, 2018.

Paun, F. (2020). *Sky is no longer a limit!: Technologie et facteur humain au coeur du nouveau paradigme de création de valeur partagée*, Éditions universitaires européennes.

Paun, F. (2021). « Hybridization of tech-push and market-pull approaches in innovation processes » in *Handbook of innovation*, Vol. 1, 2021. http://www.iste.co.uk/data/doc1-2-6-21-09-47-40.pdf

Paun, F., Richard, P. (2009). Rôle des outils collaboratifs dans la réduction et la compensation des asymétries relatives au processus de transfert de technologie; étude de cas sur la nouvelle politique, *Marché et organisations*, 59–94.

Paun, F., Vaileanu, I., O'Neal, T., Chaudron, L., Castelltort, A., Laurent, A., & Genier, L. (2022). « Nouveau paradigme d'évaluation ouverte de la valeur blockchain grâce aux outils d'agilisation de l'innovation » In *Technologie et innovation. Blockchain, open innovation et propriété intellectuelle*, Vol. 7, 2022. https://www.openscience.fr/Blockchain-open-innovation-et-propriete-intellectuelle-680

Paun, F., von Tunzelmann, N., Richard, P. (2011). Asymmetries and dynamic interactive capabilities in technology transfer between ONERA-the French Aerospace Lab TM and SMEs. *Journal of Innovation Economics*, 103–137.

Plotkinaa, D., Andreas Munzel, A., & Pallud, J. (2020). "Illusions of truth—Experimental insights into human and algorithmic detections of fake online reviews. *Journal of Business Research, 109*(2020), 511–523.

Radjou, N., & Prabhu, J. (2015). *Frugal innovation: How to do more with less. The Economist Publisher*, 272 pages..

RRI . (2019). Agile Innovation" de JIE&M . http://i-jiem.cairn.info/numero/?numero=JIE_028

Schumpeter, J. A. (1939). "*Business cycles: A theoretical, historical, and statistical analysis of the Capitalist process*". New York: McGraw-Hill.

Shkarupeta, E., Savon, A. E., & Avlasenko, L. M. (2020). « Digital ecosystem development based on open innovation model » In *Advances in economics, business and management research,* Atlantis Press, Vol. 148.

Stiglitz, J., & Weiss, A. (1992). "Asymmetric information in credit markets and its implications for macroeconomics". *Oxford Economic Papers, 44*, 694–724.

Teece, D.J. (2007). *The Role of Managers, Entrepreneurs, and the Literati in Enterprise Performance and Economic Growth*, Vita e Pensiero Editor.

Xu, Q., Chen, J., Xie, Z., Liu, J., Zheng, G., & Wang, Y. (2007). Total Innovation Management: a novel paradigm of innovation management in the 21st century. *The Journal of Technology Transfer, 32*, 9–25.

Part 2:

Innovation Ecosystems, Generation, Adoption and Diffusion of Innovation

Presentation

This second part of the book will notably analyze that innovation systems can be interconnected and lead to the formation of innovation networks in which actors interact through processes of "translation" referring to the sociology of innovation (Callon, 1986). Thus, it is essential to explain the role played by innovation ecosystems in the processes of innovation generation, adoption and diffusion, as it will be done within the different chapters of the part.

Understanding the innovation processes inherent in innovation ecosystems must be based on identifying the collaboration's factors between actors in the network. It is thus a matter of examining the different communication channels that can facilitate exchanges and the circulation of knowledge between stakeholders and that allow the establishment of consortia and cooperative processes (Laperche, 2017). These mechanisms must also be studied in light of the contextual health crisis and societal transformations induced by the ecological transition and the expanding digital revolution, and the related new vectors of creating and diffusing innovations.

Digital transformations have largely disrupted the conditions of formation, organization and deployment of innovation systems that can be related to a large range of innovative applications and sectors, including e-commerce, e-health and open innovation building on ICT dynamics. Outside-in strategies of open innovation, which involve enterprises mobilizing a wide range of actors and external sources of knowledge (including enterprises, consumers and suppliers) in order to benefit from an innovation without being at the origin from them and to create value through external innovation, are full illustrations of this (Chesbrough, 2006; Laperche, 2017), in addition of inside-out strategies of the reverse and complementary flow of open innovation (Chesbrough & Bogers, 2014) that rely on the outsourcing of knowledge or technologies initially developed within the organization. These processes will be analyzed in the chapter.

Open source, software and hardware, are also parts of this flow when organizations make the sources of technologies they have developed to be externally and universally readable (source code of computer software for open source software, plans and specifications allowing the construction of hardware for open source hardware). Moreover, various open source licenses, with singular intellectual property rights, can be adapted to different strategies (Adatto, 2021), partnerships, in particular related with open innovation ecosystems. The interest of open source hardware to face pandemic and support recovery will be detailed in the chapter.

This new era is marked by a decrease in the share of tangible capital in favor of intangible capital. This evolution is mainly stimulated by investments in training, R&D and knowledge dissemination (David & Foray, 2002; Laperche & Uzunidis, 2007). The research field of knowledge economy is particularly well suited to the analysis of this dynamic. Indeed, the knowledge economy emphasizes intangible factors related to knowledge production, scientific contributions, technical skills and "human capital" (Foray, 2013). Moreover, information as an intangible asset has also been at the center of the digital revolution, shaping much of the economic development over several decades. This informational and digital revolution involves a restructuring of economic actors around the generation, storage, processing and transfer of information (Grange & Sponem, 2021). This enhanced part of information and data is at the heart of more and more innovation ecosystems of ecological transition and digital revolution. These innovation ecosystems can involve Big Data, Open Data, Open Source, Smart City, Blockchain, Digital Factories, Bricolage, and all relevant new potential sectors. The chapters of this Part 2 will illustrated in detail for the cases of Blockchain, Bricolage, Open Source and entrepreneurial opportunity.

References

Adatto, L. (2021). Open source and open data: Filiation, analogies and common dynamics. In Uzunidis, D., Kasmi, F., & Adatto, L. (Eds.), *Innovation economics, engineering and management handbook*, Vol. 2. ISTE Ltd, London, UK and John Wiley & Sons, Inc, Hoboken, NJ, USA,, 217–223.

Callon, M. (1986). Éléments pour une sociologie de la traduction: La domestication des coquilles Saint-Jacques et des marins-pêcheurs dans la baie de Saint-Brieuc. *L'Année Sociologique* (1940/1948-), 36(troisième série), 169–208. Retrieved from www.jstor.org/stable/27889913

Chesbrough, H. (2006). Open innovation: The new imperative for creating and profiting from technology (Harvard Bu).

Chesbrough, H., & Bogers, M. (2014). Explicating open innovation: Clarifying an emerging paradigm for understanding innovation. In Chesbrough, H., Vanhaverbeke, W., & West, J. (Eds.), *New frontiers in open innovation*. Oxford: Oxford University Press, Forthcoming: 3–28.

David, P. A., & Foray, D. (2002). Une introduction à l'économie et à la société du savoir. *Revue Internationale Des Sciences Sociales, 171*(1), 13–28.

Laperche, B. (2017). *Enterprise knowledge capital.* John Wiley & Sons, Hoboken, NJ, USA.

Laperche, B., & Uzunidis, D. (2007). Le Système national d'innovation russe en restructuration: Réformes institutionnelles et politique industrielle. *Innovations, 2*(2), 69–94. https://doi.org/10.3917/inno.026.0069

The emergence of the blockchain technosystem

Raffaele Anedda[1], Didier Lebert[2]

Abstract: Patent data are increasingly used to map innovation ecosystems, especially in the blockchain domain (Marku et al., 2020; Clarke et al., 2020). We enrich the mapping method of Krafft et al. (2011). First, we choose a nomenclature more suitable for emerging technologies. Second, we augment the list of tools used for network analysis (centralities and "small worlds"). We show that the inventions around blockchain have significantly restructured the connections between the knowledge bricks that support its development. We compare two periods to give substance to this observation: a "prehistoric" period of the "blockchain technosystem" (2000–2012) and a contemporary period (2013–2019).

Keywords: Blockchain, Technosystem, Patent, Data, Information Technology, Intellectual Property Right

Introduction

Is the patent a relevant medium for representing the blockchain innovation ecosystem? A quick exploration of the Orbit Intelligence data platform, isolating the single keyword "blockchain" in patent titles, abstracts, and claims, indicates the existence of approximately 40,000 patent "families" – unique inventions – filed worldwide that include this term (January 2022). This intellectual property right therefore seems to be rich

1 Applied Economics Department, ENSTA Paris - Institut Polytechnique de Paris, France.

2 Applied Economics Department, ENSTA Paris - Institut Polytechnique de Paris and i3-CRG Ecole Polytechnique - CNRS (UMR 9217), France.

material to propose a mapping of innovation activity around blockchain. The same observation was made by Marku et al. (2020) and Clarke et al. (2020).

Blockchain is a shared database of secure transactions, so that neither fraud nor repudiation of these transactions is possible. Initially widely used as a support for the development of cryptocurrencies, this "technology of trust" has since broadly expanded its application fields (https://www.epo.org/news-events/news/2017.html), to the point where it now has a General Purpose Technology (GPT) status (Pike & Capobianco, 2020).

We use the method of Krafft et al. (2011) to map this ecosystem using patent data (PATSTAT database). The objective of this method is to study the structure and dynamics of networks (Wasserman & Faust, 1994) conceived as particular mathematical objects: "undirected and weighted graphs". The aim of this chapter is to identify the changes over time in the shape of these networks centered on the blockchain technological knowledge bricks, i.e. to identify the transformations of the "blockchain technosystem".

In these networks, the nodes are elementary units of knowledge, these "bricks" being linked together when they have a joint use. The use is joint when the same patent associates several codes of a technology nomenclature. For example, the patent *p* associated simultaneously with the nomenclature codes ("bricks") A and B corresponds to a network composed of two "nodes" linked together by a "link".

For Krafft et al. (2011), the representation of relations between knowledge bricks in the form of a network based on patent data is therefore a way of mapping technological knowledge bases. From there, these authors seek to detect the impact of this network on the industrial organization in an evolutionary framework. Indeed, in this framework, knowledge is characterized by a high degree of cumulativity and recombination, while at the same time it can go beyond by generating more radical innovations. The representation in the form of a network has the particularity of taking into account these two points of view. Indeed, radical novelty is reflected by the emergence of additional nodes in the network, while knowledge recombination is identified by the creation of new links between existing nodes.

In this chapter, compared to Krafft et al. (2011), we propose two developments. The first one is on the construction of the network itself. We use a richer technological nomenclature than the one used by these authors: the CPC (Cooperative Patent Classification) instead of the IPC (International Patent Classification), the latter being used by Krafft et al. (2011) to study the biotechnology innovation technosystem. The IPC has about 70,000 codes at its most disaggregated level, compared to 260,000 for the CPC. The latter is jointly managed by the EPO (European Patent Office) and the USPTO (its US equivalent). The CPC is considered more relevant for identifying emerging technologies (https://www.epo.org/news-events/news/2017.html).

The second development concerns the use of social network analysis tools (SNA; Wasserman & Faust, 1994). Beyond the indicators of "centrality" (i.e. relative importance) of the nodes in the network (Freeman, 1979), we propose indicators specific to the "new science of networks" (Watts, 2004), in particular to characterize the blockchain technosystem in terms of "small worlds". If this network is a small world (a highly clustered network where the average distance between nodes is small), this means that it is multipolar, and in this sense that it is characterized by innovation dynamics specific to some of its components. This indicates that the technological building blocks of blockchain do not all pull in the same direction, that they do not necessarily innovate at the same pace, and that radical internal reconfiguration can potentially occur. By comparing two periods for this emerging technosystem, it is this kind of reconfiguration that we expect to observe.

The chapter has two sections. In the first one, we define the technological perimeter of blockchain with reference to the CPC nomenclature. In the second section, we proceed to the empirical analysis of the blockchain technosystem over the periods 2000–2012 (the "prehistory" of blockchain, which identifies the bricks of the previous section and the way they are articulated before the patent boom on this theme; in short, this prehistory constitutes the soil from which the technological trajectories around blockchain have been constituted) and 2013–2019 (period of maturation of blockchain technology; cf. Figure 1), based on patents filed with the EPO and the USPTO[3].

---

3 Clarke et al. (2020) show that the technology trajectories explored in other technology markets are very similar to those found in the West. Since the CPC nomenclature has a longer track record in the EPO and USPTO, we retain only these two markets.

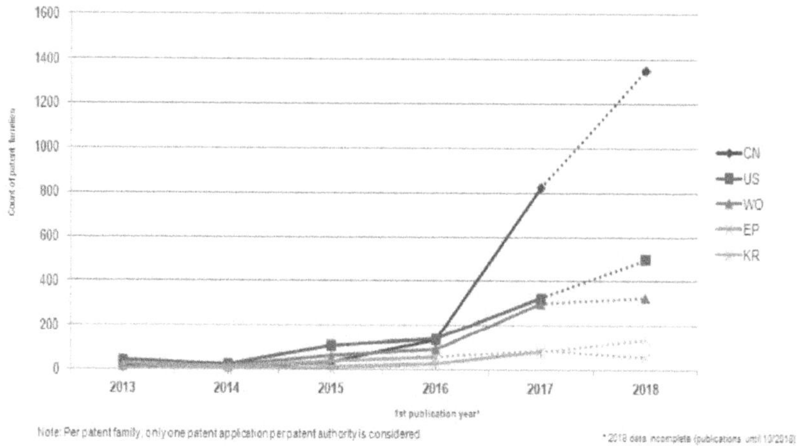

Figure 1. Number of “strict” blockchain filings by patent office (Clarke et al., 2020, p. 7)

1. The patents perimeter of the blockchain

In 2017, the European Patent Office (EPO) published a report on the Fourth Industrial Revolution (4IR) technologies as they appear in patent data. For the EPO, 4IR technologies include connected smart objects, data-driven value creation (big data, distributed computing, cloud-based data storage, new data analysis tools, 3D simulation systems, additive manufacturing) and software-driven innovation. These technologies have a wide and growing range of applications: production organization, transportation, energy systems management, finance, etc. In this EPO report, blockchain does not appear as such. However, it is cited in numerous fields of application (in finance, health, agriculture and agri-food, etc.).

In the wake of this report, a literature is developing that directly links patents and blockchain. However, this literature remains embryonic today, as it is very recent. Two contributions seem to us to be particularly interesting: Marku et al. (2020) and Clarke et al. (2020). Each of them develops a specific strategy to isolate patents that are related to blockchain.

Marku et al. (2020) favor an approach that first mobilizes the textual content of patents. In titles, summaries, and claims, they request a set of keywords associated with the technology: “blockchain”, “block chain”, etc. They identify, from the patent portfolio obtained, the IPC codes that are most present. Then they proceed to a clustering on the technological co-occurrences present in the patents referring to these codes, to finally obtain a polycentric technological map of the blockchain.

The approach of Clarke et al. (2020) is completely reversed. They seek to define the blockchain perimeter as strictly as possible. In the previous approach, indeed, the textual search may include a lot of noise – patents citing blockchain but not making it the core of the invention. Thus, unlike Marku et al. (2020), their starting point lies in a work on the technological nomenclature and, as an extension of the EPO's work mentioned above, it is the CPC nomenclature that lends itself best to this exercise, according to these authors.

This work on the CPC is done in conjunction with EPO patent experts, in order to have the most operational reading possible of this nomenclature, which is very difficult to handle because it is constantly evolving. Indeed, this nomenclature tries to take into account technical progress. This expertise of patent engineers is also necessary to understand the systemic dimension of the blockchain invention. This means that an individual patent can only be qualified as a blockchain patent when certain CPC items are present simultaneously in the patent in question. In this case, if we represent the blockchain technosystem as a network à la Krafft et al. (2011), it is in the links between certain nodes of the network that the existence of the blockchain invention is revealed, and not in the mere presence of the nodes (i.e. CPC codes).

For Clarke et al. (2020), the work on technological nomenclature is however not sufficient, even if it is systematic. A textual dimension must be added to it. Still with the expertise of EPO patent engineers, a series of keywords are associated with the CPC codes to limit the noise (false positives) transmitted by the nomenclature information alone. The authors define complex queries to search in patent databases (in their case, the Orbit Intelligence platform from Questel, and in the case of Marku et al., 2020, the Derwent platform from Clarivate) to isolate the inventions that can be most strictly attributed to the blockchain.

Once the portfolio of blockchain patents has been identified, Clarke et al. (2020) simply present quantitative results on it: temporal evolution of filings, weight of national and international offices, identification of applicants and citation relationships between them. We propose in the next section to go further in the analytical phase, and the framework drawn by Krafft et al. (2011) on the structure of technological knowledge bases will help us in this enrichment.

In this chapter, we choose to combine the approaches of Marku et al. (2020) and Clarke et al. (2020) to identify our own patent portfolio "around" blockchain. Indeed, our objective is not so much to increase the analysis of the strict perimeter à la Clarke et al. by SNA as to identify the technosystem in which the blockchain invention is embedded. From this point of view, the approach of Marku et al. (2020) has the advantage of trying to analyze blockchain as a General Purpose Technology, i.e. through its potential for diffusion within the global technological network, a diffusion that is conceived as a capacity to combine with other technologies in order to broadly irrigate the invention activity.

This conception of the diffusion of a technology consisting of equating it with the diversity of the invention processes in which it is integrated is, ultimately, the one that is apparent in the EPO's (2017) report: blockchain is nowhere on its own but is associated with other technologies that fall under multiple fields of application. From an economic analysis point of view, again using patent data, this conception of diffusion is found in Gkotis and Vezzani (2016), Meunier (2021) and Lebert (2021): a technosystem around a single knowledge brick is a star-shaped network of technology co-occurrences within patents incorporating this brick, a network sometimes simplified to consider only the existence of relationships between technologies regardless of the intensity of these relationships. Gkostis and Vezzani (2016) and Meunier (2021) show, on different technological perimeters, and from the simplified representation of the network, that the historical dynamics of the connections of the technologies of the IPC nomenclature follow a traditional S-curve and, within this framework, that it is possible to qualify each of these technologies at a given moment in time as either emerging or mature and, in Meunier's case (2021), to anticipate the potential for the diffusion of a technology over the long term (i.e. its maximal ubiquity).

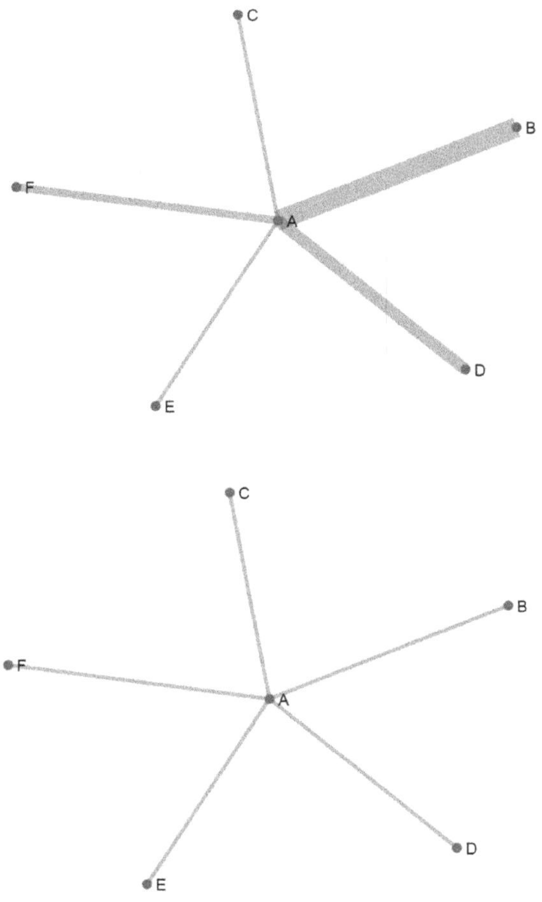

Figure 2. Network of a technology (A) for the study of its diffusion

Reading: The two networks represent the associations of technology A with technologies B, C, D, E, and F in the patents. The upper network indicates by the thickness of the connection the number of patents in which these technologies are associated with A. The bottom network only indicates the existence of connections, without information on their differential intensities. These networks are used to study the diffusion of technology A, understood here as the appearance of new branches to the star over time. The greater the number of branches, the more ubiquitous the technology. Gkotsis and Vezzani (2016) and Meunier (2021) develop diffusion models that do not consider the intensity of technology associations, unlike Lebert (2021).

In Lebert (2021), the approach is slightly different since information on the intensities of connections within technosystems is integrated into the analysis. If we focus on a single technology (a single IPC code, for example), the technosystem is thus represented graphically by a star at the center of which is the technology under study, while at the ends of each branch of the star is the set of technologies with which it combines in inventions. The links between the technologies (the branches of the star) are quantified by the number of patents in which these technologies are found together (Figure 2). The author seeks to produce a predictive tool on the extension of the technosystem of the technology studied, i.e. the addition of a branch to the star. To do this, he first identifies all the ecosystems of technologies connected to the one located at the center of the star. Some technologies belonging to these ecosystems are not directly connected to the technology being evaluated. He then defines the probabilities of future connection with these technologies that are not directly connected, assuming that the stronger the connections within the existing technosystems, the higher the probability. This hypothesis is based on Granovetter's (1973) distinction between "strong ties" and "weak ties" and can be summarized by the following analogy: in the short term, I have a better chance of becoming friends with the good friends (that I do not yet know) of my closest friends than with those of more vague acquaintances.

Thus, the "broad" approach to the blockchain technosystem, as conceived by Marku et al. (2020), is favored here. However, we limit this breadth to the blockchain technology scope identified by Clarke et al. (2020). Table 1 lists the 25 CPC codes that are related to blockchain according to these authors. Recall that in their approach, some of these codes must combine, or be associated with certain keywords to be considered "strictly" blockchain. We choose to consider these codes in isolation. This is how we can draw a rich technological environment "around" blockchain. By construction, all blockchain patents identified by Clarke et al. (2020) are included in those we identify, since we use less strict conditions to isolate patents: no combinations of codes, and no textual queries. To sum up, we precisely replicate the method used by Krafft et al. (2011) to represent a knowledge base from patent data.

Table 1. The blockchain perimeter (CPC codes from Clarke et al., 2020)

CPC	Title
H04L 9/3247	Cryptographic mechanisms or cryptographic arrangements for secret or secure communication including means for verifying the identity or authority of a user of the system involving digital signatures …
H04L 9/3249	… using RSA or related signature schemes, e.g. Rabin scheme
H04L 9/3252	… using DSA or related signature schemes, e.g. elliptic-based signatures, ElGamal or Schnorr schemes
H04L 9/3255	… using group-based signatures, e.g. ring or threshold signatures
H04L 9/3257	… using blind signatures
G06Q 20/065	Payment architectures, schemes or protocols, Payment circuits, Private payment circuits, e.g. involving electronic currency used among participants of a common payment scheme using e-cash …
G06Q 20/0652	… with decreasing value according to a parameter, e.g. time
G06Q 20/0655	… managed centrally
G06Q 20/0658	… managed locally
G06Q 20/02	Payment architectures, schemes or protocols involving a neutral party, e.g. certification authority, notary, or trusted third party …
G06Q 20/023	… the neutral party being a clearing house
G06Q 20/4014	Payment protocols authorization, identity check for transactions
G06Q 20/4016	Payment protocols authorization involving fraud or risk level assessment in transaction processing
G06Q 20/4018	Payment protocols authorization using the card verification value [CVV] associated with the card
H04L 9/3236	Cryptographic mechanisms or cryptographic arrangements for secret or secure communication including means for verifying the identity or authority of a user of the system using cryptographic hash functions …
H04L 9/3239	… involving non-keyed hash functions, e.g. modification detection codes [MDCs], MD5, SHA, or RIPEMD
H04L 9/3242	… involving keyed hash functions, e.g. message authentication codes [MACs], CBC-MAC, or HMAC
H04L 9/0637	Cryptographic mechanisms or cryptographic arrangements for secret or secure communication, encryption apparatus using shift registers or memories for block-wise coding, Block ciphers, i.e. encrypting groups of characters of a plain text message using fixed encryption transformation, modes of operation, e.g. cipher block chaining [CBC], electronic codebook [ECB], or Galois/counter mode [GCM]

(*Continued*)

Table 1. Continued

CPC	Title
H04L 9/0643	Cryptographic mechanisms or cryptographic arrangements for secret or secure communication, encryption apparatus using shift registers or memories for block-wise coding, Block ciphers, i.e. encrypting groups of characters of a plain text message using fixed encryption transformation, Hash functions, e.g. MD5, SHA, HMAC, or f9 MAC
H04L2209/38	Additional information or applications relating to cryptographic mechanisms or cryptographic arrangements for secret or secure communication, chaining, e.g. hash chain or certificate chain
H04L2209/56	Additional information or applications relating to cryptographic mechanisms or cryptographic arrangements for secret or secure communication, financial cryptography, e.g. electronic payment or e-cash
H04L2209/30	Additional information or applications relating to cryptographic mechanisms or cryptographic arrangements for secret or secure communication, compression, e.g. Merkle-Damgard construction
H04L2209/46	Additional information or applications relating to cryptographic mechanisms or cryptographic arrangements for secret or secure communication, secure multiparty computation, e.g. millionaire problem …
H04L2209/463	… electronic voting
H04L2209/466	… electronic auction

The CPC codes that appear in Table 1 are at the most disaggregated level of this nomenclature. In other words, the blockchain entries represent only about 1/10,000th of the overall technosystem (25 entries out of 260,000). Note that each entry has a complete definition of the technology corresponding to the code in question. Rather than a simple nomenclature, we are dealing with a real dictionary, extremely precise so that the experts of the patent offices can attribute the inventions to the least ambiguous fields possible. This richness in description is currently leading some patent experts and researchers to use new techniques, based on artificial intelligence, to automatically allocate inventions to these codes through the systematic processing of texts contained in patents (see for example Trappey et al., 2020), for the constitution of their state of the art (Setchi et al., 2021) and, more globally, to improve the management system of these intellectual property rights (Alderucci & Sicker, 2019). In this chapter, we will stick to categorical data (i.e. limited to CPC code information included in patents), without the use of these innovative processing techniques.

2. The blockchain technosystem revealed

We use the EPO PATSTAT database in its fall 2021 version. This database contains information on approximately 130 million patents filed in all national and international offices. We select patents filed at the EPO and USPTO between the years 2000 and 2019 and isolate the set of those that contain at least one of the 25 CPC codes listed in Table 1. These patents are grouped into INPADOC families to avoid counting the same invention filed in multiple offices multiple times (members of an INPADOC patent family have at least one priority in common with at least one other member, directly or indirectly). This base constitutes our portfolio for the analysis. For each patent in this portfolio, we identify all the CPC codes that are present. To build the network, we then consider all the possible links between these codes. For example, if there are four CPC technologies labeled A, B, C, and D in patent *p*, this results in six undirected links between them: between A and B, between A and C, between A and D, between B and C, between B and D, and between C and D. These links can be found in several patents, and we weight them by the number of patents in which they appear. Table 2 provides descriptive statistics on this portfolio by filing year.

For 2015, for example, the 25 CPC technologies are associated with 2,381 other technologies in this nomenclature (for a total of 2,406 codes). The network of connections between these technologies consists of 110,708 links with a sum of weights equal to 228,473, or an average value per link of 1.437, with a minimum value of 1 and a maximum value of 97. The density of the network, i.e. the number of effective links out of the maximum number of possible links between the 2,406 technologies, is therefore low (in the order of 0.04).

For the analysis phase, we sum the networks of all years for each sub-period ("prehistory" and contemporary) and retain only the links with a "strong" intensity. Here, we consider that an intensity is strong when technologies are found together in at least 100 patents in each sub-period. Considering only these strong links, we obtain the sub-networks of Figures 3 and 4, which include 54 nodes and 144 links for Figure 3 ("prehistory") and 143 nodes and 696 links for Figure 4 ("contemporary period"), which marks a significant complexification of the blockchain technosystem between the two periods. This is precisely how Krafft et al. (2011) proceed to map the innovation technosystem in biotechnology. The thickness of the links indicates the intensity of technological associations in the patents.

Table 2. Descriptive statistics

Year	#tech	#links	#combin	mean	min	max
2000	1112	36507	74868	1.432	1	162
2001	1851	388748	411060	1.028	1	100
2002	1655	163492	184597	1.063	1	67
2003	1482	75290	87920	1.081	1	46
2004	1483	123795	138314	1.057	1	44
2005	2182	185495	207263	1.057	1	50
2006	1276	39116	59881	1.237	1	43
2007	1048	19796	35266	1.335	1	42
2008	1339	33527	52698	1.254	1	44
2009	2234	367552	393242	1.034	1	48
2010	1362	42194	55894	1.151	1	23
2011	1690	121810	146674	1.097	1	30
2012	1686	48075	80716	1.296	1	50
2013	1836	71861	102577	1.195	1	41
2014	2105	59786	108486	1.347	1	58
2015	2406	110708	228473	1.437	1	97
2016	3433	217805	345679	1.260	1	187
2017	3638	138498	403235	1.706	1	716
2018	4120	152759	639468	2.046	1	1732
2019	3611	113945	407428	1.891	1	1309

In Figures 3 and 4, the technologies in Table 1 appear in red. In Figure 3, eight of them are present, which means that the remaining seventeen do not combine intensively enough with others (whether they are part of the blockchain perimeter or not) to appear in the figure. They therefore seem to be less central to the dynamics of invention during the "prehistory" of blockchain. The technologies represented by blue nodes do not belong to the blockchain perimeter but are part of its technosystem of invention. In the contemporary period (Figure 4), sixteen blockchain technologies contribute strongly to the structuring of the technosystem. This is another indication of an important change in the ways of inventing concerning this group of technologies.

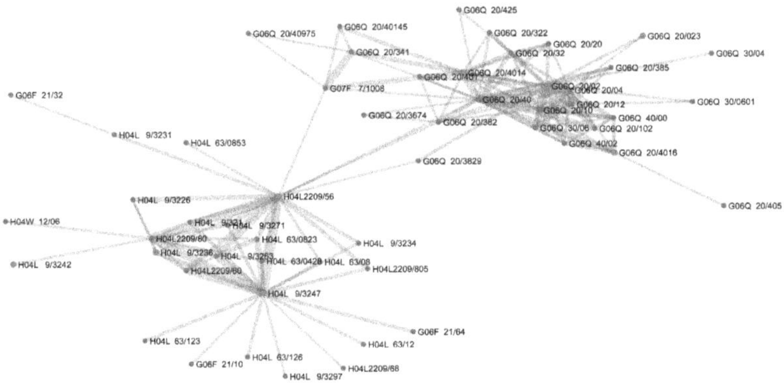

Figure 3. Blockchain innovation technosystem over the period 2000–2012

Figure 4. Blockchain innovation technosystem over the period 2013–2019

The analysis phase of these networks consists of two steps. First, we look at each of the technologies individually and determine their relative importance in the network, i.e. their "centrality" in the usual SNA terminology. In a second step, we study the network as a whole and produce indicators testing the "small world" hypothesis for the blockchain technosystem.

Table 3. Measures of technologies centrality – 2000–2012

Noms	Degree	Closeness	Betweenness	Eigenvector	Katz	h_index	Laplacian
H04L2209/56	0.358	0.582	0.583	0.098	8.269	5	600
G06Q 20/40	0.396	0.558	0.388	0.383	17.607	8	804
H04L 9/3247	0.358	0.457	0.264	0.032	5.706	5	528
G06Q 20/02	0.358	0.427	0.107	0.351	15.912	8	658
H04L2209/80	0.226	0.431	0.083	0.028	4.673	5	300
G06Q 20/382	0.151	0.482	0.076	0.186	9.088	6	276
G07F 7/1008	0.113	0.465	0.065	0.091	5.389	4	168
G06Q 20/4016	0.132	0.381	0.038	0.170	8.028	6	200
H04L 9/3231	0.038	0.376	0.038	0.010	1.858	1	46
G06Q 20/4014	0.245	0.411	0.029	0.275	12.687	8	430

Table 4. Measures of technologies centrality – 2013–2019

Noms	Degree	Closeness	Betweenness	Eigenvector	Katz	h_index	Laplacian
H04L2209/38	0.711	0.772	0.318	0.316	26.055	19	12732
H04L 9/3247	0.641	0.703	0.317	0.274	22.849	19	10516
H04L 9/3239	0.634	0.703	0.170	0.301	24.632	19	10502
G06Q 20/4014	0.183	0.500	0.090	0.079	7.384	10	1498
G06Q2220/00	0.324	0.587	0.059	0.206	16.715	18	4044
G06Q 20/02	0.197	0.546	0.036	0.135	11.296	13	2214
H04L2209/56	0.331	0.589	0.033	0.229	18.280	19	4304
G06Q 20/4016	0.134	0.488	0.031	0.072	6.648	10	1138
H04L 9/085	0.035	0.478	0.028	0.042	4.156	4	636
H04L 9/0637	0.289	0.557	0.027	0.212	16.842	19	3614

Tables 3 and 4 present measures of the centrality of the nodes that appear in Figures 3 and 4 respectively. In a network, a node can be important/central in several ways. Freeman (1979) first attempts to clarify these meanings. A node can be central based on its potential communication activity in the network. The notion of "degree" reflects this importance. Degree is measured as the number of connections a node has in the network (normalized by the maximum number of possible connections it can maintain). Alternatively, a node can be central if it is "close" to other nodes. This closeness reflects the potential independence and efficiency of a node's communication, which is least disrupted by the multiplication of transmission relays (here, the variable *Closeness* is also normalized). Finally, a node can be important when it is an obligatory passage of communication between the other nodes of the network. This betweenness is an index of the potential control of the communication by this node (*Betweenness* is also normalized).

These first three indicators are built according to the same principles: simplification of the structure of the connections to take into account only their existence apart from their intensities, and measurement based on the identification of the "geodesic paths" between the nodes (i.e. the shortest paths), with the longer connections not being included in the calculations. Other indicators respect at least some of these principles, such as the h-index, with which a node is considered important if it is directly connected to other nodes with high degrees, and the Laplacian, which is a measure of betweenness valid for weighted structures.

The other indicators (Eigenvector, Katz) consider all possible direct and indirect connections between the nodes of the network. They use the complexity of the concrete connections between the nodes and synthesize the position of each of them in the structure. The latter two indicators are therefore more general in scope (the entire structure of connections is considered in measuring node centrality) than those presented in the previous two paragraphs. Oldham et al. (2019) provide a summary of the meaning and measurement of all these indicators. They also present many other indicators, but most of the information about the relative importance of nodes in a structure is present in the ones we have selected.

Tables 3 and 4 present a hierarchy of the ten most important nodes according to the *Betweenness* indicator. According to this criterion, the most important technology is H04L2209/56 during the "prehistoric" period, which is a blockchain technology related to financial cryptography (Table 1). However, six of the top ten technologies (highlighted in gray in Table 3) are not part of blockchain. They relate to authentication of the parties to the transaction (G06Q 20/40, which is an aggregate of some of the technologies listed in Table 1, but which goes beyond the strict domain of blockchain, H04L 9/3247), communication modalities (H04L2209/80), means of payment with codes (G07F 7/1008), and transaction security protocols (G06Q 20/382, H04L 9/3231). It is on this technological ground that blockchain will explore its trajectories.

The importance of H04L2209/56 in terms of betweenness during this prehistoric phase is directly visible in Figure 3. Let us imagine that we remove this technology from the network. We would then have two disconnected components, unable to communicate with each other. Financial cryptography thus plays a major role in the way invention activity is organized at this time. It is the only brick that is capable of dialoguing between two autonomous components of technical progress, one centered on codes with a G06Q dominance (data processing systems, on the right of Figure 3), the other centered on codes with a H04L dominance (transmission of digital information, on the left of this same figure). From this point of view, we could say that this technology is "absorbing" within the blockchain technosystem, i.e. able to integrate the technologies of these two large blocks.

The situation changes significantly in the contemporary period. Blockchain technologies *stricto sensu* now constitute the core (eight out of ten technologies, Table 4), the other technologies do not belong to the previous top group of betweenness (protection of distributed file systems, G06Q2220/00, transaction security protocols, H04L 9/085), and the hierarchy of the core blockchain technologies has been disrupted. From now on, the blockchain technosystem is structured around secure communications (H04L2209/38, H04L 9/3239, H04L 9/3247). It thus takes on a broader scope than financial cryptography. This is an important feature of its new GPT status (Pike & Capobianco, 2020).

Does this technosystem of innovation have global properties, and have these properties changed between the two periods? More precisely, can it be classified as a "small world"? Watts and Strogatz (1998) show that networks of very diverse natures (social, natural, artificial) possess small-world properties, by combining a high degree of clustering with a low average length of geodesic paths (i.e. shortest paths) between nodes. This small-world characteristic moves the network under study away from a so-called regular structure, i.e. one that has low heterogeneity (the number of connections of each node is equivalent) and a low probability that two randomly chosen nodes are connected to each other. Regular graphs tend to have long geodesic paths and a high level of clustering (nodes are connected in dense groups). It also distances small worlds from random networks, which have the opposite properties of regular networks: low average short paths length, but low presence of nodes clusters.

Table 5 summarizes the properties of the different types of networks, with C an index of clustering of the concrete structure (C_r for its value in a random network) and L an index of the average length of the geodesic/short paths (L_r for its value in a random network). The blockchain technosystem will have properties of a random network if C and L have values equivalent to C_r and L_r respectively, properties of a regular network if these two values are much higher than those of a random network, and properties of a small world if it differs from the random network only by the clustering index C.

Table 5. Properties of regular, random, and small-world networks

	$C \approx C_r$	$C \gg C_r$
$L \approx L_r$	Random network	Small world
$L \gg L_r$	-	Regular network

For its measurement, the index C is equal to the number of "triangles" in the unweighted connection structure (i.e. the number of times three nodes are directly connected to each other) divided by the total number of paths of length 2 in the structure. We measure the probability that two nodes that are both connected to the same other node are also directly connected to each other. The triangle, in this case, is the primary element of a cluster, i.e. a dense connection structure between members of a network. The greater the number of triangles, the more clustered the structure is, all other things being equal.

The index L is therefore the average length of the shortest (geodesic) paths connecting the nodes. The algorithm that produces this value relies on the manipulation of the adjacent matrix associated with the network of connections. This matrix is square (let's say $n \times n$) and symmetric with respect to its main diagonal and includes a "1" at the intersection of the row of one node and the column of another if these nodes are directly connected, and a "0" otherwise. Finding the shortest paths between the nodes is equivalent to progressively increasing this adjacent matrix to the power of 1, 2, …, $n - 1$. We fill a matrix of the same format $n \times n$ by the values of these powers when this powering for the first time fills the cells with a non-zero value corresponding to the connections between the nodes. We assume that a node cannot be connected to itself in this short paths matrix and, once filled, we divide the sum of its elements by the number of non-zero cells.

To obtain these values for a random structure, C_r and L_r, we extract the number of nodes and the average number of connections of the nodes in the concrete structure (their average degree), and we proceed to make connections uniformly between these nodes while maintaining this average degree. Tables 6 and 7 show the values of these indices for the two periods.

Table 6. Small world indices – 2000–2012

C	C_r	L	L_r
0.410	0.086	2.691	2.378

Table 7. Small world indices – 2013–2019

C	C_r	L	L_r
0.287	0.065	2.395	2.326

The blockchain technosystem does have the properties of a small world: the average length of its geodesic paths is close to that of a random network, while the clustering index is higher than that of this random network. However, this characteristic tends to fade with time. The probability of finding triangles is significantly lower than in prehistoric times. It is the "multipolar" character of the technosystem that is eroding with the recent blockchain inventions. While during its prehistory this technosystem could be driven by innovation logics specific to G06Q and H04L, with a small number of absorbing technologies, cross-fertilization between these technologies now seems to be widespread, contributing to the standardization of these two domains around blockchain inventions to build a technosystem specific to this technology. In a way, we are witnessing a dynamic of technological convergence, in the sense that what was once separate is now becoming mixed and inseparable (Le Goff, 2021).

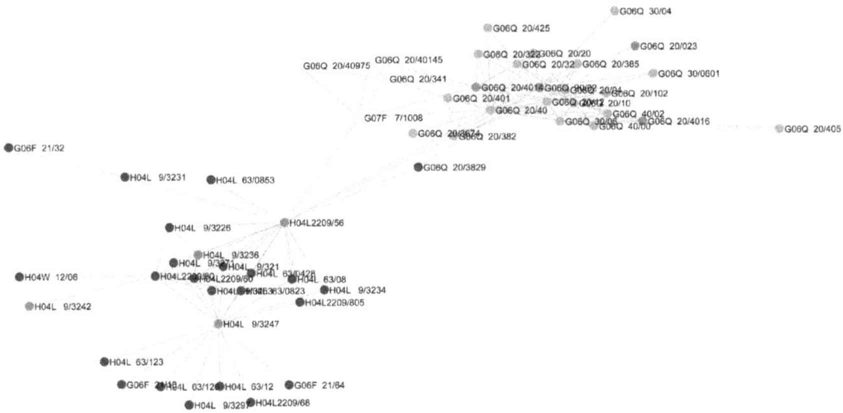

Figure 5. Detecting communities in the prehistoric blockchain technosystem – Newman (2006) – Modularity: 0.46373

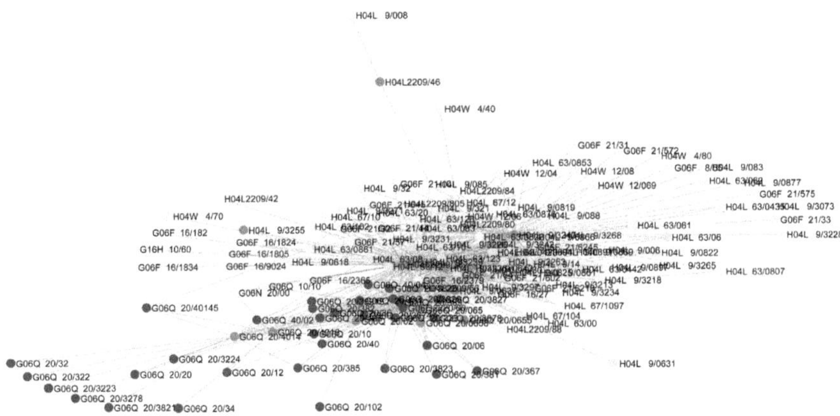

Figure 6. Detecting communities in the contemporary blockchain technosystem – Blondel et al. (2008) – Modularity: 0.32691

We seek to substantiate this finding by conducting an exercise to identify "communities" within each technosystem. We use several structural techniques to isolate groups of nodes that have particularly dense connection structures. Several methods are used in parallel, and the one that achieves the highest modularity index is chosen to fix the nodes in each community. From this point of view, Newman's (2006) method is more relevant for the prehistoric technosystem, while the so-called Louvain method (Blondel et al., 2008) is more relevant for the contemporary technosystem. In the graphs shown in Figures 5 and 6, each color corresponds to a community, and the nodes in red identify the blockchain technologies in Table 1.

Reading Figure 5 supports what has already been asserted about this period: the G06Q and H04L clusters are distributed in different communities, there is no significant mixing between these technology domains, which are held together only by the existence of a unique absorbing technology from the H04L community.

The previous intuition of a unified technosystem in the contemporary period must be put into perspective by reading Figure 6. Indeed, two of the clusters maintain a strong concentration of specific technological domains (in light blue: H04L; in dark blue: G06Q). Logics specific to these domains in terms of inventive structure thus remain present, even if they are increasingly mixed. In other words, the 2013–2019 period would mark a form of transition, not yet completed, toward the constitution of a unified blockchain technosystem. We could make the hypothesis that the source of this standardization lies in the technosystem's yellow nodes. Indeed, this community mixes components from both technological domains, and enriches the inventive outputs around blockchain (few red nodes belong to the yellow community), which reflects both the historical diversification of the application fields of blockchain and the increasing complexity of the invention processes around this technology.

Conclusion

Patents are beginning to be used to map the contours of the blockchain innovation technosystem. In this chapter, we have presented an application of the well-tested analysis method of Krafft et al. (2011) to this technology, enriching it both in terms of the data sources used to delimit the blockchain perimeter (CPC nomenclature rather than IPC) and in terms of the network analysis tools (multiplicity of centrality indices, small worlds approach). Blockchain technosystems are, at first, marked by a form of autonomy of the logics of invention around well-identified technological domains (the "prehistoric" period) and then, in a second phase, by a significant rapprochement between these domains without this process being, according to our results, completely achieved today (the "contemporary" period).

The structural method that we have implemented in this comparative statics reading has the advantage of anticipating certain technological trajectories around a complex and rapidly recomposing object (here, around financial cryptography). However, this method has also shown some limitations, precisely on the identification of technological trajectories, which should be fixed. For example, we cannot anticipate from the old map the structure of the current map. Lebert's (2021) method of constructing links, for example, only works on the basis of the existence of strong indirect connections. However, in the case of the blockchain, it seems that the reconfiguration of the invention processes is too radical for this method to be applied simply. The application of Lebert's (2021) method would have the consequence of reinforcing the trajectories at work, and therefore the weight of financial cryptography in the structuring of the blockchain technosystem. On the contrary, we note that its relative importance has been decreasing in recent years in favor of components of secure communications.

We then perceive two ways to enrich the empirical analysis of these networks. First, as proposed by Marku et al. (2020) and Clarke et al. (2020), it would be a matter of combining the textual approach and the categorical approach to identify the scope of relevant patents to be considered. We have chosen, here, to stick to the technological categories of the CPC. Proceeding as proposed by Clarke et al. (2020) would reduce the size of our portfolio. We would obtain a partial sub-network (i.e. cut out nodes and links) and the idea would be to study blockchain in the strict sense (as envisaged by these authors) within its technosystem of invention in the broad sense (as envisaged by us). The blockchain, in the perception of these authors, is not limited to the nodes in Table 1. It also includes a set of connections that are deemed necessary. The textual content of patents would add a third level of complexity in processing and analysis, capturing the noise introduced by the categorical data alone. In the end, three levels of study would interpenetrate: the network we have defined ourselves, the one taking into account only the technological combinations, and then the one integrating in addition the textual elements.

The second extension we can consider is to take into account citation data. This would allow us to define the invention processes of the blockchain, increasing the scope of technologies deemed necessary to master to develop a coherent and efficient technosystem. To our knowledge, there is not yet a study focused on a technical system using patent data that combines the analysis of technological co-occurrences (as is the case in this chapter) and the citation flows that produce these co-occurrences. This leads to the design of a network that combines undirected and weighted links between knowledge bricks, as considered here, with directed and weighted links as traditionally considered in the representation of networks of invention processes (Dosso & Lebert, 2020).

References

Alderucci, D., & Sicker, D. (2019). Applying Artificial Intelligence to the Patent System, *Technology & Innovation, 20*, 415–425.

Blondel, V. D., Guillaume, J.-L., Lambiotte, R., & Lefebvre, E. (2008). Fast unfolding of communities in large networks. *Journal of Statistical Mechanics – Theory and Experiment*. DOI: 10.1088/1742-5468/2008/10/P10008.

Clarke, N. S., Jürgens, B., & Herrero-Solana, V. (2020). Blockchain patent landscaping: An expert based methodology and search query. *World Patent Information, 61*, 101964.

Dosso, M., & Lebert, D. (2020). The centrality of regions in corporate knowledge flows and the implications for Smart Specialisation Strategies. *Regional Studies, 54*, 1366–1376.

Freeman, L.C. (1979). Centrality in social networks: Conceptual clarification. *Social Networks, 1*, 215–239.

Gkotsis, P., & Vezzani, A. (2016). The combinatorial dimension of technological diffusion: Evidence from patent data, Innovation Forum, RNI, Paris.

Granovetter, M. S. (1973). « The strength of weak ties ». *American Journal of Sociology, 78*, 1360–1380.

Krafft, J., Quatraro, F., & Saviottti, P.-P. (2011). The knowledge-base evolution in biotechnology: A social network analysis. *Economics of Innovation and New Technology, 20*, 445–475.

Le Goff, R. (2021). La convergence technologique: le cas du véhicule autonome électrique. *Technologie et Innovation, 6*(2), 11 pages, directly available at: https://www.openscience.fr/IMG/pdf/iste_techinn21v6n2_06.pdf.

Lebert, D. (2021). Sur les modèles structuraux de diffusion technologique, Club Patent Analytics, INPI, 3 mars.

Marku, E., Castriotta, M., Loi, M., & Di Guardo, M. C. (2020). General purpose technology: The blockchain domain. *International Journal of Business and Management, 15*, 192–205.

Meunier, F.-X. (2021). La diffusion des technologies d'ingénierie biomédicale: évidences sur données des brevets. *Technologie et Innovation, 6*(2), 12 pages, directly available at: https://www.openscience.fr/IMG/pdf/iste_techinn21v6n2_05.pdf.

Newman, M. E. J. (2006). Finding community structure in networks using the eigenvectors of matrices. *Physical Review E, 74*, 036104.

Oldham, S., Fulcher, B., Parkes, L., Arnatkeviciute, A., Suo, C., & Fornito, A. (2019). Consistency and differences between centrality measures across distinct classes of networks. *PLoS ONE, 14*, e0220061.

Pike, C., & Capobianco, A. (2020). Antitrust and the trust machine. *OECD Blockchain Policy Series.*

Setchi, R., Spasi, I., Morgan, J., Harrison, C., & Corken, R. (2021). Artificial intelligence for patent prior art searching. *World Patent Information, 64*, 102021.

Trappey, A. J. C., Trappey, C. V., Wu, J.-L., & Wang, J. W. C. (2020). Intelligent compilation of patent summaries using machine learning and natural language processing techniques. *Advanced Engineering Informatics, 43*, 101027.

Wasserman, S., & Faust, K. (1994). *Social network analysis: Methods and applications.* Cambridge (MA): Cambridge University Press.

Watts, D. J. (2004). The "new" science of networks. *Annual Review of Sociology, 30*, 243–270.

Watts, D. J., & Strogatz, S. H. (1998). Collective dynamics of "small-world" networks. *Nature, 393*, 440–442.

Innovation ecosystems and entrepreneurial opportunity

Yassine Mehros[1], Jean Michel Degeorge,[2]
Abdelaziz Elabjani[3]

Abstract: Entrepreneurship as a field of study has attracted considerable attention from both researchers and practitioners in recent years. The field is structured around a certain number of paradigms (Verstraete & Fayolle, 2005), of which opportunity is one of the most prominent (Vekataraman, 1997; Shane & Venkataraman, 2000; Shane, 2003, 2012). This paradigm is construed as a three-step process, corresponding to the recognition, evaluation, and seizing of entrepreneurial opportunities. The objective of this research is twofold: first, to understand the different types of links connecting entrepreneurs to other actors in their innovation ecosystems which help them to recognize, assess, and seize entrepreneurial opportunities as well as to identify the major players within this ecosystem.

To this end we present an exploratory qualitative study focusing on the key actors in the innovation ecosystem of the Loire department of France, in particular its institutions, support networks, and clusters.

Our results reveal the existence of strong connections between the different actors which make up this ecosystem. Furthermore, the creation of strong bonds of trust between these actors is facilitated by their geographical and relational proximity. Actors collaborate on projects involving businesses, and start-ups in

1 LIRE-MD and COACTIS Laboratory EA 4161, Jean Monnet University, France.

2 Mines Saint-Etienne, MRI Department, Institut Henri Fayol - Coactis Laboratory EA 4161, France.

3 FSJES Marrakesh, Department of Law, Economics and Social Sciences, Cadi Ayyad University, Morocco.

particular. All these elements combine to allow businesses to recognize and seize entrepreneurial opportunities.

Keywords: Innovation ecosystem, Entrepreneurial opportunity, Start-ups, Open innovation.

1. Introduction

In recent years, business creation has become one of the foremost priorities of economic development. In an economic context shaped by globalization, entrepreneurship offers a means of maintaining both capacity for innovation and competitiveness.

Entrepreneurship as a field of study has attracted considerable attention from both researchers and practitioners in recent years. The field is structured around a certain number of paradigms (Verstraete & Fayolle, 2005), of which opportunity is one of the most prominent (Vekataraman, 1997; Shane & Venkataraman, 2000; Shane, 2003, 2012). This paradigm is construed as a three-step process, corresponding to the recognition, evaluation, and seizing of entrepreneurial opportunities. These three steps are as relevant to the development of new opportunities by existing companies as they are to the creation of new businesses. From this perspective, entrepreneurship consists of recognizing, evaluating, and seizing opportunities to launch new goods and services, new forms of organization, new markets, new processes, and new materials utilizing organizational means which did not previously exist (Shane & Venkataraman, 2000; Shane, 2003).

In the existing literature on entrepreneurial opportunities, this process of recognizing, evaluating, and seizing opportunities is frequently regarded as an individual process undertaken by the entrepreneur (Tremblay, 2010), even if it occurs within the framework of an existing business (Degeorge & Messeghem, 2016). Although much research has been done on the influence of social capital on individuals' capacity to recognize, evaluate, and seize opportunities (Chabaud & Ngijol, 2010), none of the existing studies has fully engaged with the collective dimension of this phenomenon, particularly the importance of innovation ecosystems. These ecosystems can be defined as interorganizational, political, economic, environmental, and technological systems of innovation which contribute to the creation of an environment which is stable, dynamic, and conducive to business creation (Still et al., 2014).

Start-ups are defined by their newness and modest size (Landström, 2017). They therefore need to collaborate with other actors in the ecosystem, making use of collaborative practices such as open innovation (Chesbrough, 2003), in order to compensate for their lack of resources and skills (Vanhaverbeke et al., 2012). Fourcade (2007) describes the business environment as a source of know-how, expertise, norms, values, and relational capital. Moreover, the open innovation model may have an impact on other flows such as supply chain management, strategic alliances, networks, learning, discovery, and operational management (Van de Vrande & De Man, 2011).

From this perspective, the opportunities-focused approach and the open innovation model can provide pertinent frameworks for analyzing the roles played by different actors within innovation ecosystems with regard to the recognition, evaluation, and seizing of new opportunities by start-ups. Despite the pertinence of an opportunities-focused approach to entrepreneurship, particularly when analyzing business creation and growth, it remains under-represented in the existing academic literature. Only recently have we seen researchers begin to take an interest in an opportunities-based approach to business support (El Agy, 2019). Nonetheless, as far as we are aware, there have been no research publications dealing specifically with innovation ecosystems and entrepreneurial opportunity.

According to a study conducted by BCG & La Boussole[4] in 2018, France's entrepreneurial ecosystem is particularly dynamic: the authors identified over 10,000 start-ups.

Online software comparison tool Capterra has also analyzed[5] surveys encompassing 1,200 start-ups all over France.[6][7] According to their

---

4 BCG & La Boussole, devenir une licorne? April 2018

5 Internal survey conducted by Capterra encompassing 140 start-up founders and employees, Nov-Dec 2018.

6 Data source for the 1,200 start-ups: myfrenchstart-up.com. Data gathered and analysed for the interactive graph.

7 Data source: Statista.fr. Data not identified as being from other sources were commissioned for the purposes of this study from Statista.

analysis, the geographical distribution of start-ups in France is as follows: 51 % of start-ups are based in the Greater Paris region, with 11 % in the Auvergne-Rhône-Alpes region and 7 % in Occitanie. They are spread across a variety of sectors: 18 % in the ICT sector (the leading sector), followed by B2B services (17 %) and electronics (9 %).

Start-ups play a key role in innovation processes (Spender et al., 2017), helping to create both wealth and jobs. In 2016, a survey[8] by Dell and CSA Research found that seven out of ten start-ups created jobs, with an average of 4.5 jobs per start-up.

The aim of our research is to identify the main players in the innovation ecosystem, and also to explore and understand the importance of the connections formed within the innovation ecosystem to the entrepreneurial opportunity process as experienced by start-ups. We therefore propose to answer the following question: how does the innovation ecosystem contribute to the process of entrepreneurial opportunity for start-ups? We do so with the help of an exploratory qualitative study focusing on the key actors in the innovation ecosystem of the Loire *département* of France.

2. Literature review

2.1. Innovation ecosystem

The term "ecosystem," borrowed from life sciences, is now widely used in the industrial and academic spheres to describe national or regional business contexts.

In order to trace the development of innovation ecosystems as a concept, we should perhaps begin with Moore's (1996) definition of the business ecosystem as "*an economic community supported by a foundation of interacting organizations and individuals – the organisms of the business world. This economic community produces goods and services of value to customers, who themselves are members of the ecosystem. The member organisms also include suppliers, lead producers, competitors, and other stakeholders. Over time, they coevolve their capabilities and roles, and tend to align themselves with the directions set by one or more central companies. Those companies holding leadership roles may change over time, but the function of ecosystem leader is valued by the community because it enables members to*

8 https://www.csa.eu/media/1391/opi20160121-le-barometre-des-start-upers.pdf

move toward shared visions to align their investments and to find mutually supportive roles." (Moore, 1996, p. 9). Cooke et al. (1997) define the ecosystem in terms of the innovation made possible by "*openness to the outside world and the adoption of a more holistic understanding of the knowledge economy.*" (Cooke et al., 1997, p. 478)

The concept of innovation ecosystems began to gain traction following the publication of Adner's (2006) broader definition: "*collaborative agreements where a wide variety of partners combine their individual technologies and/or services into a coherent, customer-oriented solution.*" (Adner, 2006, p. 2). Mercan & Göktas (2011) note that innovation ecosystems comprise both economic agents and economic relations, as well as non-economic factors such as technology, institutions, sociological and cultural interactions. As such, innovation ecosystems are effectively hybrids of multiple networks and systems (Durst & Poutanen, 2013).

The term innovation ecosystem encompasses "*the complex relationships formed between actors and entities whose function is to facilitate technological development and innovation*" (Jackson, 2011, p. 2). This includes both public (public-sector research centers, public institutions, local authorities) and private-sector actors (big companies, SMEs, start-ups, private schools, venture capital firms, consultancy firms, accelerators, and incubators), working together in network mode to develop innovative projects with an economic purpose (Froehlicher & Bares, 2009). It is an innovation network that can support companies to launch innovative initiatives or bring them into contact with key actors to foster collaborations that lead to innovation (Aouinaït, 2021).

Analyzing 120 publications which discuss innovation ecosystems, Granstrand & Holgersson (2020) identify 21 more or less unique definitions. They also identify the seven components which recur most frequently in these divergent definitions of what constitutes an innovation ecosystem: actors, activities, artifacts, competition/substitutes, coevolution/co-specialization, collaboration/complementarity, and institutions. They propose the following definition: "*An innovation ecosystem is the evolving set of actors, activities, and artefacts, and the institutions and relations, including complementary and substitute relations that are important for the innovative performance of an actor or a population of actors.*" Granstrand & Holgersson (2020, p. 3).

Baiyere (2018) argues that, despite the widespread use of the term, there is no single definition of innovation ecosystems which is unanimously accepted by researchers. For the purpose of our research, we adopt the definition proposed by Gobble (2014), who holds that innovation ecosystems are *"dynamic, purposive communities with complex, interlocking relationships built on collaboration, trust, and co-creation of value and specializing in exploitation of a shared set of complementary technologies or competencies."* (Gobble, 2014, p. 55).

Unlike business ecosystems, driven by competition and value appropriation, innovation ecosystems are founded upon value creation and cooperation. The transition from the former model to the latter is closely linked to the emergence of open innovation (Gomes et al., 2018).

Of course, most businesses encounter certain obstacles when attempting to implement innovation processes, however flexible they may be. This may prompt them to work with external partners (Edwards et al., 2005), adopting the open innovation model (Chesbrough, 2003). Businesses thus engage in a form of collective intelligence founded upon collective strategies and interorganizational sharing of resources and skills with a view to attaining shared objectives (Lafaye & Berger-Douce, 2014).

The open innovation model has been studied by Chesbrough (2003) in the specific context of large companies. It involves drawing upon external innovation sources (information, knowledge, and skills) while also making better use of the fruits of internal R&D efforts.

Chesbrough (2003) proposes two graphical representations of closed and open systems which have since achieved widespread renown (Figure 1). In the 'closed' model, the innovation process is represented by a solid line whose trajectory is defined by internal R&D activities, highlighting the fact that innovation is brought to the market thanks to internal processes. The company thus remains focused on its portfolio of projects, prioritizing those that appear promising and overseeing their development and commercial launch.

In the 'open' model, on the other hand, the innovation process is represented by a dotted line, reflecting the fact that the company's boundaries are more porous. Projects and ideas may thus originate from outside the company, or else they may originate within the company but be rapidly turned outwards toward the market. The company can thus acquire and capture external sources of innovation and make use of them internally. These sources are filtered and transferred to the development phase, before being introduced to new markets. In this model, ideas circulate freely between the company and its environment (Chesbrough, 2003).

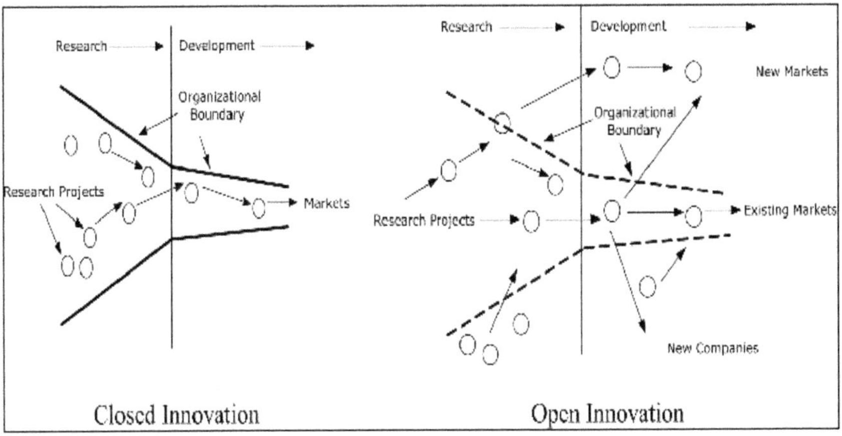

Figure 1: Closed and open innovation (Chesbrough, 2003)

Moreover, open innovation is defined as a process of innovation in which companies can and must make use of knowledge developed both internally and externally (Chesbrough, 2003). This means that all ideas, originating within the company or outside it, may be used to accelerate innovation, and may thus find a route to new or existing markets by moving beyond the bounds of the company (Chesbrough et al., 2006).

The notion of open innovation may also be linked to the concept of collective intelligence as a process of mutual learning over a long period of time, involving a group of actors committed to working on shared projects (Lafaye & Berger-Douce, 2014). Within this process, all parties become co-producers and co-consumers of information and knowledge that is useful and add value to their projects (Paul et al., 2011: quoted by Lafaye & Berger-Douce, 2014). For Lévy (2003), collective intelligence is a major source of added value and can contribute to the survival and growth of businesses.

Innovation in the open innovation model can be defined as a process of *outside-in* or *inside-out* innovation (Enkel et al., 2009), or indeed as a *coupled process* which combines both of these dynamics (Gassmann & Enkel, 2004). Some authors prefer the term *inbound* rather than *outside-in* and *outbound* for *inside-out* (Chesbrough & Crowther, 2006; Lichtenthaler, 2009; Dahlander & Gann, 2010; Chiaroni et al., 2011). The following table summarizes a number of open innovation practices with reference to these three dimensions.

Table 1: Open innovation practices (Bigliardi & Galati, 2016)

Practices	Definitions	Key texts
Inbound		
Customer involvement	Direct involvement of customers in innovation processes (e.g. developing products to meet customers' precise specifications).	Von Hippel (1986), Gasmann (2006), Van de Vrande et al. (2009), Spithoven, Vanhaverbeke, & Roijakkers (2010), Burcharth, Knudsen, & Sondergaard (2014).
External networking	Systematic collaboration with external partners in support of innovation processes (for example, with universities or research centers attached to other companies).	Chesbrough (2003), Gassmann (2006), Van de Vrande et al. (2009), Lee et al. (2010), Wynarczyk, Piperoulos & McAdam (2013), Burcharth, Knudsen & Sondergaard (2014), Harland & Nienaber (2014), Holzmann et al. (2014), Montelisciani et al. (2014).
Inbound IP licences	Buying or securing the use of intellectual property originating with external sources (e.g. patents).	Chesbrough (2003), Gassmann (2006), Van de Vrande et al. (2009), Lee et al. (2010), Wynarczyk, Piperoulos & McAdam (2013), Burcharth, Knudsen & Sondergaard (2014).
Web exploration	Systematic use of the Internet to seek out innovative ideas and technologies.	Burcharth, Knudsen & Sondergaard (2014).
Acquisition of know-how	Purchasing R&D work from third parties.	Gassmann (2006), Wynarczyk, Piperoulos, & McAdam (2013), Burcharth, Knudsen & Sondergaard (2014), Harland & Nienaber (2014), Holzmann et al. (2014).
Outbound		
Outbound IP licences	Selling permission to use patented technologies and know-how.	Gassmann (2006), Lichtenthaler & Ernst (2009), Van de Vrande et al. (2009), Lee et al. (2010), Wynarczyk, Piperoulos and McAdam (2013), Dong & Pourmohamadi (2014).
Use of knowledge	Making one's own unused innovations available to others free of charge.	Chesbrough (2003), Lee et al. (2010), Wynarczyk, Piperoulos and McAdam (2013), Burcharth, Knudsen & Sondergaard (2014).

Table 1: Continued

Practices	Definitions	Key texts
Provision of knowledge	Active involvement with other innovation projects.	Van de Vrande et al. (2009), Lee et al. (2010), Wynarczyk, Piperoulos and McAdam (2013).
Coupled		
Alliances with compatible companies	Combining *outside-in* (acquiring knowledge from external sources) and *inside-out* (bringing ideas to market) processes.	Gassmann & Enkel (2004), Enkel, Gassmann and Chesbrough (2009).

In short, open innovation is based on the implementation of collaborative innovation strategies between multiple internal or external actors (Calamel & Chabault, 2020), and innovation ecosystems are systems comprising multiple actors wherein economic and knowledge exchanges are governed by social networks (Granovetter, 1985). They form inter-organizational networks whose stakeholders share certain norms and values, building social relationships which facilitate coordination and cooperation in pursuit of a shared innovation objective (Coleman, 1994). Exchanges of information and knowledge between actors in an ecosystem may help to resolve problems and create entrepreneurial opportunities liable to enhance the performance of actors (Wenger, 1998).

In the next section, we explain our opportunities-based approach in greater detail.

2.2 An approach focusing on opportunities

Informed by the work of Verstraete & Faolle (2005), our research draws on the approach proposed by Shane & Venkataraman (2000) which holds that opportunity, broken down into successive phases, is a driving force of economic activity which is of central importance to the entrepreneurial process.

As Degeorge (2015) notes, this foundational article by Shane & Venkataraman (2000) has been the subject of much discussion and a certain number of modifications. Shane & Venkataraman (2000) and Shane (2003) launched a debate which has now run for more than twenty years, without any clear consensus as to the definition of opportunity, be it identified or created (Hansen et al., 2011). Degeorge also notes (Degeorge, 2015) that Shane (2012) and Venkataraman et al. (2012) no longer appear to agree on how to define the notion of opportunity (Sarasvathy et al., 2003). "*There is at present no agreed upon understanding, neither theoretical nor empirical, of what opportunity recognition entails.*" (Dimov, 2007: 723) Meanwhile, Singh (2000) has highlighted the need to better define the benefits of entrepreneurial opportunity, and to construct the concept with reference to other concepts.

Definition of entrepreneurial opportunity

The notion of entrepreneurial opportunity now occupies a prominent position in this field of research and sits at the heart of the business opportunity paradigm (Verstreate & Fayolle, 2005). More recently, a number of researchers working on entrepreneurship have expressed a certain consensus on the importance of the notion of entrepreneurial opportunity in this field of research (Short et al, 2010).

Various definitions have been proposed for the concept of opportunity. A brief survey of the existing academic literature on the subject of opportunity illustrates its polysemic nature. We can identify various schools of thought regarding its origins and definition. Some authors argue that opportunities are discovered, while others hold that they are created or recognized (Sarasvathy et al., 2003). For Shane & Venkataraman (2000), entrepreneurial opportunity is a business context in which goods, services, raw materials, and organizational processes can be introduced and sold at prices exceeding their cost price, requiring new relations between resources and objectives. As such, an entrepreneur might introduce new products or services into new markets by creating a new organization, thus creating value for society (Dutta & Crossan, 2005).

Entrepreneurial opportunity thus corresponds to the moment at which an entrepreneur introduces a new good or service to the market in response to pre-identified needs, delivering additional value for users (Koubaa & Schmitt, 2016).

With regard to the debate surrounding the ontological status of opportunity, Short et al. (2010) suggest that "*A reasonable middle-ground position is that some opportunities are discovered whereas others are created.*" (p. 15) Nonetheless, they also acknowledge the value of this distinction for research purposes (Short et al., 2010).

However, opportunities do not always deliver benefits; indeed, they may lead to losses (Lee & Venkataraman, 2006). Opportunity is a product of innovation, which can be invested and subsequently acquire value (Kornish & Ulrich, 2011). Davidsson (2015) proposes a reconceptualization of the notion of opportunity, insisting that this new conceptual framing must take account of actors rather than individuals. It is in this respect that our research bases itself on the concept of the innovation ecosystem i.e. a set of actors interacting among themselves to create and identify new opportunities.

2.3 The connection between the innovation ecosystem and opportunity recognition

Start-ups are characterized by a particular focus on recognizing and seizing opportunities, but also by a lack of resources and knowledge (Ortega-Argiles et al., 2009) which requires them to turn to external sources in order to boost their capacity for innovation (Huggins et al., 2012).

Within the framework of innovation ecosystems, which can be regarded as interorganizational networks, businesses strive to capitalize on the strengths of their networks of actors. They attempt to access and utilize as effectively as possible the resources and skills available both inside and outside their organizations. The innovation ecosystem is regarded as an open system based on collaboration and open innovation (Chesbrough, 2003).

The emergence of open innovation as a paradigm has illustrated the importance of access to knowledge and networks in the development of innovation (Dahlander & Gann, 2010). Inter-organizational networks play an important role in the innovation process, which is by nature complex and requires incoming and outgoing flows of knowledge between organizations (Bergenholtz & Waldstrom, 2011). Huggins and Thompson (2015) make it clear that this process is systemic, and necessarily involves complex interactions with other organizations; businesses can no longer innovate alone. The social networks in which businesses are engaged allow them to access knowledge which is not available to them internally and which is conducive to innovation (Tomlinson, 2010).

Approaches based on knowledge (Grant, 1996) and resources (Eisenhardt & Schoonhoven, 1996; Lavie, 2006) nonetheless acknowledge that businesses make use of their networks in order to meet their material needs and gain access to knowledge.

Opportunity recognition requires an understanding of the potential of the market and/or the resources required to pursue that potential (Shane, 2012). Studying a sample of 256 businesses, Singh et al. (1999) have demonstrated the positive impact of relational networks on the capacity to recognize opportunities, drawing upon social network theory. In a similar vein, Macpherson & Holt (2007) show that adopting an open approach can help companies to develop their social and organizational capital, thus contributing to the creation of knowledge with practical implications. This ensures that start-ups have strong opportunities to access new knowledge and technologies and learn from different actors in the ecosystem (Wu & Hsu, 2001). Partners operating within an ecosystem have a shared interest in exploring new knowledge and opportunities with the capacity to create value for businesses at a reduced cost (Kogut 2000).

3. Research methodology

Our research objective is to better understand how the various actors that make up the innovation ecosystem contribute to the recognition, evaluation, and seizing of new opportunities by entrepreneurs. We thus opted for a qualitative research method, justified by the scarcity of existing research on this topic (Thiétart, 2014; Mucchielli, 1996).

Although our exploratory approach does not necessarily impose any particular methodological framework, it appears that qualitative methodologies are generally used in exploratory studies since they are more effective (Charreire & Durieux, 1999). We conducted an exploratory study (multiple case studies) looking at the actors (institutions, support networks, start-ups etc.) that make up the innovation ecosystem of Saint-Etienne.

With regard to our qualitative research strategy, interviews appeared to represent the most appropriate tool for gathering data in the field. Our desire to address our research question in greater depth, seeking to identify the meanings and interpretations actors attach to innovation as a phenomenon, informed our decision to conduct semi-directive interviews with stakeholders (Rispal & Jouison-Laffitte, 2015).

3.1. The interview process

We conducted semi-directive interviews with ten directors of organizations involved with the innovation ecosystem of the Loire region.

Our interview guides focused on three main themes: the innovation ecosystem, open innovation, and the relationship between open innovation and the recognition of entrepreneurial opportunities by innovative young businesses.

4. Cases studied

We reached out to various actors in the Loire business ecosystem inviting them to take part in our study, while attempting to comply with the theoretical sampling criteria recommended by Hlady-Rispal (2002), particularly the need for diversity to achieve a comprehensive view of the ecosystem. We conducted interviews with the directors of various organizations (businesses, public institutions, associations, incubators, clusters, competitiveness clusters etc.).

The table below provides a brief profile of these organizations and their representatives who participated in our study.

Table 2: Participating organizations

Organization	Nature	Introduction
Use'In	University incubator	An incubator for innovative projects led by students and graduates in Saint-Etienne and the whole Loire department, helping them to launch businesses and attract their first clients.
Minalogic	Competitiveness cluster	A cluster which helps its members to innovate and grow, providing a boost to their international development and visibility.
Digital league	Cluster (digital industry)	Digital League is the business cluster for the digital industry in Auvergne-Rhône-Alpes. With over 500 members, it is one of the biggest digital business communities in France.
BPI France	Public investment bank	BpiFrance is a French public investment bank providing financial support for business development. The bank works with businesses of all sizes, helping them to become bigger and better. It provides financial solutions tailored to the demands of every stage in a company's life cycle.
Pôle des Technologies Médicales	Cluster (medical technologies)	A cluster for businesses specializing in implants, prostheses, medical devices, and healthcare technology. PTM helps businesses in this sector to become more competitive through innovation.
Sofimac	Venture capital firm	Specializing in the management of all forms of investment capital, supporting the development of businesses and start-ups.
Réseau Entreprendre	Support network	A network of business leaders devoted to supporting young, small and medium-sized businesses with the potential to create new jobs, helping them to launch, expand, and grow their activities.
Mines Saint-Étienne	Engineering School	Member of the Mines-Télécom Institute, Mines Saint-Étienne also plays a leading role in supporting businesses through their industrial transition, via the Mines Saint-Étienne Tech program.
Sporaltec	Cluster (sport/ health)	SPORALTEC is a business cluster for the sports sector, devoted to boosting the competitiveness of businesses through innovation.

5. Results

We conducted vertical and horizontal analyses of our interviews (Wacheux, 1996) with the leaders of various organizations associated with the innovation ecosystem in the Loire department.

After transcribing and organizing all our interviews, we performed an analysis of their content using a coding process, specifically by dividing this textual material into analytical units using the NVIVO software tool. We first performed an open, descriptive round of coding as suggested by Strauss & Corbin (1990), looking for certain themes. We then fine-tuned the coding to incorporate theoretical parameters, while also establishing a hierarchy of categories.

The principal results of our study correspond to the following themes:

Key characteristics of the innovation ecosystem

Saint-Etienne's innovation ecosystem is thriving and receives considerable support from the public sector: "*the ecosystem is very dynamic.*" (Minalogic). Public-sector organizations continue to play a major role in its development. The ecosystem is vast, dense, complex, and contains a variety of actors connected by a complex web of relationships, including competitive relations; "*the ecosystem is very dense, very diverse and, in recent years, it has really refocused and worked to establish new forms of synergy, helping businesses to foster innovation.*" (Pôle de technologies médicales) The ecosystem has no governance structure; actors work independently for the collective benefit of both businesses and the territory as a whole.

All actors support entrepreneurship and innovation at the territorial level. Actors attach particular importance to working with project leaders and start-ups, helping them to secure the support and financial backing they need to develop. The nature of this support depends on the specific needs of start-ups, and their level of maturity.

Trust and connections between actors

Within this ecosystem, most actors are connected by strong links. Trust plays an essential role in maintaining these robust, lasting connections, "*We might have slightly different approaches or systems, but the most important thing is that we know each other and trust each other. As a general rule, I attach great importance to the quality of relationships and the trust we create among ourselves.*" (Sporaltec) This trust between actors is the fruit of the various actions and activities they undertake together. The geographical and relational proximity between individuals is integral to the strong connections and sense of trust observed in Saint-Etienne's innovation ecosystem; "*We know each other and we get together almost every month, to look at projects. The projects that come in, we talk them over together. We all know each other very well, we know the projects, we trust each other.*" (BPIFrance).

Start-ups within the ecosystem

Start-ups are renowned for their strong capacity for innovation, their agility, and their ability to take risks, "*What we're seeing now is that start-ups are bringing lots more innovative ideas to the table. These days, start-ups have something that SMEs and big companies don't, and that's their agility and adaptability.*" (BPIFrance). Nevertheless, they are beset by other constraints such as a lack of resources, skills, and technologies, as well as the difficulty of breaking into markets; "*start-ups don't have access to the market, and securing that access is complicated.*" (Sporaltec)

The links between actors in the innovation ecosystem can play a role in helping start-ups to develop and succeed. Start-ups call upon actors in the ecosystem according to their needs, be they financial, technical, or commercial in nature. They also collaborate with laboratories attached to large companies and academic institutions and may benefit from support and financial assistance programs operated by incubators, accelerators, and other local actors. Collaboration between start-ups and research and teaching professionals is an increasingly prominent feature of the ecosystem: "*We do see a lot of start-ups which are very close to academic institutions. They are virtually working in partnership with research laboratories and engineering schools.*" (Minalogic).

Key players in the ecosystem

Saint-Etienne's innovation ecosystem comprises a large number of heterogeneous actors. Based on lexicographic analysis of our results, Figure 2 presents a word cloud for the actors most frequently cited in our interviews. It demonstrates the diversity of these actors and the central role occupied by businesses within the ecosystem. Alongside these businesses, we also find the Auvergne Rhône-Alpes region, Saint-Étienne Métropole, associations such as Réseau-Entreprendre, BPI France, incubators, universities and research laboratories, engineering schools clusters, competitiveness clusters etc.

All these actors strive to find new forms of synergy, in order to provide the support and financial backing that young businesses require and to galvanize innovation and development across the territory.

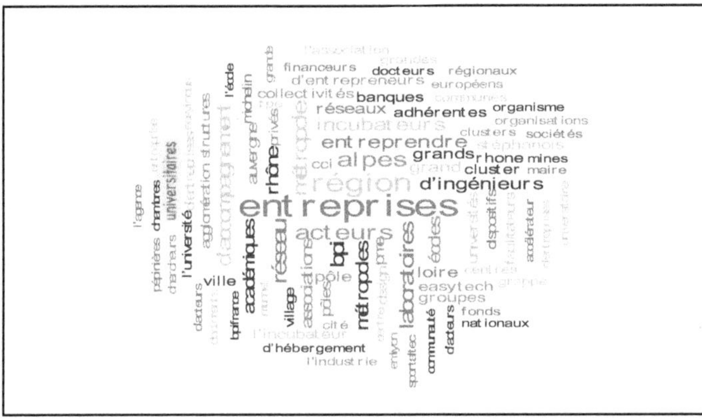

Figure 2: Word cloud (principal players in the ecosystem)
Source: Results of our study

For example, some members of this innovation ecosystem meet regularly to discuss matters of innovation, business challenges and potential solutions as part of an open innovation club. The aim of this club is to foster cohesive relations between big businesses and start-ups. The purpose of these relations is to support businesses and innovative projects, with solutions adapted to their needs and degree of maturity. Experienced actors put their expertise and skills at the disposal of start-ups, helping them to overcome any difficulties they might encounter in terms of securing financial backing, support, access to markets etc. Some actors also participate in partnerships, co-development contracts, entrepreneurial contests, hackathons, exchanges of best practices and networking opportunities involving multiple actors, with a view to fostering synergy; *"exchanges between the parties that make up the ecosystem provide opportunities for networking with partners capable of bringing new added value."* Digital League. The majority of relationships within this ecosystem are cooperative in nature, although there are examples of coopetitive relations between rival businesses. This means that some companies may find that it better suits their interests to collaborate with their rivals rather than remain in competition. Coopetition is a term used to describe complementary relations between direct or indirect rivals.

The innovation ecosystem and entrepreneurial opportunity

Start-ups suffer from a lack of resources, skills, and technologies (Landström, 2017). This can hinder the development of their innovations, and thus their growth. It therefore makes sense for young companies to reach out to other actors within their ecosystem. Our results demonstrate that the innovation ecosystem, and its component actors, help start-ups to meet the right partners, to find solutions to their problems, to save time and to create new economic models. Within this framework, entrepreneurial opportunity translates to the creation and development of a new business model. Relations with other actors in the innovation ecosystem also serve to accelerate the development of innovations and access to the market, by providing access to additional resources. In this respect, the entrepreneurial opportunity on offer pertains to the development of new products or services. Collaboration with other actors in the ecosystem helps young businesses to pick up knowledge which will be a source of value. It also serves to minimize risk by sharing it among multiple partners; "*partnerships and collaborations with partners give businesses a means of absorbing and sharing risk.*" (Pôle de technologies médicales)

Open innovation is highly beneficial for businesses, and particularly for start-ups; "*I am convinced that open innovation boosts the connectedness of businesses. These days, there are very few innovations which spring from a genius idea and just emerge fully formed.*" (Minalogic) Open innovation facilitates the acquisition of new knowledge, ideas, and technologies, which contribute to the development of new products and services and the recognition of new entrepreneurial opportunities, "*open innovation brings together actors from across the ecosystem to focus on a specific need, it gets them to discuss and develop solutions together, encouraging the transfer and sharing of skills and technologies which can serve to reveal other needs, which can translate into new opportunities to be seized by the partners.*" (Minalogic) In the same vein, the director of the *Pôle de technologies médicales* notes that: "*when a start-up collaborates with a big company, it can help them to access new and additional resources, new material and new markets, and that can lead to the development of new products which can generate healthy profits for the start-up.*" In this respect, the development of new products and markets constitutes an entrepreneurial opportunity as per the definition adopted for the purposes of our research.

6. Interpreting our results

Our research objective was to study and better understand how innovation ecosystems contribute to businesses' ability to recognize and seize entrepreneurial opportunities, identifying the actors involved and their connections within the innovation ecosystem. Our results serve to illustrate the connection between the innovation ecosystem and the recognition and seizing of entrepreneurial opportunities by start-ups. In our research, these opportunities take the form of new products, services, or business models, and the development or opening up of new markets.

An innovation ecosystem can be defined as a community of heterogeneous, interdependent actors who establish mutual relations with a view to nurturing and developing innovation (Mercan & Göktas, 2011). Our results reveal the presence of these characteristics in Saint-Etienne's innovation ecosystem, a heterogeneous network of public and private sector actors. It also displays the density and complexity of relational connections mentioned in Jackson's (2011) definition. The purpose of this ecosystem is to support entrepreneurship and innovation at the territorial level, supporting innovative project leaders and businesses, particularly start-ups.

Innovation ecosystems may thus be defined as systems of actors whose economic exchanges and exchanges of knowledge take place as part of a social network (Granovetter, 1985). Our results show that the connections between actors are generally strong, which is to say that they know one another and meet regularly. This serves to establish strong bonds of trust between actors. This is a form of structural integration founded upon trust between actors (Baum & Ingram, 2000).

Start-ups appear to be a dynamic force within Saint-Etienne's innovation ecosystem, in spite of the challenges they face. Most new businesses find it difficult to grow, and only a small proportion will develop rapidly (Barringer et al., 2005). It is for this reason that they look to other actors in the innovation ecosystem for support (Huggins et al., 2012). Our results highlight the importance of collaboration between start-ups and other actors such as big companies, laboratories, universities, incubators etc.

Our analysis identifies the key players in the innovation ecosystem. They include a variety of actors from the public and private sectors. They interact with one another, forming complex and dynamic relationships in the spirit of sharing and open innovation (Chesbrough, 2003). These dynamic relations help to foster and champion entrepreneurship and innovation at the territorial level.

Our analysis highlights some of the relations which exist between actors in Saint-Etienne's innovation ecosystem. They include support, funding, collaborations, open innovation arrangements such as co-development contracts (Van de Vrande et al., 2009; Lee et al., 2010), external networking (Chesbrough, 2003; Gassmann, 2006), hackathons, entrepreneurial contests etc.

In the academic literature, entrepreneurial opportunity is defined as a business context in which goods, services, raw materials, and organizational processes can be introduced and sold at prices exceeding their cost price, requiring new relations between resources and objectives (Shane & Venkataraman, 2000). All the examples highlighted in our results appear to correspond very closely to this definition.

Furthermore, the relations identified within the innovation ecosystem enable start-ups to meet various partners, and to exchange, transfer, and acquire new resources, knowledge and skills. Access to such resources and knowledge is crucial to the development of innovation (Dahlander and Gann, 2010). Start-ups may capitalize on their ecosystem relations to acquire vital knowledge and expertise, and thus to develop new innovations (Zahra & George, 2002). Our results thus serve to demonstrate how collaboration between actors in an ecosystem can help businesses to spread risk, to find solutions for problems, and to acquire the additional resources required for the development of new solutions. For example, start-ups often encounter difficulties with gaining access to markets; more established actors within the ecosystem can facilitate this access and lend them a sense of legitimacy. For start-ups, adopting an open innovation approach, within the framework of an innovation ecosystem, provides access to new knowledge and technologies as well as opportunities to learn from other actors, and thus to recognize and seize new opportunities for growth (Macpherson & Holt, 2007).

7. Conclusion

The existing academic literature on entrepreneurship highlights the importance of start-ups in wealth and job creation, but innovation ecosystems also play an important role in the development of innovation and regional economies. We thus chose to focus on the connection between innovation ecosystems and the recognition and seizing of entrepreneurial opportunities. Our research represents a contribution to the existing literature, exploring the impact of the web of relations which constitute the innovation ecosystem in terms of the recognition and seizing of opportunities by start-ups. We also make a contribution to our understanding of innovation ecosystems, their characteristics, their actors and the complex relations between the latter. Our research demonstrates how innovation ecosystems can contribute to the recognition and seizing of entrepreneurial opportunities, through open innovation and collaboration with other actors.

In methodological terms, our research demonstrates the advantages of adopting a qualitative approach to explore and better understand the specificities of innovation ecosystems, the connections between actors, and the nature of entrepreneurial opportunities.

At the operational level, our research casts some light on the organizational constraints and lack of resources and skills which can beset start-ups. It also constitutes a contribution to our understanding of how open innovation can facilitate the process of recognizing and seizing entrepreneurial opportunities, helping the founders and directors of start-ups to prepare more effectively.

Although we do offer some insights into the relationship between the innovation ecosystem and entrepreneurial opportunity, our research does have its limitations, both theoretical and methodological.

First, the theoretical scope of our work is restricted by the lack of a clear consensus on how to define innovation ecosystems, and the absence of a clear theoretical model for the relationship between innovation ecosystems and entrepreneurial opportunities.

In terms of methodological constraints, we were obliged to limit our investigation to ten ecosystem actors and just a single start-up, and as such we make no claim that our results are representative, certainly not of start-ups.

We nonetheless feel that our work opens up some potentially interesting avenues for future exploration, particularly regarding the connections between innovation ecosystems and entrepreneurial opportunity. A longitudinal study on the recognition and seizing of entrepreneurial opportunities by start-ups within innovation ecosystems could be highly enriching. It would also be interesting to study multiple innovation ecosystems, to obtain more general results and allow for comparisons between different ecosystems.

References

Adner, R. (2006). Match your innovation strategy to your innovation ecosystem. *Harvard Business Review, 84*(4), 98.

Aouinaït, C. (2021). Collaboration–Collaborative and open innovation in highly competitive contexts. In *Innovation Economics, Engineering and Management Handbook 1: Main Themes*, 91–99.

Baiyere, A. (2018). Fostering innovation ecosystems-Note on the 2017 ISPIM innovation forum. *Technovation, 69*(C), 1-1.

Barringer, B. R., Jones, F. F., & Neubaum, D. O. (2005). A quantitative content analysis of the characteristics of rapid-growth firms and their founders. *Journal of Business Venturing, 20*(5), 663–687.

Baum, J.A., & Ingram, P. (2000). Interorganizational Learning and Network Organization : Toward a Behavioral Theory of the Interfirm.

Baum, J. A., & Ingram, P. (2002). Interorganizational learning and network organization: Toward a behavioral theory of the interfirm. The economics of choice, change, and organization: Essays in memory of Richard M. Cyert, 191–218.

Bergenholtz, C., & Waldstrøm, C. (2011). Inter-organizational network studies—A literature review. *Industry and Innovation, 18*(6), 539–562.

Bigliardi, B., & Galati, F. (2016). Which factors hinder the adoption of open innovation in SMEs?. *Technology Analysis & Strategic Management, 28*(8), 869–885.

Calamel, L. & Chabault, D. (2020). The role of proximities in the construction of managerial innovation in a collaborative context. *Journal of Innovation Economics & Management, 32*, 107–133.

Chabaud, D., & Ngijol, J. (2010). Quels networks sociaux dans la formation de l'opportunity d'affaires?. *Revue française de gestion,* (7), 129–147.

Charreire, S., & Durieux, F. (1999). Explorer et tester. *Méthodes de research en management, 57*, 80.

Chesbrough, H. W. (2003). *Open innovation: The new imperative for creating and profiting from technology*. Harvard Business Press.

Chesbrough, H. W. (2006). *Open innovation: The new imperative for creating and profiting from technology*. Harvard Business Press.

Chesbrough, H., & Crowther, A. K. (2006). Beyond high tech: Early adopters of open innovation in other industries. *R&d Management, 36*(3), 229–236.

Chiaroni, D., Chiesa, V., & Frattini, F. (2011). The open innovation journey: How firms dynamically implement the emerging innovation management paradigm. *Technovation, 31*(1), 34–43.

Coleman, J. S. (1994). *Foundations of social theory*. Harvard university press.

Cooke, P., Uranga, M. G., & Etxebarria, G. (1997). Regional innovation systems: Institutional and organisational dimensions. *Research policy, 26*(4–5), 475–491.

Dahlander, L., & Gann, D. M. (2010). How open is innovation?. *Research policy, 39*(6), 699–709.

Davidsson, P. (2015). Entrepreneurial opportunities and the entrepreneurship nexus: A re-conceptualization. *Journal of Business Venturing, 30*(5), 674–695.

Degeorge, J. M. (2015). *Scott Shane, Une (re) définition du champ de entrepreneurship comme domaine de research*. Éditions EMS.

Degeorge, J. M., & Messeghem, K. (2016), Management entrepreneurial et nature de l'opportunity. *Finance Contrôle Stratégie, 19*/2, juin.

Dimov, D. (2007). From opportunity insight to opportunity intention: The importance of person–situation learning match. *Entrepreneurship Theory and Practice, 31*(4), 561–583.

Durst, S., & Poutanen, P. (2013). Success factors of innovation ecosystems-Initial insights from a literature review. *Co-create*, 27–38.

Dutta, D. K., & Crossan, M. M. (2005). The nature of entrepreneurial opportunities: Understanding the process using the 4I organizational learning framework. *Entrepreneurship Theory and Practice, 29*(4), 425–449.

Edwards, T., Delbridge, R., & Munday, M. (2005). Understanding innovation in small and medium-sized enterprises: A process manifest. *Technovation, 25*(10), 1119–1127.

Eisenhardt, K. M., & Schoonhoven, C. B. (1996). Resource-based view of strategic alliance formation: Strategic and social effects in entrepreneurial firms. *Organization Science, 7*(2), 136–150.

El Agy, M. (2019). Les formes et les pratiques d'accompagnement mobilisées dans le processus d'recognition et d'exploitation d'entrepreneurial opportunity: Approche exploratoire. *International Journal of Innovation and Applied Studies, 26*(3), 768–776.

Enkel, E., Gassmann, O., & Chesbrough, H. (2009). Open R&D and open innovation: Exploring the phenomenon. *R&d Management, 39*(4), 311–316.

Fourcade, C. (2007). Mise en place de milieux propices au development de la PME. Management des PME: de la création à la croissance, Chapitre, 7, 103–119.

Froehlicher, T., & Barès, F. (2009). Vers une nouvelle convention d'innovation créative au service du development régional.

Froehlicher, T., & Barès, F. (2013). Innovation ecosystem universitaire de Aalto: une contribution au repérage des acteurs impliqués lors de la phase d'émergence. *Management International/International Management/Gestiòn Internacional, 18*(1), 153–165.

Gassmann, O. (2006). Opening up the innovation process: Towards an agenda. *R & D Management, 36*(3), 223–228.

Gassmann, O., & Enkel, E. (2004). Towards a theory of open innovation: Three core process archetypes.

Gobble, M. M. (2014). Charting the innovation ecosystem. *Research-Technology Management, 57*(4), 55–59.

Gomes, J. F., Iivari, M., Pikkarainen, M., & Ahokangas, P. (2018). Business models as enablers of ecosystemic interaction: A dynamic capability perspective. *International Journal of Social Ecology and Sustainable Development (IJSESD), 9*(3), 1–13.

Granovetter, M. (1985). Economic action and social structure: The problem of embeddedness. *American Journal of Sociology, 91*(3), 481–510.

Granstrand, O., & Holgersson, M. (2020). Innovation ecosystems: A conceptual review and a new definition. *Technovation, 90*, 102098.

Grant, R. M. (1996). Toward a knowledge-based theory of the firm. *Strategic Management Journal, 17*(S2), 109–122.

Hansen, D.J., Shrader, R., Monllor, J. (2011). Defragmenting Definitions of Entrepreneurial Opportunity. *Journal of Small Business Management, 49*(2), 283–304.

Hsu, W. L., Wu, S. H., & Chen, Y. S. (2001, October). Event recognition based on the information map-INFOMAP. In 2001 IEEE International Conference on Systems, Man and Cybernetics. e-Systems and e-Man for Cybernetics in Cyberspace (Cat. No. 01CH37236) (Vol. 3, pp. 1661–1666). IEEE.

Huggins, R., & Thompson, P. (2015). Entrepreneurship, innovation and regional growth: A network theory. *Small Business Economics, 45*(1), 103–128.

Huggins, R., Johnston, A., & Thompson, P. (2012). Network capital, social capital and knowledge flow: How the nature of inter-organizational networks impacts on innovation. *Industry and Innovation, 19*(3), 203–232.

Jackson, D. J. (2011). What is an innovation ecosystem. *National Science Foundation, 1*(2), 1–13.

Kogut, B. (2000). The network as knowledge: Generative rules and the emergence of structure. *Strategic Management Journal, 21*(3), 405–425.

Kornish, L. J., & Ulrich, K. T. (2011). Opportunity spaces in innovation: Empirical analysis of large samples of ideas. *Management Science, 57*(1), 107–128.

Koubaa, S., & Schmitt, C. (2016). L'entrepreneur peut-il être «ambidextre»? Proposition d'un cadre conceptuel (No. hal-02365924).

Lafaye, C., & Berger-Douce, S. (2014). Contribuer à l'émergence d'une intelligence collective entrepreneuriale dans un projet collaboratif interorganisationnel. *Gestion, 39*(1), 93–103.

Landström, H. (2017). *Advanced introduction to entrepreneurial finance.* Edward Elgar Publishing.

Lavie, D. (2006). The competitive advantage of interconnected firms: An extension of the resource-based view. *Academy of Management Review, 31*(3), 638–658.

Lee, J. H., & Venkataraman, S. (2006). Aspirations, market offerings, and the pursuit of entrepreneurial opportunities. *Journal of Business Venturing, 21*(1), 107–123.

Lee, S., Park, G., Yoon, B., & Park, J. (2010). Open innovation in SMEs—An intermediated network model. *Research policy, 39*(2), 290–300.

Lévy, P. (2003). Le jeu de l'intelligence collective. *Sociétés,* (1), 105–122.

Lichtenthaler, U. (2009). Outbound open innovation and its effect on firm performance: Examining environmental influences. *R&D Management, 39*(4), 317–330.

Macpherson, A., & Holt, R. (2007). Knowledge, learning and small firm growth: A systematic review of the evidence. *Research policy, 36*(2), 172–192.

Mercan, B., & Goktas, D. (2011). Components of innovation ecosystems: A cross-country study. *International Research Journal of Finance and Economics, 76*(16), 102–112.

Moore, J. (1996). *The death of competition, leadership and strategy in the age of business ecosystems.* Harper Business.

Mucchielli, A. (1996). *Méthodologie d'une qualitative research.* A. Mucchielli.

Ortega-Argilés, R., Vivarelli, M., & Voigt, P. (2009). R&D in SMEs: A paradox?. *Small Business Economics, 33*(1), 3–11.

Paul, K., Donghwan, L., Youngjo, L., Chuan, H., Tamas, M. (2011). Collective intelligence ratio : Measurement of real-time multimodal interactions in team projects. *Team Performance Management, 17*(16), 41–62.

Rispal, M. H. (2002). *La méthode des cas.* De Boeck Supérieur.

Rispal, M. H., & Jouison-Laffitte, E. (2015). La contribution des méthodes qualitatives au development du champ de entrepreneurship. *Revue de Entrepreneurship, 14*(1), 15–40.

Sarasvathy, S. D., Dew, N., Velamuri, S. R., & Venkataraman, S. (2003). Three views of entrepreneurial opportunity. In *Handbook of entrepreneurship research* (pp. 141–160). Boston, MA: Springer.

Shane, S. (2012). Reflections on the 2010 AMR decade award: Delivering on the promise of entrepreneurship as a field of research. *Academy of Management Review, 37*(1), 10–20.

Shane, S. A. (2003). *A general theory of entrepreneurship: The individual-opportunity nexus.* Edward Elgar Publishing.

Shane, S., & Venkataraman, S. (2000). The promise of entrepreneurship as a field of research. *Academy of Management Review, 25*(1), 217–226.

Short, J. C., Ketchen Jr, D. J., Shook, C. L., & Ireland, R. D. (2010). The concept of "opportunity" in entrepreneurship research: Past accomplishments and future challenges. *Journal of Management, 36*(1), 40–65.

Singh, R. P. (2000). *Entrepreneurial opportunity recognition through social networks*. Psychology Press.

Singh, R., Hills, H., & Lumpkin, G. T. (1999, June). Examining the role of self-perceived entrepreneurial alertness in the opportunity recognition process. In 13th UIC/AMA Symposium on Marketing and Entrepreneurship Interface, Nice, June.

Spender, J. C., Corvello, V., Grimaldi, M., & Rippa, P. (2017). Start-ups and open innovation: A review of the literature. *European Journal of Innovation Management, 20*(1), 4–30.

Still, K., Huhtamäki, J., Russell, M. G., & Rubens, N. (2014). Insights for orchestrating innovation ecosystems: The case of EIT ICT Labs and data-driven network visualisations. *International Journal of Technology Management 23, 66*(2–3), 243–265.

Strauss, A., & Corbin, J. (1990). *Basics of qualitative research*. Sage Publications.

Thiétart, R. A. (2014). *Méthodes de research en management* (4ème éd.). Dunod.

Tomlinson, P. R. (2010). Co-operative ties and innovation: Some new evidence for UK manufacturing. *Research policy, 39*(6), 762–775.

Tremblay, M. (2010). Recognition collective d'entrepreneurial opportunities: une étude exploratoire (Doctoral dissertation, Université du Québec à Trois-Rivières).

Van De Vrande, V., & de Man, A. P. (2011). A response to" Is open innovation a field of study or a communication barrier to theory development?". *Technovation, 31*(ARTICLE), 185–186.

Van de Vrande, V., De Jong, J. P., Vanhaverbeke, W., & De Rochemont, M. (2009). Open innovation in SMEs: Trends, motives and management challenges. *Technovation, 29*(6–7), 423–437.

Vanhaverbeke, W., Vermeersch, I., & De Zutter, S. (2012). Open innovation in SME's: How can small companies and start-ups benefit from open innovation strategies?.

Venkataraman, S. (1997). The distinctive domain of entrepreneurship research (Vol. 3, pp. 119–38).

Verstraete, T., & Fayolle, A. (2005). Paradigmes et entrepreneuriat. *Revue de lEntrepreneuriat, 4*(1), 33–52.

Wacheux, F. (1996). Méthodes qualitatives de researchs en gestion (No. hal-00157140).

Wenger, E. (1998). Communities of practice: Learning as a social system. *Systems thinker, 9*(5), 2–3.

Zahra, S. A., & George, G. (2002). Absorptive capacity: A review, reconceptualization, and extension. *Academy of Management Review, 27*(2), 185–203.

From bricolage to ecosystems of resource-poor firms

Son Thi Kim Le[1]

Abstract: The emergence of resource-constrained innovations has reshaped innovation towards reducing resource consumption. Bricolage is often referred as an innovation pathway in a resource-constrained environment. Through analyzing bricolage capabilities, this chapter explores the advantages of bricolage in driving innovation towards frugality and sustainability. In particular, bricolage enables resource-poor firms to overcome scarcity and introduce products that are good enough and affordable for the scarce environment, to seek innovative solutions to social needs by make use of all available resources, to minimize consumption of resources and raw materials as well as waste and hazardous emissions. Further, the networking capabilities of bricolage practices also facilitate the development of an innovation ecosystem of resource-constrained enterprises.

Keywords: Bricolage, Resource-constrained context, Innovation ecosystem.

Introduction

The circular economy has been attracting the attention of business and government leaders. Their imaginations have been captured by improving efficiency at all stages of the production process, while minimizing resource waste and the environmental impact (Gallaud & Laperche, 2016). This principle of the circular economy appears to be crucial to assist in dealing with the resource-constrained contexts which

[1] Research centre on Innovation and Industrial Strategies (ISI/Lab.RII), ISCID-CO Business School, University of Littoral Côte d'Opale, Research Network on Innovation, France.

have attracted global warnings. Among the potential solutions, reshaping innovation toward reducing resource consumption has informed the development of resource-constrained innovations. Several previous studies have argued that the dedication of resources is central to the innovation process, thus scarcity is often known to be a critical obstacle to innovation (Galia & Legros, 2004; Segarra-Blasco et al., 2008; Iammarino et al., 2009). However, the emergence of resource-constrained innovations indicates the reality of "doing more with less", such as "low-tech" innovation (Alexander & Yacoumis, 2018), good-enough innovation (Mazieri et al., 2017; Weyrauch & Herstatt, 2017), grassroots innovation (Smith et al., 2014), reverse innovation (Giannetti & Rubera, 2020), frugal innovation (Agarwal et al., 2017; Le Bas, 2016), or bricolage (Senyard et al., 2014), etc.

Among such resource-constrained innovation, bricolage has emerged as an innovation pathway of resource-constrained enterprises (Senyard et al., 2014). The literature on bricolage has, indeed, emphasized the possibility to innovate in unconventional settings. In a nutshell, this literature states that constraints and resource scarcity hamper conventional innovation processes and, for that reason, may also have a stimulating effect, leading to new innovation strategies. Actors may then try to overcome resource shortcomings by imagining new uses from what they find at hand. As such, scholars emphasize the possibility of a "resourceful" innovation that highlights the ability of making do with whatever is at hand (Baker & Nelson, 2005). In coping with resource-constrained settings, entrepreneurs might have two options: creatively searching for other resources or abandoning the intention to pursue identified opportunities (Baker & Nelson, 2005). When entrepreneurs cannot assemble more resources, they tend to avoid this constraint by creatively using "existing undervalued, slack, or discarded resources" (Desa & Basu, 2013, p. 29). Such negative resources tend to be considered as liabilities of both businesses and the broader society or economy. Nevertheless, Wu et al. (2021) argued that "*well-managed entrepreneurial bricolage can transform these liabilities or constraints into opportunities, redefining waste materials as valuable resources*" (p. 230). As such, could bricolage drive innovation toward reducing pollution or facilitating environmental sustainability?

In the literature on innovation, the concept of bricolage has been studied when exploring how resource-poor entrepreneurs mobilize and combine their limited resources "at hand" in developing innovation and their businesses. This bricolage behavior of entrepreneurs appears to be a possible strategy to overcome scarcity. Prior work on bricolage has indeed noticed the importance of dealing with a lack of affluent customers, financing, human resources, skills, technology, and knowledge (see Baker & Nelson, 2005; Duymedjian & Rüling, 2010; Cunha et al., 2014). As a result, bricolage is also a trigger for innovation in scarcity settings such as in nascent and young enterprises (Senyard et al., 2014), small enterprises (Baker & Nelson, 2005), and enterprises in developing countries (Srinivas & Sutz, 2008; Linna, 2013; Gurca & Ravishankar, 2016; An, Zhang, et al., 2018), informal entrepreneurship (Holt & Littlewood, 2017; Afutu-Kotey & Gough, 2022), social enterprises (Desa & Basu, 2013; Di Domenico et al., 2010; Langevang & Namatovu, 2019), etc. In addition, bricolage is also an antecedent of frugal innovation (Ernst et al., 2015; Sharmelly & Ray, 2018) in emerging markets, especially when those markets are affected by resource scarcity (Santos et al., 2022). As such, the next question to be addressed is: whether bricolage could play a trigger role for innovation in an ecosystem of resource-limited enterprises.

Based on resource-based theory, Baker and Nelson (2005) and Desa and Basu (2013) investigated how resource-poor enterprises acquire standard resources by mobilizing slack, discarded, or undervalued resources that others have rejected. These enterprises adopt typically creative processes to combine various existing resources to seek workable approaches to solve problems or seize opportunities and may create differential value, which is known as bricolage. Baker and Nelson (2005) expanded on Lévi-Strauss's ideas on bricolage and offer the concept of entrepreneurial bricolage as a critical explanation for an innovativeness pathway for resource-constrained enterprises. Baker and Nelson (2005, p. 333) indicated that entrepreneurial bricolage is a process of "*making do by applying combinations of the resources at hand to new problems and opportunities*". In particular, instead of being constrained by resource-poor contexts, certain enterprises are able to find a specific way to use and combine their resources "at hand" which range from physical resources (such as materials, skills, labor), social resources (from customers and markets), to institutional resources (standards and regulations) (Baker & Nelson, 2005), even though these resources are "nonstandard resources" or "discarded and undervalued resources". Bricolage is considered to be the re-construction and re-use of under-utilized resources to produce new meaning, purpose, and value (Salunke et al., 2013). The novel combination of "*nonstandard resources*" can sometimes "*reach brilliant unforeseen results*" (Lévi-Strauss,

1967, p. 17). Under scarcity, bricolage is thus considered as enterprises' creative behavior to solve problems, which often results in emerging innovation (Baker & Welter, 2018). The bricolage concept is widely accepted as denoting innovation in resource-constrained environments (Baker & Nelson, 2005; Baker & Welter, 2018; Cunha et al., 2014; Fisher, 2012; Senyard et al., 2014; Welter & Xheneti, 2013; Witell et al., 2017).

Bricolage is a recent concept, but it is an innovation method for numerous types of resource-poor enterprises. It has already demonstrated empirically positive consequences for enterprises' growth (Baker et al., 2003), performance (Senyard et al., 2009), innovation (Baker & Nelson, 2005; Senyard et al., 2014), etc. More details on the consequence of bricolage for innovation under a resource-constrained environment have been extensively explored (e.g. An, Zhang, et al., 2018; An, Zhao, et al., 2018; Garud & Karnøe, 2003; Halme et al., 2012; Linna, 2013; Senyard et al., 2014; Stenholm & Renko, 2016). Regarding the origin of bricolage, most have emphasized only external factors, such as resource-constrained environments (e.g. Baker & Nelson, 2005; Desa & Basu 2013; Fisher, 2012; Shen, 2018; Welter & Xheneti, 2013), and individual-level (managerial) factors (e.g. An, Zhang, et al., 2018; Shen, 2018; Stenholm & Renko, 2016). More precisely, scarcity appears to be a trigger for the bricolage behavior of entrepreneurs in various contexts (Baker et al., 2003; Senyard et al., 2014; Garud & Karnøe, 2003; Linna, 2013). Some studies suggest that the fundamental influence of scarcity is to stimulate enterprises to search for new opportunities, manage with the resources at hand, and seek a variety of novel resource recombinations (Baker & Nelson, 2005). Further, internal factors (e.g. internal firm capabilities) related to bricolage's emergence in resource-constrained environments may be associated with internal managerial discretion (e.g. Barney et al., 2001; Pitelis, 2007). Baker and Nelson (2005) suggested that enterprises may differ systematically in their ability to engage in bricolage and proposed extensively examining other bricolage antecedents (internal firm capabilities) rather than only emphasizing the trigger role of a poor environment for bricolage. This gap in bricolage predictors limits our understanding of why certain enterprises adopt bricolage and others do not (An, Zhang, et al., 2018; Shen, 2018). In this chapter, we thus provide a summary about the emergence, determinants, and importance of bricolage for the innovation ecosystem and then for the emergence of a new socio-economic paradigm: the circular economy.

The emergence of bricolage: An innovation pathway of resource-limited enterprises

Definition of bricolage

French anthropologist Claude Lévi-Strauss (1967) introduced the concept of bricolage and bricoleurs, described as those who solve resource problems by exclusively relying on "*whatever is at hand*". Baker and Nelson (2005) expanded upon Lévi-Strauss's ideas and offer the concept of entrepreneurial bricolage as a critical explanation for the innovativeness pathway for resource-constrained enterprises. Bricolage is a process of "*making do by applying combinations of the resources at hand to new problems and opportunities*" (Baker & Nelson, 2005, p. 333) whereby the enterprises are required to have an improvisation ability (Baker & Nelson, 2005; George et al., 2012; Halme et al., 2012) in mobilizing and combining existing resources in a novel way to compensate their missing resources (Rosenzweig et al., 2016). In other words, this process has been characterized as "*a refusal to accept limitations by combining and using abandoned or lower-quality resources in an unorthodox way*" (Rönkkö et al., 2014, p. 44). Innovative outputs obtained due to bricolage behavior might be pre-planned (Baker et al., 2003) or unforeseen because, in both cases, the improvisation through a novel combination of "*non-standard resources*" can create a "*brilliant unforeseen result*" (Lévi-Strauss, 1967). Bricolage, therefore, not only creates new from old but it also generates "*something from nothing*" or "*doing more with less*" (Baker & Nelson, 2005). Various social science research areas, including innovation management (Garud & Karnøe, 2003), entrepreneurship studies (Baker et al., 2003), and management and organization studies (Duymedjian & Rüling, 2010; Perkmann & Spicer, 2014), have analyzed the paradigm of bricolage behavior.

A literature review study by Clough et al. (2019) indicates that bricolage is predominantly employed as a resource mobilization strategy and as a response to resource scarcity setting. It further shows that entrepreneurs use bricolage creatively as a form of innovation in resource-constrained environments by employing existing resources along with mobilizing traditional factual knowledge (Baker & Nelson, 2005). Bricolage, thus, is referred to as a form of resource transfer that requires entrepreneurs to be better at realizing the "hidden" potential of a certain resource at hand (Clough et al., 2019). Therefore, instead of following conventional resource mobilization strategy, entrepreneurs practicing bricolage could engage in non-conventional, informal, or even cost-free resource mobilization strategy to achieve "good-enough" solutions (Fisher, 2012). Synthesized by Baker and Nelson (2005) from various literatures, the concept of bricolage is a constraint-shattering mechanism which includes: "resources at hand"; "recombination of resources for new purposes"; "making do".

First, the "resources at hand" of entrepreneurs are very diversified, they vary from "*existing organizational mechanisms, forms and "junk routines"*" to "*social myths and fragments of myths*", ""*models, analogies, conventions, concepts" of existing institutional principles*", "*available materials "such as wood and lorry gears," other "modest resources" and miscellaneous "embedded" individuals*", "*existing social network contacts*", "*constitutional and legal fragments*", and "*previously learned skills and coping mechanisms*", etc. (Baker & Nelson, 2005, p. 333). In summary, Baker and Nelson (2005) concluded that "resources at hand" could be cheap or free and could be those that others judge to be useless or substandard resources. For instance, to successfully produce a wind turbine, Danish engineers choose to actively source and use or reuse materials that can be obtained from scrap dealers rather than purchasing or making newly manufactured wind turbine components like their American counterparts (Garud & Karnoe, 2003).

Second, a "recombination of resources for new purposes" emphasizes the enterprises' ability to "create something from nothing" through exploiting, combining, and reusing all physical, social, or institutional inputs that others view as useless in a way that is more novel than its original purpose in order to give new meaning and new value to such resources (Salunke et al., 2013). For instance, the example of the wind turbine competition of Garud and Karnoe (2003) described the way of combining and reusing existing resources of Danish enterprises to solve the problem of scarcity and exploit new opportunities in order to successfully produce a wind turbine. The recombination of resources for new purposes sometimes serves as a mechanism to promote the emergence of innovations from existing resources (Baker & Nelson, 2005).

Third, the main principle of bricoleurs is "*always make do with 'whatever at hand'*" (Lévi-Strauss, 1967, p. 17). Thus, "*making do implies a bias toward action and active engagement with problems or opportunities rather than lingering over questions of whether a workable outcome can be created from what is at hand*" (Baker & Nelson, 2005, p. 334). Even though it is a "making do" process, the outcomes of bricolage are not always highly imperfect solutions but, in some cases, "*brilliant unforeseen results*" (Lévi-Strauss, 1967, p. 17). Further, making do should start with behavior of a "*refusal to enact limitations*" (Baker & Nelson, 2005, p. 334). Consistently, Baker and Nelson (2005) observed a sample of small enterprises and found a similar tendency of such resource-constrained enterprises, which is known to be "*to disregard the limitations of commonly accepted definitions of material inputs, practices, and definitions and standards, insisting instead on trying out solutions, observing, and dealing with the results*" (p. 334).

Baker and Nelson (2005) also suggest that in resource-constrained contexts, bricolage stimulates innovation in two ways. While resource constraints may discourage enterprises from trying new approaches, bricoleur firms are willing to experiment to tackle innovation challenges. Furthermore, entrepreneurs practicing bricolage tend to realize the potential value of resources that other enterprises might consider worthless. This is particularly useful when doing business in resource-constrained environments. Due to the main characteristics of bricolage as discussed above, an extensive literature indicates the importance of entrepreneurial bricolage in pursuing opportunities under resource-constrained contexts (An, Zhao, et al., 2018; Witell et al., 2017). From a resource-constrained perspective, prior studies also show that bricolage enables the emergence of frugal innovation (Ernst et al., 2015), especially in emerging markets (Santos et al., 2022; Sharmelly & Ray, 2018). The rationale is that frugal innovation focuses on offering value at an affordable cost and practicing bricolage allows the enterprises to reduce costs by employing existing resources, raw materials, and tools in new applications or unconventional processes for product development (Cunha et al., 2014; Ernst et al., 2015); emphasizing the reuse and recycling of by-products (Iqbal et al., 2021); devising low-cost, value-added products, and services for customers through improvisation and an experimental learning process in enterprises with higher entrepreneurial bricolage (Cai et al., 2019)

Given this approach, it is not coincidental that authors have considered bricolage to be a relevant perspective to study innovation in the resource-constrained environment of developing countries. Those countries are replete with examples of resourceful innovation: relying on combinations of existing devices, inventing new uses and, sometimes, creating new markets. The following box provides various examples of bricolage in developing countries, including Africa (in Box 1) and Asia (e.g. Vietnam in Box 2).

Box 1: Bricolage in Africa

It's been the dream of sci-fi enthusiasts and inventors for decades, but has this Nigerian man created a flying jet car that can dodge traffic? Kehinde Durojaiye, or "Kenny Jet", is attempting to build an aero-amphibious jet car. He's driven it on sea and land. Now it's only the air that he has left to conquer.

(Source CNN: https://edition.cnn.com/2017/11/16/africa/gallery/africa-innovations-that-could-change-the-world/index.html)

The Hippo Water Roller, known previously as the Aqua Roller and renamed in 1993 to give it a more "African" flavor, was invented in 1991 by two South Africans, Pettie Petzer and Johan Jonker. It meets a pressing social need. Women in rural areas often carry water for long distances, balancing buckets on their heads. This is not only exhausting and uncomfortable but can also lead to neck injuries. The tough plastic drum, which won a SABS Design for Development Award in 1992, rolls along easily with a full load of 90 litres of water and does not need to be lifted and carried.

(Source: https://showme.co.za/lifestyle/great-south-african-inventions-part-2/)

Box 2: Bricolage in Vietnam

The invention of a homemade air-cooler, for example as below, is a prominent example of the bricolage process in a developing country – Vietnam. Applying the three-component framework by Baker and Nelson (2005), Figures 1 and 2 provide a visual display of the bricolage process, more particularly the use of resources at hand. It shows how this equipment is created from three main things: a common fan, cold water/ice in bottles, and a box.

Figure 1: '*Resource at hand*' of a homemade air-cooler

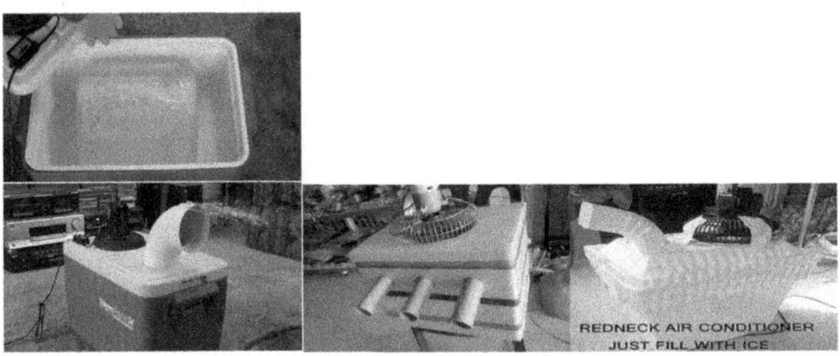

Figure 2: '*Recombining resources at hand for a new purpose*' of a homemade air-cooler

Obviously, those elements are much cheaper than those comprising an actual air-cooler.

Figure 3: '*Making do*' to create 'good-enough' outputs

These elements exist independently and are combined on purpose to fulfil a different function than initially intended. Finally, this air-cooler has an undoubtedly lower performance than common modern industrial air-coolers, as shown in Figure 3.

Consequences of bricolage

Bricolage's consequences have been extensively studied (e.g. Baker & Nelson, 2005; Di Domenico et al., 2010; Garud & Karnøe, 2003; Halme et al., 2012; Linna, 2013; Senyard et al., 2014; Stenholm & Renko, 2016), and most prior studies indicated that the bricolage behaviors of enterprises result in positive effects on innovation (Senyard et al., 2014), the enterprises' performance (Senyard et al., 2009), and growth (Baker et al., 2003). More precisely, Senyard et al.'s (2014) quantitative study on an efficacy measurement of entrepreneurial bricolage based on 658 new and typically small and resource-constrained enterprises in Australia found a positive link between bricolage and entrepreneurial innovativeness in terms of a novel product/process and marketing methods. In another resource-constrained context, the quantitative study of Gundry et al. (2011) on 113 social entrepreneurs found that social innovation could depend on the extent to which social entrepreneurs can engage in entrepreneurial bricolage by combining and employing resources at hand in useful and creative ways. Di Domenico et al. (2010), in the context of social enterprises, extended a bricolage concept and proposed the definition of social bricolage. Bricolage is essential for the sustainability and performance of social ventures (Desa & Basu 2013; Di Domenico et al., 2010; Bacq et al. 2015). Moreover, Salunke et al. (2013) showed that bricolage positively affects supportive service innovation. In recent times, bricolage is found to be an antecedent of frugal innovation in a resource-constrained environment (Ernst et al., 2015; Cai et al., 2019). In summary, these studies provide empirical evidence that enterprises can attain innovation outputs due to bricolage behavior.

In innovation literature, bricolage behavior has thus been presented as a coping mechanism (Johannisson & Olaison, 2007) against scarcity and, in some instances, as unintentionally creating innovation outcomes. In spite of the positive "image" of bricolage in the innovation process of resource-poor enterprises, the outcomes of this problem-solving process are very different. For instance, some bricoleur companies have reported better results than other well-resourced counterparts (Gibbert et al., 2007; Senyard et al., 2014) whereas "good-enough" solutions (Berchicci & Hulsink, 2006) or lower or inferior quality outcomes (Garud & Karnoe, 2003) emerged due to bricolage behavior in certain enterprises. Innovativeness owing to bricolage behavior also varies greatly from product innovation (Cunha et al., 2014), technology innovation (Gurca & Ravishankar, 2016), service innovation (Witell et al., 2017) or market-based innovation (Linna, 2013) to public service innovation (Fuglsang, 2010), etc. Even so, bricolage is also explored as an approach to new product development (Senyard et al., 2014; Wu et al., 2017) but innovation through bricolage is more likely to be incremental and minor (Nelson et al., 2014) rather than a radical innovation. Undeniably, "*bricolage is usually associated with second best solutions, maladaption, imperfection, inefficiency, incompleteness, slowness*" and "*the outcomes of it are hybrid, imperfect, transient artifacts.*" (Lanzara, 1999, p. 347).

Extensive literature on bricolage currently presents numerous examples of bricolage that drives innovation toward environmental sustainability and frugality. For example, Musona et al. (2020) show that bricoleur-entrepreneurs combine waste and other resources at hand to generate new green products and services such as the conversion of biomass waste into briquettes as an alternative green energy solution. Vilchez and de la Hiz (2018) show the example of BASF – a German chemical company – who used the by-products of one plant as an input to another to reduce resource consumption, logistics costs, hazardous gas emissions, and to strengthen synergies between plants. Further, an example of frugal innovation that has emerged from bricolage in India is presented by Dhavale (2013): Due to the poor infrastructure of public transport and the popularity of a simple means of transport – bicycles – in India, Nokia has introduced a phone charger for the Indian market, whose energy is generated through pedal power. In addition, a Chinese fiberglass manufacturer improvises and bricolages to find a new value of fiber waste and precipitation sludge and then decides to recombine fiber waste with new raw materials to create fiberglass, as well as by mixing precipitated sludge with coal to obtain new fuels (Wu & Liu, 2022). Due to bricolage, they were successful in recycling both fiber waste and precipitated sludge and reducing the use of raw materials. Similarly, the bricolage approach enables the minimizing of costs to achieve frugal innovation in the case of developing Hyundai Eon for Indian markets. Hyundai India significantly reduced manufacturing cost and resource consumption by eliminating non-essential waste through re-engineering numerous core product development processes, reusing common raw materials, and reducing process rejections (Sharmelly & Ray, 2018).

Prerequisites of bricolage

a. Resource-constrained environment

Scarcity represents a double-edge sword, which simultaneously triggers and hinders enterprise performance (Bradley et al., 2011). While more resources are often required to fuel organization innovation (Levinthal & March, 1981), this does not mean that all enterprises with limited resources face problems in becoming innovators. Resource constraints might be a trigger for creative searching processes and entrepreneurial behaviors to be termed innovativeness (Bradley et al., 2011). Recent research on entrepreneurship has paid more attention to which patterns of behavior allow some resource-constrained enterprises to innovate.

Under the scarcity context, a "*refusal to be constrained by limitation*" (Baker & Nelson, 2005) and a social mindset combined with "resourcefulness" should be the starting point of bricolage behavior (Linna, 2013). A recent stream of research on bricolage (Baker et al., 2003; Garud & Karnøe, 2003) focused on identifying patterns of business behavior and processes that may enable resource-constrained enterprises to overcome scarcity and to innovate (*e.g.* Baker & Nelson, 2005; Katila & Shane, 2005; Senyard et al., 2014; Cunha et al., 2014; Gurca & Ravishankar, 2015). The fundamental influence of scarcity is to stimulate enterprises to search for new opportunities, manage with resources at hand, and seek a variety of novel resource recombinations (Baker & Nelson, 2005). Likewise, Penrose's (1959) growth theory proposes that resource slack creates an opportunity for enterprise growth by recombining existing resources.

Enterprises with financial constraints often embrace risk and raise their acceptance of experimentation because limited financial resources prevent them from acquiring more external resources (Keupp & Gassmann, 2013). Being forced to accept their limited resources (Hoegl et al., 2008), these enterprises are more likely to increase efficient resource allocation (Mosakowski, 2002) and seek novel resource recombinations (Bradley et al., 2011; George, 2005). From an RBV perspective, enterprises may differ in identifying slack, discarded, or undervalued resource potential and knowing how to creatively combine them to create value (Desa & Basu, 2013; Garud & Karnøe, 2003). Enterprises that effectively combine such resources might create heterogeneous value and thus engage in bricolage (Desa & Basu, 2013). In that regard, bricolage has been extensively discussed as a constraint-shattering approach of entrepreneurs when faced with resource-poor contexts (Baker & Nelson, 2005; Garud & Karnøe, 2003; Johannisson & Olaison, 2007). Bricolage behavior allows "*resource-constrained firms to exploit their potential for agility and freedom of action by making creative use of their limited resources*" (Senyard et al., 2014, p. 213).

Existing literature on bricolage has also developed valuable insights on the trigger role of the scarcity condition in driving bricolage. For instance, Desa and Basu (2013) investigated the environment-level antecedents of bricolage using a sample of 202 ventures operating in 42 countries and found that such ventures were likely to adopt a greater degree of bricolage in environments of very low and very high resource munificence. Similarly, Fisher's (2012) qualitative case studies based on six consumer internet ventures also concluded that the degree of resource slack might affect bricolage. Further, one of the prominent examples of "doing more with less" by engaging in bricolage behavior is the emergence of wind turbines in Denmark. Garud and Karnøe (2003) described and compared wind turbine emergence in Denmark and the United States. They found that financially constrained actors in Denmark created a viable wind turbine by searching for possible materials from scrap dealers and labelled it as bricolage. Conversely, the US actors' breakthrough approach used considerable intellectual and financial resources to build their wind turbines, but they failed in their competition with Denmark.

b. Enterprises' capabilities: Absorptive capacity and networking

Beyond the traditional trigger – a penurious environment – bricolage seems to be more sensitive to internal managerial discretion than external penurious environments (Pitelis, 2007). For instance, Baker and Nelson (2005) observed the variation in the frequency and scope of bricolage among 29 resource-constrained mainly small enterprises. They noticed that "*firms varied significantly in their capacity to make use of inputs that were at hand*" (p. 336). Further, "*bricolage behavior is fundamentally different when it comes to sourcing and applying resources*" (Baker & Welter, 2018, p. 151). Desa and Basu's (2013) arguments using the RBV implied that bricolaging ventures might recognize potential uses of resources that are different from their intended uses and unconventionally combine these resources to create value. This variation is partly derived from the difference in the capabilities of developing and renewing specific resources and assets gathered into organizational routines.

Based on the RBV perspective to identify when enterprises may engage in bricolage, Desa and Basu (2013) argued that when enterprises cannot afford resource acquisition, they may structure resources (e.g. discarded or undervalued resources considered useless) and creatively bundle resources (effectively unconventionally recombining resources). Thus, they may create differential value. However, the abilities of enterprises in recognizing potential resource uses and recombining existing resources (Desa & Basu, 2013) may vary widely due to an enterprise's dynamic capabilities to develop and renew resources and assets (Teece et al., 1997). Certain capabilities such as absorptive capacity and social networking are central factors driving the enterprise's ability to engage in the bricolage approach under a resource-constrained environment.

Absorptive capacity is the enterprise's ability "*to recognize the value of new information, assimilate it, and apply it*" (Cohen & Lévinthal, 1990, p. 128). Absorptive capacity is a firm-level measure that captures the firm's ability to recognize and exploit external knowledge (Zahra & George, 2002). Enterprises having a higher absorptive capacity tend to be better at assimilating both tacit knowledge and explicit knowledge (Scaringella & Burtschell, 2017). Regarding SMEs, Laperche and Liu (2013) argued that absorptive capacity supports SMEs accumulating and building up their knowledge capital, which allows enterprises to better recognize resources' value and combine these to create value. This ability is expected to raise an enterprise's probability of solving problems by relying exclusively on the (re)combination of all resources at hand (see Baker & Nelson, 2005). Along with absorptive capacity, bricolage also necessitates networking with external partners to mobilize external resources (Perry et al., 2012). Through social networking, external partnerships support enterprises to obtain more access to external resources (Liu & Laperche, 2015). Integrated with enterprises' at-hand resources, those external resources give them access to more novel resource combinations to better cope with resource constraints (Witell et al., 2017). Regarding SMEs, they often rely on external relationships (Fréchet & Goy, 2017) and networks to build up their knowledge capital (Laperche & Liu, 2013; Uzunidis & Boutillier, 2012) because an extensive social network enables access to and transfers of much-needed knowledge/technologies and external resources among its members in an active manner (Inkpen & Tsang, 2005), especially new or missing resources which enterprises cannot acquire or internally develop. As a consequence, there is no doubt that the knowledge and information transferred through the social networks provide opportunities to enlarge a firm's knowledge base or to build connections with external bundles of resources. Furthermore, "*social links, through trust, empathy, emotional relationships, are all qualities that enable knowledge to be acquired more quickly and to promote innovation*" (Casadella & Uzunidis, 2017, p. 142). This therefore clarifies the importance of networking for raising bricolage capabilities during the process of generating, adopting, and disseminating innovation in the innovation ecosystems.

Bricolage capabilities – The integration of an enterprise's capabilities in terms of "making do", improvising, and networking

Bricolage capabilities were proposed by Witell et al. (2017) in a study about the bricolage perspective on service innovation, which comprised four specific capabilities: (1) addressing resource scarcity actively, (2) making do with what is available, (3) improvising when recombining resources, and (4) networking with external partners. It should be noted that the ability to address resource scarcity actively and to "make do" with all resources at hand are the most basic capabilities linked directly with the nature of bricolage behavior. Still, improvisation is able to play the role of bridging to close the gap produced by the scarcity condition by actively using the existing resources at hand to compensate for missing resources (Rosenzweig et al., 2016). At the same time, the ability to network is a necessary condition to support the other bricolage capabilities above. This nuance about bricolage capabilities highlights the activating role of bricolage in the emergence of innovation in an ecosystem of resource-limited enterprises.

a. Making do

The first construct of bricolage (as defined by Lévi-Strauss (1967)) – making do – is referred to as a process in which bricoleurs can use and recombine resources in novel ways to meet challenges and to respond to opportunities. In general, the "making do" process involves three main approaches to acquire and construct resources, including (1) "*creating something from nothing*" (such as creating a new market/product/service that did not exist before); (2) using resources available cheaply or for free for new purposes that were not originally pre-intended; and (3) using resources that other enterprises fail to recognize or use adequately (Baker & Nelson, 2005).

Di Domenico et al. (2010) provided examples of social enterprises for each of the above aspects of "making do". For the first aspect of making do – "*creating something from nothing*" – they showed the success of a social enterprise that is part of a small community that was poor, with a lack of amenities and facilities, high unemployment, and a high crime level. This enterprise was initially founded with the purpose of training skills and raising employment opportunities for local people and improving safety on the properties by making available social amenities (such as public housing and a community guardian network). The achievement of such an enterprise led to rapid business growth and created an even larger demand for services that were then offered over a wider geographical area. For the second aspect of making do – "*using resources available cheaply or for free towards new purposes*"- they showed the evidence of another social enterprise which recycles and refurbishes unused computers for community use. Starting only from a local community initiative aimed at improving employment skills through computer literacy, the success of such an enterprise demonstrated that the creation of social value is not predetermined but is mainly shaped by existing resources at hand. For the third aspect of making do – "*using resources that other firms fail to recognize or use adequately*" – they analyzed the example of a sustainable wind energy project that was established from thinking (in a pub-type conversation) that the natural environment is an asset, particularly wind.

However, to be able to clarify "making do", the fieldwork of Baker and Nelson (2005) observed "*a conscious and frequently wilful tendency for firms in our sample to disregard the limitations of commonly accepted definitions of material inputs, practices, and definitions and standards, insisting instead on trying out solutions, observing, and dealing with the results*" (p. 334). The analysis of Baker and Nelson (2005) thus extends beyond the conceptualizations of "*making do*" to include a "*refusal to enact limitations*" whereby "*actors consciously and consistently tested conventional limitations*" (p. 335). Further, Baker and Nelson (2005) highlighted an entrepreneurial refusal to be constrained by scarcity conditions induced by institutional or culture settings and proposed that "*making do includes a bias for testing received limitations*" (p. 335). Similarly, "making do" has also been characterized as "*a refusal to accept limitations by combining and using abandoned or lower-quality resources in an unorthodox way*" (Rönkkö et al., 2014, p. 44). In more detail, the work of Di Domenico et al. (2010) on social enterprises also confirmed a refusal to enact limitations by showing a strategic response to limitations of resources which include: "*trying out solutions to counteract limitations imposed by institutional and political settings and subverting the limitations imposed by available resource environments on their ability to create social value*" (p. 694).

Thus, in the entrepreneurship literature on bricolage, bricoleurs are defined as those who can "make do" with cheap and free resources that others regard as worthless (Baker & Nelson, 2005). To overcome resource constraints and even to possess innovativeness, enterprises should engage in a stopgap tactic of "making do" with resources and skills available perhaps in an unconventional way rather than doing nothing (Le, 2018). The "making do" capability, at least, might cope with new challenges and opportunities with all available resources, although it may create "good-enough" solutions. In the resource-poor environment of developing countries, "making do" with all the cheap and free resources at hand, with reuse and recombination, combining resources for new purposes (Linna, 2013), are known as a leveraging step for the emergence of such "good enough" solutions as products/services that meet the specific requirements of local markets. For example, Cai et al. (2019) has indicated that enterprises with a high bricolage capacity have the potential to merge existing technologies with locally available resources to create "good-enough products" for low-income consumers in emerging markets. Bricolage, therefore, facilitates affordable and valued-added innovations or frugal innovation for BOP consumers. Beyond this, Christensen et al. (2013) argued that in the first period, "good-enough" solutions may only attract the attention of less demanding customers but during the time when such solutions are well-developed and mature, they can disrupt current markets thanks to the emergence of a new value constellation.

b. Improvising

Improvisation could be linked to flexible and creative thinking and working to counteract resource limitations (Miner et al., 2001). The work of Di Domenico et al. (2010) provided evidence that improvisation is necessary and considered to be a "toolkit" of social entrepreneurs to respond to the constraints of limited resources, as well as to potential opportunities. Even so, social entrepreneurs have confirmed that they will be willing to improvise to figure out solutions to social problems, despite the fact that they may be exposed to a higher risk of failure than other alternative ways that are "less community-driven strategies". Considering the role of improvisation in supporting the emergence of bricolage for service innovation, Witell et al. (2017) also showed that an enterprise's capabilities in actively addressing resource constraints and improvising can result in improving innovation outcomes. For instance, the ability to improvise in terms of intuition, imagination, and creativity leads to novel solutions that are sometimes highly appreciated by customers (Duymedjian & Rüling, 2010).

In general, improvisation is referred to as an organizational tactic to mobilize and combine resources in a new way (Weick, 1993). Theoretically, improvisation often emerges when the design and execution of a novel action occur at the same time (Miner et al., 2001) and there is no, or only a very small "room" to identify in advance the resources/materials necessary for an activity and how to obtain them (Janssen et al., 2018). For that reason, the occurrence of improvisational activity seems to imply the emergence of bricolage (Baker et al., 2003). Improvisation often emerged due to intuition, creativity, and problem-solving but, at first, also requires enterprises to accumulate knowledge and experience to a certain extent (Duymedjian & Rüling, 2010). Further, trial-and-error experimentations emerged during the improvisation, allowing enterprises to progressively accumulate knowledge and skills by learning from the failures or successes of improvised experiments (Duymedjian & Rüling, 2010). In turn, the more prior knowledge and experiences the enterprises accumulated during the operating process, the more resources and capabilities they possess to boost their "making do" capacity.

According to the resource-based view, entrepreneurs tend to mobilize, assess, and allocate resources when they need resources but these activities may not be relevant in a context where resources are scarce or entrepreneurs are not able to have their expected resources. Instead, entrepreneurs may engage in bricolage behaviors in such cases through experimenting and improvising to create unforeseen solutions to unexpected challenges (Kerr et al., 2014). A typical example is the case of the Apollo 13 mission: when the prior plan was forced to be modified, the astronauts of Apollo 13 relied on bricolage in order to figure out solutions from unplanned resources such as clothing, duct tape, and unused pages of instruction manuals (Rerup, 2001)

c. Networking

Prior works suggest that bricolage requires the ability to network through mobilizing resources and collaborating with external partners in order to better confront resource constraints (Perry et al., 2012). This is because contact with external partners supports enterprises in gaining access to resources generated by or transferred from these partners, which can be combined with internal existing resources to cope with new challenges or to identify and exploit new opportunities through innovation (Subramaniam & Youndt, 2005). In the case of small enterprises or SMEs, often resource constrained, networking could allow SMEs to enrich resources "at hand" for the emergence of bricolage. Similarly, in the context of developing countries where firms often do business in a resource-constrained setting, firms tend to rely heavily on relationship-based strategies to achieve their business goals (Peng & Luo, 2000; Park & Luo, 2001). Social relationships are therefore an effective way for enterprises to access services, knowledge, and information. An extensive social network is considered in such countries as a valuable asset that allows enterprises to obtain access to knowledge/technology and resources that have been externally developed by other enterprises in their network (Nichter & Goldmark, 2009). Prior studies highlighted the importance of a social network as the bedrock of innovativeness (Zheng, 2010). The literature points out the critical roles of a social network for business, such as facilitating the creation of new knowledge within organizations (Tsai, 2001), encouraging informal communications, and enhancing the knowledge exchanged among members within social networks (Morris & Lancaster, 2005). The process of distributing knowledge and up-to-date information among members of a social network in such a way would help enterprises to accumulate a diverse knowledge base that can be integrated with prior knowledge in a manner that enables them to draw novel associations and linkages that develop new ideas and innovations (Baker et al., 2016). These novel ways of combining and applying the resources available, therefore, are known as a part of the bricolage process that can result in the emergence of innovation outputs under resource-constrained contexts. There is also no doubt that in an innovation network, the collaboration modalities between actors in the network and the communication channels that are likely to facilitate the exchange and flow of knowledge among stakeholders in the network play an important role in the process of generating and disseminating innovation (Laperche, 2017). As a result, bricoleur-firms engaging in a network are more likely to become bricoleur-innovators together due to the effects of social networks above.

In addition, the extant literature on entrepreneurial bricolage also addressed two categories of bricolage: individual and collective bricolage. Regarding the concept of collective bricolage, Garud and Karnoe (2003) applied a network-based collective bricolage approach in studying the development of the Danish wind turbine industry. More precisely, they described the joint contribution of all stakeholders in a network, including manufacturers, users, regulators, and evaluators, in order to generate a profitable technology path for the wind turbine industry. According to Baker and Nelson (2005), bricolage can be harmful if applied only to the top administrative level of organization, but it can be beneficial if implemented widely among many interested parties (such as collective bricolage). Research about the Taiwanese plastic waste industry by Wu et al. (2021) also showed the role of a network-based collective bricolage in facilitating the transformation from waste materials into valuable assets and thus to support the formation of a circular economy. Indeed, this entrepreneurial process of collective bricolage in Taiwan has attracted new ventures and incumbents to join the waste recycling sector. This case of Taiwanese SMEs can be seen as further evidence for the dual importance of networking and collective bricolage and subsequently for the development of an innovation ecosystem of resource-constrained enterprises.

Conclusion

As environmental issues emerge strongly, due to the linear pattern of production and consumption, the concept of the circular economy is gaining in popularity all over the world. The circular economy promotes a sustainable way of life where resources are used more efficiently and retained in the economy for as long as possible. This is the main principle of the circular economy as well as of industrial ecology strategies (Boldrini, 2018; Gallaud & Laperche, 2016). Circular economy conceptualizations and models are mainly based on developed country contexts (Kirchherr & van Santen, 2019). However, in resource-constrained settings such as resource-constrained firms (e.g. small firms, young firms, social ventures, etc.) and the low-income context of developing markets, the scarcity of resources on a daily basis motivates individuals and businesses to undertake resource-conserving innovative activities in order to retain the value of materials and goods in circulation. Among emerged concepts, bricolage is a potential candidate that results from scarcity and can result in innovation.

Based on the philosophy of "necessity is the mother of invention", the literature on innovation has developed a view under which scarcity does not exclusively play a hampering role in innovation but may also sometimes be the source of innovative activities. For the last few years, a series of studies has offered explanations of the seeming paradox of innovation under resource-constrained settings. This literature, indeed, identifies a resource-scarce environment as a main trigger of new innovation strategies. This idea is explicitly derived from the concept of bricolage first mentioned by Lévi-Strauss (1967). 'Bricolage' is often described as making do with "*whatever is at hand*" (Lévi-Strauss, 1967, p. 17). Applying his insight at the firm level, in the last few years, this metaphor of bricolage has gained legitimacy among scholars to enlighten strategy-making in resource-poor environments (e.g. Baker & Nelson, 2005; Senyard et al., 2014).

Recent research shows that bricolage allows enterprises to innovate with limited resources at hand; thus, bricolage behavior is crucial for resource-constrained enterprises including small enterprises, new enterprises, social ventures, developing country enterprises, etc. Despite the importance of bricolage for the innovation process, enterprises are not always at the same bricolage level and their different bricolage ability derives from the absorptive capacity and social network (Le, 2018).

This chapter thus contributes to a better understanding of a constraint-shattering mechanism – bricolage – mainly induced by a resource-constrained environment. Bricolage enables enterprises to exploit new opportunities or tackle challenges by recombining and re-using the resources at hand in the presence of resource scarcity (Baker & Nelson, 2005; Senyard et al., 2014). Therefore, social ventures rely on bricolage because they seek to provide innovative solutions for social needs by making do with, or creating, anything possible using any resources at hand (Desa & Basu 2013; Di Domenico et al., 2010; Molecke & Pinkse, 2017). This constraint-shattering approach is mainly aimed at overcoming scarcity and introduced affordable and good-enough products for the scarcity environment. However, on the other hand, it has also allowed the reduction of resource and raw materials consumption, as well as waste and dangerous emissions. In doing so, bricolage and entrepreneurial bricolage play a trigger role in driving innovation toward frugality and sustainability, especially in resource-constrained settings. Further, this process of pursuing frugal innovation also requires bricoleur-enterprises to build collaborations and partnerships with various stakeholders (Sharmelly & Ray, 2018) and, therefore, establish a collaborative ecosystem, also known as an innovation ecosystem, which includes stakeholders such as suppliers, customers, competitors, financial, social and technology institutions, and regulatory agencies (Iansiti & Levien, 2004; Laperche, 2017).

References

Afutu-Kotey, R. L., & Gough, K. V. (2022). Bricolage and informal businesses: Young entrepreneurs in the mobile telephony sector in Accra, Ghana. *Futures*, *135*, 102487.

Agarwal, N., & Brem, A. (2017). Frugal innovation-past, present, and future. *IEEE Engineering Management Review*, *45*(3), 37–41.

Alexander, S., & Yacoumis, P. (2018). Degrowth, energy descent, and 'low-tech' living: Potential pathways for increased resilience in times of crisis. *Journal of Cleaner Production*, *197*, 1840–1848.

An, W., Zhang, J., You, C., & Guo, Z. (2018). Entrepreneur's creativity and firm-level innovation performance: Bricolage as a mediator. *Technology Analysis & Strategic Management*, *30*(7), 838–851.

An, W., Zhao, X., Cao, Z., Zhang, J., & Liu, H. (2018). How bricolage drives corporate entrepreneurship: The roles of opportunity identification and learning orientation. *Journal of Product Innovation Management, 35*(1), 49–65.

Bacq, S., Ofstein, L. F., Kickul, J. R., & Gundry, L. K. (2015). Bricolage in social entrepreneurship: How creative resource mobilization fosters greater social impact. *The International Journal of Entrepreneurship and Innovation, 16*(4), 283–289.

Baker, T., & Nelson, R. E. (2005). Creating something from nothing: Resource construction through entrepreneurial bricolage. *Administrative Science Quarterly, 50*(3), 329–366.

Baker, T., & Welter, F. (2018). Contextual entrepreneurship: An interdisciplinary perspective. *Foundations and Trends® in Entrepreneurship, 14*(4), 357–426.

Baker, T., Miner, A. S., & Eesley, D. T. (2003). Improvising firms: Bricolage, account giving and improvisational competencies in the founding process. *Research Policy, 32*(2), 255–276.

Baker, W. E., Grinstein, A., & Harmancioglu, N. (2016). Whose innovation performance benefits more from external networks: Entrepreneurial or conservative firms?. *Journal of Product Innovation Management, 33*(1), 104–120.

Barney, J., Wright, M., & Ketchen, D. J., Jr. (2001). The resource-based view of the firm: Ten years after 1991. *Journal of Management, 27*(6), 625–641.

Berchicci, L., & Hulsink, W. (2006). Of bikes and men: Innovation patterns and strategic entrepreneurship in the human-powered vehicle sector. *Strategic Entrepreneurship: The Role of Networking, Vrije Universiteit Amsterdam.*

Boldrini, J. C. (2018). The value co-creation in a collaborative project of innovation: A case of transition towards circular economy. *Innovations, 55*(1), 143–171.

Bradley, S. W., Wiklund, J., & Shepherd, D. A. (2011). Swinging a double-edged sword: The effect of slack on entrepreneurial management and growth. *Journal of Business Venturing, 26*(5), 537–554.

Cai, Q., Ying, Y., Liu, Y., & Wu, W. (2019). Innovating with limited resources: The antecedents and consequences of frugal innovation. *Sustainability, 11*(20), 5789.

Casadella, V., & Uzunidis, D. (2017). National innovation systems of the south, innovation and economic development policies: A multidimensional approach. *Journal of Innovation Economics & Management, 23*, 137–157.

Christensen, C., Raynor, M. E., & McDonald, R. (2013). *Disruptive innovation*. Brighton, MA, USA: Harvard Business Review.

Clough, D. R., Fang, T. P., Vissa, B., & Wu, A. (2019). Turning lead into gold: How do entrepreneurs mobilize resources to exploit opportunities?. *Academy of Management Annals, 13*(1), 240–271.

Cohen, W. M., & Lévinthal, D. A. (1990). Absorptive capacity: A new perspective on learning and innovation. *Administrative Science Quarterly, 35*(1), 128–152.

Cunha, M. P., Rego, A., Oliveira, P., Rosado, P., & Habib, N. (2014). Product innovation in resource-poor environments: Three research streams. *Journal of Product Innovation Management, 31*(2), 202–210.

Desa, G., & Basu, S. (2013). Optimization or bricolage? Overcoming resource constraints in global social entrepreneurship. *Strategic Entrepreneurship Journal, 7*(1), 26–49.

Dhavale, S. (2013). Connecting the masses. *Smart Innovations, 6*(2), 521.

Di Domenico, M., Haugh, H., & Tracey, P. (2010). Social bricolage: Theorizing social value creation in social enterprises. *Entrepreneurship Theory and Practice, 34*(4), 681–703.

Duymedjian, R., & Rüling, C.-C. (2010). Towards a foundation of bricolage in organization and management theory. *Organization Studies, 31*(2), 133–151.

Ernst, H., Kahle, H. N., Dubiel, A., Prabhu, J., & Subramaniam, M. (2015). The antecedents and consequences of affordable value innovations for emerging markets. *Journal of Product Innovation Management, 32*(1), 65–79.

Fisher, G. (2012). Effectuation, causation, and bricolage: A behavioral comparison of emerging theories in entrepreneurship research. *Entrepreneurship Theory and Practice, 36*(5), 1019–1051.

Fréchet, M., & Goy, H. (2017). Does strategy formalization foster innovation? Evidence from a French sample of small to medium-sized enterprises. *M@n@gement, 20*(3), 266–286.

Fuglsang, L. (2010). Bricolage and invisible innovation in public service innovation. *Journal of Innovation Economics & Management, 5*, 67–87.

Galia, F., & Legros, D. (2004). Complementarities between obstacles to innovation: Evidence from France. *Research Policy, 33*(8), 1185–1199.

Gallaud, D., & Laperche, B. (2016). Circular economy, industrial ecology and short supply chain. John Wiley & Sons.

Garud, R., & Karnøe, P. (2003). Bricolage versus breakthrough: Distributed and embedded agency in technology entrepreneurship. *Research Policy, 32*(2), 277–300.

George, G. (2005). Slack resources and the performance of privately held firms. *Academy of Management Journal, 48*(4), 661–676.

George, G., McGahan, A. M., & Prabhu, J. (2012). Innovation for inclusive growth: Towards a theoretical framework and a research agenda. *Journal of Management Studies, 49*(4), 661–683.

Giannetti, V., & Rubera, G. (2020). Innovation for and from emerging countries: A closer look at the antecedents of trickle-down and reverse innovation. *Journal of the Academy of Marketing Science, 48*(5), 987–1008.

Gibbert, M., Hoegl, M., & Valikangas, I. (2007). In praise of resource constraints. *Sloan Management Review, 48*(3), 15–17.

Gundry, L. K., Kickul, J. R., Griffiths, M. D., & Bacq, S. C. (2011). Creating social change out of nothing: The role of entrepreneurial bricolage in social entrepreneurs' catalytic innovations. *Advances in Entrepreneurship, Firm Emergence and Growth, 13*(7), 1–24.

Gurca, A., & Ravishankar, M. N. (2015). A bricolage perspective on technological innovation in emerging markets. *IEEE Transactions on Engineering Management, 63*(1), 53–66.

Halme, M., Lindeman, S., & Linna, P. (2012). Innovation for inclusive business: Intrapreneurial bricolage in multinational corporations. *Journal of Management Studies, 49*(4), 743–784.

Hoegl, M., Gibbert, M., & Mazursky, D. (2008). Financial constraints in innovation projects: When is less more? *Research Policy, 37*(8), 1382–1391.

Holt, D., & Littlewood, D. (2017). Waste livelihoods amongst the poor–Through the lens of bricolage. *Business Strategy and the Environment, 26*(2), 253–264.

Iammarino, S., Sanna-Randaccio, F., & Savona, M. (2009). The perception of obstacles to innovation. Foreign multinationals and domestic firms in Italy. *Revue d'économie industrielle*, (125), 75–104.

Iansiti, M., & Levien, R. (2004). *The keystone advantage: What the new dynamics of business ecosystems mean for strategy, innovation, and sustainability*. Harvard Business Press.

Inkpen, A. C., & Tsang, E. W. (2005). Social capital, networks, and knowledge transfer. *Academy of Management Review, 30*(1), 146–165.

Iqbal, Q., Ahmad, N. H., & Halim, H. A. (2021). Insights on entrepreneurial bricolage and frugal innovation for sustainable performance. *Business Strategy & Development, 4*(3), 237–245.

Janssen, F., Fayolle, A., & Wuilaume, A. (2018). Researching bricolage in social entrepreneurship. *Entrepreneurship & Regional Development, 30*(3–4), 450–470.

Johannisson, B., & Olaison, L. (2007). The moment of truth—Reconstructing entrepreneurship and social capital in the eye of the storm. *Review of Social Economy, 65*(1), 55–78.

Katila, R., & Shane, S. (2005). When does lack of resources make new firms innovative?. *Academy of Management Journal, 48*(5), 814–829.

Kerr, W. R., Nanda, R., & Rhodes-Kropf, M. (2014). Entrepreneurship as experimentation. *Journal of Economic Perspectives, 28*(3), 25–48.

Keupp, M. M., & Gassmann, O. (2013). Resource constraints as triggers of radical innovation: Longitudinal evidence from the manufacturing sector. *Research Policy, 42*(8), 1457–1468.

Kirchherr, J. W., & van Santen, R. (2019). Research on the circular economy: A critique of the field. *Resources, Conservation and Recycling, 151*, 104480.

Langevang, T., & Namatovu, R. (2019). Social bricolage in the aftermath of war. *Entrepreneurship & Regional Development, 31*(9–10), 785–805.

Lanzara, G. F. (1999). Between transient constructs and persistent structures: Designing systems in action. *The Journal of Strategic Information Systems, 8*(4), 331–349.

Laperche, B. (2017). *Enterprise knowledge capital*. Hoboken, NJ: John Wiley & Sons.

Laperche, B., & Liu, Z. (2013). SMEs and knowledge-capital formation in innovation networks: A review of literature. *Journal of Innovation and Entrepreneurship, 2*(1), 1–16.

Le Bas, C. (2016). The importance and relevance of frugal innovation to developed markets: Milestones towards the economics of frugal innovation. *Journal of Innovation Economics Management, 21*(3), 3–8.

Le, S. T. K. (2018). Innovation strategies in developing countries – The case of Vietnamese Small and Medium enterprises. Thèse de Doctorat, Université Toulouse 1 Capitole.

Levinthal, D., & March, J. G. (1981). A model of adaptive organizational search. *Journal of Economic Behavior & Organization, 2*(4), 307–333.

Lévi-Strauss, C. (1967). *The savage mind.* Chicago, IL: University of Chicago Press.

Linna, P. (2013). Bricolage as a means of innovating in a resource-scarce environment: A study of innovator-entrepreneurs at the Bop. *Journal of Developmental Entrepreneurship, 18*(3), 1–23.

Liu, Z., & Laperche, B. (2015). The knowledge capital of SMEs: The French paradox. *Journal of Innovation Economics Management, 2*(17), 27–48.

Mazieri, M. R., Vils, L., & de Queiroz, M. J. (2017). Frugal innovation beyond emerging countries: The key role of developed countries. *Revista Gestão & Tecnologia, 17*(4), 232–257.

Miner, A. S., Bassof, P., & Moorman, C. (2001). Organizational improvisation and learning: A field study. *Administrative Science Quarterly, 46*(2), 304–337.

Molecke, G., & Pinkse, J. (2017). Accountability for social impact: A bricolage perspective on impact measurement in social enterprises. *Journal of Business Venturing, 32*(5), 550–568.

Morris, T., & Lancaster, Z. (2005). Translating Management Ideas. *Organization Studies, 27*(2), 207–233.

Mosakowski, E. (2002). Overcoming resource disadvantages in entrepreneurial firms: When less is more. In Hitt, M. A., Ireland, R. D., Camp, S. M., & Sexton, D. L. (Eds.), *Strategic entrepreneurship: Creating a new mindset* (pp. 106–126). Oxford, UK: Blackwell.

Musona, J., Sjögrén, H., Puumalainen, K., & Syrjä, P. (2020). Bricolage in environmental entrepreneurship: How environmental innovators "make do" at the bottom of the pyramid. *Business Strategy & Development, 3*(4), 487–505.

Nelson, R. E., Stinchfield, B. T., Rodriguez-Lluesma, C., & Companys, Y. E. (2014). Levi-Strauss' types and the subjectivist-objectivist debate in entrepreneurship. *Academy of Management Proceedings*, 1, 12801.

Nichter, S., & Goldmark, L. (2009). Small firm growth in developing countries. *World Development, 37*(9), 1453–1464.

Park, S. H., & Luo, Y. (2001). Guanxi and organizational dynamics: Organizational networking in Chinese firms. *Strategic Management Journal, 22*(5), 455–477.

Peng, M. W., & Luo, Y. (2000). Managerial ties and firm performance in a transition economy: The nature of a micro-macro link. *Academy of Management Journal, 43*(3), 486–501.

Penrose, E. (1959). *The theory of the growth of the firm*. Oxford, UK: Oxford University Press.

Perkmann, M., & Spicer, A. (2014). How emerging organizations take form: The role of imprinting and values in organizational bricolage. *Organization Science, 25*(6), 1785–1806.

Perry, J. T., Chandler, G. N., & Markova, G. (2012). Entrepreneurial effectuation: A review and suggestions for future research. *Entrepreneurship Theory and Practice, 36*(4), 837–861.

Pitelis, C. N. (2007). A behavioral resource-based view of the firm: The synergy of Cyert and March (1963) and Penrose (1959). *Organization Science, 18*(3), 478–490.

Rerup, C. (2001). "Houston, we have a problem": Anticipation and improvisation as sources of organizational resilience. Snider Entrepreneurial Center, Wharton School.

Rönkkö, M., Peltonen, J., & Arenius, P. (2014). Selective or parallel? Toward measuring the domains of entrepreneurial bricolage. In *Entrepreneurial resourcefulness: Competing with constraints* (pp. 43–61). Emerald Group Publishing Limited.

Rosenzweig, S., Grinstein, A., & Ofek, E. (2016). Social network utilization and the impact of academic research in marketing. *International Journal of Research in Marketing, 33*(4), 818–839.

Salunke, S., Weerawardena, J., & McColl-Kennedy, J. R. (2013). Competing through service innovation: The role of bricolage and entrepreneurship in project-oriented firms. *Journal of Business Research, 66*(8), 1085–1097.

Santos, L. L., Borini, F. M., Oliveira, M .d. M., Rossetto, D. E., & Bernardes, R. C. (2022). Bricolage as capability for frugal innovation in emerging markets in times of crisis. *European Journal of Innovation Management, 25*(2), 413–432.

Scaringella, L., & Burtschell, F. (2017). The challenges of radical innovation in Iran: Knowledge transfer and absorptive capacity highlights—Evidence from a joint venture in the construction sector. *Technological Forecasting and Social Change, 122*(C), 151–169.

Segarra-Blasco, A., Garcia-Quevedo, J., & Teruel-Carrizosa, M. (2008). Barriers to innovation and public policy in Catalonia. *International Entrepreneurship and Management Journal, 4*(4), 431–451.

Senyard, J., Baker, T., & Davidsson, P. (2009). Entrepreneurial bricolage: Towards systematic empirical testing. *Frontiers of Entrepreneurship Research, 29*(5), 5.

Senyard, J., Baker, T., Steffens, P., & Davidsson, P. (2014). Bricolage as a path to innovativeness for resource-constrained new firms. *Journal of Product Innovation Management, 31*(2), 211–230.

Sharmelly, R., & Ray, P. K. (2018). The role of frugal innovation and collaborative ecosystems: The case of Hyundai in India. *Journal of General Management, 43*(4), 157–174.

Shen, T. (2018). *When less is more: Exploring the antecedents of entrepreneurial bricolage and its innovation implication* (Doctoral dissertation, Rutgers University-Graduate School-Newark). Retrieved from https://rucore.libraries.rutgers.edu/rutgers-lib/57388/PDF/1/

Smith, A., Fressoli, M., & Thomas, H. (2014). Grassroots innovation movements: challenges and contributions. *Journal of Cleaner Production, 63*, 114–124.

Srinivas, S., & Sutz, J. (2008). Developing countries and innovation: Searching for a new analytical approach. *Technology in Society, 30*(2), 129–140.

Stenholm, P., & Renko, M. (2016). Passionate bricoleurs and new venture survival. *Journal of Business Venturing, 31*(5), 595–611.

Subramaniam, M., & Youndt, M. A. (2005). The influence of intellectual capital on the types of innovative capabilities. *Academy of Management Journal, 48*(3), 450–463.

Teece, D. J., Pisano, G., & Shuen, A. (1997). Dynamic capabilities and strategic management. *Strategic Management Journal, 18*(7), 509–533.

Tsai, W. (2001). Knowledge transfer in intraorganizational networks: Effects of network position and absorptive capacity on business unit innovation and performance. *Academy of Management Journal, 44*(5), 996–1004.

Uzunidis, D., & Boutillier, S. (2012). Globalization of R&D and network innovation: What do we learn from the evolutionist theory?. *Journal of Innovation Economics & Management*, 10, 23–52.

Vilchez, V. F., & de la Hiz, D. I. L. (2018). Lessons on frugal eco-innovation: More with less in the European business context. In *The critical state of corporate social responsibility in Europe*. Emerald Publishing Limited.

Weick, K. E. (1993). Organizational redesign as improvisation. Organizational Change and Redesign: Ideas and Insights for Improving Performance, 346–379.

Welter, F., & Xheneti, M. (2013). Reenacting contextual boundaries–Entrepreneurial resourcefulness in challenging environments. In Katz, J. & Corbett A. (Eds.), *Entrepreneurial resourcefulness: Competing with constraints* (Vol. 15, pp. 149–183). Bingley, UK: Emerald Group.

Weyrauch, T., & Herstatt, C. (2017). What is frugal innovation? Three defining criteria. *Journal of Frugal Innovation, 2*(1), 1–17.

Witell, L., Gebauer, H., Jaakkola, E., Hammedi, W., Patricio, L., & Perks, H. (2017). A bricolage perspective on service innovation. *Journal of Business Research, 79*(C), 290–298.

Wu, L., & Liu, H. (2022). How bricolage influences green management in high-polluting manufacturing firms: The role of stakeholder engagement. *Business Strategy and the Environment.*

Wu, L., Liu, H., & Zhang, J. (2017). Bricolage effects on new-product development speed and creativity: The moderating role of technological turbulence. *Journal of Business Research, 70*, 127–135.

Wu, C. Y., Hu, M. C., & Ni, F. C. (2021). Supporting a circular economy: Insights from Taiwan's plastic waste sector and lessons for developing countries. *Sustainable Production and Consumption, 26*, 228–238.

Zahra, S. A., & George, G. (2002). Absorptive capacity: A review, reconceptualization, and extension. *Academy of Management Review, 27*(2), 185–203.

Zheng, W. (2010). A social capital perspective of innovation from individuals to nations: Where is empirical literature directing us?. *International Journal of Management Reviews, 12*(2), 151–183.

Medical devices building on open paradigm

Laurent Adatto[1]

Abstract: The pandemic context has led to an increase in global cooperation in emergency domains under pressure. They include Personal Protective Equipment (PPE), health components, and clinical devices, in particular, critical medical ventilators. In parallel, linked consortia and innovation ecosystems have emerged to this end, incorporating stakeholders with the necessary skills, potentially private and public, and with the support of government agencies. To maximize the potential for cooperation, as will be shown in this chapter, some of these initiatives were based on open innovation ecosystems: innovation ecosystems related to open paradigm features. In this perspective, complementary elements and symbioses in terms of involved open innovation ecosystems include the cooperation of open innovation, 3D printing open elements, open requirements and open-source hardware. This chapter, therefore, will analyze relevant case studies linking the design and manufacture of medical devices for the purpose of supporting pandemic care and recovery.

Keywords: Innovation ecosystem, Open-source hardware, 3D printers, Additive manufacturing, Open innovation, Covid-19

1. Introduction

Innovation ecosystems aim to foster the emergence of innovation through systemic processes. The related processes involve stakeholders from various sectors and industries, which perhaps did not work together

---

1 Research centre on Innovation and Industrial Strategies (ISI/Lab.RII), University of Littoral Côte d'Opale, Research Network on Innovation, France.

before. Through cooperative actions, when aggregated in ecosystems these plan to create and achieve required solutions (Laperche et al., 2019).

The formation of innovation ecosystems can be linked, in particular, to a customer, a governmental support agency, and an organizational group such as a consortium (Mahmoud-Jouini et al., 2020). Related to innovation ecosystems, the field of academic research seeks in particular to examine the elements and contexts of their emergence. An additional key theme is to foster the genesis of innovation ecosystems in a knowledge and digital economy, regarding its key role in promoting progress.

This chapter intends to contribute to the advancement of this task in a context that is unprecedented on this scale, which required the urgent use of innovation in the response to the Covid-19 pandemic.

Through the analysis of relevant case studies, it shows that such innovation ecosystems, which are boosted by open dynamics, have been set up for the rapid, efficient, and flexible development of quality solutions in order to support the care of pandemic patients by the design and production of dedicated medical devices, including ventilators.

2. Context, background and design

Unforeseeable pandemic, non-adapted health infrastructures and insufficient medical devices

Covid-19 led to severe failures of international health systems. The sudden phases of the pandemic have significantly affected several areas worldwide, in particular with the capacity of hospital infrastructure and medical devices. Most dramatically, this saturation point concerned medical ventilators. Medical ventilators are indeed devices that assist patients in respiratory distress, a complication of severe forms of the associated disease. Tragic mortality is correlated with an extreme tension on these important medical devices.

Unusual demand for specific medical devices

Countries or areas lacking medical infrastructure and materials are particularly at risk in the case of a pandemic outbreak. In addition, sudden infectious diseases can lead to an unusual demand for medical devices that some countries could have in adequate quantities in normal times, in particular those related to Covid-19, medical ventilators.

Respiratory distress and the vital need to avoid a shortage of dedicated devices

The pandemic is indeed related to the SARS-CoV-2 coronavirus, or Severe Acute Respiratory Syndrome: CoronaVirus – 2. The complete title rightly emphasizes the respiratory distress that complications can cause. Therefore, respiratory support equipment, particularly medical ventilators, have a crucial role in preserving lives. That is why saturation point for these devices must be avoided by all available means.

Open-source hardware and 3D printing as innovative vectors for local production of medical devices

From this perspective, this chapter proposes to show that open source in its hardware version (known as open-source hardware, sometimes simplified as open hardware), 3D printing (also known as additive manufacturing), and related technologies and processes gathered in dedicated innovation ecosystems, can substantially reduce these risks by contributing to the production of medical devices.

In an intrinsic way, open-source hardware and 3D printing enable an autonomous production. Indeed, by definition, open-source hardware is fully informationally codified, in the form of freely available and implementable digital files. So implementation simply requires availability of the components and tools that allow the production of the related devices. Additive manufacturing is based on the use of suitable 3D printers and digital files containing the 3D virtual modeling of future manufactured devices.

Confluences between open-source hardware and 3D printing

These common features of open-source hardware and 3D printing, including digital support for tangible production, the non-dependence on a unity of place, and an autonomy in realizing this production, thus create opportunities for cross-acting and symbiotic confluences.

These two sectors, which are parts of the open paradigm, are very frequently linked in terms of development and use (Adatto, 2018). In particular, within fab labs, the manufacturing laboratories and workshops where innovative machines and technologies are made available to "makers" (notably engineering and computer students at universities, the concept was initiated by the MIT) who can put their teaching and knowledge into practice in an open-source way of creating ICT commonalities.

Design and prospective

Within this work, we will discuss these crucial issues and analyze innovative ways to design and produce key medical devices related to Covid-19 building on open-source hardware, 3D printing, open organizations, and innovation ecosystems, as we will develop.

Before studying their role in the development of highly operational medical devices during the pandemic, the issues and dynamics, in particular related to innovation, of open-source hardware and 3D printing, will be analyzed.

Then we will analyze operative cases that exemplify the value of implementing these agile, cooperative, and innovative manufacturing processes. Following Yin (2014): "*Compared to other methods, the strength of the case study method is its ability to examine, in-depth, a 'case' within its 'real-life' context*". While this work constitutes a book chapter and is intended to be didactic, we will adopt the most appropriate methodology for this type of exploratory research aimed at making discoveries in a specific context. In our case, open organizations and innovation ecosystems relate to the medical devices that support pandemic care, and implementing elements of the open paradigm, in particular, open innovation, 3D printing, open features, open requirements, and open-source hardware. Indeed, these elements of the open paradigm are, by definition, optimal boosters for developing, in the most flexible and open way, emergency devices in a pandemic context. For that purpose, we conducted systematic analyses of available internal data and published external documents of the exploratory cases. This includes project stakeholder statements, figures, established processes and organizational charts.

3. Open-source hardware: Analyzing the issues of an innovative breeding ground

Open source and field of open innovation

Open-source software and hardware belong to open innovation. Highlighted by Chesbrough (2003), the related academic field constitutes a major vector of prospects and strategies for innovation (Chesbrough, 2006; Gassmann, 2006; Enkel et al., 2009; Bogers, 2011; West & Bogers, 2014; West et al., 2014). It details innovation processes that involve open, shared, internalized, or externalized technology and data and, further, the relevant business models to develop and capture value (Chesbrough, 2006; West, 2014).

Analyzing the evolution of the field, Chesbrough and Bogers (2014) refined their definition of open innovation: "*as a distributed innovation process based on purposely managed knowledge flows across organizational boundaries, using pecuniary and non-pecuniary mechanisms in line with the organization's business model. These flows of knowledge may involve knowledge inflows to the focal organization (leveraging external knowledge sources through internal processes), knowledge outflows from a focal organization (leveraging internal knowledge through external commercialization processes) or both (coupling external knowledge sources and commercialization activities)*".

Gassmann and Enkel (2004) indicate that open-source software "*is the most prominent example of the revolutionising of the conventional innovation process*" and constitutes a pioneering step of the open paradigm. Jullien and Zimmermann (2009) consider open-source software as an optimal case of open innovation. Open-source software is related to an open call for contributions by all organizations and agents that wish to develop and improve a computing program. To this end, the source code is available to allow improvements, under the rules of its open-source license. The vectors of this distant collaboration are primarily the Internet and support building on IT tools and servers. The goal is to create community dynamics related to the project. Open-source software has become a highly effective part of the open paradigm. Massive contributions, including those of firms, mainly shape key open-source projects.

From open-source software to open-source hardware

In the matrix of software engineering, open-source software emerged as an innovative development sector. It combines a process innovation and a legal innovation. A process innovation is characterized by freedom in use, modification, redistribution, and access to the source code. The legal innovative aspect refers to intellectual property rights. It builds on the concept of copyleft, which is based on an etymological analogy with copyright. The regulation of copyleft allows us to set the level of recursivity and propagation of openness and, thus, to generate the unique and sophisticated range of open-source licenses. In particular, these licenses are adapted to the different strategies of project initiators. Moreover, the freedom attributes conferred by open source are the vectors of possible unlimited cooperation (Adatto, 2021). The open nature optimizes verification and development abilities, leading to potential continuous improvements. For example, these innovations induced by open-source software have resulted in the creation of high-level programs. Among open-source software currently used as standards by the digital sector are the Linux kernel-related operating systems and the Apache HTTP server, which is the most-used software in its range. Following the success of the movement, a material counterpart, open-source hardware generic is sometimes simplified in open hardware.

From the centrality of the source code for open-source software to that of production specifications for open-source hardware

The software opening highlights the source code. That is the part of the program that is readable and writable by developers. It contains instructions formulated according to the rules and syntax of a programming language. By the vector of an adapted computing process, this source code is ultimately transformed into a corresponding software device. This device can take the form of an operating software program or an application.

By analogy, open-source hardware is based on the openness of all information required for the construction of related material. This information includes specifications and may include plans, schemas, design procedures, calibration, and computer-aided elements. All this information is mainly edited as digital files. Because of that, updates of these information files of open-source hardware can be instantly accessible from storage on remote computer servers, an analogy of the source code's permanent availability of the open-source software projects. Moreover, the software part of open-source hardware is logically formatted as open-source software.

The licenses of open-source hardware are also built on this analogy, adapting the spirit of pioneering open-source software to the technical specificity of material projects. The renowned CERN (European Council for Nuclear Research) has developed, and continues to develop,.an open-source hardware license that is largely used in different projects: the CERN Open Hardware License (OHL).

Variations of processes and replication costs between open-source software and hardware

Operatively, the download of open-source software allows the diffusion of new occurrences. By analogy, open-source hardware is the matrix of a free hardware replication. In addition, the inherited universal call for contribution features leads to continuous improvements in the technology and in the manufacturing process of the equipment concerned.

A fundamental difference between open-source software and hardware is the cost of technological implementation. Related to the first movement, this implementing cost can be considered to be imperceptible. Indeed, all the devices (source code and operating software) are fully digital. In the case of open-source hardware, this cost must include the purchase of the necessary components and the expenses incurred from material production. In addition, not all parts may be available locally, especially if they include components that are not widely distributed. Also, the tools needed for production can cover the widest range of shapes and associated availability. Cost issues related to the components and means of production are central. In particular, they can constitute a barrier to material production in case of emergency, such as the Covid-19 pandemic.

3D Printers as tools for open-source hardware development

To develop open-source hardware, an additional innovative technology can be incorporated: 3D printing. A fundamental analysis of the 3D printing technological field will be developed, in the manner of open-source hardware. Both of these developments constitute theoretical prerequisites for analyzing the applications of these two fields related to the production of medical devices within open innovation ecosystems in the pandemic context.

4. 3D printing: Technology principles and relationship with the medical sector

3D printing, also known as additive manufacturing, is an innovative mechanical construction technology that combines chemical reaction, fusion, and computing processes.

3D printing is also a manufacturing vector of autonomous productions. It is therefore suitable for local development. As we will show, the synergies between open-source hardware and an implementation within 3D printing can play a key role in overcoming the lack of medical devices, especially in areas without sufficient health infrastructure. From this perspective, this technology will now be analyzed theoretically.

Additive manufacturing is the generic industrial term for automatic material-additional processes of production. It is in contrast to subtractive manufacturing, previously known as machining, that builds on material-removal production processes. Included in additive manufacturing, and commonly merged with this (Lipson & Kurman, 2013), 3D printing particularly focuses on the computer-aided manufacturing of three-dimensional objects. More than twenty years after the first prototypes of 3D printers, additive manufacturing has seen a spectacular boom, particularly in relation to technological refinement and progress. Analysts at IDC (International Data Corporation) highlighted the fact that global spending on 3D printing appeared to reach $14 billion in 2019 (+21 % compared with 2018).

3D printing constitutes a disruptive innovation (Rayna & Striukova, 2016) and the matrix of a very broad range of applications and related markets. 3D printing is a main driver of a new industrial revolution, in sync and in synergy with the development prospects of high-tech fields (Gausemeier et al., 2011). 3D printing combines low-volume production and mass customization. 3D printing is also a booster for co-creation and user innovation (Rayna et al., 2015). Related to this technology, user innovation, online platforming and community dynamics are components of openness strategies that can mix complementary open and proprietary components (West & Kuk, 2016).

Innovations and 3D printers

In an analogical perspective that is similar to that of open-source hardware, the 3D printing sector is a vector of innovation dynamics and high-level evolutionary prospects. Additive manufacturing is innovative in several ways. The technology builds on an innovative hardware architecture around components including extruder, filament, guidance mechanism, and laser. 3D printers are controlled by a computer process. This process is itself innovative. CAD software (Computer Assisted Design) enables the modeling of the 3D object as a digital file through slice structuring. The calibrated file allows unlimited potential replication of the modeled artifact. During the 3D printing process, the spatial shape of the digital file is physically recreated by stacking layers of material.

3D printing: Innovative applications related to the medical sector

Related to this mechanism, 3D printing allows the shaping of highly complex designs. The printing technique of materials in layers (potentially with a very high finesse, according to the models) makes additive manufacturing adaptable to high-tech developments, particularly in the innovative engineering, aerospace, and medical fields. As an illustration, in the medical field, 3D printers can integrate biomaterials, materials with skin-like properties, or transplant media in which complex electronic elements can be incorporated. Bionic prostheses have already been developed following this pattern. Due to these characteristics, 3D printing has emerged as one of the most promising technologies for disruptive innovations in the medical sector.

For Covid-19's medical device projects based on additive manufacturing, mid-range 3D printers can be used as production tools. Furthermore, this range benefits from large availability and their distribution is easy. In addition, some models of open-source hardware 3D printers have been created to have the ability to be replicable. The most common replicable 3D printer is the RepRap (Replication Rapid prototyper) model. The model was initiated by the University of Bath in the UK, under the open-source license GPL (GNU General Public License). This has generated a very active global community engaged in the continuous improvement and dissemination of the project.

5. The open paradigm and innovation ecosystems: Winning synergies for manufacturing medical devices in the emergency context of a pandemic

Building on the preliminary theoretical analysis of open-source hardware and 3D printing technologies and processes in this chapter, this part will show the interest, particularly symbiotic, in the production of Covid-19 related medical devices, potentially boosted by the dynamics of innovation ecosystems. Some major cases will be analyzed in these developments.

3D printing of standardized masks and filters

Among these medical devices, the initiatives of volunteers to continuously produce 3D printing components of masks, filters, and protective visors have been publicized. In this context, specifications of several protective designs have been made available free of charge by standardization bodies, including Afnor in France. The materials used to produce these devices may in particular be thermoplastic elastomers and microfiber.

As an illustration, additive manufacturing has played a key role in supplying masks and protective devices against the spread of the virus, including by providing them to the most exposed caregivers and hospital workers.

Innovative design of protective masks produced using 3D printing technology and open-source hardware

Among the innovative projects related to these protections implementing health standards, the 3D printer manufacturer Copper3D has made an open source STL (STereo Litography) file related to a new design of 3D printed mask (NanoHack mask) freely available. The aim is to reach the US standard N95 (the specification that is close to the European standard FFP2). The company has already produced devices for the medical sector, notably based on antibacterial materials developed from copper micro-particles, and relied on the expertise of health specialists. The mask design is the subject of a patent application. A free license for the future patent is planned to shape the intellectual property of the architecture within open-source hardware.

Transforming diving masks into respiratory masks: 3D printing technology with open specifications

Another project is the transformation of diving masks by the sportswear retailer Decathlon into respiratory masks for hospital use, first in Italy, then in France and other countries. The interconnection valve that made this transformation possible was developed using 3D printing technology and open-source hardware. The Italian start-up Isinnova, an expert in 3D printing design technology, developed this invention to transform Decathlon's's Easybreath diving mask model into a breathing mask by producing a bypass component as an interface for hospital pipes. To that end, the created component fully complies with medical standards. Decathlon also contributed to the project by providing the CAD scheme of its model. The Italian start-up was able to ensure the component's connection to the medical ventilator based on this scheme, the 3D technical drawing, disassembly, and a highly detailed study of the mask. Then, the interconnection valve, named Charlotte, could be produced rapidly and in sufficient volume.

Before being put into use, a battery of tests was carried out at the Chiari Hospital in northern Italy to ensure the safety and effectiveness of the device. The 3D printing development enabled this high reactivity of shaping and production.

Isinnova patented the valve, but only to guarantee its freedom of diffusion and use in every hospital that wished to use the device, according to the philosophy of intellectual property rights associated with open-source hardware, as we analyzed in the previous theoretical part. The 3D printing file of the valve was rapidly and freely downloadable from the start-up's website. For hospital staff, a professional tutorial video about the interconnection of the valve, mask, and pipes was released, and is also freely available. In addition to the Decathlon model, the start-up has produced adapted versions of the Charlotte valve for other models of diving masks related to the Ocean Reef and Mares brands. The aim was to maximize the number of respiratory masks and, thus, to contribute to pandemic care through the production of medical equipment, which is designed and achieved through the symbiotic effects of 3D printing and open-source hardware.

Ventilators as complex medical devices

Along with these masks, the most critical medical devices related to Covid-19 are ventilators. As mentioned in the introduction, these devices are the major devices that can assist patients with high breathing distress. The shortage of ventilators was probably the most tragic episode during the pandemic. From the technical perspective, ventilators were the most sophisticated medical devices that had to be built during the pandemic. Their components include ventilation, electronics, connectors, pipes, filtration, engine, belts, and power supply. Its requirements are related to details of the different elements, design, and multiple procedures for calibration, assembly, device functioning, monitoring, probe, and safety norms. Related to this sophistication of shaping, projects can be developed by the use of open-source hardware and 3D printing elements, as will be analyzed in the case studies.

Ranges of ventilators with open architecture and 3D printing elements related to the pandemic

Two ranges of medical ventilators, as discussed below, have emerged from pandemic-related projects: medical ventilators created as open-source hardware, and existing medical ventilators designed by the medical industrial sector, whose specifications were opened specifically in relation to the pandemic. Both categories include components that can be implemented using the 3D printing method.

Open-source hardware/3D printing ventilators created specifically in the Covid-19 context

AmboVent

In relation to the first category, one pioneering project was the AmboVent ventilator, which emerged from an open innovation ecosystem launched by the University of Technion in Israel. The project, initiated by more than 40 scientists and engineers, began with the development of around twenty prototypes at an approximate cost of $200,000. These prototypes were inspected by external worldwide specialists to provide third-party expertise and to bring the prototypes together in a model. Hospital tests were also conducted.

Full data needed for the open production of the model (architectural, electronic, mechanical, software, and 3D printing data) were then made universally accessible and available on the open-source development platform GitHub.

The ventilator has an electronic speed controller. A connected system of probes enables the transmission of monitoring details for a patient who is connected to the ventilator to a specific application for caregivers.

The open-source hardware manufacturing model and the strategic choice to use 3D printing components, or common and inexpensive ones, facilitate the production of ventilators and also reduce the cost of a unit down to around $500, whereas full proprietary models can cost $40,000.

OxyGEN-IP and OxyGEN-M

In the same category, a dual open-source hardware project of medical ventilators related to an open innovation ecosystem was provided by the Catalan mechanical and industrial engineering design company Protofy.xyz, the scientific and medical expertise of the Barcelona Clínic and Germans Trias i Pujol hospitals, and the city's university.

Two designs of open-source hardware ventilators have been created and implemented for two types of shaping:

> The OxyGEN-IP medical ventilator, for machined production, which includes metal work and is labeled by the Spanish medical agency related to medical devices, ESMA. The automobile firm Seat joined the project with the aim of promoting the industrialization of design.

The OxyGEN-M medical ventilator, whose design is specifically adapted for local build by requiring the usual tools and components.

The requirements and elements necessary for the development of these medical ventilator models are fully available on the project's website.

Existing ventilators from the medical industrial sector, whose requirements are opened for the pandemic: The Medtronic Covidian PB 560 case

As indicated, an additional category makes available the requirements and designs of medical ventilators to support local production by third-party agents and is related to medical ventilators developed by the health-care industrial sector.

One major case is the Covidian Puritan Bennett 560 medical ventilator. This device belongs to the multinational medical engineering company Medtronic (NB: the associated name Covidian was not related to Covid-19 but to the Irish medical firm Covidian, acquired in 2015 by Medtronic, of which the medical ventilator is an extension). Its availability to allow an implementation by any agent during the pandemic is a relevant contribution in the war against Covid-19. This initiative was endorsed by Elon Musk, the world-famous entrepreneur and President of SpaceX and Tesla.

Medtronic is a highly innovative firm that created the first pacemaker in 1957 and has since produced millions of units. Medtronic's turnover reached 23 billion dollars in 2018 and the firm has around 80,000 employees.

The medical ventilator builds on a compact and operational design developed in 2010. The openness of this singular architecture was chosen to be in sync with open development collaboration. It could mainly include the contribution of start-ups and medical organizations. Furthermore, various components of the medical ventilator can be made by 3D printing to support the implementation of the design.

Medtronic develops models of medical ventilation devices that require more parts, more than 1,500 components, and a large number of specialized engineers. However, such medical ventilators are not suitable for the contextual need to make available the requirements of a model to be implemented by external technicians who are not specialized in the development of niche designs and who do not have the factories, tools, and infrastructure of the parent firm.

The choice is therefore to make the requirements of the Covidian PB 560 medical ventilator with an easier-to-implement design and with fewer components to boost its open production. A permissive license to supervise its development by third parties meets the emergency context and runs until 1 October 2024, or when the pandemic is over.

This disclosure of the essentials for public implementation of an existing design of the medical industry related to the pandemic is consistent with the FDA (Food and Drug Administration) pandemic directive.

Safety requirements for ventilators as critical medical devices

The Covidian PB 560 ventilator has been launched and running for a decade. Thus, the model is associated with a long-term trial in hospital use. In addition, the model was fully certified by medical regulatory bodies, such as the FDA in the United States.

In this context, its safety has been certified for a long time within production that conforms to all the published elements of implementation. These elements include specifications, tools, components, and manufacturing processes. Thus, for legal protection issues, the terms of the license protect the firm from potential misuses or errors in implementation by third-party producers.

Indeed, the safety features of ventilators are crucial. Critical medical devices, such as respiratory aids, must ensure continuous functionality for the vital functions involved.

In the specific case of ventilators, the medical literature refers to models previously produced outside the pandemic's stress period and mainly following the standards established in the 1990s that led to a series of pulmonary injuries and traumas. In addition, ventilators can be a field of nosocomial infections. The danger is amplified by the fact that treated patients may be in a state of general weakness in relation to the respiratory disease. Thus, procedures were established to avoid these potential flaws. All models, including those of open-source hardware, must conform to these recommendations. In emergency health situations, standardization bodies with fast-track procedures can play a major role in accelerating the certification of these medical devices. In a related area, Covid-19 treatment research, these fast-tracking procedures have already been deployed.

The main UK medical industrial project related to the pandemic: The VentilatorChallengeUK case

As shown, several countries have collaborated in open innovation ecosystems dedicated to medical ventilators. This was notably the case with the British VentilatorChallengeUK consortium.

(NB: Official website of the VentilatorChallengeUK Consortium: https://www.ventilatorchallengeuk.com)

National importance of the innovation ecosystem initiated by the UK Government

The analysis, as an in-depth case study, of the VentilatorChallengeUK consortium constitutes a special national project. As will be shown, it is the innovation ecosystem set up by the UK government to meet the country's essential manufacturing needs for medical ventilators and this, in an accelerated way, in relation to the pandemic emergency. In its organization, operation, and innovative results, this consortium is compliant with a high-quality innovation ecosystem.

The project started on 19 March 2020. From the outset, the consortium's goal was to produce around 15,000 medical ventilators to fully address the country's equipment shortages in the context of the pandemic. Such a target was directly ordered by the British government with accompanying facilities and state support.

Dick Elsy was appointed at the head of the consortium's organization, following the approval of the UK government. This designation is linked to his recognized role as the CEO of High Value Manufacturing Catapult, a British network of manufacturing research labs that provide firms and organizations with innovative and high-quality processes and technologies for the manufacturing sector. In his interviews and public statements, he has elaborated in detail the contributions of the VentilatorChallengeUK consortium.

Composition and types of ecosystem stakeholders

The VentilatorChallengeUK innovation ecosystem acted as a breeding ground where the expertise and added value of each stakeholder was stimulus for a creative and productive symbiosis.

To this end, the innovation ecosystem formed by the consortium has been joined by leading stakeholders from all the necessary sectors. They include healthcare, industrial engineering, and the automotive and aerospace fields.

Among these industrial stakeholders is the innovative firm that has revolutionized the cordless vacuum cleaner industry, Dyson. This firm's industrial experience in airflow engineering on portable devices and its high capacity for innovation gave the initiative an additional global impact.

Another icon in the UK is the internationally famous stakeholder: Rolls-Royce. The developing excellence of the firm radiates worldwide, particularly in engineering linked to the automotive and aeronautical sectors, with the creation of high-level engines.

The other stakeholders include: Catapult High Value Manufacturing, of the CEO, Dick Elsy. Concerning the aeronautical industry: Airbus. Related to the transport and logistics sector: DHL. Concerning the automotive industry: Ford, in addition to Rolls Royce. Related to the industrial sector: Thales, Unilever, Siemens, and its subsidiary company Siemens Healthineers for its airflow expertise. Linked to firms in the IT sector: Microsoft, Dell Technologies. Related to the innovative Formula 1 domain: McLaren, AMG Petronas, Renault F1 Team, Red Bull Racing, Williams Advanced Engineering, Haas F1 Team, BWT Racing. Concerning suppliers and supporters: Dassault Systèmes, Aerospace, Advanced Manufacturing Research Centre of the University of Sheffield, Rexroth, a subsidiary of Bosch, Metro Aluminium Treatment Specialists. In relation to innovation-centered firms: Renishaw Apply Innovation, Flowstore Innovative Solutions That Work. And many more firms and organizations.

In addition to the central government founder, the innovation ecosystem has also received financial support from the Welsh government.

Setting up two complementary designs of medical ventilators

In a search of complementarity for hospital uses, two designs of medical ventilators have been engineered, as in the other case study in Barcelona. For an accelerated start, necessitated by the medical emergency, these designs have incorporated proven medical engineering components and special innovative elements, also at the level of development processes, with the aim of increased flexibility for accelerated developments.

The technologies and elements used to develop two designs were chosen according to their:

- experience feedback,
- reliability,
- practicality of use,
- manufacturing using readily available materials and components,
- potential to be combined and interfaced to facilitate the meshing processes of two medical ventilator designs.

Development of new production lines within the consortium and organizational innovations

Specifically for this innovation ecosystem, new production lines have been created, incorporating elements already in operation in factories of the automotive, aeronautical, and extra industries associated with the consortium stakeholders.

Organizational innovations have been made in particular in the logistics, routing, and supply chains of the consortium. In addition, new supplier chains have been solicited.

Innovation by recombining processes to save time in an emergency situation

In addition, an adaptation of industrial tooling was conducted. Moreover, the consortium also innovated in the major use of new combinations of experienced industrial processes. Thus, and with the aim of accelerating the development, these combinations enabled new and adjusted contributions to be brought to functional processes. In a related way, there was a beneficial contribution by the improved development processes by stakeholders from different sectors.

Innovative implementation of parallel supply chains

A further innovation is the use of parallel processes to save more time. In particular, parallel supply chains have been implemented.

This innovation ecosystem has enabled industrial realization at an unprecedented rate, involving increased flexibility. The consortium has also initiated innovations in the new field of the industrial organization of parallel factories. This allowed a symbiosis of the different parallel and complementary production chains.

Agile process and team autonomy within the consortium

The team autonomy set up by the consortium is close to the usual processes of open-source projects. There were no strict formal guidelines for development tasks. Instead, there were agile-type processes. A high level of creativity was given to the engineering teams.

Aiming for success on the first attempt to meet timelines

Regarding the need to rapidly achieve the objectives of the UK Department of Health, a key factor was to develop a functional prospective and to implement it with a high probability of success on the first attempt. Upstream work was carried out with relevant stakeholders to reach these objectives. At the same time, it provided flexibility to the team in the innovation ecosystem.

Flexibility but with the will to avoid distance from the initial mission

Indeed, another key factor in the success of the consortium is based on autonomy. Thus, the importance of the mission's framework was extensively considered. The flexibility that was implemented was accompanied by a determination to complete the original mission.

Ecosystem organization and concentric circles

The consortium set up teams in concentric circles dedicated to differential tasks. These included requirement developments, logistics, supplier relations, and manufacturing. In addition, these teams were not closed. This facilitates interactions and open communication between different circles.

Human factor and maintenance of voluntarism

The involvement, motivation, and cooperation of teams and contributors were also essential. The human factor was at the center of the innovation ecosystem. In particular, a high degree of trust was established between the stakeholders of the consortium.

Key roles given to experts

The consortium has assigned key roles to the most qualified experts for the allocated tasks. Again, this is also a high-level process found in major open-source projects.

Decision-making and expertise with the trust of other stakeholders

In the phases requiring decision-making, the innovation ecosystem solicited the most qualified people in the related fields. The quick acceptance of decisions by other stakeholders was crucial to creating this environment of trust.

Engineering innovation and reshaping

Through this innovation ecosystem, engineers and technicians have been able to move from manufacturing aircraft or automotive parts to medical ventilators through intelligent reshaping using their knowledge, skills, and procedures, thanks to a high degree of flexibility to link engineering adaptation to new medical designs.

Openness to new stakeholders joining the innovation ecosystem

It is also important to analyze that the innovation ecosystem was open from the start by launching a permanent call for contributions. Although, of course, the level of expertise and suitability was fully considered in order to allow the best entries as new stakeholders or supporting actors of the consortium.

Learning and industry intelligence acquisition strategies related to the innovation ecosystem

A major strategy that was adopted builds on the concept of learning by doing. An important factor was also linked to the optimization of information and data collecting related to the development of the production lines, in sync with the knowledge economy.

At the same time, an accelerated learning process of the operational members of the stakeholders is also related to the success of the innovation ecosystem. Digital and distance learning vectors have been used as part of the learning process. Virtual and Augmented Reality processes have also been implemented in the acquisition of industrial knowledge in the innovation ecosystem.

Importance of quality controls and safety

The role of tests and quality controls was emphasized, especially in accordance with sanitary aspects. Indeed, safety was essential in relation to the theme of the design and production of medical devices, as also analyzed in the chapter's previous case studies. For that purpose, stakeholders in the medical sector contribute their experience and know-how to the consortium. In addition, high-level health security for the stakeholders' representatives was provided during face-to-face work to protect them from the pandemic.

The innovative digital twin concept extensively applied by the consortium

The consortium is also linked to the innovative process of the digital twin. The innovative concept of the digital twin is based on the creation of a virtual model specially designed to be a replication of a physical object, a process, or a system. It allows simulation of all the phases of the product life through digital replication. It is also possible to simulate the different constraints that can occur in the real world.

The digital twin concept implements, in particular, Artificial Intelligence, high level data computing, and automatic learning. The aim is to generate a high number of digital elements to optimizing the simulation. Moreover, the digital twin concept is considered a "*mise en abyme*" of learning: the more the learning system is used, the more it becomes reinforced by learning.

Digital twins constitute a cutting-edge innovative technology. R&D in the fast-growing field of the Internet of Things highlights the concept of the digital twin.

The consortium has established an innovation in itself by such a use of digital twins in the context of a health innovation ecosystem that needs to be operational rapidly.

The digital twin concept was notably used in the consortium to simulate the layout of a development factory for medical ventilator components in an improved time frame.

This has enabled acceleration of the tooling and assembly of the factory from virtual simulation to the real world.

It was also being used to reformat the machined manufacturing of one of two medical ventilator designs in the innovation ecosystem.

Innovation by recombination

The consortium also engaged in innovation by recombining systems and components of anesthesia equipment. The aim was to reshape the system into an innovative medical ventilator design that did not previously exist in this form. This new design had to be approved by the British health authorities. An accelerated procedure could be set up thanks to the combined work of the stakeholders.

Creating complementary designs of medical ventilators

As we analyzed, medical ventilators are devices with a high need for security and sophistication. Hence the choice to create only two complementary and sufficient designs. And being able to include elements and processes that have already given guarantees, the need is to create, through innovative and adapted recombination, according to the short time available.

Indeed, considering the medical emergency, the innovation ecosystem has focused on the possibilities of starting with existing quality elements. Numerous sites and factories of various stakeholders were involved.

This allowed the creation of a network of redesigned industrial sites and factories.

Soliciting the leading innovation sector of Formula 1

The consortium has in particular set up an assembly of high-level electronic parts. Firms well-known for their experience in the highly innovative field of Formula 1, including McLaren as mentioned, have been solicited for the implementation of high-quality on-board electronics. In particular, McLaren has set up supply chains for electronic components as a stakeholder of the innovation ecosystem.

Outstanding success of the case

The success of the consortium allowed the UK government to obtain a sufficient number of medical ventilators for the entire country thanks to the dynamics of these innovation ecosystems. Indeed, when the consortium realized a number of 13,437 units (including both designs for optimized flexibility of use), the UK Department of Health could put the implementation on hold, as the sufficient threshold had been reached. However, the production of this high number of medical ventilators could be obtained in the early summer of 2020, i.e. only three months after the project started: a great success.

This innovation ecosystem is also an achievement because the UK, like many countries in the globalized world, usually outsources numerous processes. In order to develop this consortium, it was necessary to recreate a sufficient system of supply chains locally, at the peak of the pandemic, when global trade was very limited.

Among the contributions of this innovation ecosystem: the repurposing of the role of engineers and technicians for this process of reindustrialization, following the successful constitution of high-level local supply chains; the massive use of new technologies and digital including, as we have seen, the concept of digital twins; a public commissioning support.

Perspectives learned from the successful VentilatorChallengeUK innovation ecosystem to support British industrial policy

Thus, this successful innovation ecosystem is also instructive for the development of relocation and short circuit policy, and the process of reindustrializing the United Kingdom. The British authorities have judged that the positive experience of the VentilatorChallengeUK consortium has the potential to extend to the entire national manufacturing sector. The role of public intervention in orchestrating these reindustrialization strategies has been highlighted in this case study.

VentilatorChallengeUK innovation ecosystem achievement report

As analyzed, within the VentilatorChallengeUK consortium, high production levels in line with the UK Department of Health's schedule were established and in an accelerated timescale to achieve this success. This was crucial, as it saved the lives of many patients who were able to benefit from the medical ventilators that had been designed.

The current production lines were also solicited by the reassembly of operational elements incorporated in the two designs created by the consortium. In addition, the stakeholders solicited the best specialists and human resources from their internal projects to develop these two medical ventilator designs.

The success of this innovation ecosystem has demonstrated the preeminent role of industrial digital technologies, in particular, as we have seen, Virtual and Augmented Reality, co-creation through remote virtual networks, industrial e-learning, ICT tools for teamwork and the high adaptability of stakeholders in terms of flexibility and autonomy, while respecting the specifications of the mission to be accomplished.

In addition, a process of transfer and dissemination of the knowledge acquired through experimentation was a full part of the innovation ecosystem. The fields of health and manufacturing, and beyond, benefit from the new knowledge and processes implemented with feedback from the industrial success of this unprecedented innovation ecosystem, which has enabled the mass production of high-level, certified medical ventilators.

The manufacturing sector, at the center of this innovation ecosystem, is also considered by most experts in the field of industrial economics as crucial in reindustrialization policies and, in a related way, a relocation of technological supply chains, implementing short circuits. These reindustrialization policies are also considered to be determining factors for the recovery of the post-crisis economy.

Conclusion

Particularly related to the Covid-19 pandemic context, this work analyzed that the combination of open-source hardware and additive manufacturing, boosted within open innovation ecosystems, can be a key symbiotic vector of the creation of dedicated medical devices. These devices include masks, filters, valves, to the most critical elements, breathing medical ventilators.

In a crisis situation, the combination of 3D printing, open-source hardware, and open innovation dynamics, allow the production of such medical devices by overcoming market tensions and trade slowdowns concerning these crucial ranges of devices.

Indeed, because of the autonomous manufacturing process, endogenous to both open-source hardware and 3D printing, the tools and means of production can be established in their area of use. So the usual and potentially flawed supply chain can be effectively bypassed.

Instead of sending medical devices, only the elements necessary for their production are transmitted. And when it comes to digitized information files, as for open-source hardware's files and 3D canvas's printing files, they are instantaneously accessible via the Internet in any part of the world connected to the global digital network. In addition, digital support allows the most recent versions to be had following the real time files' availability, which contain the latest project developments. This reactivity is parallel to that of the open-source hardware and 3D printing communities.

In the Covid-19 context, this open cooperation within innovation ecosystems extends to all categories of actors that can contribute to the improvement of concerned medical devices. It includes, in particular, health institutions, medical firms, start-ups, research laboratories, hospitals, and universities and, beyond that, an unlimited range of potential contributors including health specialists, computer developers, mechanics, and electronics engineers.

These additions of complementary efforts can also be promoted through government actions. Especially in a time of pandemic crisis, organizations such as the FDA have provided guidelines for opening medical architectures. Firms in the sector, as shown in the case of Medtronic, can play an important role by opening their specifications and medical designs.

Also, open-source hardware associated with 3D printing optimizes the free access and circulation of digital files containing all the specifications and elements enabling production, open cooperation, flexibility of deployment, best practices in situ, technological developments, feedback, and increased knowledge. All these elements lead to a continuous improvement of the related devices.

In addition, the generated knowledge is recorded in registers that are universally accessible by definition. The expression of these open-source hardware and 3D printing registers is twofold: from digital files coding all the technology and construction processes, to the materialized and functional medical devices. i.e. from digital commons to material commons as medical devices. Thus, these processes generate a universal common good that is fully in line with the perspective drawn up by Elinor Ostrom (Ostrom & Hess, 2007) moreover, in a crucial field: health care.

As shown, regarding the vital importance of medical devices as ventilators, operating safety must always be a priority, from traditional production of the medical industry to production using open-source hardware and additive manufacturing. In this way, in a time of pandemic, fast track procedures should be favored by regulators and medical authorities in connection with the need for quick and safe action.

These projects linking 3D printing and open-source hardware analyzed in the context of the Covid-19 pandemic are also an "*avant garde*" of a major economic and industrial development.

Indeed, they illustrate the shift from a "1.0" industry linked to in situ production, where product delivery requires supply chains, freight, and transport (chains that are highly susceptible to breakdowns, which can lead to the unavailability of crucial products, in the event of tensions, over-auctions or conflicts of interest on the markets caused by a global crisis such as the Covid-19 pandemic)

...to a range of production tools that are flexible, modular, autonomous, and transportable, as shown in this work for additive manufacturing, building on commonly available material resources. And digital information resources established as open collaboration, scalable, instantly updated, and freely accessible on the Internet for local production, according to open-source hardware's analyses. The trend toward a "2.0" digital factory, connected and decentralized, will only increase as technological progress evolves to the high potential of 3D printing supported by open-source hardware. Because this technology should significantly shape the future, regarding its major potential, it is already considered to be a pivotal part of the Fourth Industrial Revolution.

This work shows the great utility of combining open-source hardware and additive manufacturing in innovation ecosystems in the current context of the Covid-19 pandemic.

For that purpose, the developed case studies for this chapter led to the generation of knowledge based on experiments and feedback from the analyzed organizations. The linked innovation ecosystems demonstrated their capabilities by conceiving new designs for medical ventilators, which constitute vital care support during the pandemic.

In theoretical knowledge case studies, our work analyzed that the search for complementary partnerships to establish related innovation ecosystems may have been spontaneous, sometimes with small-sized ultra-innovative structures as start-ups or research labs, or sponsored by government institutions in order to compensate the shortcomings of health systems, in particular with regard to strategic and critical medical equipment in the context of a pandemic. We particularly focused on medical ventilators because they constitute the most crucial health devices in the context of Covid-19, as we have detailed.

We also showed that these innovation ecosystems could have been at the origin of device designs and provided the specifications and requirements for an open and free implementation of an unlimited number of instances, in particular for regions and countries lacking such equipment.

We showed that, in a complementary way, innovation ecosystems have also been able, in addition to creating designs, to lead to high industrial production of these health devices.

Thus, we analyzed that these innovation ecosystems are highly enlightening objects of study, according to various facets, which include organizing relations between stakeholders, creating symbiotic effects, transformations induced by the practice and the problems encountered in the field from potential initial plans, codifying innovation and, in our context, the contributions of elements from the open paradigm to optimizing the development and dissemination of induced production in innovative ways.

References

Adatto, L. (2018). Additive manufacturing and standardization: A key step for an industrial growth. *Transitioning 3D Printing from Niche to Mainstream Markets. Research Workshop of École Polytechnique*, Paris 1 June, Conference chairs: Thierry Rayna (École Polytechnique), Joel West (KGI), Frank Piller (RWTH Aachen).

Adatto, L. (2021). Open – Open source and open data: Filiation, analogies and common dynamics. In Uzunidis, D., Kasmi, F., Adatto, L. (Eds.), *Innovation economics, engineering and management handbook 2 – Special themes.* ISTE and Wiley, September. 332 pages.

Bogers, M. (2011). The open innovation paradox: Knowledge sharing and protection in R&D collaborations. *European Journal of Innovation Management, 14*(1), 93–117.

Chesbrough, H. (2003). *Open innovation: The new imperative for creating and profiting from technology*. Boston, MA: Harvard Business School Press.

Chesbrough, H. (2006). *Open innovation: Researching a new paradigm.* Oxford: Oxford University Press.

Chesbrough, H., & Bogers, M. (2014). Explicating open innovation: Clarifying an emerging paradigm for understanding innovation. In Chesbrough, H., Vanhaverbeke, W., & West, J. (Eds.), *New frontiers in open innovation.* Oxford: Oxford University Press, Forthcoming: 3–28.

Enkel, E., Gassmann, O., & Chesbrough, H. (2009). Open R&D and open innovation: Exploring the phenomenon. *R&D Management, 39*(4), 311–316.

Gassmann, O. (2006). Opening up the innovation process: Towards an agenda. *R&D Management, 36*(3), 223–228.

Gassmann, O., & Enkel, E. (2004). Towards a theory of open innovation: Three core process archetypes. *R&D Management Conference*: 1–18, Lisbon, Portugal.

Gausemeier, J., Echterhoff, N., Kokoschka, M., & Wall, M. (2011). *Thinking ahead the future of additive manufacturing – Analysis of promising industries.* Paderborn: Heinz Nixdorf Institute.

Jullien, N., & Zimmermann, J. B. (2009). Firms' contribution to open source software and the dominant user skill. *European Management Review, 6*(2), 130–139.

Laperche, B., Lima, M., Seuillet, E., & Trousse, B. (dir.). (2019). *Les écosystèmes d'innovation : regards croisés des acteurs clés.* L'esprit économique, Economie et Innovation, Paris: L'Harmattan, April. 326 pages.

Lipson, H., & Kurman, L. (2013). *Fabricated: The new world of 3D printing.* Indianapolis: Wiley. 280 pages.

Mahmoud-Jouini, B., Charue-Duboc, F., Huet, J. M., & Zeitoun, H. (2020). Qu'est-ce qu'un écosystème d'innovation? *Special Issue: Chroniques d'experts chaire salesforce, Innovation. Harvard Business Review.*

Ostrom, E., & Hess, C. (2007). *Understanding knowledge as a commons: From theory to practice.* Cambridge, MA: MIT Press. 382 pages.

Rayna, T., & Striukova, L. (2016). From rapid prototyping to home fabrication: How 3D printing is changing business model innovation. *Technological Forecasting and Social Change, 102*, 214–224.

Rayna, T., Striukova, L., & Darlington, J. (2015). Co-creation and user innovation: The role of online 3D printing platforms. *Journal of Engineering and Technology Management, 37*, 90–102.

West, J. (2014). Challenges of funding open innovation platforms: Lessons from Symbian Ltd. In Chesbrough, H., Vanhaverbeke, W., & West, J. (Eds.), *New frontiers in open innovation.* Oxford: Oxford University Press, pp. 71–93.

West, J., & Bogers, M. (2014). Leveraging external sources of innovation: A review of research on open innovation. *Journal of Product Innovation Management, 31*(4), 814–831.

West, J., & Kuk, G. (2016). The complementarity of openness: How MakerBot leveraged Thingiverse in 3D printing. *Technological Forecasting and Social Change, 102*, 169–181.

West, J., Salter, A., Vanhaverbeke, W., & Chesbrough, H. (2014). Open innovation: The next decade. *Research Policy, 43*(5), 805–811.

Yin, R. K. (2014). *Case study research design and methods* (5th ed.). Thousand Oaks. CA: Sage. 282 pages.

Part 3:

Evolution of Innovation Ecosystems Facing New Societal Issues

Presentation

Innovation has been the subject of many studies and literature to understand its creation process, its emergence framework, its characteristics, and the levers that are favorable for its diffusion. Innovation ecosystems are also investigated through these features in order to better understand the stakes and the means to generate efficient and collaborative solutions. In a sensitive time, where climate change induces many structural, political, economic, environmental, and societal changes, innovation is put at the core of multidisciplinary solutions that are expected to improve responsible behaviors and support economic development towards limitation of resources' waste. The innovation ecosystem concept entails long-lasting exchanges and relations between organized actors around a common project.

The role played by innovation ecosystems and their integrated economic actors within the processes of generation, adoption, and diffusion of innovation, as well as their evolution respecting the current societal transformations are investigated in this book. This part is dedicated to analysing this evolution in the face of new societal challenges (i.e. climate and environment, access to basic needs and digital transformations) and inherent multilevel consequences.

Different ideologies of innovations were used and diffused during the last decades. Example of three orientations include linear technoscientific innovations, managerial and administrative innovations, and social innovations. Economic growth is mainly based on industrial production specified in techno-engineering process that circulated globally and was largely used. However, the productivist innovation vision depicts some limits in the face of modern and global systemic issues that concern many sectors, populations, territories, and economies. One chapter of this part therefore presents the need for and importance of humanist education and knowledge to be developed to design new innovation pathways.

Environmental pressures push actors to structure themselves and create ecosystems to find innovative solutions. Thus, the agricultural sector is developing and applying innovations in this logic like digital innovations. Digitization has benefited from consumers' interests and increasing expectations in a frame of health disturbance (i.e. the rise of the Covid-19 pandemic between 2020 and 2022). One chapter focuses on short food supply chains applying innovative digital solutions to cope with these diverse issues in diverse settings.

Furthermore, innovation must be responsible and at the service of a more sustainable development (Mobhe Bokoko, 2020). It can take several forms, includings eco-innovation (Arundel & Kemp, 2009); social innovation (Richez-Battesti et al., 2012); frugal innovation (Haudeville & Le Bas, 2016) and reverse innovation (Hussler & Burger-Helmchen, 2016; Laperche & Lefebvre, 2012). The geographical context embodies crucial conditions for an efficient organization of innovation ecosystems and its functioning. In this frame, territorial organization can be structured for greater resilience, especially regardless of climate and environmental challenges, using resource-constrained innovations. Actors shall be structured following different criteria such as their diversity, their territorial presence, the direction of institutions' activities and their socio-economic involvement amongst others. A new avenue for resource-constrained innovations is gaining importance and many actors are successfully generating them, supported by territorial systems of innovation. The third chapter of this part deals with managing resource-constrained innovations for a stronger resilience of territories in a frame of climatic and environmental challenges.

Finally, the last chapter of the third part is looking at digital dependency and the activities of clusters. A focus is put on the "translocal" innovation networks, highlighting a nomadic dimension of these networks. The virtual facet of innovation networks is adding a supplementary element of the theory of network performance which was initially developed on territorial complementarity between actors. Digitization is thus an innovative tool to serve new organizations of actors that are physically distant while being very close on others features (e.g. cognitive proximity, institutional proximity).

References

Arundel, A., & Kemp, R. (2009). *Measuring eco-innovation*. United Nations University. UNU-MERIT. OECD Org. 2009–2017. https://www.oecd.org/greengrowth/consumption-innovation/43960846.pdf.

Haudeville, B., & Le Bas, C. (2016). L'innovation frugale, paradigme technologique naissant ou nouveau modèle d'innovation ?. *Innovations, 3*(3), 9–25. https://doi.org/10.3917/inno.051.0009

Hussler, C., & Burger-Helmchen, T. (2016). Inversée vous avez dit inversée ? – Une typologie stratégique de l'innovation inversée. *Revue Française de Gestion, 42*(255), 105–119. https://doi.org/10.3166/rfg.2016.00024

Laperche, B., & Lefebvre, G. (2012). The globalization of Research & Development in industrial corporations: Towards "reverse innovation": The cases of General Electric and Renault. *Journal of Innovation Economics & Management, 2*(2), 53–79. https://doi.org/10.3917/jie.010.0053

Mobhe Bokoko, D. (2020). Responsible innovation and social innovation. *Journal of Innovation Economics & Management, 32*(2), 229. https://doi.org/10.3917/jie.032.0229

Richez-Battesti, N., Petrella, F., & Vallade, D. (2012). L'innovation sociale, une notion aux usages pluriels : Quels enjeux et défis pour l'analyse ?. *Innovations, 2*(2), 15–36. https://doi.org/10.3917/inno.038.0015

Innovation diversity in human societies

JEAN CLAUDE RUANO-BORBALAN[1]

Abstract: Innovation must be considered in its dual nature. It designates practices which are multiple, ranging from consumption and marketing to techno-scientific processes, from industrial production to public policies. It also, and this will be the main object of analysis of this article, designates a set of analysis and, above all, discourses of promotion and justification. Those discourses can be categorized in three main orientations: linear technoscientific innovations; managerial and administrative innovations; social innovations. In the past half century, those discourses have become the common credo of a world focused on techno-scientific engineering, industrial economic development, and economic growth, and can be considered as a kind of global and ubiquitous ideology, spread all around the planet, particularly in urban behavior and within productive and managerial processes of contemporary organizations.

This ideology and practices of innovation face a huge and almost insurmountable problem: it is powerless, at least, and surely more harmful, to resolve some of the main systemic challenges that are currently occurring (global warming, persistence of inequalities, etc.). This paper pledges to consider reinforcing regulation and public policies, but mainly proposes a bet on the relevance of humanist education and knowledge, i.e a radical transformation of higher education in order to develop new ways for new innovation.

Keywords: Ideology, Doctrines of innovation, Responsible innovation, Knowledge, Universities and research, Sustainable future

---

1 Conservatoire National des Arts et Métiers (CNAM Paris), Chair of Mediation of Technology and Science in Society, France.

Introduction

Innovation must be considered in its dual nature. It designates practices, which are multiple, ranging from consumption and marketing to techno-scientific processes, from industrial production to public policies. It also, and this will be the main object of analysis of this article, designates a set of analysis and, above all, discourses of promotion and justification. Those discourses (and related practices) can be categorized in three main orientations: linear technoscientific innovations; managerial and administrative innovations; social innovations. In the past half century, those discourses have become the common credo of a world focused on techno-scientific engineering, industrial economic development, and economic growth. The rise of civilization and the industrial and commercial mode of production dates from the 18th and early 19th centuries in Europe and at least the second industrial revolution at the end of the 19th century for the world as a whole. (Freeman & Louçã, 2001). For the most recent period, science, technology, and industry have been, and remain, seen by all political leaders and elites as a necessary horizon, whatever the political regime (Clerc & Landes, 2001) Innovation has not always been the ubiquitous doctrine we know, nor the credo of managerial and industrial elites: its birth as a mobilizing discourse for nations, organizations, and individuals (in different ways) dates from the 1960s. It reached a peak in the 2000s, and then splintered and cracked. It is now singularly challenged because of the major systemic problems and risks facing human societies (Ruano-Borbalan, 2021).

Fragmented discourses and practices

The most widespread form of innovation today is fundamentally techno-industrial (encompassing public policy and scientific production on a macroscopic scale), known as "linear", i.e. it takes place in linear sequences, from scientific or techno-scientific conception and discovery to engineering and product development procedures, and finally to marketing and adoption by consumers (Joly, 2017). This "linear" innovation is, however, only one manifestation of a protean reality. In the administrations of companies and the public service, a vision in terms of innovation has come to cover a deepening of the processes of standardization of change, which were present long before this. This vision of innovation, developed on the 'mezzo' scale of industrial, governmental, and knowledge-producing organizations and institutions (universities/research), combines the classic concepts of organizational change, cost reduction, and technological innovation. If we look at public administration the accompanying discourses have corresponded, to the generalization of "new public management" in western countries. In developing countries (excluding China), it is the interventions by international regulatory or lending bodies that have conveyed these, as well as the phenomena of diffusion and imitation that are well described by managerial and organizational sciences. They have accompanied and continue to accompany organizational rationalizations and the reduction of state intervention in the economy. If there is anything 'new', beyond the rhetoric, it is the generalization of so-called collaborative or project-based managerial forms, using new justifications such as design thinking and generating new practices in the midst of hybrid places and devices known as 'labs'. It is also and primarily through the introduction and modernization of communication infrastructures, IT/office automation, and today the use of artificial intelligence or massive data (Rival & Ruano-Borbalan, 2017).

A third concept of innovation, social innovation, has emerged in the last few years. It corresponds to the development of associative and "citizen" mobilizations and discussions around urban, environmental, or techno-science impact problems. It proposes solutions and ways of solving problems (Fossati et al., 2018), of "deliberative democracy" or "participative sciences" or "technical democracy" (Ruano-Borbalan, 2018).

This contemporary collaborative and "citizen" form is increasingly valued, both academically and in urban or public policy. In part, it takes up the traditions of social and political protest of the 20th century, but it goes well beyond this by integrating a number of contemporary societal concerns, particularly those that are cultural and identity related (Richez-Battesti et al., 2012). It asserts its radical break with the linear industrial and techno-scientific innovation regime, while reusing the doctrinal vocabulary of innovation promotion. Like administrative innovation, it uses and reinforces collaborative practices, often stemming from the educational or social movements of previous periods. It has also appropriated the tools recently developed by communication technologies and the collaborative doctrines stemming from higher education in engineering, which are widespread in these sectors of social innovation or public administration and policy.

Social innovation, and this is a crucial point, is considered to produce knowledge of a new, multidisciplinary nature: knowledge that is said to be "co-constructed", i.e. produced within practical or mobilization processes by actors from different backgrounds (Moulaert, 2013). This "co-constructed" knowledge is considered essential for the implementation of innovations in the field, particularly through the so-called "citizen" promotion actions that it supports.

Innovation: A "religion" like any other?

The discourse of promoting innovation was imposed and established as a hegemonic doctrine at the end of the Cold War, including in countries still formally claiming to be Marxist.[2] Innovation was advocated at the macro-economic level by the major international organizations (primarily the OECD) as a means of transformation and economic development. It was also embodied in the same period of the 1950s and 1960s within specific epistemic communities and practices, particularly rural studies and agricultural technology development, as historian Matthew Wisniovski shows in a forthcoming book (Wisniovski, 2022). It was precisely from 1955 onward that a doctoral student, Everett Rogers, on the campus of the University of IOWA, studied the forces of technical change and its diffusion in agriculture, and his book "Diffusion of Innovations", published in 1962 by Free Press, has become the second most cited social science book to date.

In fact, this global generalization of the promotion of innovation has been affirmed relatively recently as an imperative, notably through scientific or knowledge development, which is progressively considered as an engine of economic growth (Popp-Bermann, 2013). Having become a powerful doctrine to accompany industrial and economic development, the discourse of promoting innovation has been extended – for more than half a century – to national public policies, urban policies and practices, companies and individuals (associated with the promotion of creativity in this case) (Burger-Helmchen, 2019). The spectacular success of this vision of economic and social or political development in terms of innovation/creativity/entrepreneurship stems not only from generalization of the industrial and market production system over the past half-century,

2 Placed in a broader historical perspective, it can be considered that innovation, which for a long time had been seen as of little interest in economic doctrine, except under the heading of "scientific and technical revolution", mainly in the Soviet vision, has come to crown the historical process of industrial growth in the present period.

but also and particularly from its effectiveness for material growth in a now fully interconnected and globalized world.[3]

Discourses advocating techno-industrial or managerial innovation reached a peak at the end of the Cold War, from the 1990s to the 2000s (Lechevalier, 2019). Although strongly supported by overabundant research production, the doctrine (supported by the media and professional and administrative consultants or discourses in particular) was restricted to economic, managerial, and political circles: it became what it is today, the common thought of economic circles, engineers and managers, modernist reformers, and urban individuals from the upper middle class, for the most part.[4]

The persistence of discourses and doctrines promoting innovation, even if it is considered to be "responsible", stems first and foremost from the power and influence of the elites (knowledge rooted in professional

---

3 The contemporary world has been undergoing accelerated change for half a century; if we take a simple economic and societal point of view (and not geo-strategic conflict), several major trends are at work, more or less, in all countries, albeit with different realities and at different speeds:

first, changes in the regulation and growth of productive systems (transformation of industry under the effects of digitalization and artificial intelligence, but also of managerial changes and innovation; development of the knowledge economy, etc.).

second, the essential role of organizational and institutional analysis at all levels, but particularly at the urban and territorial level;

third, the necessary linkage of techno-scientific knowledge and engineering sciences with knowledge from the social sciences and humanities, which have themselves become - as the English sociologist Anthony Giddens has emphasized - elements of argumentation and socio-political rhetoric and of individual reflexivity;

Last, but not least, the increasingly prevalent concern with anticipation and foresight: the question of the meaning and ethics of political, managerial, or individual action is becoming a priority, taking into account 'citizen' narratives and wills, social uses, as well as narratives produced by multiple social and urban cultures, compatible with the dominant managerial and industrial ideology, framed by the doctrine of innovation, which is far from being the only justification and belief framework in contemporary societies.

4 It seems that the worsening of systemic crises in the recent period (ecology, climate, pandemics, geostrategic crises) has led to a decline in faith in innovation and in the possibility of solving "complex" problems through creativity and innovation. Added to this is the relative failure of the promise of cooperative forms of training, such as training in innovation through creativity and projects which, after a clear blossoming in the years 2000 to 2015, have been reduced and "trivialized". Cf. Ruano-Borbalan J.C. (2019).

functioning, mastery of the media, dominant public policies and doctrines of economic and managerial justification, production of institutions of higher education and research, based on economic science, as the sociologist Elizabeth Popp Bermann has recently shown) (Popp-Bermann, 2022). The doctrine now feeds into education and training systems, particularly around creativity and entrepreneurship development schemes[5], although the penetration of conceptions in these terms is extremely variable across countries and education sectors.

The discourses accompanying innovation policies and practices can be considered to be one of the great ideologies of our time. It is probably the only one that is shared today by all the elites and urban middle classes of the contemporary world. Like all ideologies, it has its designers and creators of doctrine ("apostles"), namely the great theorists of innovation and the famous "triple helix", now refined into a "quadruple" or "quintuple" helix of innovation (Carayannis, 2012). It has its propagators ("priests"), who are the tens of thousands of teachers and researchers in engineering and business schools, thousands of journalists, and hundreds of thousands of consultants, but also government officials and their administrations at all levels, etc. It has its institutions ("churches"): engineering schools, business and management schools, professional associations or meetings, international agencies and institutions. It has its celebrations and seminars: colloquia, forums, meetings, workshops of all kinds (with names that sound like managerial-innovative Newspeak) that propagate entrepreneurial doctrines and hymns to innovation.

---

5 These mechanisms are derived from the forms of project implementation developed in engineering schools at the turn of the 1970s and 1980s (see Ruano-Borbalan, 2019), op cit. Embodied in higher education by innovation-based training, they are most often indebted to the actions carried out through networks originating from MIT (fab labs) or Stanford (design school) and take their spirit of competition through action and fabrication. These forms of pedagogy by collaborative and multidisciplinary project privilege design thinking and creativity as almost universal doctrines of pedagogical justification. In view of the spread of doctrines and discourses promoting innovation, they now coexist within education systems with other traditions, stemming from the active pedagogy implemented within education in the 19th and early 20th centuries, but the two 'traditions' do not really cross-fertilize, with rare exceptions, such as the interdisciplinary teacher training center in Paris (Taddei, F. (2015). Trusting innovative systems. *Cités*, 63, 55–68).

In teacher training, the educational sciences dominate, with different references to the traditions of active pedagogy, socio-constructivist epistemologies, or humanistic psychology.

The persistence of a voluntarist discourse around innovation can be read as one of the classic phenomena, from a historical point of view, of the propagation of ideas, which the anthropologist Dominique Desjeux has just analyzed by studying the advent of rabbinic Judaism and Christianity (over a period of eight centuries) in the light of theories of innovation (Desjeux, 2022). From the point of view of the doctrine of innovation, the speed and rapidity of diffusion, which is very different from that of Christianity, for example, is of course linked to the strength of the state apparatus, public policies and media control, but it also stems from the fact, as we have said, of the efficiency of industrial innovation practices (Kroll & Frietsch, 2022).

In fact, this great "ideology" constitutes, on the basis of multiple studies and analyses from the social sciences, economics, and engineering sciences[6], the justifying discourse of public policies and economic or entrepreneurial practices centered on techno-scientific innovation. It also constitutes a "cultural discourse" and a set of basic, often tacit, knowledge or beliefs associated with corresponding professional or consumer practices. Here again, the scales of observation and organization of discourses and practices carry different justifications.

At the level of central public policies, for example, we note the unification of discourses around the promotion of "national and local innovation systems" within the large OECD countries and emerging countries (role of districts, knowledge production regimes, social and labor regulation, etc.).[7] At the individual and social interaction levels, innovation discourses are above all about consumption (through the usual propaganda of innovation and novelty) or, on the contrary, if we place ourselves from the point of view of innovation and social mobilization, rather than on a radical critique of consumption and growth.

Can innovation be "responsible"?

To this day, scientific, engineering, and management discourses continue to value the development of innovation and industrial development in the same terms as those which prevailed during the industrial boom

6 See for example https://www.francophonieinnovation.org/articles/h/rapport-de-suzanne-berger-sur-les-dispositifs-de-soutien-a-linnovation-en-france.html

7 https://www.oecd.org/fr/innovation/

of the last two centuries. However, despite the emergence of forms of social innovation, the impact of which is still weak in reality, the discourse promoting innovation is having difficulty in coping with the growing concern and distrust of industrial and techno-scientific development, particularly because of the worsening of systemic, technological, or industrial health (Ruano-Borbalan, (2022-1) and climatic and other risks (Ruano-Borbalan, 2021-1). This is all the more true given that attempts to make innovation the path to sustainable growth or a green industry (responsible innovation) (Von Schomberg & Hankins, 2019), particularly within the policies of the European Union, are currently in their infancy and that the possible successes of proactive industrial policies are rather mixed.

However, at least the dominant form of techno-scientific and industrial development promoted by this ideology of innovation and the practices it covers has not yet proved its contribution to the transformation of human activities in the direction of the "sustainability" of natural "eco-systems", and consequently weighs on the future. In fact, many analysts believe that the opposite is true, since this vision favors competition, economic growth, and consumption, and therefore has a negative impact on ecosystem resources and environmental balance (Fassin, 2022). It is mainly the "linear" vision (Joly, 2017) of innovation, and above all its environmental or social consequences, that many analysts are denouncing today, particularly from the perspective of promoting ecological transition and combating inequalities.[8] Admittedly, concerns about "responsible" innovation have been asserting themselves for several decades (Gauthier & Benjaminsen, 2012). But the dominant conception of innovation and economic development, like the human industrial activity it accompanies, remains "concomitant" with the destruction of natural eco-systems or global warming.

This dominant vision of innovation is strongly criticized for containing an ideological bias (Godin & Winck, 2017), which is very present

---

8 For the philosopher Dominique Bourg, one of the recognized analysts of the risks and orientations that are necessary from the point of view of the ecological crisis: "We are thus caught between, on the one hand, resources that are absolutely necessary to our economies and that are becoming increasingly scarce and, on the other hand, considerable planetary upheavals that will lead to major population movements during this beginning of the 21st century", in Bourg, D. (2012) Transition écologique plutôt que Développement Durable, *Vraiment Durable*, 2012 N°1, pp 77–96.

in management studies, for example, and which leads to two assertions, often implicit, which are contradicted by the history of human societies and contemporary realities. The first statement could be summarized as follows: "A country or a company can only develop more and more, otherwise it will decline, be overtaken, and its inhabitants will lose their security and well-being. The second would be: "there is no other solution than to innovate through science, technology, and industry to offset the inequalities and 'negative externalities' caused precisely by the past development of industry and human population growth and mass consumption." Many polemicists now believe, particularly when compared with historical societies that have disappeared abruptly, that our contemporary societies could only escape the impasses of growth innovation by major internal or external conflicts and major risks of "collapse". A review of the literature on these subjects shows that catastrophist fear and utopia constitute a counterpart that is just as doctrinal as the vision of a resolution of systemic crises through techno-scientific or industrial innovation (Middleton, 2017).

Beyond innovation and its doctrines

The issue of our time is not – at least not only – to develop innovation and competition between firms or entrepreneurial and individual "creativity". It is obviously to face systemic risks and form economical to ecological or geopolitical ones, without forgetting pandemics. And it is increasingly recognized that the answers to the systemic challenges human societies are facing will not be only, if not primarily, techno-scientific, or innovative (Lechevalier, 2019). In its 2030 Agenda the UN has, for example, identified 17 key goals for a "sustainable" future. Among these major goals there are two types of issues, strongly connected: on the one hand, the reduction of inequalities and, on the other hand, the need for "ecological transitions", neither of which can only be solved with just "more innovation".[9] The latter – although much criticized[10] – has become

[9] In a few years, in order to overcome the weaknesses of a conception in terms of "sustainable development" stemming from the dominant political conceptions of the 1960s and 1970s, the political notion of "ecological transition" has been asserted (Bourg, 2012).

[10] The French historian Jean-Baptiste Fressoz, in numerous press articles and interviews, indicates that the energy transition is a myth, present in contemporary discourse,

essential in the design and implementation of contemporary public policies[11], as indicated, to take only one example, by the eponymous title (Ministère de la transition écologique) of a ministry in France, for example. If we consider the situation at the level of the major countries, we can also see a strong rise in concern about systemic risks: in China, in a different register, in 2012, the 18th National Congress of the Chinese Communist Party (CCP) put forward the construction of an "ecological civilization". China has since emphasized the need to "build a society that conserves resources and develops ecological awareness" (Mouton, 2019). However, these intentions can be qualified by the fact that, for the Chinese authorities, environmental protection and energy management are linked to the country's economic performance, which depends precisely on the development of increasingly important techno-scientific and industrial innovation. In the United States, the planet's main industrial power, the authorities for a time refused to accept the common observation of an increasingly irreversible degradation of the planet's ecosystemic balances in terms of climate or the environment during the presidency of Donald Trump. The Democrat administration of President Biden has, at least intentionally, returned to international cooperation. The United States, like the governments of the other major world economies (European Union, China), is once again putting the issue of reducing the impact of human activities on environmental systems at the forefront of

and totally absent from human history. Cf Fressoz, J.B. (2022) Énergie et matières premières: le mythe de la transition, Omniprésent dans les discours, la transition est absente dans l'histoire matérielle de l'humanité, pour la Science n° 535.

11 The agreement is thus almost general, to reduce in several fields the desire for the transformation of human activities, so that they become, if possible, "sustainable". These orientations, policies or actions are interrelated and can be applied according to the sectors of activity or countries: at all levels of social activity or public policy, territorial or urban, but also of course entrepreneurial and industrial.

It is obviously a question, on a global scale as well as on a national or territorial level, of thinking and acting in the economic field (regulation, adaptation of production systems, etc.) or in organizations and institutions (efficiency and taking into account the challenges of transitions), in terms of infrastructures (energy, transport, techno-sciences), but also in terms of the orientation of policies or actions of civil society (local action, social innovation and consumption, citizenship and behavior).

The challenges relate in particular to the need to adapt innovation, production, and consumption systems. The aim is to reinforce the changes in social practices, particularly those linked to technological and scientific developments: production, mobility and transport, consumption, work, health, leisure, etc.

its concerns. One of the major objectives of the President of the United States was to put in place a "green new deal" for the energy transition (against global warming, for sustainable urban development, the development of clean energy accessible to all, responsible consumption and production, etc.)[12]

Though considering all dimensions of possible actions, the declarations and political orientations that maintain the hope that techno-scientific innovations, combined with economic regulation, could, through "sustainable" industrial policies, counteract the environmental degradation caused by human activity, are not tenable. A large body of scientific literature focuses on "transitions", particularly in energy production and consumption and in industry (social and environmental responsibility of companies and public institutions). Using the theoretical frameworks of economics or management studies, this literature examines the various forms of implementation of industrial policies and their constraints and contrasting results, even in countries that are very committed to respecting international commitments in environmental or climate matters (Johnstone et al., 2021). However, from a strictly public policy point of view, the observation is clear, as demonstrated by the economist Dani Rodrik, who emphasizes the extreme difficulty of balancing normal economic functioning with the possible requirements of public policies intended – hopefully – to make growth sustainable (Rodrik, 2014). As we know, in the recent period, it was only – and very temporarily – the consequences of the global Covid-19 pandemic that caused a decrease in greenhouse gas emissions, for example: this was quickly made up for as soon as the confines were removed (Sovacool et al., 2020).

However, despite the declarations, international conferences, and industrial or public policies for a more "virtuous" economy and consumption, the objectives of reducing negative human externalities, which have been reiterated for decades now, are in frequent, if not systematic, contradiction with the reality of real industrial or economic development: as we know, only the period of containment in the Covid pandemic slowed down and even reduced the growth in greenhouse gas emissions, which immediately caught up in the following period. From this article's point of view, the drivers of human action in society and its "industry" – in the very general sense of the word – are, in the medium and long term, quite

---

12 https://joebiden.com/climate-plan/

different from the talk of "responsible" innovation or the consideration of any environmental sustainability. And no green industry or technology that is not embedded in the constraints and forms of human social, political, and economic reaction as historically constructed can seriously emerge. They are framed by powerful anthropological, political, and economic infrastructures, including the reality of nation states, institutional systems, etc. It is not, in this perspective, beliefs, values or discourses and ideologies that ultimately determine human and societal capacities for action, but rather the long-term institutional and socio-legal norms or frameworks that play the central role in the tacit constraints they impose on social actors and communities of practice. For example, the frameworks of individual property, the forms of techno-industrial and scientific development, the geo-strategic securing of energy supplies, the constraints of political action, etc. All of this is absolutely banal to an evolutionary historian or anthropologist, for example, and is summarized by the political need for power for states and welfare for citizens, in the context of a globalized "world system" (Graeber & Wengrow, 2021).

Can the contradiction between industrial development and the preservation of eco-systems be resolved?

According to this approach, there is a clear contradiction between, on the one hand, an increasingly prevalent doctrine on the capacity for techno-scientific and industrial innovation, one of the virtues of which is to enable the development of "sustainable" industry and human activities and, on the other hand, the – difficult – observation of the inability of political communities and industrial systems to reduce the negative impacts on an environment that has long been anthropized and violently degraded (Moore, 2015). Countless researchers and analysts have tried for at least two decades to resolve the contradiction (Guston et al., 2014). However, despite many speeches in this direction, innovation – even if it is responsible – is not a solution to environmental and social challenges.

Certainly, the challenges of economic and social development are debated within political communities, both in democratic and authoritarian forms of society. These debates are leading everywhere to increasingly important public policies, as well as attempts at international regulation of ecological and social issues. They are taking place at all levels of socio-economic organization, from neighborhoods to cities and states to international relations.

To take just one example, environmental concerns have become an essential part of Chinese urban policies, whose recent industrial development and urban gigantism was initially unconcerned with preserving energy resources or limiting environmental and climatic impact.

However, China, like many developed countries, is currently struggling to reduce the environmental impact of its growth, despite the authorities' apparently very firm commitments and wishes. In China, these difficulties are linked in particular to the resistance of local and urban authorities, which are in competition with each other and are ideologically driven (Guilhot et al., 2018). But this observation is absolutely the same in western democracies and we must everywhere add the passive and active resistance of the populations, as illustrated recently in France by the social movement of the "Gilets Jaunes", protesting against the hypothesis of a tax on carbon emissions into the atmosphere by motor vehicles, a tax that mainly penalizes the inhabitants of the working classes and the active population of the country's small towns.

Beyond these known differences, there is a strong convergence of increasingly standardized administrative mechanisms and everywhere the 'machinery' of government is playing a central role, with specific constraints and standards of 'internal' efficiencies, focused essentially on procedures and 'good execution', particularly because measuring the effectiveness of public policy outcomes is a challenge (Heath, 2020).

More generally, the 'concrete' issues and challenges of transitions to 'sustainable' and socially responsible development are of formidable systemic complexity. They require responses at all levels and there is no simple solution that innovation, in any form, could solve. Just think of the issues of mobility; urban mobility in an "energy transition" perspective, ecology, and economic efficiency (Le Breton, 2019). The electric car, for example, which seems to be a solution, does not answer, or at least only partially answers, the questions raised. Atmospheric and noise pollution, accidents, and the loss of billions of hours for urban dwellers in individualized transport, can possibly be resolved in the long term by the development of public transport and autonomous, non-polluting, shared vehicles. But in no case are the current solutions (including electric vehicles) a panacea: neither from the point of view of social use, nor from the point of view of a global energy or environmental balance sheet which remains negative, in particular because of the costs and consequences of the extraction of multiple minerals, their transport, and the difficulties or impossibility of recycling the components

Many innovation actors, governments, cities, associations, or private actors are betting on the development of eco-innovation solutions and methods that accompany the substitution of services for products (economy of functionality) as in the case of car-sharing systems or energy efficiency.[13] All categories of eco-innovations can or should be combined for the same ecological solution, as in the case of a rethought eco-mobility, following the example of the city of Singapore, which is at the forefront of these issues, for obvious geographical and societal reasons[14]. It is true that contemporary eco-innovations are likely to disrupt market structures and induce behavioral changes at the margin. They affect all sectors and all professions to the point that, according to some analysts, they constitute one of the greatest economic opportunities of the 21st century, with a booming global market (Nicolaï & Faucheux, 2015). However, to date they have had no significant effect on the major issues of energy supply or industrial production, particularly given the inertia of production methods and value creation models. The sole economic and ecological goals of eco-innovation must be complemented by a concern for the long term. And their usefulness must be measured in terms of the common good and equity between the various human populations, and not just in terms of the manufacture of new products or services that generate profits on a global market.

[13] Some of them are said to be radical, such as green chemistry and smart grids, while others are "incremental", i.e. they involve improving existing processes in agriculture or elsewhere. So-called "added" eco-innovations do not prevent pollution, but treat it afterwards (e.g. particle filters for diesel engine pollution). Integrated" eco-innovations, on the other hand, act preventively, by promoting the use of less polluting raw materials, the substitution of causes of pollution, and the design of reusable and/or recyclable products.

[14] https://www.lesechos.fr/industrie-services/tourisme-transport/mobilite-urbaine-singapour-en-tete-dun-classement-mondial-1151409

Guiding ongoing transformations: Wishful thinking or serious solutions?

Does it make sense to want the modification of innovation processes, particularly to deal with ecological and social emergencies? A priori, no, if we want massive and immediate modifications: awareness of dangers or potentially irreversible processes does not provide any particular key to modifying the normal course of institutions and human activity. At best, it can be said that possible actions could (should) be carried out at several levels at the same time, but certainly not that one level of action alone is capable of solving the problems (neither individual action alone, nor public regulations and policies alone, etc.).

The challenges are such that only transformations on a state or inter-state level would be able to cope with them. The regulations must concern the institutional foundations and frameworks, primarily the forms of intervention and structuring of the state. However, if we can write the corresponding sentences, we cannot decree the implementation of these regulations: the States and the international system will not change "voluntarily" as the currents of analysis of international relations, which show that the forces behind the constitution of the global order are of an evolutionary and systemic nature, agree to do (Adler, 2019).

As a counterpoint, however, we note that a struggle between urban or federal forms and centralized forms of governance is underway. It concerns in particular the forms of citizen participation and the questions of ecological or energy transitions but does not concern industrial questions, which remain state and inter-state questions. It is not new, and dates from the emergence of the state from in the 3rd millennium before the Common Era (Scott, 2017). But it is singularly important for the future of our societies. We can see that city-states, towns, and small regions are at the forefront of ecological and social transition concerns. It is probably on this scale, provided that these territorial scales have the minimum autonomy to do so, that – paradoxically – global and cooperative solutions seem able to be developed. But we are a long way from any possibility of global regulation of innovation policies that take into account environmental challenges. It certainly could not be the firms and players in the real economy, on which some people base their hopes, particularly because the driving forces of their activity, at the micro-economic level, are not primarily the search for the common good. The question is different if we take the point of view of a political economy of the commons, as we know from the work of Nobel Prize winner Jean Tirole (Tirole, 2016).

Using knowledge?

Understanding and orienting industrial transformations, with the help of public policies and the transformation of contemporary innovation discourses and practices, requires the transformation of knowledge production systems. Indeed, administrations, production systems, but also the educated population itself consume knowledge in almost exponentially increasing quantities. It is first and foremost a question of devoting a significant proportion of energy and socio-economic resources to the quality of knowledge production systems, certainly in terms of innovation and transfers between research and industry, as advocated by all the government agencies and world-class consultancy firms, but above all in a radically new way: if utilitarian or market goals remained dominant or even exclusive, both as a doctrine and as legal or contractual institutions and norms, then the ability to really initiate ecological and social transitions would be irremediably compromised.

One of the possible policy directions directly available to governments is to support and reorient the education, training, and knowledge production systems (research and higher education). The last period has seen the development of a dominant and polarized system of massive scientific knowledge production on an international scale.[15] This is now totally oriented toward the strengthening of new techno-sciences

[15] In this field, the United States is clearly dominant, since American universities were and remain the world's leading universities. Europe remains a significant power in terms of techno-scientific production. However, as we know, new players are emerging: India has the largest higher education system in the world, with almost 750 universities and around 35/380 million students, but it does not have any institutions that are currently well placed in international rankings. China, on the contrary, has built up a leading higher education sector in less than two decades. It should also be remembered that in 2020, China will have nearly 2,600 universities or higher education establishments with nearly 32 million students (doctoral, masters, and bachelor's degrees), nearly half a million of whom come from abroad. Just as spectacular is the country's colossal production of scientific articles, which has now surpassed that of the United States: from fewer than 87,000 articles in 2003 to 426,000 in 2016. Cf: Ruano-Borbalan, J.C. (2022), editorial, European Journal of Education, special issue (ed. Ruano-Borbalan, J.C.,) *Reducing inequality in higher education: Limitations and possibilities,* Volume 57, Issue 2, June 2022, Pages 161–167.

(biology, nano-technologies, artificial intelligence, communication, etc.) (Pestre, 2015), and toward the development of industrial innovation.

This massive system of production is characterized by a standardization of knowledge and the institutions of its production, an ancient but recently globalized process (Ruano-Borbalan, 2017), through the unification of institutional forms of higher education and standards of evaluation or research, but also within the training of engineers and business schools, whose impact on the structuring and management of productive systems is colossal. It is completely oriented toward the objectives conveyed by the doctrines of promoting techno-scientific and managerial innovation, particularly through the creation of entrepreneurial and innovation universities (17,000 out of 18,000 in the world today). The observation is similar for research, which is now focused on industrial transformation and "challenges", as defined by governments or international institutions, whose ideological and conceptual frameworks are based on standard economic theory.

But - and this is a hypothesis based on historical analysis of the "functions" of higher education and education (Ruano-Borbalan, 2022-3)- the systems of training and knowledge production are also, and still are, the breeding ground for the possible transformation of the doctrines of social and industrial or urban innovation, or for the accompaniment of multiple forms of human creativity. It is within higher education and research circles that analyses are developed and expressed that strongly advocate a humanist vision of innovation. Universities, or at least certain areas of research and training, can possibly constitute a significant element of political solutions to contemporary challenges... on the condition that the States "let go" and that the forced managerial transformation that has been taking place, particularly in Europe, for the last thirty years in the higher education and research sector is reoriented.

It would be a question of changing the now exclusive focus on the production and transfer of knowledge that is "useful" for techno-scientific and economic innovation in the name of a response to inequalities and the consideration of common goods, following the invitations of the philosopher Martha Nussbaum or the Nobel Prize winner in economics Amartya Sen, for example. The latter, referring to older pedagogical or philosophical traditions, believe that it is increasingly urgent today to develop knowledge institutions and education from a humanistic, artistic, or creative perspective, and not only from a techno-scientific or managerial one. Moving in this direction is possible without major institutional or value changes. The world's teachers and researchers are a priori committed to these objectives of self-fulfillment through knowledge and deliberation or creative curiosity, which constitute the foundation of modern science. Abandoning the subjugation of knowledge production and transfer systems to the imperatives of industrial innovation, trusting youth and social actors to define common goals, and aggregating knowledge at global levels (as in the case of the climate change review) are likely to reduce looming environmental or geopolitical shocks. Such orientations can provide individuals with a strong reflexivity and a benevolent understanding of others as much as, if not more than, professional viatics, which are often obsolete before they are used (Nussbaum, 2010).

It will surely seem surprising to many that education and training actions can contribute to solving geostrategic, economic, or industrial problems in the medium and long term. It will not, alone! But one must remember that the promotion of innovation and useful knowledge at all costs are very recent doctrinal inventions, counter-intuitive for humans in a social situation or learning commitment. The proof, for this ideology as for others, is that these doctrines must be powerfully and daily reaffirmed and that colossal sums of money and powerful media resources must be invested in them, for the benefit of market and economic efficiency, but not necessarily for the common good of humans. Innovation, as a doctrine valuing creativity and entrepreneurial projects, is a blind ideology and does not particularly correspond to the pillars of human action. These are based on many other imperatives: energy saving (by routine as much as by techno-scientific and innovative resolution), social sharing, and curiosity, which can take forms of innovation oriented in science, technology, or industry, but not only and not primarily: and perhaps, above all, the political "game".

Conclusion

The voluntarist position advocating a liberal and humanist type of education can be retained as a necessary horizon, as much as the development of techno-scientific innovation or economic efficiency. This position would be reinforced by the irrepressible human need for freedom, social creativity, and reflexivity, the reality of which has been demonstrated by both humanistic psychology and anthropology. The generalization of secondary education in the last half of the 20th century in the main countries of the world, and today the equally massive development of higher education, have positive consequences from this point of view. In fact, in the industrialized and post-industrial countries, between 40% and 60 % of an age group will have completed a university course, and lifelong learning is also becoming more widespread. It is therefore these privileged moments of reflexivity, for a significant part of the human population, that can become the framework of possibility and elaboration of proposals and action for the common good: the production of knowledge is by definition universal if, precisely, it is recognized as such.

But a possible reorientation would only generate systemic transformations under the conditions of a major change of orientation, based on creative capacity, art, and empathy between all humans and therefore by renunciation, by the States and their agents, of an industrialist instrumentalization, through doctrines that promote innovation. No one would believe in this renunciation if, on the one hand, the forms of education and training through creativity and the project had not been used with good results in the motivation for learning for more than two centuries and if, more fundamentally, the potentially fatal economic, social, and political crises did not risk imposing themselves on States and societies.

The worst for humanity, in terms of the degradation of eco-systems, is likely under current conditions. A priori, no techno-scientific answer (Johnson, 2017) has a chance to solve the challenges, however sophisticated it may be. But the worst is never certain, and, paraphrasing the philosopher Pascal, it is appropriate to "gamble". We must advocate an education that develops the "humanistic" capacity of individuals and human groups, left free to define the meaning of their actions. We must also argue, with philosophers of higher education such as Ronald Barnett (2018), for a reversal of the trends at work in higher education, through the development of free academic institutions, taking up some of the strong traditions of self-governance in western higher education, ridding them – needless to say – of the scoriae of aristocratic corporatism, and integrating students and all stakeholders in their governance.

Let us finally conclude with an affirmation of the value of the "European historical experience". One can consider that this part of Eurasia, regularly downgraded in comparison with the historical civilizations of the Middle East, India, and China (Morris, 2010), but capable of having produced great creators, is capable of unprecedented military or scientific, but also political and artistic, achievements, due to its very eccentricity and internal chaos (Levy, 2008). Europe, with its complex and contradictory political anthropologies, its diverse institutions and languages, its gaping historical wounds, its colonial and genocidal guilt, but also its university history favoring open freedom, its capacity for initiative and rebound, can constitute a laboratory, a response, if it too reorients itself toward a humanism that it has invented. In the heart of Europe, princes adopted a motto that should be taken up again with despair: “Il n’est pas necessaire d’espérer pour entreprendre, ni de réussir pour persévérer” (there is no need to hope to undertake, nor to succeed to persevere).

References

Adler, E. (2019). *World ordering: A social theory of cognitive evolution.* Cambridge University Press.

Bengtsen, S. S., & Barnett, R. (2018). *The Thinking University: A philosophical examination of thought and higher education.* Springer.

Birner, R. (2018). Bioeconomy Concepts, in Lewandowski, I. (ed.), *Bioeconomy: Shaping the Transition to a Sustainable, Biobased Economy*, 17–38. Cham: Springer.

Bourg, D. (2012). Transition écologique plutôt que Développement durable. *Vraiment Durable*, 2012 N°1, pp. 77–96.

Burger-Helmchen, T. (2019). Innovation studies and knowledge generation. *Journal of Innovation Economics & Management, 30*, 245–251.

Carayannis, E. G., Barth, T. D., & Campbell, D. F. (2012). The Quintuple Helix innovation model: Global warming as a challenge and driver for innovation. *Journal of Innovation and Entrepreneurship, 1*, 2.

Clerc, D., & Landes, D. S. (2001). “Richesse et pauvreté des nations”. *L’Économie politique, 11*(3), 107–112.

Desjeux, D. (2022). Le marché des dieux, comment naissent les innovations religieuses, du judaisme au christianisme. PUF.

Fossati, E. C., Degavre, F., & Lévesque, B. (2018). ‘Social innovation: Back on the steps of a theoretical and practical construction’. *Revue de la régulation* [Online], 23 | online 05 July 2018.

Fassin, D.(dir.). (2022). *La société qui vient.* Le seuil.

Fressoz, J.B. (2022). Énergie et matières premières: le mythe de la transition, Omniprésent dans les discours, la transition est absente dans l’histoire matérielle de l’humanité, pour la Science n° 535.

Freeman, C., & Louçã, F. (2001). *As time goes by: From the Industrial Revolutions to the Information Revolution*. Oxford University Press.

Gauthier, D., & Benjaminsen, T. A. (2012). Environnement, discours et pouvoir, l'approche Political ecology. Quae, 2012.

Godin, B. (2006). The Knowledge-Based Economy: Conceptual Framework or Buzzword? *The Journal of Technology Transfer, 31*, 17–30.

Godin, B., & Vinck, D. (2017). *Critical studies of innovation, alternative approaches to the pro-innovation bias*. Elgar Publishing.

Graeber, D., & Wengrow, D. (2021). *The dawn of everything: A history of Humanity*. MacMillan, 2021.

Guilhot, L., Meunié, A., & Pouyanne, G. (2018). "Chinese cities, key actors in the fight against air pollution?". *China World, 56*(4), 51–58.

Guston, D. H., Fisher, E., Grunwald, Armin, Owen, R., Swierstra, T., & van der Burg, S. (2014). Responsible innovation: Motivations for a new journal. *Journal of Responsible Innovation, 1*(1), 1–8.

Heath, J. (2020). *The machinery of government, public administration and the liberal state*. Oxford University Press.

Johnson, S. A. (2017). *Why did ancient civilizations fail?*. Routledge.

Johnstone, P., Rogge, K. S., Kivimaa, P., Farné Fratini, C., & Primmer, E. (2021). Exploring the re-emergence of industrial policy: Perceptions regarding low carbon energy transitions in Germany, the United Kingdom and Denmark, *Energy Research & Social Science, 74*, Elsevier.

Joly, P. B. (2017). "Beyond the competitiveness framework? Models of innovation revisited." *Journal of Innovation Economics & Management, 22*(1), 79–96.

Kroll, H., & Frietsch, R. (2022). China's changing role in global science and innovation, Discussion papers innovation systems and policy analysis no. 73. Karlsruhe: Fraunhofer ISI.

Le Breton, E. (2019). "How mobility fractures cities". *DARD/DARD, 1*(1), 50–57.

Lechevalier, S. (2019). *Innovation beyond technology: Science for society and interdisciplinary approaches*. Springer, 324 pp.

Lévy, J. (2008). *L'invention du Monde, une géographie*. Presses de Sciences Po.

Middleton, G. D. (2017). *Understanding collapse, ancient history and modern myth*. Cambridge University Press, 2017.

Moore, J. W. (2015). *Capitalism in the web of life, ecology and the accumulation of capital.* Verso.

Morris, I. (2010). *Why the west rules-for now: The patterns of history, and what they reveal about the future.* Farrar, Status & Giroux.

Moulaert, F., (2013). *The international handbook of social innovation, collective action, social learning and transdisciplinary research.* Edward Elgar.

Mouton, G. (2019). The energy transition "with Chinese characteristics": Geopolitical dimensions of a public policy, article published on 2 December: http://asie1000mots-cetase.org/La-transition-energetique-aux

Nicolaï, I., & Faucheux, S. (2015). Business models and the diffusion of eco-innovations in the eco-mobility sector. *Society and Business Review, 10*(3), 203–222.

Nusbaum, M. C. (2010). *Not for profit, why democracy needs humanities.* Princeton University Press.

Pestre, D. (2015). *Histoire des sciences et des savoirs.* Le Seuil.

Popp Bermann, E. (2013). *Creating the Market University: How academic science became.* Princeton University Press.

Popp Bermann, E. (2022). *Thinking like an economist: How efficiency replaced equality in U.S. Public Policy.* Princeton University Press.

Richez-Battesti, N., Petrella, F., & Vallade, D. (2012). Social innovation, a notion with plural uses: What issues and challenges for analysis?. *Innovations, 38*(2), 15–36.

Rival, M., & Ruano-Borbalan, J. (2017). The making of co-constructed public policies: Ideology and innovative practices. *Politiques & Management Public*, 1–2, 5–16.

Rodrik, D. (2014). Green industrial policy. *Oxford Review of Economic Policy, 30*(3), 469–491.

Ruano-Borbalan, J. C. (2017). La grande standardisation et la transformation de la connaissance technoscientifique en société. *Innovations, 1*(52), 17–41.

Ruano-Borbalan, J. C. (2018). La démocratie technique au prisme des Sciences Sociales. *Technology and Innovation*, ISTE OpenScience, *18*(4).

Ruano-Borbalan, J. C. (2019). Pluridisciplinary programs for innovation: Realities and limits of a promising form of learning. *European Journal of Education*, 54. 10.1111/ejed.12370.

Ruano-Borbalan, J. C. (2021). Risques technoscientifiques en société, contribution to the report of the Allianz "New Risks" Chair, to be published.

Ruano-Borbalan, J. C. (2022–1). Chapter 37. Transformations de l'innovation à la lumière de la crise sanitaire. In: Cappelletti, L. (Ed.), *Crise de la connaissance et connaissance de la crise: Les points de vue du Conservatoire national des arts et métiers* (pp. 389–402). EMS Editions.

Ruano-Borbalan, J. C. (2022–2) Doctoral education from it's medieval foundations to today's globalization andstandardisation. *European Journal of Education*, "special Issue on Doctoral Education". In Gabor, H. & Ruano-Borbalan, J. C. (Ed.), Wiley-Blackwell.

Ruano-Borbalan, J. C. (2022–3). Reducing inequality in higher education: Limitations and possibilities. *European Journal of Education*, special issue (dir. Ruano-Borbalan, J.C.), *57*(2), 161–167, June 2022.

Scott, J. (2017). *Against the grain, a deep history of earliest states.* Yale University Press.

Sovacool, B. K., Del Rio, F. D., & Griffiths, S. (2020). Contextualizing the Covid-19 pandemic for a carbon-constrained world: Insights for sustainability transitions, energy justice, and research methodology. *Energy Research & Social Science, 68*, 101701.

Tirole, J. (2016). *Economics for the common good.* Princeton University Press.

Von Schomberg, R., & Hankins, J. (Eds.). (2019). *International handbook on responsible innovation*. Edward Elgar.

Wisniovski, M. (2022). "Every American an innovator: How innovation became a way of life", forthcoming.

Evolution of the food sector in innovation ecosystems

Camille Aouinaït[1]

Abstract: The food sector is experiencing fast and intensive changes. Environmental pressures, economic disturbances and social requirements are enhancing changes that society, firms, and economic agents have to undertake. For several years we have been witnessing an increasing interest in the strengthening of social ties, on the one hand, and regional and local food products, on the other hand. The chapter deals with the importance of short food supply chains, in a health, economic, ethical, environmental, and social context that is uncertain. The COVID-19 pandemic has impacted many sectors in an economic dimension as well as a social dimension. Nevertheless, it has also brought opportunity for improvement and changes on an ecological dimension. The agri-food sector has benefited from a boost in consumer interest and in the innovation development time window. In this chapter there is a focus on digitization and the use by short food supply chains of digital innovations in an ecosystem innovation perspective.

Keywords: Digitization, Short food supply chain, Resilience, Sustainability

Introduction

The standardization of food products and industrial production chains over the last few decades has been increasingly criticized by actors in the agricultural sector themselves and by consumers. The proliferation of raw and processed products that travel hundreds (or even more) kilometers

[1] AGROSCOPE, Switzerland and Research Network on Innovation, France.

before being consumed is moving toward a "re-territorialization" of the food system (Poulain, 2013). This localization of the food system has a positive impact on local economies, as argued by Benedek et al. (2020). Alternative supply chains have thus been developed, whether through producer or consumer-driven initiatives. Short food supply chains are developing and spreading around the world in various forms such as direct farm sales, community supported agriculture (CSA), farmers' stores and markets, digital platforms offering agricultural products, and many others (Belletti et al., 2012; Chiffoleau & Dourian, 2020; Kneafsey et al., 2013; United Nations Industrial Development Organization, 2020). Actors structure themselves in such a way that this energizes the ecosystem and produces innovations such as the appearance of CSAs, Association de Maintien de l'Agriculture Paysanne (AMAP), and other forms of baskets of products that consumers can buy from producers, with or without a subscription. The direct relationships that are created between producers and consumers are an important motivation for using these types of food chains (Belletti et al., 2012; Benedek et al., 2020). Technological and non-technological, social, marketing, or environmental innovations are developed and implemented at a local scale. One of the advantages of using these short food chains is that producers obtain a better price, due to the higher margin capture, dedicated to intermediaries in longer chains (Malak-Rawlikowska et al., 2019).

Innovation can have an important role in responding to the current and future challenges that our society is facing. Many sectors can be impacted by responsible, appropriate, and smart innovations like the sectors of food, housing, clothing, health care, heating, and energy for instance.

Innovation can be seen as a process or a system that depicts a capacity for change at different levels such as technical, organizational, and managerial. Innovation also implies the involvement of actors that constitute an ecosystem (Laperche et al., 2019). However, even without a unique definition of an innovation ecosystem, Granstrand and Holgersson (2020) identified more than 20 definitions of innovation ecosystems, concluding with: *"An innovation ecosystem is the evolving set of actors, activities, and artifacts, and the institutions and relations, including complementary and substitute relations that are important for the innovative performance of an actor or a population of actors."*

The goal of the chapter is to analyze the evolution of the organization of food chains by focusing on short food supply chains (SFSCs). Through an analysis of the literature, the innovations that are the most adapted for SFSCs in a context of development of digital tools and ecological transition are presented. The role of innovation ecosystems and the economic agents in the creation, dissemination, and adoption of innovations is highly important. This first part of the chapter focuses on describing the evolution of SFSCs in different geographical areas, and the anchoring of these chains and the stakes they have in sustainable development and ecological transition. The second part relates the implications of the pandemic. Finally, the use of digital technology by short food supply chains ends the chapter.

1. The evolution of short food supply chains and their impact on sustainability

The next paragraph highlights the relationship that the elements of relational proximity and geographical proximity, both in developed and developing countries, have with the innovation ecosystem. The latter is structured with several actors that display interactions of different natures (i.e. social, hierarchical, institutional, and technical). This ecosystem can reply to changes and stimuli like ecological transition and the digital revolution by developing and implementing innovations.

1.1. Short food supply chains in Europe

According to Chiffoleau et al. (2007), Short Food Supply Chains (SFSCs) can be categorized taking into account the number of intermediaries, the dimension (individual versus collective) and the geographical distance. Thus, the authors ended up with a categorization (see Figure 1).

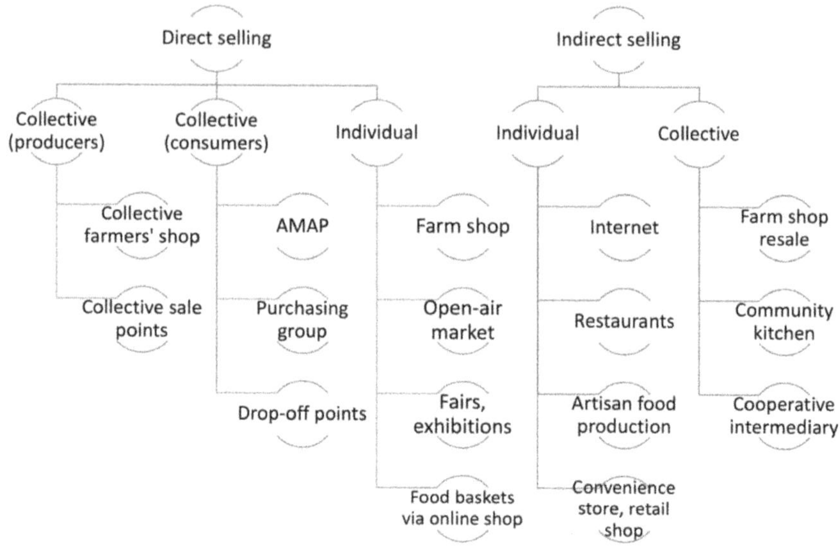

Figure 1. SFSC categories based on (Bounameaux, 2015; Chiffoleau, 2007)

The main definition of SFSCs does not follow a consensus. Various criteria can be used to define what is a short chain, and weighting of these criteria can also differ according to the actors' role. Is a short chain "short enough" if it includes one intermediary? Or is it possible to include two intermediaries? For processed products, where does the short chain start, and where does it end? There is a list of three actors: the producer of primary products (e.g. beef, milk, fruit), the processor (e.g. slaughterhouse, dairy processing), and the final consumer.

The concept of short food supply chains was nevertheless framed by the EU in the EU's rural development regulation (1305/2013) as a "supply chain involving a limited number of economic operators, committed to cooperation, local economic development, and close geographical and social relations between food producers, processors and consumers."

At a political level, the development of SFSCs is one answer to the Common Agricultural Policy to improve European competitiveness. Following this definition, in the EU's rural development policy for 2014–2020, SFSCs were defined for the first time. This policy supported and fostered production in SFSCs by co-financing producers through the European Agricultural Fund for Rural Development ("Rural development", 2022).

Marsden et al. (2000) argued that SFSCs have the capacity "to 're-socialize' or 're-spatialize' food". This characteristic induces a notion of food value. It is also an element that is often cited by consumers when one is asking for the motivation of buying food products from this type of supply chain.

Furthermore, the locality and the specific farm are of interest in the definition of SFSCs. The level of proximity is quite high and there is a personal aspect included in SFSCs. Consumers get to know the products and the producers that are behind these. Moreover, Marsden et al. (2000) highlighted the need for clear information (i.e. during face-to-face contacts at the point of sale, or on food packaging) to be transferred to consumers. They argued that "it is not the number of times a product is handled or the distance over which it is ultimately transported which is necessarily critical, but the fact that the product reaches the consumer embedded with information."

In turn, Kneafsey et al. (2013) stated that SFSCs can be categorized from the simplest to the most complex forms. The simplest one is direct sales from the producer to the consumer (e.g. on-farm, farmers' markets, internet deliveries). Other forms are box delivery schemes, community-supported agriculture (CSA), or "pick your own". These forms are characterized by the financial support of consumers for local producers.

Marsden et al. (2000), and later Renting et al. (2003) identify three main types of SFSC, all of which engender some form of "connection" between the food consumer and producer: spatial proximity, spatially extended, and face-to-face.

Furthermore, the definition of sustainable diets by the Food and Agricultural Organization of the United Nations organization is the following:

> "diets with low environmental impact that contribute to food and nutrition security and healthy lives for present and future generations. Sustainable diets help protect and respect biodiversity and ecosystems, are culturally acceptable, economically equitable and accessible, affordable, nutritionally safe and healthy, and optimize natural and human resources".

The development of short food supply chains is increasing in different countries, in Europe at least. In the case of Belgium, the definition includes different aspects like better eating (i.e. unprocessed food that is preferably local, organic, and seasonal), reducing food waste along the value chain.

In this regard, sustainable food can be understood "as a set of practices, from the production to the consumption of food goods, that are economically viable, socially sustainable and environmentally responsible" (Yuna Chiffoleau & Prévost, 2012). Therefore, the development of SFSCs is depicted as a sustainable solution providing sustainable food items. Consequently, the three poles put forward are economic, social, and environmental.

Through these definitions that were taken from the European context, we can see that many concepts often come up, but with different particularities.

1.2. Definition of short food supply chains outside Europe

In Montreal, a study has emphasized the need to combat food deserts by creating collaboration and alliances between actors in the conventional sector and local actors. The goal is to benefit from current infrastructures (Lefèvre & Audet, 2016).

In Latin America, characteristics of SFSCs that are more common than in European developed countries have been studied in Latin America have been studied. The weight of the industrialized agri-food sector is quite important, as well as the urbanization rate. Also, initiatives of alternatives markets on long food supply chains are increasing in order to valorize familial production of food items (e.g. localized agri-food systems, labeling on environmental advantages, or based on geographical origin, amongst others) (Requier-Desjardins, Roudart, 2019).

The commercialization of açaí has been developed, in addition to traditional consumption, for the middle class in Brazil and abroad, by valorizing the nutritional qualities of the fruit. Moreover, the actors of this sector are in relation with each other, but not only within short circuits. One of the determining factors is the processing of the fruit, which can be carried out on site, with the Brazilian middle class and tourists as the main consumers. The short circuits act as a "vector of reinforcement of a development dynamic" at the level of a territory. The construction of localized agricultural and food markets in the south of the country has been made possible by supporting public policies for supplying school canteens and vulnerable people, organic certification, and the creation of farmers' markets. The public policies implemented sought to enhance the value of the territory while relying on the collective action of actors in the ecosystem (Requier-Desjardins & Roudart, 2019).

Moustier and Renting (2015) studied the potential innovations in SFSCs in southern countries. They found that food safety is one main issue that needs to be secured in order to perform SFSCs. Moreover, supermarkets' requirements can hinder producers in southern countries, as the producers cannot supply large volumes of food products, in time delivery, and food quality standards. Furthermore, the limited scale of production hinders producers to compete with larger production plots that reach the necessary economies of scale. In this context, the diversification of market sales can be an efficient solution. Farmer's markets combined with supply to local restaurants is an example given by the authors.

Short food supply chain examples that (Moustier & Renting, 2015) inventoried include:

- "Online food shops (e.g. the Jingle online store in Beijing that delivers seasonal vegetables, fruit, eggs, milk, oil, poultry meat, etc.) produced by several cooperatives of peri-urban producers to the staff of government offices and universities in Beijing that order these food products through the Jingle website"
- Food products that are directly delivered to restaurants, hotels, schools, and institutions by producers from cooperatives (such as the Van Noi Cooperative in Hanoi)
- "Food buyers' cooperatives (for example, the Canastas Comunitarias in Ecuador): groups of the urban poor that bi-weekly collectively buy a basket of ca. 15 food items from ecological producers in the city region."

The authors also reviewed 26 innovative short food chain initiatives designed in developing countries (Renting & Dubbeling, 2013) and other cases developed in Asia, Africa, and Brazil (Moustier, 2013). They found that all these initiatives depict some differences and common characteristics.

The divergences include the type of food products, distribution methods, quality attributes (e.g. farmers' fair prices, ecologically grown, regional location of production, etc.), the certification type and degree, or "the degree of external support received". Common characteristics include the marketing messages that target specific consumers' needs that also correspond to motivations that push consumers to purchase their food products in SFSCs (e.g. support for the local economy and especially small-scale producers, the reduction in agro-chemicals use, or food safety). This brings concrete results through the creation of a niche market that can provide better price margins, thanks to the exclusion of intermediaries in the value chain and the valorization of products.

These elements highlight the sustainable advantage that a short food supply chain can have in the context of southern countries. Fresher products, with a higher quality due to the reduction of agricultural inputs, can be economically valorized, for the advantage of producers. However, SFSCs cannot be the only food supply chains that will nourish the entire population. Moustier (2017) argues that SFSCs are complementary to longer chains, mainly because of comparative advantages and drawbacks for each supply chain. One main advantage of SFSCs is their capacity to manage fresh and perishable products and which are efficient in cases where transport logistics are difficult. However, for land pressure regions and where transport management is improved, longer chains are more efficient than SFSCs.

Geographical proximity appears to be very important in the context of developing countries, as well as the relational proximity for urban food supply. On the one hand, geographical proximity is related to the link between food origin and its perishability and the difficulty of transportation. In order to supply fresh and perishable food products, the production location should be close to the consumption location. This is frequently the case in developing countries. On the other hand, relational proximity corresponds to the frequency of interactions between value chain actors, especially intermediaries, producers, and consumers. The latter can ask for information on food production systems, or the origin of food, for example.

Moustier et al. (2017) studied the case of Vietnam and other countries in Asia, Africa, and Latin America. They found that geographical proximity favors relational proximity. In this regard, Aubry and Kebir (2013) designed a food chain typology based on the degrees of geographical and relational proximities. Based on a scale from low to high for both geographical proximity and organized proximity, different supply chains can be categorized in Figure 2.

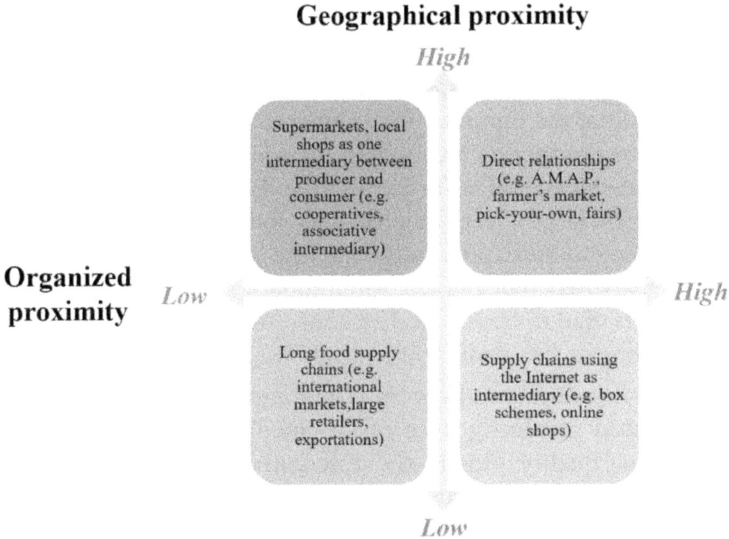

Figure 2: Categorization of food supply chains based on organized and geographical proximity (based on Aubry and Kebir (2013))

Disparities between long and short food supply chains include the commitment level between farmers and consumers, which is lower in short than in longer chains. Consumer concerns focus more on food safety and support for local family agriculture by public authorities than concerns about the environment, which is a more important topic in developed countries.

Transport limitations are another concern for SFSCs in developing countries. Geographical proximity is of great importance in this context and can support the supply of perishable products.

1.3. Short food chains as a resilience tool

In a context of resource scarcity, limitations, and pressure at economic, environmental, and social levels, alternative value chains are increasing all over the world. Sustainability is one of the drivers of the increase in initiatives from different actors in the agri-food sector. Short food supply chains are one of these alternative solutions[2].

The various food supply systems depict diverse features. Bounameaux (2015) states that the domestic food system is characterized by the proximity between production location and consumption location. The surpluses are transferred to family members and the organization is mainly managed at the family level. A proximity food system has a few intermediaries, geographical proximity, and the producer's expertise is not officially recognized. For the territorial food system, there can be more intermediaries than the other food systems, and the geographical proximity is also different (i.e. from 100 to 1,000 km).

The agro-industrial food system is characterized by the mass market, no geographical proximity, a lot of intermediaries, and standardization of the product quality. Finally, the differentiated quality food system is highlighted by labels that guarantee the products' quality, more expensive food products, and diverse quality (e.g. organic, halal products, terroir products).

The resilience of actors in the food ecosystem is possible through the implementation of short circuits. Food dependency can be reduced by increasing the number of producers, increasing their autonomy, and resistance to long-distance actors such as supermarkets (Bounameaux, 2015). Diversification of products to reach several markets reduces risk-taking. Moreover, the development of know-how can strengthen the skills of the actors and thus also strengthen the ecosystem. Innovation comes into play in this context via the development and implementation of new products, more or less incremental, depending on the companies and actors involved.

The short food supply chains also enable power to be given back to the actors located upstream of the value chain, i.e. the producers. Downstream actors such as consumers or citizens have, moreover, active decision making. They can give more meaning to their food by selecting, through their involvement in the choice of producers and products in particular.

---

2 By "alternatives" we are suggesting that the development of these value chains is not overwhelming the mass market. However, the success of local initiatives in different localities is confirmed and the term "alternatives" can no longer be correct in this regard.

Hendry et al. (2018) showed the importance of different collaboration directions (e.g. horizontal and vertical) within the ecosystem to build resilience. This resilience involved the firms' capability to innovate in order to maintain and/or increase their competitiveness (Requier-Desjardins & Roudart, 2019).

2. Short food supply chains during the pandemic

The pandemic created a great lever for acceleration of the ecological transition. It pushed the development of SFSCs, in particular digital purchases of local food products. As food consumption is vital and everyone is concerned by this sector, the health crisis has led to the acceleration of the development of trends that had already been established for some years (Bourdoncle, 2022; Galanakis et al., 2021; Nemes et al., 2021).

The pandemic caused by the SARS-CoV-2 or Covid-19 had a substantial impact on many sectors, countries, and populations. Regarding the agri-food sector, several publications and scientific articles have been published since 2020 (i.e. the date of the onset of the pandemic). The rise of direct on-farm sales, the development of sales online, the interest of consumers for local producers' markets, the development of digital innovations to satisfy the need of consumers during lock-downs, and the survival of producers' and firms', were highly important (Dannenberg et al., 2020; Galanakis et al., 2021). It was also the case of social innovations where Chiffoleau et al. (2018), Cranfield et al. (2012) and Nemes et al. (2021) found the necessity for consumers and individuals to recreate social links and share with others, as a community seeks to sustain itself.

In a context of a health crisis, consumers wish to buy their food products directly from producers, mainly because they can gain knowledge on how the food is produced, where, and by whom. Small and medium-sized enterprises had to cope with these new societal challenges: economic, health, and social crises. Innovations in SFSCs thus represent a means to find new solutions, to adapt the business, and attract new consumers.

Many innovations were developed during the pandemic, being included in food system models categorized as "domestic", "proximity", "agro-industrial", and "differentiated quality". Existing models before the pandemic were indeed accelerated and combined with each other: home deliveries and drive-by supermarkets, traditional actors in SFSCs who were developing and implementing digital platforms or new sales areas; and adaptation of certification systems for food quality (Touzard, 2020).

Short food supply chains can benefit from innovations and improving changes. Societal issues applied to daily challenges can be related to the need for innovations by SFSCs. Their growth, to combine personal beliefs, has less of an impact on the environment, supports farmers financially, creates social links, and focuses on health and nutrition, amongst others. SFSCs are locally embedded and can benefit from the existing ecosystem, with the diversity of actors who are present. Granstrand and Holgersson (2020) identified the definition of the innovation ecosystem. The elements can be found in various SFSCs. Thus, these innovations have different advantages:

2.1 Optimization of costs

Digitization thus represents an efficient and adapted innovative tool in this unprecedented situation. It allows producers to gain critical size and increase sales, supporting their activities by optimizing costs (Chiffoleau et al., 2018).

Mutualization and cooperation are facilitated using digital innovations, as different actors can collaborate. Chiffoleau et al. (2018) take the example of an ordering platform, which can be used by several producers, and a carpooling platform, also used by producers to optimize deliveries and reduce carbon costs and time spent at the same time.

2.2 Trust and consumer loyalty

Consumer loyalty can also be increased by digital innovations. Even with physical distance, the social relationship between producers and consumers, which is one of the main motivations for SFSC product consumption, is ensured (Chiffoleau et al., 2018). Furthermore, at the beginning of the pandemic, anxiety, fear, and weariness were spreading among consumers. There are many motivations for the consumption of local food products, comprising economic, social, environmental features, and health benefits (Cranfield et al., 2012). The pandemic brought the opportunity for diverse consumers to question themselves about food security, origin, and how it is produced, leading to a questioning of the reliability of the food system (Hobbs, 2020).

Furthermore, consumers have the possibility to look for information on various products and topics such as composition, production process, origin of products, and other elements (Chiffoleau et al., 2018).

2.3 Consumer governance in SFSCs

In a French participatory approach entitled "Ici.C.Local" ("here it is local"), consumers have the possibility to signpost SFSC products in retail outlets at the local level. A community of consumers manages this platform, which aims to target all actors including farmers, processors, retailers, and craftsmen. In this regard, digital technology is seen as a driver of a development of food democracy for a transition to food systems that are more environmentally, socially, and economically sustainable.

The Covid-19 pandemic returned the need for food traceability to the main landscape. Thus, this was an opportunity for digital innovation to be developed in this domain (Galanakis et al., 2021). Rowan and Galanakis (2020) discuss blockchain technology that is a "security-proof" approach, ensuring a recording of transactions in a digital form. The potential of this technology is substantial and disruptive. It can also be applied to the food sector, for food safety and quality aspects, food waste improvements, recycling, and traceability.

Besides the boost to the ecological transition fostered by the pandemic, another result of this health crisis was the digital revolution (Bourdoncle, 2022). Short food supply chains also had the opportunity to increase since direct-to-consumer services have been in high demand by consumers. Initiatives were developed in this context, while traditional shops also went into the niche of online sales (Galanakis et al., 2021). Indeed, there were significant requests for online food trade, and a substantial increase in demand was observed.

A study by Nemes et al. (2021) concerned the implications of the Covid-19 crisis as an opportunity for ecological transition with alternative food supply chains. The authors included 13 countries from Europe, North America, Asia, and South America. They found that alternative networks like SFSCs are able to satisfy the social needs inherent to the initiatives of this type of short food chain. Innovations were then used during the pandemic to adapt the value chain to disruptive changes.

Digitization and the implementation of innovations in agriculture and short food supply chains are presented in more depth in the third part of this chapter.

SFSCs have social implications, specifically in terms of economic and environment impacts. Besides, different actors of the ecosystem can benefit from these positive implications.

The social implications of SFSCs have been investigated through the negative side, as these can create divergences and affordability issues for certain economic and social categories of the population. The biases also concern gender, race, and class (Goodman et al., 2012; Nemes et al., 2021). Food and nutrition are now widely recognized to be linked to health; the importance of purchasing and consuming this kind of food products is essential. However, the price can be a barrier for consumers for some food products sold in SFSCs.

3. Adaptation of short food supply chains using digital innovations

3.1. *Digitization of short food chains*

As mentioned above, digitization provides a great opportunity for supply chains through increased visibility for food products, improved transparency, logistics optimization, and real-time data collection, for instance (Goodman et al., 2012; Nemes et al., 2021). Many actors in food supply chains can therefore implement these types of innovations. Farmers can gain time in different agricultural activities with robots, big data, even the Internet of Things, and with the agriculture of precision. Digital technologies appear to support sustainability and ecological transition with the development of tailored solutions for every crop to adapt, with a high level of accuracy, the need for inputs (fertilizers, water, treatments, etc.). They can also help the decision-making process, by providing real-time data such as crop stress, according to diverse parameters.

Blockchain technology can also prevent the deterioration of raw materials throughout the transformation process. Processors and actors that deal with these raw materials directly benefit from this digitization of the supply chain. Furthermore, retailers also exploit digitization via certification of the food supply chain from start to finish. Consumers can also get information about product history. This added value is one piece of precious information that retailers use for communicating about the product (Bigliardi et al., 2022). Finally, the concept of the circular economy can be supported by digital technologies, specifically by blockchain technology. This will ensure transparency and timely information. Short food supply chains and the existing ecosystem would thus profit from this innovation.

Since the advent of the Internet in the 1980s, the digital revolution has continued to permeate many facets of our lives. The use of digital technology has been complexified and many sectors are economically based on many technological tools. Agriculture and SFSCs also follow this evolution through the implementation of innovations in diverse activities such as marketing, management of the farm (e.g. administrative tasks), logistics, and increasingly deliveries. Even if the purchase of food products is still a small proportion of total revenues in agriculture, there is a trend that was promoted during the pandemic that has potential for the future. The "drive" business model designed by big supermarkets has, for instance, democratized purchasing on the Internet (Naumowicz, 2019).

A striking example of the use of digitization in agriculture can be explained thanks to a French case. The collaborative economy observed a new business movement via La Ruche Qui Dit Oui, a French firm (Chiffoleau et al., 2018). It provides farmers, producers, and craftsmen with the possibility to connect with consumers through an online platform for selling. The platform takes a 20 % commission. Most of the producers' farms are located near the city and the concept of this farm is to support these "hives". In 2011, 71 firms were registered on the platform. There was a significant increase one year later, with 517 hives. The following years witnessed a different evolution (stagnation and reduction), reaching a total of 789 hives in 2019, extended at a territorial level (Naumowicz, 2019). In this context, digital technology seems to be an easy and accessible tool to foster behavior change and to support new interactions, like modifying our way of consumption by choosing and switching ways of purchasing food toward more sustainable systems (Chiffoleau et al., 2018; Naumowicz, 2019)

The advantages and the disruptive features of the digital revolution within the development of SFSCs include innovations borrowed from many models. Furthermore, at a governance level, digital technology supports the co-construction operation, while enlarging the social dimension (Chiffoleau et al., 2018).

Different European research programs have the objective to support rural development with actions and concrete activities. The European project SMARTCHAIN[3] aims to encourage and accelerate the shift to collaborative short food supply chains and to introduce new sound business models and innovative practical solutions that improve the competitiveness and sustainability of the European agri-food system. In this frame, a platform presenting innovations that were developed by different firms, associations, or cooperatives related to short food supply chains was designed in 2019. The goal of this inventory of innovations was to propose a place that is available to anyone who is looking for ideas, inspiration, or information on SFSC innovations. This platform was used to select technological innovations in the context of the chapter of this book.

Three categories of innovations were therefore identified: technological, social, and organizational. There is high diversity of innovations and comprises quality schemes, a disinfection system, a robot for harvesting activities in fruit production, a food radar system, vending machines, mobile juice trailers, biodegradable packaging, a predictive analytic of orders, a smart greenhouse, an aerial crop analysis system, smart label application, temperature monitoring labels, virtual farmers' market application, and traceability, amongst others. All these innovations were collected from producers and small farms, cooperatives, or professionals in the short food supply chains system. The extended range of innovations highlights the diversity of tools, devices, and strategies that this sector is using to cope with climate change, environmental pressures, and increasing socio-economic constraints.

3.2. Consumer involvement and support for SFSCs

Lankauskienė et al. (2022), in their article on the evolution of SFSC theory and practice, focused on the post-industrial food system and analyzed through three different paradigm innovation systems the importance of changes in the food ecosystem, their components, and the position of their actors. The authors stated the importance of food users in the innovation ecosystem. These became key players, and their needs have to be understood and fulfilled by all the actors in food supply chains.

---

3 https://www.smartchain-platform.eu/en/innovation-inventory-new?combine=&field_innoinv_type_value%5B%5D=Organizational&sort_order=ASC

Furthermore, as consumption of food products is playing an increasing role in sustainability, user-driven innovations are increasingly important and also developed. Users can directly innovate and/or think about innovative solutions that they could use for their personal needs. These users are actively involved in the innovation process. The trend of urgent needs related to food waste, valorization of by-products, and the circular economy can be partially solved with the involvement of these users.

The authors also pinpointed the change in the market economy to a platform-based network economy. This economy is focusing on value creation through the use of collaborative networks. For SFSCs, famers and consumers directly transact using platform resources. This can bring them different advantages: the network is stimulated via the platform; and value co-creation activities can be developed.

Beaudoin et al. (2018) studied the consumer's perception and experience regarding SFSCs. The consumer "sees himself as responsible, enlightened, capable of making production systems evolve" (one consumer answer). This is opposed to what another consumer defines as "when you are an unthinking consumer". In this regard, there is an important advantage to being an active and recognized consumer. The concept of "consom'acteur" is crystallized here. Consumers take back control of their food consumption.

Moreover, the ecological aspect is one driver for consumers to buy food products from SFSCs. Beaudoin et al. (2018) highlighted the fact that this consumption is "more respectful of the environment" and a reduction in the negative impact on the environment (e.g. pollution) was also one element that consumers pinpointed. Consumers have a perception that food product consumption from SFSCs is less polluting than consuming products from longer chains. Production methods and distances for supply are both perceived as more positive for SFSCs.

Beaudouin et al. (2018) investigated the temporal dimension of the experience of SFSCs. The temporal dimension is one crucial element that distinguishes the longer food supply chains with the shorter ones. The authors collected data from consumers that confirmed the time-consuming aspect of SFSCs, and the "slowing down of the rhythm of life", with the notion of entertainment through various events such as demonstration, tastings, visits. Nevertheless, SFSC initiatives can be driven by producers and consumers that are actively involved in the monitoring and success of the initiative. Innovative short food chains were developed, some through producer impulse (e.g. farm sales), third party impulse (e.g. La Ruche Qui Dit Oui), and consumer impulse (e.g. Association de Maintien d'une Agriculture Paysanne) (Beaudouin et al., 2018).

Over the last ten years, raw milk distributors have spread in many locations in France. These vending machines were initially installed by producers or cooperatives. This offer was then extended to other food items such as cheese, fruit, and vegetables in the form of farm racks and refrigerated parcels, in shops that can be opened from early to late in the day, facilitating accessibility for consumers (Chiffoleau et al., 2018).

Digital technology allows a critical size to be reached that is economically interesting for farms and cooperatives. Nevertheless, the transparency of the short supply chain is still guaranteed as structure size is not modified with the economic equilibrium that is targeted.

At a social level, the digitization implemented in SFSCs responds to a need by consumers for tools that are easy to access and too complex to understand (i.e. instead of blockchain technology used in longer food chains) (Chiffoleau et al., 2018). Finally, the relationships between producers and consumers can be improved through the re-allocation of time to more personal links, discussions, and explanations of production methods to consumers, for instance.

Different organizations and actors, partly from the public sector, bring their support to actors in SFSCs. Therefore, the ecosystem is creating opportunities to find solutions, and innovation can emerge from that.

Sales support provided by institutions was strong in France in the late 2000s. Before this support, producers were sustained by European rural development policy and social cohesion. The short food chain concept emerged in the European Leader Observatory of Innovative Actions from 1997. Ten years later, this concept of an alternative food network was scaled up to national level and the Grenelle de l'Environnement emphasized this distribution channel as "one of the means, among others, of sustainable agriculture". At the governmental level, in 2008 the Minister of Agriculture created a working group to develop a network and delineate actions for its development. This network will then bring in organizations with public institutions (Chiffoleau, 2017).

Conclusion

The goal of this chapter was to draw a picture of the interesting potential offered by short food supply chains in a frame of ecological transition and digital revolution. Environmental pressures are increasing and climate change is increasingly crystallized through highly concrete consequences (e.g. extreme weather events, development of new diseases and pests for crops, fatal viruses for humans).

Many people want to take steps to have a positive impact on the environment. Consuming food products directly from producers using short food supply chains can be a part of a greater solution.

For many years initiatives in SFSCs have grown in popularity (Lankauskienė et al., 2022). Many consumers have a greater awareness of the implications of the food production system for the environment, but also at social and economic levels. The "good-dominant logic" versus the "service-dominant logic" was defined by Lankauskienė et al. (2022). The latter logic can be compared to the "servitization of farming" concept, which creates value for the supply chain with a focus on services (i.e. goods) that are distributed along this chain. It can foster a production strategy that pushes consumers to purchase food products that satisfy their personalized demands. Furthermore, it supports the creation of long-term relationships between actors in the supply chain, especially farmers and consumers. The transition of a globalized, capitalist, and mass-market food system to a more customized and local food system is "a new model of growth which harnesses the potential of digital services and technologies without forgetting the importance of social inclusion and ecological sustainability" (Valenduc, 2018).

Implementing sustainable business models is possible in the agricultural and food sectors. Innovation represents an efficient tool to reach this aim. Farmers, in particular farmers that have a part of their sales dedicated to the short food supply chain, are confronted with this trend and need.

The chapter highlighted different specific issues that SFSCs are coping with in both developed and developing countries. The logistics issue, difficulty to reach a sufficient critical size, food security, visibility, marketing, and unstable production can build great barriers for SFSC actors. Geographical and organizational proximity are also important and have significant weight in the functioning of the sectors but also of the territorial ecosystem.

Furthermore, consumer behavior that is shifting toward more local food, interest in the origin of the product, and traditional production methods, partially explains the increase in SFSC attendance and development. Besides the economic and ecological motivations, there is a social aspect in many SFSC initiatives. Moustier and Renting (2015) talk about the facilitation of fair market prices for small urban producers, the possibility of job creation for young people, or the facilitation of access to healthy food from known sources. Strengthening the role of farmers in food delivery to consumers is fairly or very important for 80 % of European citizens surveyed in 2016 (EUFIC, 2021).

At the European level, the European Commission supports multi-actor projects that use a participatory approach, including researchers, farmers, and other agri-food practitioners (i.e. advisers, cooperatives, trade bodies) in the project's consortium. This ensures efficient cooperation with concrete results and solutions that can be diffused to all actors in the ecosystem. The innovations are developed following a protocol of co-creation, expected to be positive on a long-term scale to many actors, and which supports rural development (EUFIC, 2021).

In addition to the important increase in interest in short food supply chains and the implementation of the implementation of innovations, encouraged by the health crisis, the social crisis, and environmental deterioration, technological innovations are used as a smart tool for many actors in the agricultural supply chains. The agri-food industry is influenced by digitization. Different steps of the supply chain are benefiting from these technologies, including cultivation, production, storage, or sales. Data generation and analysis that meet supply chain actors' needs are increasingly used in the sector (Bigliardi et al., 2022). The landscape of active players in the sector has broadened, especially in longer food chains with farmers, input producers (i.e. feed and seed producers), breeders, processors, transporters, distributors, wholesalers, retailers, and consumers.

Digitization is a trend and likewise a crucial mechanism for the improvement and competitivity of many agricultural firms. Innovations that come from abroad or from other supply chains have the potential to be implemented, with adaptations and modifications, so that actors of SFSCs can benefit from interesting positive impacts. In this context in which each actor (e.g. producer, processor, retailer, consumer) of the supply chain is concerned, external actors have a role to play. Policymakers, private firms, public bodies, researchers, companies, and civil society actors must be involved through an active approach to understand and encourage the process of digital change in order to be sustainable. The innovation ecosystem makes sense in that case.

However, a difficult challenge that SFSCs have to cope with in a context of ecological transition is to be recognized as a high-quality alternative to longer food supply chains, and also to have greater impacts at the local level. However, the initiatives that are developed in the short food supply chain system are mainly between an innovation approach and a transition approach, to go beyond the local framework of local impact. Lefèvre and Audet (2016) argue that it can be seen as a compromise system that wishes to solve social and environmental issues that are spreading at a global level.

Furthermore, at an environmental level, the efficiency of SFSCs is questioned. The number of intermediaries is at the core of the SFSC definition, as well as the short distance that consumers travel to purchase food products on sale directly to consumers. However, economies of scale are difficult to achieve since the production volumes are often limited and logistics can be hazardous (Requier-Desjardins & Roudart, 2019).

References

Aubry, C., & Kebir, L. (2013). Shortening food supply chains: A means for maintaining agriculture close to urban areas? The case of the French metropolitan area of Paris. *Food Policy, 41*(C), 85–93.

Beaudouin, V., Sugier, L., & Robert-Demontrond, P. (2018). Une lecture expérientielle du phénomène de consommation en circuit court alimentaire. *Management Avenir, 106*(8), 133–153.

Belletti, G., Casabianca, F., & Marescotti, A. (2012). Local food quality and local resources. In *Local agri-food systems in a global world. Market, social and environmental challenges*, 278. Cambridge Scholars Publishing. Consulté à l'adresse https://hal.archives-ouvertes.fr/hal-01354016

Benedek, Z., Fertő, I., & Szente, V. (2020). The multiplier effects of food relocalization: A systematic review. *Sustainability, 12*(9), 1–18.

Bigliardi, B., Filippellia, S., Petroni, A., & Tagliente, L. (2022). The digitalization of supply chain: A review. *Procedia Computer Science, 200*, 1806–1815. https://doi.org/10.1016/j.procs.2022.01.381

Bounameaux, D. (2015). *Le circuit court, une stratégie efficace pour lutter contre le gaspillage alimentaire des consommateurs à Bruxelles ?* Université Libre de Bruxelles, Bruxelles. Consulté à l'adresse https://mem-envi.ulb.ac.be/Memoires_en_pdf/MFE_14_15/MFE_Bounameaux_14_15.pdf

Bourdoncle, M. (2022). La pandémie et l'agriculture : un virus accélérateur de mutations ?Thierry Pouch et Marine Raffray. *Paysans & Société, 393*(3), 51–53. https://doi.org/10.3917/pes.393.0051

Chiffoleau, Y. (2007). *Vente directe et circuits courts : évaluations, définitions et typologie* (Les cahiers de l'observatoire CROC No. 1). Montpellier.

Chiffoleau, Y. (2017). Dynamique des identités collectives dans le changement d'échelle des circuits courts alimentaires. *Revue Française de Socio-Économie, 18*(1), 123–141. https://doi.org/10.3917/rfse.018.0123

Chiffoleau, Y., Bouré, M., & Akermann, G. (2018). Les circuits courts alimentaires à l'heure du numérique : quels enjeux? Une exploration. *Innovations Agronomiques,* (67), 37–47. https://doi.org/10.15454/FDWTG6

Chiffoleau, Y., & Dourian, T. (2020). Sustainable food supply chains: Is shortening the answer? A literature review for a research and innovation agenda. *Sustainability, 12*(23), 9831. https://doi.org/10.3390/su12239831

Chiffoleau, Y., & Prévost, B. (2012). Les circuits courts, des innovations sociales pour une alimentation durable dans les territoires. *Norois, 224*(3), 7–20. https://doi.org/10.4000/norois.4245

Cranfield, J., Henson, S., & Blandon, J. (2012). The effect of attitudinal and sociodemographic factors on the likelihood of buying locally produced food. *Agribusiness, 28*(2), 205–221. https://doi.org/10.1002/agr.21291

Dannenberg, P., Fuchs, M., Riedler, T., & Wiedemann, C. (2020). Digital transition by COVID-19 pandemic? The German Food Online Retail. *Tijdschrift Voor Economische En Sociale Geografie, 111*(3), 543–560. https://doi.org/10.1111/tesg.12453

EUFIC. (2021). *Short food supply chains exist in many forms across Europe. Multi-actor projects like Strength2Food and SMARTCHAIN are exploring ways to stimulate them.* Consulté à l'adresse https://www.eufic.org/en/food-production/article/short-food-supply-chains-reconnecting-producers-and-consumers

Galanakis, C. M., Rizou, M., Aldawoud, T. M. S., Ucak, I., & Rowan, N. J. (2021). Innovations and technology disruptions in the food sector within the COVID-19 pandemic and post-lockdown era. *Trends in Food Science & Technology, 110*, 193–200. https://doi.org/10.1016/j.tifs.2021.02.002

Goodman, D., Dupuis, E., & Goodman, M. (2012). *Alternative food networks: Knowledge, practice and politics, alternative food networks: Knowledge, Practice, and Politics*,. https://doi.org/10.4324/9780203804520

Granstrand, O., & Holgersson, M. (2020). Innovation ecosystems_ A conceptual review and a new definition | Elsevier Enhanced Reader, *Technovation*. https://doi.org/10.1016/j.technovation.2019.102098

Hendry, L. C., Stevenson, M., MacBryde, J., Ball, P., Sayed, M., & Liu, L. (2018). Local food supply chain resilience to constitutional change: The Brexit effect. *International Journal of Operations & Production Management, 39*(3), 429–453. https://doi.org/10.1108/IJOPM-03-2018-0184

Hobbs, J. E. (2020). Food supply chains during the COVID-19 pandemic. *Canadian Journal of Agricultural Economics/Revue Canadienne d'agroeconomie, 68*(2), 171–176. https://doi.org/10.1111/cjag.12237

Kneafsey, M., Eyden-Wood, T., Bos, E., Sutton, G., Santini, F., Gomez y Paloma, S., … Institute for Prospective Technological Studies. (2013). *Short food supply chains and local food systems in the EU: A state of play of their socio-economic characteristics.* Luxembourg: Publications Office. Consulté à l'adresse. http://dx.publications.europa.eu/10.2791/88784

Lankauskienė, R., Vidickienė, D., & Gedminaitė-Raudonė, Ž. (2022). Evolution of short food supply chain theory and practice: Two-sided networks and platforms. *Energies, 15*(3), 1137. https://doi.org/10.3390/en15031137

Laperche, B., Lima, M., Seuillet, E., & Trousse, B. (2019). *Ecosystèmes d'innovation: regards croisés des acteurs clés*. L'Harmattan – Collection L'esprit économique - Economie et Innovation. Consulté à l'adresse https://hal.inria.fr/hal-02418541

Lefèvre, S., & Audet, R. (2016). La mise en marché alternative de l'alimentation à Montréal. De la niche d'innovation à une transition du secteur alimentaire ?, *Revue Interventions économiques. Papers in Political Economy*, (54). https://doi.org/10.4000/interventionseconomiques.2689

Malak-Rawlikowska, A., Majewski, E., Wąs, A., Borgen, S. O., Csillag, P., Donati, M., … Wavresky, P. (2019). Measuring the economic, environmental, and social sustainability of short food supply chains. *Sustainability, 11*(15), 4004. https://doi.org/10.3390/su11154004

Marsden, T., Banks, J., & Bristow, G. (2000). Food supply chain approaches: Exploring their role in rural development. *Sociologia Ruralis, 40*(4), 424–438. https://doi.org/10.1111/1467-9523.00158

Moustier, P.. (2013). Short urban food chains in developing and emerging countries: Signs of the past or of the future? Montpellier.

Moustier, P. (2017). Short urban food chains in developing countries: Signs of the past or of the future?. *Natures Sciences Sociétés, 25*(1), 7–20. https://doi.org/10.1051/nss/2017018

Moustier, P., & Renting, H. (2015). Urban agriculture and short chain food marketing in developing countries [book_section]. https://doi.org/10.4324/9781315716312-11

Naumowicz, F. (2019). *Numérique et circuits courts alimentaires* (Mémoire de Master). Université Toulouse Jean Jaurès. Toulouse: Consulté à l'adresse https://www.hdigitag.fr/wp-content/uploads/Rapport-StageDigitAg-M2-2019-Flora-Naumowic.pdf

Nemes, G., Chiffoleau, Y., Zollet, S., Collison, M., Benedek, Z., Colantuono, F., … Orbán, É. (2021). The impact of COVID-19 on alternative and local food systems and the potential for the sustainability transition: Insights from 13 countries. *Sustainable Production and Consumption, 28*, 591–599. https://doi.org/10.1016/j.spc.2021.06.022

Poulain, J.-P. (2013). Chapitre 1 – La mondialisation et les mouvements de délocalisation et relocalisation de l'alimentation, *Quadrige*, 19–34.

Renting, H., & Dubbeling, M. (2013). Synthesis report: Innovative experiences with (peri-) urban agriculture and food provisioning; lessons to be learned from the global South, in *Leusden. RUAF Foundation*, 43.

Renting, H., Marsden, T. K., & Banks, J. (2003). Understanding alternative food networks: Exploring the role of short food supply chains in rural development. *Environment and Planning A: Economy and Space, 35*(3), 393–411. https://doi.org/10.1068/a3510

Requier-Desjardins, D., & Roudart, L. (2019). Introduction. Les circuits courts alimentaires : regards croisés entre l'Amérique latine et l'Europe occidentale. *Économie rurale. Agricultures, alimentations, territoires*, (367), 7–11.

Rowan, N. J., & Galanakis, C. M. (2020). Unlocking challenges and opportunities presented by COVID-19 pandemic for cross-cutting disruption in agri-food and green deal innovations: Quo Vadis?. *Science of The Total Environment, 748*, 141362. https://doi.org/10.1016/j.scitotenv.2020.141362

Rural development. (2022). Consulté 31 juillet 2022, à l'adresse https://agriculture.ec.europa.eu/common-agricultural-policy/rural-development_en

Touzard, J.-M. (2020). Innover pour se nourrir au temps du coronavirus [Blog Alternatives Economiques]. Consulté 16 juillet 2022, à l'adresse http://blogs.alternatives-economiques.fr/reseauinnovation/2020/05/13/innover-pour-se-nourrir-au-temps-du-coronavirus

United Nations Industrial Development Organization. (2020). *Short food supply chains for promoting local food on local markets | UNIDO Knowledge Hub* 53. United Nations Industrial Development Organization. Consulté à l'adresse https://tii.unido.org/node/2879

Valenduc, G. (2018). Technological revolutions and societal transitions. SSRN Scholarly Paper, Rochester, NY. https://doi.org/10.2139/ssrn.3180000

Territorial development in the face of climate change

MICHELLE MONGO[1], AUDREY TANGUY[2],
VALÉRIE LAFOREST[3], ERIC PIATYSZEK[4]

Abstract: Climate change and its effects on human and natural systems call for rethinking territorial organization in favor of greater resilience. This implies the territory being able to develop a capacity to adapt, recover, and regenerate in the face of major events and crises (Martin & Sunley, 2007). The territorial ecosystem must also integrate a diversity of actors interacting around socio-economic, environmental, and institutional issues promoting resilient territorial development. Beyond the static maps of the resilience of the territories, it seems essential to better understand the organizational dynamics structuring the territory and which make it possible to increase the capacity for resilience. The study of territorial systems of innovation and their evolution regarding climate challenges makes it possible to underline the importance of innovations that are constrained by resources in the dynamics of local development.

Keywords: Resource-Constrained Innovations, Territorial development, Resilience, Climate change

[1] Mines Saint-Etienne, Institut Henri Fayol - Coactis Laboratory EA 4161, France.

[2] Mines Saint-Etienne, Université Lyon, Université Jean Moulin, Université Lumière, Université Jean Monnet, ENTPE, INSA Lyon, ENS Lyon, CNRS, UMR 5600 EVS, Institut Henri Fayol, Département GEO, France.

[3] Mines Saint-Etienne, Université Lyon, Université Jean Moulin, Université Lumière, Université Jean Monnet, ENTPE, INSA Lyon, ENS Lyon, CNRS, UMR 5600 EVS, Institut Henri Fayol, Département GEO, France.

[4] Mines Saint-Etienne, Université Lyon, Université Jean Moulin, Université Lumière, Université Jean Monnet, ENTPE, INSA Lyon, ENS Lyon, CNRS, UMR 5600 EVS, Institut Henri Fayol, Département GEO, France.

Introduction

Many IPCC reports warn of global warming and its consequences on the human (technosphere) and natural (biosphere) systems of the planet (IPCC, 2018). Indeed, the latter tends, among other things, to increase the number of extreme weather events in the world (Dourte et al., 2015; IPCC, 2014; Ouzeau et al., 2016) which also contributes to an increase in systemic risks (economic, geopolitical, environmental, societal, and technological). Coupled with the recent COVID-19 crisis, these different events show to what extent our globalized and interconnected societies are fragile and vulnerable (Maldonado, 2020). However, despite these facts, CO_2 emissions continue to increase (UNEP, 2017). Therefore, it becomes urgent to act quickly by not only reducing our CO2 emissions but also by implementing measures allowing us to increase the resilience of societies and individuals in the face of climate change (Hawchar et al., 2020).

Resilience "is not only the ability to cope with major events and absorb crises. It is also the ability (of the city) to constantly renew itself and to assimilate recurring or future disturbances and crises by adapting and anticipating these events" (Laganier & Serre, 2017).

In this sense, it constitutes a means of thinking about the maintenance or adaptation of a territory whose components and functioning can be analyzed according to the principles of sustainability (Thomas & Da Cunha, 2017). The resilient territory is therefore part of a multifunctional strategy (Ahern, 2011) whose deployment is largely dependent on socio-economic, environmental, and ecological factors driving local dynamics (Graziano & Rizzi, 2016; Pickett et al., 2004).

In this perspective, achieving the objectives of economic growth, social equity, and environmental preservation is a necessary condition for territorial development (Dermine-Brullot & Torre, 2020). Local production systems are therefore profoundly modified and the territorial innovation ecosystems making it possible to guarantee the attractiveness and competitiveness of the territories are evolving toward a greening of the practices of stakeholders (Torre, 2019). Industrial ecology and more broadly the circular economy illustrate these developments by reconsidering the economic systems of exchange and production, to move toward greater efficiency in the use of resources, the minimization of the environmental impact, and the development of wellbeing of individuals (Geldron, 2014). The circular economy, although widely recognized and at the heart of the European Commission's long-term strategy (European Commission, 2018), focuses on efficiency strategies in which innovation driven by R&D is central. However, these eco-efficiency strategies supported by environmental innovations self-maintain the consumerist logic of our societies based on a linear economy. This techno-centered vision is dominant, despite the limits observed (Stahel, 2014), particularly in terms of the existence of the rebound effect (Font Vivanco et al., 2016; Ness, 2008) or even mining controversies relating to the extraction of green transition metals (Merlin, 2021).

The current context of constraints in terms of the availability and use of resources invite us to reconsider lifestyles, the use of resources, institutions, the organization of production and consumption patterns. Innovation must also be multidimensional (Joly, 2020) in which technological, social, environmental, cultural and/or institutional dimensions can be integrated. Initiatives that develop in contexts of resource scarcity, such as "low-tech" (Tunzelmann & Acha, 2005) and/or frugal innovations or "Jugaad[5]" advocate doing better with less (Radjou & Prabhu, 2015). Also referred to as Resource Constrained Innovations (RCI), these offer a varied vision of innovation in which the social dimension is largely present. They thus allow better social inclusion by increasing socio-political capacity and access to the resources necessary to meet human needs (Hillier et al., 2004).

The question is therefore to know how innovations constrained by resources contribute to a stronger resilience of territories with regard to climatic and environmental challenges.

This contribution proposes to answer this research problem by taking as a theoretical basis the work on territorial development. The analysis of territorial innovation systems and their evolution regarding climate issues and resource constraints thus justify the particular attention paid to analysis of the processes of the emergence of Innovations Constrained by Resources. This work contributes to a better understanding of the role of ICRs in the resilience of territories. The remainder of this section is organized as follows. The first section sets out the main climatic and environmental crises that are straining the resilience of territories. Section 2 presents the evolution of analyses in terms of territorial innovation

5 "Jugaad" is a popular Hindi word that could be translated as "improvised solution born out of ingenuity and intelligence, using simple means".

systems and discusses the contributions and limits of this work. Finally, Section 3 presents the characteristics of the ICRs and presents some examples of good practices initiated within this framework at the local level.

1. Territorial resilience put to the test

1.1 Climate and environmental crisis: Contextual elements

According to the 5th report of the IPCC, climate change is largely engaged (IPCC, 2014) and is reflected in an increase in average temperatures on the planet, an upward trend in sea levels, and the melting of ice. Indeed, the warming of the global average temperature of the air at the surface of the land and of the water at the surface of the oceans is very clear. Before the industrial era, the evolution of temperatures was fairly stable and this then accelerated until the 1980s to reach completely new levels, i.e. +0.74° compared to the average of the 20th century. In France, for example, the summer of 2022 is the second hottest ever observed with, according to Météo France[6], an average temperature of around 22.7°C over the June–July August quarter, i.e. an anomaly of more than 2.3°C compared to normal. Similarly, according to the 5th IPCC report, the rate of sea level rise rose to nearly 3.2 mm per year over the period 1993–2010. The work of the IUCN (Ceballos et al., 2017) warns of the loss of biodiversity which is characterized by the gradual disappearance of a certain number of vertebrate species (mammals, birds, reptiles, amphibians).

6 https://meteofrance.com/actualites-et-dossiers/actualites/changement-climatique-lete-2022-et-ses-extremes-meteorologiques

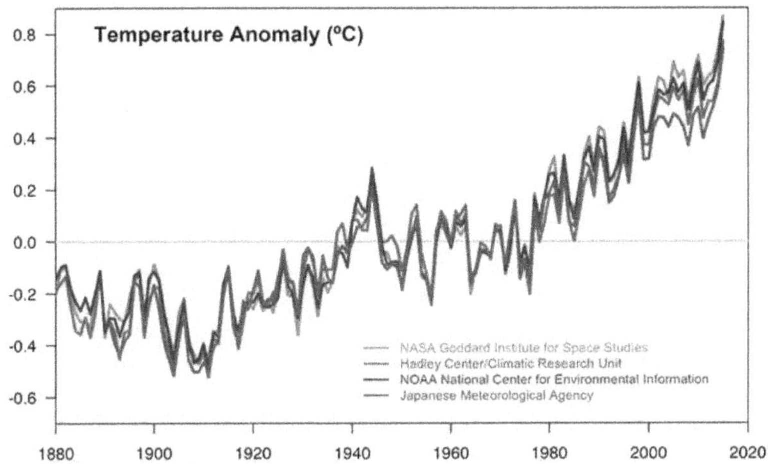

Figure 1: The rise of Earth's temperature over time
Source : https://climate.nasa.gov/

According to IPCC experts, these disturbances to human and natural systems will contribute to increasing the frequency of extreme phenomena such as: storms, floods, droughts. Ecosystems will be increasingly disrupted with the extinction of nearly 20 % of animal and plant species, posing risks in terms of food security, sources of conflict and migration, but also health risks likely to promote the transmission of animal diseases that are dangerous to humans (Morris et al., 2016). The ecological footprint is an estimate of the land area needed to support people. It thus makes it possible to measure the pressure exerted by man on nature. This depends on lifestyles in particular: the type of diet (omnivorous, vegetarian, vegan…) and the origin of the food (local…), the quantities of waste emitted, the modes of transport (soft modes, car, train, plane, etc.) and distances traveled, the heating methods, origin of the electricity used, etc.

According to the Global Footprint Network[7], a human's way of life currently requires 1.7 planets for their resource consumption to be compensated globally. This anthropogenic pressure exerted on the planet amplifies the systemic risks on the planet. These relate to the shocks (flooding, industrial accidents, storms) or slow disturbances (socio-economic

[7] https://www.wwf.ch/fr/vie-durable/calculateur-d-empreinte-ecologique

crisis, coastal erosion, loss of biodiversity, etc.) suffered by the territories (Centeno et al., 2015).

In view of these contextual elements, it is the responsibility of the public authorities but also of all stakeholders to identify solutions allowing greater resilience of our societies in the face of the effects of climate change.

1.2 Territorial resilience

Resilience has gradually replaced the notion of vulnerability, which was relatively fashionable in the 1990s, particularly with the World Conference on Natural Disaster Reduction, which took place in Yokohama, 1994. (UN. Office for Disaster Risk Reduction,1994). Indeed, the disasters of early 2000 (Katrina in New Orleans, September 11 attacks, 2001, etc.), and climate changes challenged this concept of vulnerability (invulnerability!). If it is no longer possible to avoid disasters, it is necessary to adapt to them (Rufat, 2011).

Since then, a real enthusiasm has arisen around the concept of resilience, which has contributed to its sometimes contradictory polysemy: resistance, (ability to cope, ability to adapt, ability to respond, return to balance, absorption of shock), reconstruction (building, political and social, symbolic), bifurcation, self-organization, transition, sustainability, durability. This leads some to say that "resilience is an incantatory storytelling of the post-disaster period" (Rufat, 2011), which is part of political discourse and that the favor that surrounds it is due to its positive connotation. Therefore carrying out risk management through the prism of resilience provides a more optimistic view that is less anxiety-provoking than using the (negative) term vulnerability (Vale et al., 2005). Moreover, in a context of climate change (uncertainty, unpredictability, impossibility of controlling risks), "the resilience that opposes a feeling of fatality, expectation, or resignation, ... offers a response to the anxieties of citizens by presenting itself as a means of coping.... to adapt" (Quenault, 2013).

Territorial resilience was initially and very often approached through the prism of sudden disturbances of a "disaster" type in a context of risk prevention (for example UNISDR, 2005, CGDD 2017). However, in recent years, resilience has extended to all types of shocks and more or less slow changes and is no longer confined solely to the field of disasters (mass immigration, water shortage, economic depreciation, etc.) (Meerow et al., 2016).

The polysemy of the term resilience is also found in the concept of urban or territorial resilience. Thus, Meerow et al. (2016) identify no less than 25 definitions of urban resilience in the literature. However, the following definitions can be put forward:

Territorial resilience can be defined as the ability of territories to adapt, recover, and regenerate (Martin & Sunley, 2007). Resilience "is not only the ability to cope with major events and absorb crises. It is also the ability (of the city) to constantly renew itself and to assimilate recurring or future disturbances and crises by adapting and anticipating these events" (Laganier & Serre, 2017). It is the result of a multifunctional strategy combining socio-economic, environmental, and ecological factors (Ahern, 2011). It involves bringing together the various actors (companies, elected officials, citizens, professionals) within a sustainable ecosystem allowing collective processes for the co-construction of favorable projects for territorial development (Cerema, 2018).

This multitude of definitions does not help to operationalize the concept. "The problem with resilience is the multitude of different definitions and turning any of them into operational tools." (Klein et al., 2003). However, many have tried to build resilience indicators or methods/tools to quantify it (e.g. Annelli et al. (2022), Zaher Sedar et al. (2022), Leobons et al. (2019), and Gonzalez et al. (2018)).

For example, based on a study on the Italian provinces, Graziano and Rizzi (2016) propose a grid of indicators to measure the level of resilience of these territories (Figure 2). These include various data on innovation, employment, social capital, biodiversity, etc.

Economy	Society	Environment
1. Size of the local economy	1. Social infrastructure and leisure	1. Biodiversity
1.1 Population growth rate	1.1 Libraries/population	1.1 Urban green areas
1.2 Business Density	1.2 Gyms/population	
1.3 Value added per capita	1.3 Shows/population	
	1.4 Nurseries/population (0–3 years)	
2. Availability of resources for enterprises	2. Health infrastructure	2. Sustainable production and consumption
2.1 Return on Equity	2.1 Rate of nursing staff	2.1 Separate Waste collection (percentage waste)
2.2 Liquidity Ratio	2.2 Rate of medical staff	2.2 Composite index of eco-management for public administration
2.3 Loans to firms	2.3 Rate of hospital beds used	2.3 International Organization for standardization (ISO) 14000 – certified industries
3. Availability of resources for households	3. Social capital	3. Public policy for environment
3.1 Amount of pensions per capita	3.1 Newspapers sold/inhabitants Voluntary service organizations /population	3.1 Pedestrian areas
3.2 Families bank deposits per capita	3.2 Foundations/inhabitants	3.2 Restricted access areas
3.3 Non-food consumption/total consumption	3.3 Recreational, cultural art associations/inhabitants	3.3 Cycle paths
3.4 Intensity of residential real estate market		3.4 Composite index of policies for renewable energy
4. Innovation	4. Human capital	
4.1 Italian patents submitted	4.1 Lifelong learning	
4.2 Italian applications of designs		
4.3 Italian applications of models		
4.4 European applications of trademarks		
4.5 European applications of designs		
5. Economic infrastructure		
5.1 Rail infrastructures		
5.2 Broadband services		
5.3 Electrical network		
5.4 Energy networks		

Figure 2: Variables of economic, social, and environmental resilience
Source : Graziano and Rizzi (2016)

Although very interesting, this type of work provides a static representation of territorial resilience. However, it seems essential to better understand upstream the organizational dynamics of the territory which make it possible to increase this capacity for resilience. In short, it is a question of studying the local dynamics of development. These are presented at the end of this section.

2. Territorial systems of innovation: Resilience in the face of climate and environmental challenges

2.1 Territorial systems of innovation and local development

The typology of approaches to the problem of regional development and innovation depends both on the interpretation of technical progress (endogenous or exogenous) and on that attributed to the spatial component (Ratti, 1992). Before the 1980s, technical progress was considered exogenously (as given or known) and space as a simple territorial support. Since the mid-1980s, this trend has changed, with new growth theories reconsidering the origin and role of technical progress in explaining growth. We therefore see the emergence of a current of thought analyzing technical progress as an endogenous variable (Romer, 1990) and space as an active component of regional development.

In this context, works from territorial innovation systems attempt to provide an explanation for local development based on the potential for innovation. For Torre and Tanguy (2014), these works are based on two affiliations: on the one hand the particularities specific to the territory (regulations, laws, economic policies, etc.) and on the other hand innovation as a systemic approach. The idea being that the territory generates a potential for the creation of new knowledge, new technologies, new processes which, through a physical, organizational, and social infrastructure, allow industries to be more competitive and dynamic on the markets (Porter, 2003). Territorial innovation systems derive, in short, from national innovation systems (Lundvall, 2007), except that the local dynamics of innovation depend on the interactions between the different actors in the territory (economic and non-economic). The different categories of Territorial Systems of Innovation (TSI) make it possible to better understand the logic of development. These are categorized according to four major currents:

- **Industrial districts**: analyses of industrial districts historically stem from the work of Marshall (1919), which highlights an example of an endogenous development model consisting of companies located in the same territory. Becattini, in his work on the industrialization of Tuscany (Becattini, 1999), shows the importance of external economies and the sense of belonging (Becattini, 1979). In order to explain the dynamics of the district (composed of family SMEs and local communities) and its means of generating profits, Becattini distinguishes several dimensions essential to its functioning. He analyzes the notion of "system of values" (ethics of work and activity, of the family, of reciprocity and of change) and admits that the latter can be relayed and disseminated from one generation to another within the district through rules and institutions (market, family, school, church, etc.).
- **Localized Production Systems (LPS)** are based on the agglomeration dynamics of different actors (companies, households, consumers, etc.). In the SPL, companies are mostly large, which does not make room for analysis of local dynamics on the model of industrial districts.

- **The "milieux innovateurs"** offer a territorialized analysis of innovation by highlighting the role of the environment and more specifically that of the circles in the innovation process. Aydalot's hypothesis is that *"the innovative company does not exist before local environments, it is secreted by them. Innovative behavior essentially depends on variables defined at the local or regional level. Indeed, the past of the territories, their organization, their ability to generate a common project, the consensus that structures them are the basis of innovation. Access to technological knowledge, the presence of know-how, the composition of the labor market and many other components of local environments determine areas of greater or lesser innovativeness"* (Aydalot, 1986, p. 10).
- **Clusters**: Porter (1998) defines the cluster as *"a network of companies and institutions that are geographically close and interdependent, linked by common professions, technologies and know-how (…) The cluster has a positive influence on innovation and competitiveness, worker skills, information and long-term entrepreneurial dynamics"* (Porter, 1998, p. 199). Torre and Tanguy (2014) admit that despite recognition of the virtues of geographical proximity in the dynamics of territorial innovation, these assertions seem to be blurred due to the development of digital technology, which makes face-to-face contacts less essential for collaboration. The authors also underline the potential risks induced by the co-location of firms (industrial espionage, high mobility of specialized workers, "between oneself", etc.) as well as the existence of other forms of proximity such as cognitive proximities.

However, beyond the criticisms levelled at the factors explaining the local innovation dynamics of ITS, it should be recognized that these forms of territorial organizations centered on economic objectives of competitiveness and territorial positioning raise questions about their ability to respond to climate and environmental challenges.

2.2 Toward a "greening" of practices within territorial innovation systems

Beyond their international and national dimensions, the issues raised by climate change, the loss of biodiversity, and the challenges of energy and ecological transition also find an echo at the local level and concern all stakeholders. This awareness of the limits of the "classic" models of territorial development contributes to the development of new innovative approaches to wealth creation based on strong territorial anchoring and the consideration of environmental issues (Torre, 2019). Ginelli et al. (2020) speak of the "greening of practices" to describe these developments which have tended to develop at the local level over the past ten years. These concern approaches such as the circular economy or industrial ecology (Maillefert & Screnci, 2016).

The circular economy (CE) is based on different strategies whose objective is to reorganize production and social systems into environmentally-friendly closed circuits (De Jesus et al., 2016). One operational implementation of the circular economy is based on the principle of the 4Rs, namely the Reduction or minimization of the use of resources, the Reuse of materials/goods, the Recycling and finally the Recovery of waste which can also serve as an energy source (Kirchherr et al., 2017).

The circular economy could constitute, according to Torre (2019), *"an innovative solution to territorial challenges in terms of competitiveness, resilience, and valorization of specific local resources, even mobilization of actors around questions of territorial governance" (translation from French by the authors).* For Torre (2019), the territorial organization of CE production and/or consumption activities is based on logics of interaction that are quite similar to those of territorial systems of innovation and in which geographical proximity constitutes an antecedent to territorial dynamics of innovation. The innovative business models of CE companies, by managing to reconcile the objectives of economic profitability with those of minimizing the use of resources, contribute to the creation of the value of the territories (Maillefert & Robert, 2017).

For its part, industrial ecology (another operational axis of circular economy) is characterized by the grouping of companies established, for example, in an industrial area or park with the common objective of increasing economic, environmental, and social efficiency by focusing on reciprocal collaboration between the actors. The drivers are synergies in terms of flows, information systems, services, etc. In France, the deployment of industrial ecology is relatively recent and local public decision-makers as well as companies are showing growing interest in it. For Brullot et al. (2012), territorial industrial ecology constitutes a rational opportunity for local development with a view to sustainability. Indeed, according to Maillefert and Screnci (2016), despite its focus on the industrial sector, it could, *"promote original strategies of territorial anchoring based on several pillars: the articulation of market and non-market flows (for coordination), recycling flows and materials on a local scale (for the loop dimension) and better integration of the production and consumption cycle (for the dimension of finding short circuits)" (translation from French by the authors).*

In their publication, Morales et al. (2021) integrate resilience in industrial ecology about two periods of action. First, the identification and analysis of the threshold beyond which shocks lead to a structural change in the system. Second, the description of its behavior after a disturbance. The transdisciplinary character of resilience in industrial ecology is not only affirmed in the organizational and technical aspects, but also in the cultural components, which are decisive in a social system, in order to develop a capacity to withstand disruption and sustain change (Dron, 2013 cited by Morales et al.(2021)). Because the keys to industrial symbiosis are collaboration and synergetic possibilities offered by geographical proximity, the resilience capacity of such strategies is demonstrated by the presence of stabilisers (collaboration and synergetic possibilities) (Chertow, 2007 cited by Morales et al.(2021)). These collaborations are determinant for the success of an industrial symbiosis. In order to help decision makers and territorial actors in the implementation of industrial ecology strategies, many tools and methodologies exist. We can note in particular the ADALIE® tool[8], which allows us, in the upstream phase of ideation, to characterize the territories, the artisanal zones, and the companies with the aim of identifying the potential synergies (Laforest & Derail, 2019). Consideration of the actors is essential for the strategies to be sustainable and ensure territorial resilience.

However, faced with the virtues advocated by these innovative initiatives, more and more work is being developed to question the level of sustainability of these practices (Arnsperger & Bourg, 2016). Sustainability refers to the idea of growth that is compatible with the well-being of populations and is based on physical, natural, human, social, and institutional capital. At the regional level, this implies designing local development based on the principles of sustainable development. Unlike strong sustainability, weak sustainability emphasizes the possibility of unlimited economic growth due to the substitutability between natural capital and physical capital (possible thanks to the capacities offered by new technologies to replace the depletion of resources) (Loiseau et al., 2016). Torre

[8] https://www.cap-ter.com/home

(2019) admits that the circular economy strategies implemented at the territorial level as well as the analysis of their direct and indirect effects on the environmental, economic, and social levels, remain largely oriented toward weak sustainability objectives.

Besides, the implementation of environmental strategies by way of more eco-efficient production devices are likely to increase business productivity and to lead to potential rebound effects (Font Vivanco et al., 2016). This phenomenon thus tends to cancel out the initial objective of reducing environmental impacts. The energy transition can, for its part, lead to a strong demand for resources, thus contributing to accelerating their scarcity. The tensions caused by the availability of water are good examples[9]. Hence, if the objective is the decentralization of technological idealisation and economic profitability, industrial ecology could be in line with a strong sustainability model (Morales et al. 2021).

Thus, the real challenge with regard to climate and environmental issues lies in (1) promoting changes in the production system along with changes to consumption patterns and (2) accounting for their dynamics when implementing new solutions in order to avoid rebound effects. This implies developing systemic approaches to circularity, not only focused at a product level but also at user and organizational levels. This implies considering the scarcity of resources as a new deal in the development of territories. The initiatives developed in contexts of scarcity of resources, such as "low-tech" (Tunzelmann & Acha, 2005) and/or frugal innovations or "Jugaad", which advocate doing better with less (Radjou & Prabhu, 2015), are promising examples to address this challenge. These solutions and their potential link to resilience are presented later in this section.

3. Local development and resource constrained innovations

3.1 What are resource-constrained innovations?

Resource-Constrained Innovations (RCIs) refer to innovations that develop in order to address shortages of material, financial, and human

9 https://theconversation.com/les-pressions-sur-leau-face-ignoree-de-la-transition-energetique-154969

resources (Agarwal et al., 2017; Baker & Nelson, 2005). In recent years RCIs have developed in particular in developing countries. They have contributed to the development of a rich theoretical and empirical literature that attempts to understand the ways in which ICRs can solve problems such as poverty reduction (Prahalad et al., 1999), social inclusion (George et al., 2012), environmental issues, or even the transfer of these innovations to developed countries (Hussler et al., 2016). Although rich and promising, the work on ICRs does not reach a consensus on the definition and the methods of dissemination of the different forms of innovations developed in situations of resource constraints.

On the one hand, the concept of "low-tech" covers a set of socio-technical systems imagined to be "both socially beneficial, ecologically sustainable and politically democratic" (Abrassart et al., 2020). The steps taken in this context call into question the relationship between men and new technologies, and in this sense are opposed to "high-tech". Nevertheless, it would be simplistic and counterproductive to see it as "only a return to the candle". A reflection on "low-tech" invites us to question the underlying mechanisms of current production and consumption systems, in a multidimensional way, as evidenced by the multidisciplinary research on the subject (engineering, design, economics, anthropology, and history of techniques…).

On the other hand, frugal innovation not only involves doing things at a lower cost but also developing products that are accessible to all (simplicity), sustainable (environmental dimension), and of quality (Haudeville & Bas, 2016; Kalogerakis et al., 2014; Tiwari & Herstatt, 2012). Whether "low-tech" or frugal, these different forms of innovation, also known as Resource-Constrained Innovations (RCI), constitute an alternative path to the purely technological and competitive model of innovation and presuppose an evolution of the analysis of the very nature of the innovation process. Integrated within the framework of a circular economy strategy, Innovation Constrained by Resources invites us to feed the reflections around the different scenarios (according to different geographical scales) favoring strategies of "sobriety". In this scenario production would, for example, be decentralized, carried out on a small scale, for local communities and with minimal use of technologies (an example of less intensive organic farming) (Bauwens et al., 2020). All this with the aim of reducing the consumption of resources (through strong cognitive and emotional engagement on the part of consumers), CO2 emissions, and increasing the resilience of societies (Figge et al., 2014).

3.2 Some examples of local initiatives favorable to the deployment of ICRs

Initiatives at the territorial level are developing around sobriety practices allowing the emergence of innovation constrained by resources. In France, for example, the Low Tech Lab[10] brings together a group of actors engaged in activities aimed at promoting the principle of living better with less, the adoption of more sober and more collaborative modes of consumption or production. In this context, the collective undertakes several collaborative projects and low-tech experiments by questioning the needs, the relationship to technology, and the dominant consumerist model. Among the projects we can mention are those relating to sustainable habitats or the Low-Tech automobile or Agami model experienced in Bangladesh, Madagascar, and France. These two examples have in common the prioritization of the frugality of the materials, energetic frugality, and frugality in technicality.

Figure 3: Example of a Low-Tech housing project
Source : Lévêque and Chabot (2018)

[10] https://lowtechlab.org/fr

Figure 4: Example of a Low-Tech automobile project
Source : https://lowtechlab.org/fr

Conclusion

The proliferation of extreme phenomena is being felt all over the world. In India and Pakistan the heat wave recorded between March and April 2022 was made 30 times more likely due to human-induced climate change (Zachariah et al., 2022). In France, the summer of 2022 is considered by Météo France to be one of the hottest ever recorded. The latter was also the cause of many fires in the territory. Far from being a long-term prospect, climate change is already underway and it is the responsibility of the authorities and all stakeholders to identify solutions allowing greater resilience of our societies. At the local level, resilience is understood not only as a city's ability to cope with disturbances but also its capacity to constantly renew itself and assimilate recurring disturbances and crises or those to come by adapting and anticipating these events. It involves multifunctional strategies to integrate socio-economic, environmental, institutional, and ecological dimensions. Although a certain number of indicators are being developed in order to measure the resilience capacity of cities (Graziano & Rizzi, 2016), it seems essential to better understand upstream the organizational dynamics of the territory, which makes it possible to increase this capacity for resilience. In short, it is a question of studying the local dynamics of development.

The work carried out within the framework of territorial systems of innovation offers a relevant structure for analysis of the interaction processes between the actors at the origin of the local dynamics of the innovation source of territorial development. However, it should be recognized that this work, largely centered on the economic dimension of local development, must evolve to take into account the challenges raised by climate and environmental issues. From this point of view, research on new organizational forms of territories is emerging and tending toward an ecologization of practices in terms of territorial development (Ginelli et al., 2020). Approaches such as the circular economy, the industrial economy (to name but a few) constitute alternatives to "classic" local development by proposing production/consumption systems based on closed loops and oriented toward minimizing the use of resources associated with economic profitability objectives (Maillefert & Robert, 2017). Although highly relevant, these developments show the path still to be traveled due to the still too strong pressure exerted by human activities (Boutaud & Gondran, 2020). The rebound effects resulting from eco-efficiency strategies, as well as the controversies around the extraction of transition metals, invite us to reconsider our production/consumption methods with regard to the pressures exerted on the planet and the availability of resources. Resource constraints are a new factor to be taken into account in territorial development strategies and to increase the resilience of territories. Initiatives developed in contexts constrained in resources such as "low-tech" (Tunzelmann & Acha, 2005) and/or frugal innovations or "Jugaad" which advocate doing better with less (Radjou & Prabhu, 2015) constitute as many initiatives as possible that can be instructive in the context of sobriety scenarios. But research in this context is still fragmented, which justifies our interest in these forms of innovation constrained by resources for the development of more resilient territories. This is ultimately the ambition which has been the focus of this research work.

References

Abrassart, C., Jarrige, F., & Bourg, D. (2020). Introduction au dossier Low-Tech : Low-tech et enjeux écologiques : quels potentiels pour affronter les crises ? *La Pensée Ecologique* , *5*(1).

Agarwal, N., Grottke, M., Mishra, S., & Brem, A. (2017). A systematic literature review of constraint-based innovations : State of the Art and future perspectives. *IEEE Transactions on Engineering Management, 64*(1), 3–15. https://doi.org/10.1109/TEM.2016.2620562

Ahern, J. (2011). From fail-safe to safe-to-fail: Sustainability and resilience in the new urban world. *Landscape and Urban Planning, 100*(4), 341–343. https://doi.org/10.1016/j.landurbplan.2011.02.021

Aneli, D., Tajani, F., & Ranieri, R. (2022). Urban resilience against natural disasters: Mapping the risk with an innovative indicators-based assessment approach. *Journal of Cleaner Production, 371*, 133496.

Arnsperger, C., & Bourg, D. (2016). Vers une économie authentiquement circulaire. *Revue de l'OFCE, 145*(1), 91–125. https://doi.org/10.3917/reof.145.0091

Aydalot, P. (1986). *Présentation de Milieux innovateurs en Europe* (GREMI).

Baker, T., & Nelson, R. E. (2005). Creating something from nothing: Resource construction through entrepreneurial bricolage. *Administrative Science Quarterly, 50*(3), 329.

Bauwens, T., Hekkert, M., & Kirchherr, J. (2020). Circular futures: What will they look like? *Ecological Economics, 175*(May), 106703. https://doi.org/10.1016/j.ecolecon.2020.106703

Becattini, G. (1999). L'industrializzazione leggera della Toscana, Milan, Franco Angeli.

Becattini, G. (1979). Dal settore industriale al distretto industriale : alla ricerca dell'unità d'indagine della economia industriale. *Revista di economia e politica industriale, 1*.

Boutaud, A., & Gondran, N. (2020). *Les limites planétaires* (Repères Ec). La découverte.

Brullot, S., Payen, A., & Harpe, C. (2012). L'écologie infdustrielle et territoriale (EIT): des représentations à l'action. *Association de Science Régionale De Langue Française*, 1–19.

Ceballos, G., Ehrlich, P. R., & Dirzo, R. (2017). Biological annihilation via the ongoing sixth mass extinction signaled by vertebrate population losses and declines. *Proceedings of the National Academy of Sciences of the United States of America, 114*(30), E6089–E6096. https://doi.org/10.1073/pnas.1704949114

Centeno, M. A., Nag, M., Patterson, T. S., Shaver, A., & Windawi, A. J. (2015). The emergence of global systemic risk. *Annual Review of Sociology, 41*, 65–85. https://doi.org/10.1146/annurev-soc-073014-112317

Cerema. (2018). *Pourquoi mon territoire est-il forcément concerné par des risques ?*

Chertow, M. R. (2007). Uncovering Industrial Symbiosis. *Journal of Industrial Ecology, 11*(1), 11–30. www.mitpressjournals.org/jie

Commission europenne. (2018). *Une planète propre pour tous Une vision européenne stratégique à long terme pour une économie prospère, moderne, compétitive et neutre pour le climat.*

de Jesus, A., Antunes, P., Santos, R., & Mendonça, S. (2016). Eco-innovation in the transition to a circular economy: An analytical literature review. *Journal of Cleaner Production, 172*, 2999–3018. https://doi.org/10.1016/j.jclepro.2017.11.111

Dermine-Brullot, S., & Torre, A. (2020). What sustainability for territorial development? A reflection on the spatial components of circular economy. *Natures Sciences Societes, 28*(2), 108–117. https://doi.org/10.1051/nss/2020034

Dourte, D. R., Fraisse, C. W., & Bartels, W. L. (2015). Exploring changes in rainfall intensity and seasonal variability in the Southeastern U.S.: Stakeholder engagement, observations, and adaptation. *Climate Risk Management, 7*, 11–19. https://doi.org/10.1016/j.crm.2015.02.001

Dron, D. (2013). La résilience : un objectif et un outil de politique publique son apparition en france, et quelques perspectives. *Annales Des Mines - Responsabilité et Environnement, 4*(72), 12–16. https://doi.org/10.3917/re.072.0012

Figge, F., Young, W., & Barkemeyer, R. (2014). Sufficiency or efficiency to achieve lower resource consumption and emissions ? The role of the rebound effect. *Journal of Cleaner Production, 69*, 216–224. https://doi.org/10.1016/j.jclepro.2014.01.031

Font Vivanco, D., Kemp, R., & van der Voet, E. (2016). How to deal with the rebound effect? A policy-oriented approach. *Energy Policy, 94*, 114–125. https://doi.org/10.1016/j.enpol.2016.03.054

Geldron, A. (2014). Fiche Technique Economie Circulaire : Notions. In *Fiche Technique – ADEME.*

George, G., Mcgahan, A. M., George, G., Mcgahan, A. M., & Prabhu, J. (2012). Innovation for inclusive growth : Towards a theoretical framework and a research agenda. *Journal of Management Studies, 49*(4), 661–683. https://doi.org/10.1111/j.1467-6486.2012.01048.x

CGDD. (2017). Théma. La résilience des territoires aux catastrophes. Rapport du Commissariat Général au Développement Durable. Direction de la recherche et de l'innovation. Décembre 2017.

Ginelli, L., Candau, J., Girard, S., Houdart, M., Deldrève, V., & Noûs, C. (2020). Écologisation Des Pratiques Et Territorialisation Des Activités : Une Introduction. *Développement Durable et Territoires*, *11*(Vol. 11, n°1), 0–12. https://doi.org/10.4000/developpementdurable.17272

Gonzalez, D. P., Monsalve, M., Moris, R., & Herrera, C. (2018). Risk and resilience monitor: Development of multiscale and multilevel indicators for disaster risk management for the communes and urban areas of Chile. *Applied Geography*, *94*(2018), 262–271.

Graziano, P., & Rizzi, P. (2016). Vulnerability and resilience in the local systems: The case of Italian provinces. *Science of the Total Environment*, *553*, 211–222. https://doi.org/10.1016/j.scitotenv.2016.02.051

Haudeville, B., & Bas, C. Le. (2016). L' innovation frugale : une nouvelle opportunité pour les économies en développement ? 1. *Mondes En Développement*, *173*(1).

Hawchar, L., Naughton, O., Nolan, P., Stewart, M. G., & Ryan, P. C. (2020). A GIS-based framework for high-level climate change risk assessment of critical infrastructure. *Climate Risk Management*, *29*(May), 100235. https://doi.org/10.1016/j.crm.2020.100235

Hillier, J., Moulaert, F., & Nussbaumer, J. (2004). Trois essais sur le rôle de l'innovation sociale dans le développement territorial. *Geographie Economie Societe*, *6*(2), 129–152. https://doi.org/10.3166/ges.6.129-152

Hussler, C., & Burger-Helmchen, T. (2016). Inversée vous avez dit inversée ? – Une typologie stratégique de l'innovation inversée. *Revue Francaise de Gestion*, *42*(255), 105–119. https://doi.org/10.3166/rfg.2016.00024

IPCC. (2014). Climate change 2014 Part A: Global and sectoral aspects. In *Climate Change 2014: Impacts, Adaptation, and Vulnerability. Part A: Global and Sectoral Aspects. Contribution of Working Group II to the Fifth Assessment Report of the Intergovernmental Panel on Climate Change*. Retrieved from papers2://publication/uuid/B8BF5043-C873-4AFD-97F9-A630782E590D

IPCC. (2018). *Global warming of 1.5 Degrees*. Retrieved from https://report.ipcc.ch/sr15/pdf/sr15_spm_final.pdf

Joly, P.B. (2020). Reimagining Innovation, in Innovation Beyond Technology – Science for society and interdisciplinary approaches, ed. By Lechevalier S., Springer, 25-46

Kalogerakis, K., Tiwari, R., & Kalogerakis, K. (2014). *Frugal innovation and analogies : Some propositions for product development in emerging economies* (Vol. 49). Retrieved from http://www.global-innovation.net/publications/PDF/Working_Paper_84.pdf

Kirchherr, J., Reike, D., & Hekkert, M. (2017). Resources, conservation & recycling conceptualizing the circular economy : An analysis of 114 definitions. *Resources, Conservation & Recycling, 127*(September), 221–232. https://doi.org/10.1016/j.resconrec.2017.09.005

Klein, R.J., Nicholls, R.J., & Thomalla, F. (2003) Resilience to Natural Hazards: How Useful is the Concept?. *Environmental Hazards, 5* (1-2), 35–45

Laforest, V., & Derail, C. Démarche territoriale ADALIE : Un outil innovant au service des acteurs du territoire pour booster les projets en faveur de l'économie circulaire. Séminaire Apport de l'économie circulaire pour répondre aux enjeux de la transition industrielle et écologique. Entretiens Jacques Cartier 2019, Montréal, 4–6 novembre 2019

Laganier, R., & Serre, D. (2017). Les conditions et la mise en oeuvre de la résilience urbaine. In Thomas, I. & Da Cunha, A. (Eds.), *La ville résiliente, comment la construire ?* (Collection, p. 322). Montréal.

Leobons, C.M., Gouvêa Campos, V. B., & Mello Bandeira, R.A.de. (2019). Assessing Urban Transportation Systems Resilience: A Proposal of Indicators. *Transportation Research Procedia*, *37*, 322–329. https://doi.org/10.1016/j.trpro.2018.12.199

Lévêque, P.-A., & Chabot, C. (2018). *Habitat Low-Tech.*

Loiseau, E., Saikku, L., Antikainen, R., Droste, N., Hansjürgens, B., Pitkänen, K., … Thomsen, M. (2016). Green economy and related concepts: An overview. *Journal of Cleaner Production*, *139*, 361–371. https://doi.org/10.1016/j.jclepro.2016.08.024

Lundvall, B.-Å. (2007). National innovation systems — Analytical concept and development tool. *Industry and Innovation*, *14*(1), 95–119. https://doi.org/10.1080/13662710601130863

Maillefert, M., & Robert, I. (2017). Nouveaux modèles économiques et création de valeur territoriale autour de l'économie circulaire, de l'économie de la fonctionnalité et de l'écologie industrielle. *Revue d'Économie Régionale & Urbaine, Décmbr*(5), 905. https://doi.org/10.3917/reru.175.0905

Maillefert, M., & Screnci, N. (2016). *Ecologie industrielle et nouveaux modèles économiques . Quels enjeux de développement pour les territoires ?* 1–26.

Maldonado, V. (2020). Collapsologie, la crise systémique: comment y faire face ? *LIREC, 62*, 2.

Martin, R., & Sunley, P. (2007). Complexity thinking and evolutionary economic geography. *Journal of Economic Geography, 7*(5), 573–601. https://doi.org/https://doi.org/10.1093/jeg/lbm019

Merlin, J. (2021). Les ressources controversées de la transition écologique. *Natures Sciences Sociétés, 29*, 91–95. https://doi.org/https://doi.org/10.1051/nss/2021056

Morales, M.E., Diemer, A. & Cervantes, G. (2021). Combining efficiency and resilience assessments in industrial symbiosis value chains: a comprehensive flow analysis. *International Journal of Engineering Research and Applications, 11*(11), 51-65. Doi: 10.9790/9622-1111015165

Meerow, S., Newell, JP., Stults, M. (2016). Defining urban resilience: A review. *Landscape and urban planning, 147*, 38-49. https://doi.org/https://doi.org/10.1016/j.landurbplan.2015.11.011

Morris, A. L., Guégan, J. F., Andreou, D., Marsollier, L., Carolan, K., Le Croller, M., … Gozlan, R. E. (2016). Deforestation-driven food-web collapse linked to emerging tropical infectious disease, mycobacterium ulcerans. *Science Advances, 2*(12). https://doi.org/10.1126/sciadv.1600387

Ness, D. (2008). Sustainable urban infrastructure in China: Towards a Factor 10 improvement in resource productivity through integrated infrastructure systems. *International Journal of Sustainable Development and World Ecology, 15*(4), 288–301.

Ouzeau, G., Soubeyroux, J. M., Schneider, M., Vautard, R., & Planton, S. (2016). Heat waves analysis over France in present and future climate: Application of a new method on the EURO-CORDEX ensemble. *Climate Services, 4*, 1–12. https://doi.org/10.1016/j.cliser.2016.09.002

Pickett, S. T. A., Cadenasso, M. L., & Grove, J. M. (2004). Resilient cities: Meaning, models, and metaphor for integrating the ecological, socioeconomic, and planning realms. *Landscape and Urban Planning, 69*(4), 369–384. https://doi.org/10.1016/j.landurbplan.2003.10.035

Porter, M. E. (2003). The economic performance of regions. *Reg. Studies, 37*, 549–578.

Porter, M. E. (1998). *On competition* (Harvard Bu).

Prahalad, C. K., Arbor, A., & Hart, S. L. (1999). *Strategies for the bottom of the pyramid : Creating sustainable development.*

Quenault, B., (2013). Du double affrontement ontologique/axiologique autour de la résilience aux risques de catastrophe : les spécificités de l'approche française. *VertigO - la revue électronique en sciences de l'environnement, 13*(3). https://journals.openedition.org/vertigo/14510#quotation

Radjou, N., & Prabhu, J. (2015). Frugal innovation: How to do more with less. *The Economist.*

Remigio, R. (1992). *Innovation technologique et développement régional* (PU de Lyon). Lyon.

Romer, P. M. (1990). Endogenous technological change. *Journal of Political Economy, 98*(5), 71–102.

Rufat, S. (2011). Critique de la résilience pure.

Stahel, W. (2014). Reuse is the key to the circular economy. Retrieved from Eco-innovation Action Plan – European Commission website: https://ec.europa.eu/environment/ecoap/about-eco-innovation/experts-interviews/reuse-is-the-key-to-the-circular-economy_en

Thomas, I., & Da Cunha, A. (2017). *La ville résiliente* (Presses de; PUM, Ed.). https://doi.org/10.4000/books.pum.11789

Tiwari, R., & Herstatt, C. (2012). *Open global innovation networks as enablers of Frugal Innovation: Propositions based on evidence from India.* Retrieved from http://www.global-innovation.net/publications/PDF/Working_Paper_72.pdf

Torre, A. (2019). *L 'économie territoriale circulaire. Un pas vers la soutenabilité des territoires ? T ORRE (André), D ERMINE- B RULLOT (Sabrina), « L ' économie territoriale circulaire . Un pas vers la soutenabilité des territoires ? », Systèmes.* (December), 27–47. https://doi.org/10.15122/isbn.978-2-406-09829-4.p. 0027

Torre, A., & Tanguy, C. (2014). Les systèmes territoriaux d'innovation : fondements et prolongements actuels. In *Principes d'économie de l'innovation* (pp. 1–17).

Tunzelmann, V., & Acha, V. (2005). *Innovation in "low-tech" industries.* Oxford: Oxford University.

UNEP. (2017). *The Emissions Gap Report 2017 UNEP Emissions Gap Report.*

Vale, J. V., Campanella, T. J. (2005). The Resilient City. How modern cities recover from disaster, New York, Oxford University Press, 392 p.

Zachariah, M., T, A., AchutaRao, K., Saeed, F., Jha, R., Dhasmana, M. K., … Otto, F. E. (2022). Climate Change made devastating early heat in India and Pakistan 30 times more likely. *World Weather Attribution*, 43. Retrieved from https://www.worldweatherattribution.org/climate-change-made-devastating-early-heat-in-india-and-pakistan-30-times-more-likely/

Clusters and the digital dependency

CHEIKH ABDOU LAHAD THIAW[1]

Abstract: Nowadays, digital industry strengthening and the proliferation of its technological solutions removing physical borders between organizations challenge the usual processes of emerging innovations within collaborative networks (see Covid-19). Indeed, a set of situations leads us to question the metamorphoses of the framing angle of innovation territorialization models, considering the emergence of "translocal" innovation networks concepts that are nomadic (*Thiaw, 2018*). Without rejecting classic models of clusters based on the "local thesis" and the search for complementarity between geographically nearby actors, the contribution of the virtual allows optimization of traditional innovation network models by expanding the potential of the intellectual and knowledge capital stock of the organizations involved. Therefore, it is an increase in the innovation potential of the co-evolution between science, technology, and innovation by bringing together distant actors to form a nomadic innovation network.

Keywords: Digital revolution, Localized networks, Nomadic clusters, Innovation, Science-technology-innovation coevolution

Introduction

This chapter aims to discuss the concept of innovation networks in the sense of clusters (Porter, 2000) and the co-evolution between science, technology, and innovation (ST-I) (Thiaw, 2018), but from an analysis perspective bearing on the challenges of the digital technology revolution and the strengthening of an economy based on knowledge. Moreover, it

[1] Polytechnic School (ESP) / Cheikh Anta Diop University (UCAD), Senegal.

evokes the possibility of encouraging the not necessarily territorialized concentration of innovation dynamics that are conducive to growth and economic development.

Innovation has always and unequivocally been the founding principle of the evolution of the human being and of life on earth. Indeed, to permanently embrace the realities of his time while following the evolution of his environment, man has always striven to adapt himself to the environment in which he lives by constantly pushing back the limits of his intrinsic possibilities. In the economic and industrial field, this same process is exercised through innovation and the taking of entrepreneurial initiatives.

Therefore, as guarantors of strategies designed to stimulate the development of national economies, public authorities rely more on innovation as a variable to implement appropriate policies. For nearly forty years now, these kinds of policies have been strongly oriented toward the organization of territorial socioeconomic dynamics based on the promotion of innovations and a desire to structure socioeconomic actors. From then on, they have been manifested as a delegation of competencies, in terms of employment, industrial development, education or research, from central and state services to regional and sub-regional services. The main objective is to always adapt to the new requirements of the modern economy, by mobilizing local communities to implement a governance aimed primarily at the development of local resources and know-how.

In this continuity, we are challenged by a new wave of evolution characterized by the advent and spread of digital technology in all spheres of the economy. It accentuates the habitual consequences of the vagaries of the global economy, the opening of markets, and the persistent "globalization" of production factors, as for the usual processes of the emergence of innovations. In this context, how should the environment of innovation networks be articulated in this digital era, marked by the disappearance of spatial borders, the instantaneousness of exchanges, and the conversion of spaces from localization to timing and virtualization? In this era of knowledge and the immaterial economy, we consider the opportunity of envisaging a co-evolution between ST-I without a spatial and local base, and while considering the subsistence of the collective character of innovation. Certainly, the localization of innovation remains one of the most decisive quotients among the factors for promoting fruitful entrepreneurship and local job creation for national economies, but here in a distanced and virtual way.

Indeed, as the Covid-19 pandemic has already demonstrated over the last almost three years, there is today a growing role for the possibilities allowed by the digital industry, notably with the suppression of borders, and therefore, for us, the constitution of a set of factors leading us to question the metamorphoses of the framing angle of the models of territorialization of innovation, by envisaging the emergence of innovation networks concepts we name "translocal clusters" and which are more or less "nomadic" (Thiaw, 2018). This "nomadic cluster" concept could concern all forms of innovation networks (clusters, competitiveness clusters), but which, from now on, would no longer be based simply on a territorial and local dimension, with the exploitation of the externalities of physically neighboring actors, but which goes beyond that, considering other criteria such as the complementarity of actors, the sharing of common interests, the completeness of an industry's value chain, etc. From then on, it is no longer geographical proximity that is considered, but other forms of proximity such as sharing of a common industry, specializations, technologies, value chains, etc. In other words, this concept could also refer to the co-evolution between science, technology, and innovation, but not necessarily with a physical approach of the actors forming the network, but with the possibility of their distancing.

The literature has already dealt extensively with issues about innovation and territorial innovation networks (Schumpeter, 1939; Porter, 2000; Thiaw, 2013), but very few have sketched the issue of the advent of innovation ecosystems that ignore geographical proximity. Today's innovations are still mostly the result of a collective process involving several actors and diverse sources of knowledge (ST-I). In fact, the structuring of the modern economic environment no longer allows each actor (company, researcher) to be able to innovate efficiently while being isolated. In our proposed nomadic innovation system, the issue is to outperform the close territories, by linking physically distant actors using the possibilities allowed by digital technologies.

As history reminds us, the substitution of a human driving force by animal power for agriculture, then by machines through the Industrial Revolution, or the advent of the steam engine in the past, then of electricity with a potential multiplication of the productive capacities of men, it is possible today, with the Internet and the digital revolution, to consider a redefinition of the organizational basis of innovation networks. This new determination could be based on an unprecedented economic era placing digital technology at the heart of the system. The literature on this subject has already referred to the classic industrial revolutions and the economic evolution phases mentioned above.

Since the beginning of the 1980s, scientific (teaching and research), technological and innovation-related activities in firms have attracted particular attention from researchers, who have attempted to analyze them and study their interrelations (Thiaw, 2021). At the same time, the localization of innovation within territorialized ecosystems began to be established as the ideal economic model to respond to the new demands of the contemporary economy: effects of globalization, changes in habits and customs (consumption habits), rise of ICTs, and later the strengthening of the digital economy as a driving force of economies.

Nowadays, the consolidation of the digital economy has a major influence on the structuring of modern innovation networks, with a pressing need for adaptation to take full advantage of the opportunities allowed (1). Rather than considering traditional innovation networks as outdated and deserving to be put aside, they remain innovation ecosystems based on the "Science, Technology and Innovation" trilogy, and are therefore still relevant (2). However, it is now necessary to consider a new form of cluster adapted to the realities of the new economy (3). Indeed, the digital revolution is currently the most decisive element in determining the organizational basis of a "new economy" based on networks and nomadic clusters.

1. Innovation and the new global economy: When the digital revolution forces adaptation

Already stabilized throughout the world, globalization has caused a forced rapprochement of cities and countries. This proximity and the relationships it generates have in turn led to interdependence between areas once physically distant, and now close to each other, and which constitute what might be called interconnected urban networks (UINs). In the literature, this interconnection was first questioned from different angles of analysis and measurement: by infrastructure networks, according to the specificity of the firms, by forms of inter-organizational collaboration relations, by transport channels (air, rail, sea flows), etc.

For more than thirty years now, the global economy has been immersed in a new dynamic evolution marked by the importance of innovation, knowledge, and immateriality. Now, with the digital technologies imprint, these variables have become correlative factors determining the performance of companies as well as the competitiveness and growth of nations (1.1). To cope with this new situation while performing through innovation, the development of networking methods and the territorialization of innovation have been advocated as *sine qua non*-solutions (1.2.).

Moreover, the appearance of new markets made up of the emerging economies have metamorphosed the *geo-economic* of innovation and the traditional innovation processes. Indeed, innovation in these new economic environments is provided by innovative models that are different from those developed in western countries and related to new concepts that distort traditional innovation processes. For instance, this is the case with frugal innovation (FI), which was conceived in southern countries, and which then has impacts on the innovation processes of certain multinational companies from northern countries. In order to adapt to the new economic conditions, other innovative forms of innovation have also appeared in recent years: frugal innovation, open innovation, social innovation, etc. (1.3.).

1.1. The knowledge and immaterial economy and the rise of the digital era

History has shown that the evolution of the global economy is not set in stone. At each period of history different facets of the global economy, with their own prerogatives and priorities, appear. Correlatively, the evolution of practices within organizations has taken place according to the required development priorities, and in parallel with this advance in economies. Thus, from the pre-modern era marked by a totally agrarian and artisanal society, relying on human energy, we moved, from the 18th century onwards, to an Industrial Revolution marked by the advent of mechanical energy, the development of production techniques, communication, commerce, and industry (Thiaw, 2017).

Today, these successive mutations have led to the establishment of a knowledge-based economy, which imposes immateriality as a decisive lever for the growth of economies. In this way, while in the past, wealth in terms of raw materials, the weight of manufacturing industries, and the volume of material capital available to each nation conditioned its economic success, today, the real wealth is not concrete and material, but abstract and immaterial (Levy & Jouyet, 2006). In other words, "*the share of knowledge-intensive jobs has increased considerably, the economic weight of the information sectors has become decisive, and the share of intangible capital has exceeded that of tangible capital in the real capital stock*" (Foray, 2000).

Nowadays, the intersection between the significant increase in the share of intangible capital (education, training, etc.), the spectacular eruption of ICTs, and the continuous diffusion of innovations (permanent innovation) in the economy has led to an "*expansion of investments, a proliferation of 'knowledge' activities and a technological revolution that radically changes the conditions of production and transmission of knowledge and information.*" This set of coincidences is reflected in the economy through three main effects (ibid.).

The first concerns the increase in the share of intangible capital in national economies, resulting from the performance of triptych education (*education and training*), R&D (*practical knowledge acquired*), and organizational structures (*managerial structures, information systems, control, marketing, user services*). In other words, today's economic development is not enabled by the unique contribution of natural and environmental resources but requires more investment in human capital and in the main variables related to knowledge and which offer potentialities for creating economic value. Otherwise, countries like the Democratic Republic of the Congo and Niger in Africa would be among the world's leading economies.

Moreover, the second effect related to the development of the knowledge industry confirms this trend. Nowadays, the expansion of knowledge-intensive activities is one of the main indicators of development, and the contribution of ICT industries to the gross national product (GNP) of countries has increased significantly, making the intangible and immaterial capital approach a tool to shed light on the real value of economies.

The third effect concerns the development of the tertiary sector and the constant increase in highly qualified jobs. From a historical point of view, the growing importance of tertiary activities in the economy of industrialized countries began to be felt in the 1970s. For example, they already accounted for nearly two thirds of job creation and total wealth production in Canada (Polèse, 1974), and the share of tertiary[2] activities

---

[2] Tertiary activities include the service sector, public administration, finance, insurance, real estate, trade, transport, logistics, communications, etc.

rose from 24 % in 1870 to 63 % in 1971. The same observation was also made in other countries like France, where DATAR[3] had recorded a clear decrease in the share of jobs from industrial activities in favor of the tertiary sector. Today, a country like France has nearly 76 % of its jobs in the tertiary sector (INSEE, 2015)[4].

In these new sectors of activity dominated by service professions, the importance of knowledge is not limited to production mechanisms, the dominance of manual practices, and the multiplication of industrial equipment. Technological changes influence the criteria for measuring productivity and the growth of the workforce and, through their synergies, allow for accelerated economic growth. Henceforth, labor and capital yields are now measured by the role of science and technology in advanced industries. Knowledge contributes significantly to the growth of national economies by spurring on new industries, improving competitiveness, and achieving productivity gains. However, benefiting from such advantages implies, beforehand, prerequisites and an effective consideration of the organizational changes brought about by the importance of the "knowledge" variable in economies.

In the modern economy dominated by knowledge and immateriality, the success of organizations depends largely on their degree of integration within networks. They differ from each other "*in terms of maturity, the amount of knowledge required and the way in which the different knowledge bases are linked*" (Burger-Helmchen et al., 2018). Thus, they need to use combinations of knowledge to develop new ideas. In this context, networking allows them to benefit from externalities to complete their knowledge bases, particularly for the benefit of innovation. Because key knowledge is not always present within the company and can be held by multiple sources (suppliers, partners, industrial or academics).

---

3 DATAR : Délégation interministérielle à l'aménagement du territoire et à l'attractivité régionale (Interministerial Delegation for Regional Planning and Attractiveness, France).

4 According to the INSEE (National Institute of Statistics and Economic Studies) Employment Survey (2015), 25.8 million people are employed as defined by the International Labor Office (ILO), in metropolitan France: 13.9 % in the industry sector, 6.6 % in construction, 2.8 % in agriculture, and 75.7 % in the service sector.

1.2 Networks and territorialization of innovation

Nowadays, innovation is the main determinant of economic growth (Uzunudis, 2008) and a major variable in the socio-economic dynamism of territories (Mongo, 2021). Indeed, companies increasingly favor belonging to a "network" to ensure the long-term performance and competitiveness of their activities. For them, it is a way of increasing their efficiency and strengthening their "backbone" while protecting themselves from competition. In the same way, more and more means are deployed by public authorities to encourage the networking of companies in localized geographical areas to boost job creation and economic growth. Thus, the network, representing both an instrument of protection for enterprises and a job creation device (Thiaw, 2013), is today an increasingly decisive form of organization (Loilier & Tellier, 2005). On the other hand, the effectiveness of the network is more accentuated when it is associated with a territory (regional, national), because in this typical case, it allows us to establish a sustainability of existing jobs while supporting the creation of new ones for the local workforce. Therefore, all around the world, government measures have been introduced to encourage companies working together and collaborating with other public and private organizations located in their area. These clustering and cluster effects are the focus of countless major innovations, particularly in the field of new technologies. From now on, the development of national economies will be based more on the network's logics, or even innovation networks, than on the efficiency of solitary industrial players.

To discuss these network logics, it is important at the outset to question the literature in order to understand their theoretical foundations, which initially originated in the work led by Alfred Marshall (1890, 1919) on industrial districts, before undergoing a revival nearly a century later under the impetus of contemporary authors such as Becattini (1979, 1987) and Porter (1990, 2000, 2004). In the 1990s, upheavals in the global economy and the changes brought about by globalization and its effects caused a multiplication of network configurations and a disparity of conceptualizations that led Veltz (1996, p. 70) to speak of a "semantic penumbra" relative to this notion of the network, which does not facilitate its understanding. From this disparity of conceptual models and distinct names, we retain industrial districts (Bagnasco & Trigilia, 1977, 1984, 1988; Becattini, 1979, 1989), clusters (Porter, 1990, 1994, 1998, 2000, 2004), innovative milieus (Aydalot, 1986; Maillat, 2003), business parks, local innovation systems, technopoles, science parks, competitiveness clusters (Thiaw, 2013), growth clusters, and business ecosystems. Today, most innovations are developed within these networks, and very often follow a territorial logic.

As for the notion of territory, it covers quite varied contours referring to geographical, economic, sociological, and political dimensions. Territory can be defined as a geographical space with natural, cultural, and economic features appropriated by groups of individuals who take possession of its natural resources and develop material means and symbolic expressions (Thiaw, 2017). Because of the appropriation action that characterizes it, the territory covers a historical perspective referring to an "experience," "practices" and "meanings" that are granted to it (Di Méo & Buléon, 2007, p. 85; Saives & Desmarteau, 2010).

Thus, as a social construction, the territory is an axis of the emergence and development of dynamic capacities of interaction between diversified actors, and a vector of learning for localized companies. In this context, the study of the literature allows us to identify different forms of territorialization, or activation and co-construction of territorial resources and skills. According to Saives (2002), taking the territory of French agri-food firms as a reference, there are four contingent strategic constructs that enable firms to strengthen their competitiveness: consumption, conservation, contagion, and co-option (*see* Figure 1).

From this perspective, the localization of innovation responds to a set of criteria and targets specific objectives in terms of creating localized jobs, supporting business performance, and stimulating economic growth from local to national and supranational spheres (Thiaw, 2017).

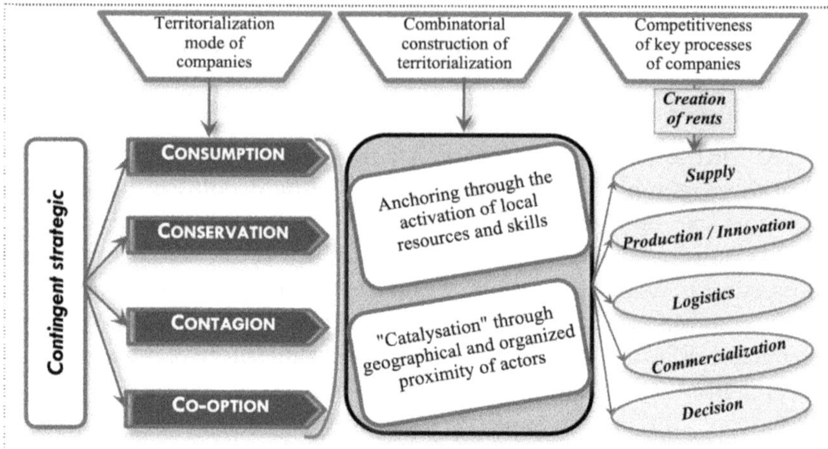

Figure 1: Modes of territorialization and benefits for localized companies
[Sources: Author, Adapted from Saives (2002): French agri-food sector]

1.3. *Emergence of innovative forms of innovation:* From frugal innovation to contribution of the digital in support of innovation networks

The new global environment, combined with upheavals in the global geo-economy and the emergence of new economic powers (emerging economies), have given rise to new forms of innovation. From a micro-economic point of view, this is the case with frugal innovation, social innovation, open innovation, or the permanent innovation phenomenon. From a more meso and macroeconomics point of view, the new condition resulting from the stabilization of the digital era and its scaling is shaping the foundations of a new form of clusters that we conceptualize under the name of "virtual innovation networks" or "nomadic clusters."

Frugal innovation is originated from less developed (emerging and developing) countries. These are countries with significant development and growth potential that remains relatively under-explored or unexplored, and which represent dynamic places where large multinational companies operate to stimulate innovation, but also where domestic companies are moving to find innovative solutions to the socio-economic problems of the populations. However, alongside this important development potential, these countries also face innumerable constraints to innovation. These include the lack of means for economic stakeholders (infrastructure, equipment, human resources, weak capitalization, financing, education, etc.), the absence of support structures for innovation, the disparity and dichotomous nature of the societies in place (either very poor or very rich), or the principles of the population's way of life (politics, habits and customs, religion, etc.).

To face these challenges and offer products and services to people in emerging economies, local and multinational companies are adopting original strategies and operational orientations. Indeed, bypassing the pitfalls that are hostile to innovation and the lack of support mechanisms for R&D, local actors have been proactive in developing innovative capabilities. The concept of frugal innovation (Radjou & Prabhu, 2013) is presented as a reverse innovation process based on a focus on the needs of "disadvantaged" populations (from emerging or developing countries in Africa, South Asia, or South America). Its particularity is that the products and technologies generated are designed and developed within these countries, to serve the less affluent population. It can also make use of technologies designed elsewhere by adapting and giving them innovative usages.

The concept of frugal innovation (FI) is defined with disparate but consistent connotations (Radjou et al., 2013; Haudeville & Le Bas, 2016; Eagar et al., 2011). It is given an economic role because it allows innovation by reducing costs. Similarly, FI is attributed a societal purpose, as it aims to serve the less affluent populations as a priority and is presented as a means of inclusion for fragile populations. Therefore, it is also sometimes assimilated to a means of providing answers to new needs, to "*low-cost*", and offering extended accessibility. In concrete terms, it consists in generating innovations for low-income populations to meet local needs that are not yet satisfied, thanks to simplification, conversion, and the adaptation of innovations already designed elsewhere. This is a process that reverses the traditional innovation cycle and allows products with very high added value to be obtained from low production costs. These products are going to be offered to mass markets, at low prices, while having a satisfactory price/performance ratio (Thiaw, 2018). Once domestic markets have been conquered, the products resulting from reverse innovation are subsequently disseminated to other countries with equivalent levels of development.

As for the concept of innovation networks or nomadic clusters, this refers to a modification of the space of existence of territorial clusters (*with a conversion of the local territorial space into a temporal and virtual place*) which considers other variables in the framing angle of the models of territorialization of innovation. Indeed, we envision the emergence of concepts of "translocal" innovation networks that are nomadic (Thiaw, 2018). This could concern all forms of innovation network (clusters, competitiveness clusters), but would no longer be based only on a territorial and local dimension, and aiming to exploit externalities from physically neighboring actors, but which goes beyond the local space by considering other criteria that could be the complementarity of actors, the sharing of common interests, the completeness of an industry's value chain, etc. From then on, it is no longer geographical proximity that is considered, but other forms of proximity such as sectors of activity, specializations, technologies, value chains, etc. In other words, this concept could also refer to the co-evolution between science, technology, and innovation, not with a necessarily physical approach of the actors forming the network but with the possibility of their distancing. In this form of network, the territorial hierarchy tends to be articulated according to an interconnection following two main levels: a local one exploiting the geographical proximity of the actors and a more global or regional one taking advantage of the increase in connection nodes between distant actors. This notion will be discussed in detail in Part 3 of this chapter.

2. Classic innovation networks: Innovation ecosystems through a trilogy of science, technology, and innovation

Since the early 1980s, networked working models have become widespread and continue again today to spread and "grow" as economies and technologies evolve. This expansion is deeply linked to the expansion of science, technology, and innovation. This double expansion is marked by issues related to innovation and their impact on the economic growth of nations and companies. Indeed, innovation is the surest way for firms to gain a competitive advantage (Christensen, 2001; Porter, 2000) and to sustain their activities. Similarly, promoting innovation is a sure way for countries to foster productivity, meet the socio-economic needs of their populations, and stimulate employment and economic growth.

Today, the new realities of the global economy have led researchers and practitioners to revisit the classic forms of networking, with a view to proposing models that are more in line with the structuring of the modern economy: globalization, knowledge-based and immaterial economy, territorialization of innovation, etc. (1.1). In this context, the models of propelling a parallel evolution between science, technology, and innovation are presented as being most in line and crucial for the development of economies on the way to emergence (1.2).

2.1. The co-evolution between science, technology, and innovation

Described as a knowledge economy, the contemporary global economy is marked by the existence of strong dependencies between both variables, *science*, and technology. In concrete terms, this interconnection is manifested through innovation which, as the result of the interaction process, has substantially engaged literary debates to the detriment of the first two variables mentioned above. Indeed, the literature on the relationship between *science* and *technology* remains relatively limited "*even though a particular vision of this relationship is always present behind the choices made by public authorities to promote the innovation capacities of their respective countries and thus their economic growth*" (Encaoua, 2010).

For the sake of conceptual simplification, by *science* we mean *basic research*; and by *technologies*[5], we understand *applied research* and *development*. Basic research deals with questions aimed at advancing knowledge, whereas the primary focus of "applied research" is on developing industrial and commercial applications. That is to say, the former makes it possible to explore a phenomenon to deepen our understanding of it, without aiming to discover specific applications. Thus, it makes it possible to surpass the limits of science, by extending the field of knowledge toward levels never reached before. The activities of such research make it possible, for example, to "lift technological locks," i.e. to "remove" the pitfalls and "bottlenecks" that prevent companies from innovating (Thiaw, 2013). For so-called "applied" research, this focuses on well-defined objects and purposes. It does not necessarily aim to advance science, but rather to

---

5 Technology: Its etymological meaning is "the study of tools and techniques", but the concept is more akin to "the application of science to the useful arts" in the sense of Bigelow (1829) who had generalized the use of the word through his emblematic work: "Elements of technology"..

achieve specific application objectives. The two forms of research are therefore distinguished by their purpose.

However, a second point of distinction can be considered: the result obtained. The result of basic research activities is a discovery, whereas the result of applied research activities is an invention. In the industrial world, applied research implies a connotation of commercialization, that is, the research work undertaken has as its main objective the finding of new scientific knowledge to fulfill specific commercialization objectives, in reference to products, processes or services (Thiaw, 2018). "*Invention is the first appearance of an idea into a new product or process, while innovation is the first attempt to convert that idea into practice*"[6] (Fagerberg, 2004).

As a result, innovation is also distinct from *discovery* and *invention*, from which it can be derived. Similarly, the terms "*discovery*" and "*invention*" appeared in the literature long before innovation (Thiaw, 2013). According to Alter (2000, p. 8–9), "*innovation represents the bringing to market and/or integration into a social milieu of inventions.*" He also believes that the inventor *or* designer[7] (of an object or an organization) may be a genius devoid of practical sense, but not the innovator, who is responsible for finding a market or a use for these discoveries, that "*invention is therefore not comparable to innovation,*" because "*the first is never mechanically followed by the second*". The entrepreneur is therefore the one who valorizes a discovery by introducing it into the company and the economy but he is not necessarily its inventor.

Subsequently, it is through the second function of technology (i.e. development) that commercial information is translated *(e.g. concerning the needs, expectations, and demands of consumers*) to introduce the technical result of applied research into the market, in the form of an innovative product or process, and therefore of an innovation. This marketing of innovation requires the operationalization of a long process including a set of successive steps, each one stamped with uncertainties, to be validated one after the other. Indeed, '*if invention is a creative idea, innovation requires the gathering of a whole set of factors such as technical*

6 "*invention is the first occurrence of an idea for a new product or process, while innovation is the first attempt to carry it out into practice*" Fagerberg (2004).

7 The designer is "anyone who imagines some arrangement to change an existing situation into a preferred one" (Simon, 1991, p. 113).

skills, the availability of financial resources, commercial and legal skills, etc.' (Encaoua, 2010).

As for technology, which refers to applied research, it underlies an association between scientific theory (knowledge) and practical competence (empirical). In this sense, scientific understanding allows for the enrichment of techniques.

Based on this analysis, the co-evolution between "Science, Technology and Innovation" appears as a parallel evolution between "fundamental research" and "applied research". It suggests that it is from this bidirectional process that innovation is generated and contributes to sustaining economic growth. Moreover, it is in this context that innovation is beneficial and can contribute to boosting the competitiveness of companies and nations. This also explains the proliferation of development policies in favor of innovation in advanced countries, but also those issued to develop and strengthen inter-organizational collaborative relationships around R&D between researchers (research laboratories, universities), industrial companies (large groups and innovative SMEs), and institutional actors (Thiaw, 2021). We are talking here about innovation networks such as clusters, technopoles, industrial districts, innovative environments, local production systems, competitive clusters, and other forms of innovation ecosystems.

Within the framework of this tripartite co-evolution, public policy intervention aims to simultaneously propel the three variables of science, technology, and innovation. More specifically, it is about promoting innovation as a result of co-evolution, as well as the sharing of knowledge and skills between different socio-economic actors from both spheres (basic and applied research). However, the spectrum for developing the activities is wide. It can range from basic research (collaboration between several public and private research laboratories) to applied research subsidized by public authorities under the condition of a certain level of cooperation between partners working together to develop new technologies.

2.2. Classic forms of innovation networks

Territorial innovation networks (TINs) to implement the concept of localized innovation refer to networks that are both dedicated to portions of territories (local, regional, national, etc.) and which are the result of efforts made by public authorities to promote innovation and territorial development dynamics (Thiaw, 2013). From our research on their theoretical foundations we found that this form of economic activity location has existed for more than a century, with Alfred Marshall's (1890) work on industrial districts as a prelude. Later, Marshall's industrial districts became, in a general way, the theoretical basis of innovation networks and influenced the models that have since been conceptualized in national economies.

This diversity of concepts makes it difficult to understand the phenomenon and leads to the establishment of different classifications. Our study of the literature has resulted in a classification that considers a logic of historical evolution which unfolds with the progress of economies and the transmutations of the development priorities of the times. Thus, since economic progress was once dependent on the density of the production industry, the networks of the time were rather 'production'-oriented: Italian industrial districts (Bagnasco & Trigilia, 1977, 1984; Becattini, 1979, 1989), the flexible specialization of Piore and Sabel (1984), Benko et al. (1996), the new industrial spaces of Scott (1988), Storper and Scott (1988), Storper (1997), and the local productive systems (Courlet, 1994), etc.

Maillat (2003, p. 8) defines the territorial production systems (TPS) as *'a set characterized by the proximity of productive units in the broadest sense (industrial and service companies, research and training centers, interface organizations, professional organizations, etc.), which maintain market and non-market relationships of varying degrees of intensity' (Gilly, 1987)* and which generate a productive dynamic of ensembles. These network models are different from the others because they are derived from local development theory (Chabault, 2006).

Subsequently, the consolidation of innovation as a central driver of economic growth and the competitiveness of firms make way for networks that are more marked by the preponderance of innovation: innovative environments (Maillat, 1993), Porter's clusters (1990, 1998), French competitiveness clusters (Thiaw, 2013), etc. Thus, toward the beginning of the 1990s, the acceleration of the process of globalization of economies and the metamorphosis of the competitiveness of companies, as well as the spectrums of competition, ended up raising questions about the role of *territorial networks* in an economy where ICTs, as facilitators of exchanges, make it possible to go beyond the natural physical borders of countries.

Indeed, since these networks provide countries with added value that promotes the performance of firms and stimulates their growth (Rocha, 2004), the changing contours of the modern economy must necessarily have an impact on their forms and the way in which they generate competitiveness factors. Thus, in this context, innovation has once again become the central theme of the new forms of *territorial networks* and has been highlighted as an important element in the competitiveness of companies and the economic growth of countries. These new models are moving toward a point of convergence that treats the development prospects of territories according to paradigms based on the 'innovation' variable. Based on innovation, this new system of territorial configuration is presented as '*the organization of a set of actors and entities (companies, public and private organizations, institutions) interacting to generate together new economically useful knowledge, which they use and disseminate in their production and innovation processes*' (Thiaw, 2013).

Thus, innovation coupled with the notion of territory makes it possible to broaden the initial concept of the territorial system of production (STP) for the benefit of the territorial system of innovation (STI). It is even a construct used as a generic name to evoke the different regional models of innovation in which local institutional dynamics play a significant role (Moulaert & Sekia, 2003 p. 291). These ITSs can be consolidated into the following two groups of approaches:

- — Economic approaches based on Marshall's (1890 1919) concept of the external economy: Porter's Cluster (1990, 1998, 2004), Krugman's New Geographic Economics (1991);
- — Network approaches like the Geography of Innovation, Innovative Milieux of Aydalot and GREMI researchers, the Nordic School of Innovation and Learning, and the institutional approach.

However, if we retain this distinction between Territorial Production Systems (TPS) and Territorial Innovation Systems (TIS) based on a focus on the evolution of the models' precepts (Chabault, 2006), other typologies based on distinct classification criteria also exist and can be considered. This is the case of the typology highlighted by Moulaert and Sekia (2003), which distinguishes three groups (*see* Box 1).

Box 1 Classification of territorial innovation systems models

Based on the existing literature, Moulaert and Sekia (2003) distinguished three families of innovation territory models.

The first family includes the French model of "Milieux innovateurs," which was the basis of the synthesis carried out by GREMI (Aydalot, 1986), the models of Industrial Districts, and the Local Production Systems. According to both authors, the endogeneity of the institutions that play a primordial role in the research processes constitutes one of the major characteristics shared in this group. These networks are also characterized by their great capacity to generate innovative and dynamic enterprises, and the prominent place they give to cooperation and partnership relations during the innovation process.

The second group is more in line with the literature about the "Broader Systems of Innovation" considered by Edquist (1997) as a transfer of the institutional coordination principles of sectoral and national innovation systems to a regionalized level of development or, according to Cooke (1996), an evolutionary interpretation of the "Regional Learning Economy" (Cook & Morgan, 1998).

The third model identified relates to the work of the Californian School of Economic Geography, which specifies the "new industrial spaces" (Stopper & Scott, 1988), Saxenian (1994). It includes a concept that has fewer similarities with the regional economy, but which is close to the innovation cluster model developed by Porter (1990, 1998). This is the Spatial Innovation Cluster model.

[1] *GREMI: Groupe de recherche européen sur les milieux innovateurs (European Research Group on Innovative Environments)*

3. What conceptual articulation for "nomadic" innovation networks?

From what has been said above, it appears that establishing collaborative relationships without a spatial basis is possible. Whether on a transregional or interregional scale, companies are important actors in the structuring of networks. By studying the evolution of the structuring of their inter-organizational relations, we notice explanatory factors for a possible new trend of clusters, giving way to a preponderant role of the impact of digital transitions, and which would not leave indifferent the conditions in which innovation networks are formed. Indeed, in the same way that firms expand toward a particular industry in vogue, the phenomenon of the increasingly persistent adoption of the opportunities brought by ICT to cope with the hazards of distancing and the forced confinements linked to the Covid-19 pandemic can also be considered as a transition factor likely to influence the dynamics of networks. This is because, during these periods of the forced distancing of actors, most firms continued operating, ignoring the inherent barriers. Companies that belonged to the same innovation network also continued to work in a distanced way, using digital technologies to keep in touch with other stakeholders.

From a literary point of view, few works have approached the issue of innovation networks from the perspective of analyzing interrelationships based on the virtual and the non-localization of actors. As mentioned above, the literature has focused more on the study of inter-organizational collaboration relationships emanating from the geographical proximity of actors, and therefore from their spatial location. Nowadays, in the same way that the digital revolution (*computerization of activities and advent of the Internet*) has enabled the metamorphosis of a company's organization, digital technologies and the adoption of their modern solutions are leading today's organizations to opt for networking practices and a massive outsourcing of part of their activities. From then on, the "new economy" advocates organizational modes being the antithesis of traditional practices inherited, for example, from "Fordism," such as hierarchization, concentration of large production units, standardized mass production, etc. Instead, it is based on work in autonomous teams, the networking of companies, or flexibility and "customization" (Muet, 2006). We can notice similar changes affecting relationships between firms within networks, whether they involve links between competing firms (coopetition), customers, or suppliers.

Subsequently, "nomadic" cluster forms could resemble innovative networks that existed in the IT sector and congregate companies within networks (Cisco, IBM, Microsoft, Hewlett Packard, etc.). Therefore, it would refer to a structuring around the Internet and digital solutions that would allow a network of organizations (companies, research laboratories, and other bodies) to form partnerships that would foster innovation.

3.1- Forms and characteristics of "nomadic" innovation networks

Innovation networks play an active role in the development and attractiveness of their territories. They can take several forms, but the quintessence of their existence remains the same: to stimulate territorial development by promoting the interconnection of the socio-economic actors. Thus, it is a matter of exploiting the positive externalities generated through collaborative relationships.

In addressing an innovative issue related to both notions of territory and digital technology in order to consider a nomadic cluster form, we want to sketch a new research issue. By a territorial cluster, we mean a community of organized actors belonging to a network and based nearby, aiming to exploit their complementarities. This type of territorial and innovation ecosystem is currently undergoing a threefold change. First, the transmutation of markets. Second, the continuous transformation of territories. And finally, the socio-economic stakeholders themselves. Therefore, new clusters are emerging nowadays to meet the present-day realities.

"Nomadic clusters" or virtual innovation networks, are defined as translocal innovation spaces, based on the pooling of knowledge and skills for the benefit of actors from industry (companies), the academic sector (universities, research laboratories), and institutions (state bodies, public agencies, associations, etc.) deciding to collaborate while not necessarily being located nearby in the same physical space. This virtualization trend is a continuation of recent trends of clusters favoring the mutualization of services within local spaces in order to try out new modes of innovation based on the sharing of know-how and skills.

Thus, network virtualization extends the potential for increasing the stock of the available intellectual capital of the organizations involved. As the OECD reminds us, innovation is the result of an accumulation process by which firms increase their stock of intellectual capital (OECD, 2019; Ahmad & Seymour, 2008). To innovate, firms create, associate, and recombine a set of assets such as technology, specialized skills and know-how, data and trademarks, organizational arrangements and processes, or business models and networks (OECD, 2021). Knowing that it is now proven that access to knowledge and skills is facilitated by membership of a network and the geographical proximity with other actors, this accumulation process could be optimized by the virtualization of networks.

Because in this very case, the virtual innovation network extends these possibilities of access to assets beyond the only positive externalities permitted by geographical proximity, on the assumption that digital solutions eliminate distances to potential partners and grant access to distant knowledge and skills.

From then on, we consider the advent of nomadic clusters that are materialized by the networking of actors forming innovation spaces and efficient services, with the combination of a localized physical basis (*territorial basis*) supported by remote working mechanisms (*virtual basis*).

The territorial basis is composed of infrastructure and diverse resources (material, human, etc.) based on an organization of integrated services deployed by various actors who are physically distant. It is managed by the governance body of the network and by animation services.

The second non-physical and virtual basis relies on digital solutions to facilitate collaboration between actors and the sharing of their knowledge. It concentrates the cooperation activities deployed by the network's stakeholders working together on collaborative innovation processes.

3.2- *Possible application criteria (for nomadic clusters):* Virtualization, sharing of a common industry, complementarity, common interests, and value chain

Thus, the COVID-19 pandemic has accelerated the digital transformation of companies (especially SMEs) and boosted their engagement in innovation activities. As a consequence, it has made them ready to engage in a "virtual" network mode, with the possibility of having geographically distant companies work together. As they were seeking to adapt to the situation led by the pandemic, survive and sustain their activities, companies have accelerated the dematerialization of their operations and business processes. Similarly, we have witnessed the development and expansion of a range of remote and online work platforms (Zoom, Google Meet, Microsoft Teams, Cisco Webex Meetings, Blue Jeans), allowing economic actors to have a continuity of interrelations with their markets, partners, suppliers, and customers. This is even more the case since these changes made by companies in strengthening their digital capabilities are likely to last over time in view of the expected benefits and the significant investments made. According to a study made by Facebook, the OECD, and the World Bank (2020), almost 78 % of the companies concerned affirm that these improvements will remain permanent.

Concerning the innovation ecosystems, these play an essential role in the dynamics of innovations and their processes of generation. The success of innovations depends on the quality of inter-organizational collaborative relationships within the network. For example, in the French competitiveness cluster model (2005), collaborations between academic and industrial actors were promoted to generate innovations ready for market access, whereas this was not possible during the first phase (2005–2008) and second phase (2009–2012), because the structuring of the clusters presented notable pitfalls for innovation at that time (cf. reports from CM International & Boston Consulting Group, 2008; and Bearing Point-Erding-Technopolis, 2012). In fact, the collaborative relationships could not cover the entire process which fades once prototypes are acquired (Thiaw, 2013). The corrective measures brought by phase 3 of the French competitiveness cluster policy (2013–2018) have therefore improved the model by complementing the collaborative innovation process with an orientation toward economic outlets and employment creation.

In virtual mode, "nomadic" clusters represent an optimized model of classic innovation networks. By relying on complete communication channels, they extend the scope of cooperation opportunities and allow the establishment of consortia (collaborative relationships) with physically distant actors. The facilitation of the exchanges allowed by this model also results in an optimized quality of knowledge flow between stakeholders. As we already know, the interest and benefit of networks and cooperative innovation processes lies in the exploitation of the knowledge and skills of the actors involved, namely their knowledge capital (Laperche, 2018), as well as the expertise and know-how that stem from them.

On the other hand, the nomadic cluster can originate from the interconnection between different innovation ecosystems. In this context, the set of gathered stakeholders, which is formed into a consolidated network, allows interactions between heterogeneous actors around the innovation process. The application criteria for these original clusters are not far removed from those considering traditional innovation networks of the type of cluster (Porter, 1994). Like them, the nomadic cluster aims to exploit externalities and complementarities between actors hoping to complete their knowledge bases. Furthermore, they also offer the possibility of doing so on a larger scale of space by not limiting their target only to geographically close actors. In other words, we are considering the opportunity of doing similar activities, but by seeking to expand the options for collaboration beyond the local space and considering additional criteria other than territory and the geographical proximity of actors. As mentioned above, these criteria can be the proximity of a sector, the existence of close competences comprising a shared value chain of an industry, etc.

Thus, the main distinction between traditional and nomadic clusters concerns the non-localization of the network actors, i.e. their distancing and the use of digital technologies and sophisticated means of communication to promote telework. For this reason, nomadic clusters will help to increase business performance. As Coenon and Kok (2014) advocate, telecommuting (*or remote working*) tends to maximize the performance of teams involved in developing new projects. While the organization of periodic meetings to maintain face-to-face exchanges is preached (ibid.), it is not necessarily decisive for the success of innovation processes. Indeed, the transmission of tacit knowledge that is useful for innovation does not necessarily require the location of actors and geographical proximity (Massard & Torre, 2004). In fact, it is recognized that the transmission of knowledge within a group of actors in the same sector of activity is facilitated (ibid.).

Conclusion

By discussing the co-evolution between science, technology, and innovation (ST-I) in the digital era and in an environment marked by the stabilization of knowledge and the immaterial economy, we encourage the establishment of virtual innovation networks or so-called nomadic clusters. More precisely, it is an incentive to a non-forcibly-territorialized concentration of innovation dynamics conducive to growth and economic development. That is to say, the actors in this type of network do not group together according to a spatial and local logic. As the transformations of the digital revolution (Shift Project, 2018) have impacts on the organization of our society and the development modalities of innovation systems, this model of cluster structuring is a dedicated response.

This does not mean calling into question the classic model of clusters based on the promotion of the “local” and the search for complementarity between actors who are geographically nearby, as advocated by certain authors (Soltwedel & Laaser, 2003; Cairnrcross, 2001). Nonetheless, if spatial proximity remains fundamental in the dynamics of collaborative innovation (Aouinaït, 2021; Thiaw, 2013; Uzunidis, 2010), this obvious and persistent trend toward virtualization seems inescapable, as recent evolution disrupts the organization of our society and its socio-economic structures. Moreover, it legitimately questions the relevance of maintaining this "local thesis" (Santamaria et al., 2021; Bottazi & Peri, 2003; Audretsch & Feldman, 1996; Jaffe, 1989) and pushes us to explore modern and complementary models.

Indeed, the crisis produced by the Covid-19 pandemic and its effects guided public authorities to react by implementing measures aimed at limiting the damage to health and economic situations. Among these, social distancing, and successive confinements (Wang et al., 2020) have allowed the development of remote work using the possibilities allowed by digital technologies (Aguilera et al., 2016; Pontier, 2014; Taskin, 2003). With these digital solutions, it becomes achievable to remove physical boundaries while guaranteeing an optimized level of work quality for socio-economic actors (Coenen & Kok, 2014).

This is what led us to question the framing angle of the models of territorialization of innovation, by considering the emergence of these concepts of so-called "translocal" and virtual innovation networks, which would be nomadic (Thiaw, 2018). Indeed, it is in the continuity of the attempts of researchers, practitioners, and public authorities to adapt to the permanent evolution of the economic environment by always proposing innovative models such as open innovation (Chesbrough, 2006; Laperche 2017), collaborative platforms, the system of integrated services, coworking spaces, FabLabs and Living Labs (Béjean et al., 2021), business incubators, resource and training centers, etc., that we sketch out the proposal of nomadic clusters. This model extends the concept of the classic cluster model by incorporating, in addition to the territorial and local dimension, remote work modalities. Thus, in addition to exploiting externalities between geographically close actors and focusing on complementarities and the sharing of common interests, the aim is to facilitate the transmission of knowledge that is useful to the innovation process while increasing the scope of possibilities by reaching physically distant actors. It is therefore an increase in the potential of the co-evolution between science, technology, and innovation by bringing together distant actors to form an innovation network.

In addition to the advantages linked to the reduction in costs (travel, equipment) and the speed of execution allowed by this new way of networking (decisions, activity management), some disadvantages of the nomadic cluster model, which can certainly be overcome, can be considered. They concern risks inherent to digital security, which may be likely to lead to cyber attacks by malicious actors, but also the digital gaps that are the feature of some ill-prepared or ill-equipped companies (OECD, 2021). Therefore, prior preparation is essential, particularly in terms of raising awareness among stakeholders, acquiring the needed skills, making the necessary investments, and securing and locking down data. It is at both the macro and micro levels that preparation and awareness actions must take place, as is currently the case with the proactive role of public authorities in the digital transformation of companies (OECD, 2021). Thus, it is necessary to include the promotion of nomadic clusters among the measures that aim to create a National Innovation System (Laperche et al., 2019). The main role of the latter is to organize the actors of a country by encouraging their connection and the creation of interactions between them to promote the generation of innovations.

As promising as it is, this model of nomadic innovation networks deserves to be perfected. Indeed, the implications of our work aimed at proposing an innovative model of virtual clusters suggest very interesting future research perspectives that could try to answer some remaining questions. They will contribute to giving this concept a more accomplished design and to answer issues related to the ideal articulations to be prioritized for these translocal innovation spaces, to the forms of inter-organizational collaboration to be promoted in a virtual environment, to integration services to be set up, to possible emergence modalities, to the probable pitfalls and key success factors, or to the possible successes and brakes of the innovation processes within them.

References

Aguilera, A., Lethiais, V., Rallet, A., & Proulhac, L. (2016). Le télétravail, un objet sans désir?. *Revue d'Economie Regionale Urbaine,* (1), 245–266.

Ahmad, N., & Seymour, R. (2008). "Defining entrepreneurial activity: Definitions supporting frameworks for data collection". OECD Statistics Working Papers, No. 2008/01, OECD Publishing, Paris, https://doi.org/10.1787/243164686763.

Alter, N. (2000). *La gestion du désordre dans l'entreprise*, Nouvelle édition. Paris: L'Harmattan, 207 p.

Aouinaït, C. (2021). Innovation collaborative et innovation ouverte : caractéristiques de leur mise en œuvre. *Technologie et innovation, 6*(1), 1–12.

Audretsch, D. B., & Feldman, M. P. (1996). R&D spillovers and the geography of innovation and production. *American Economic Review, 86*(3), 630–640. https://doi.org/10.2307/2118216

Aydalot, P. (Ed.). (1986). *Milieux innovateurs en Europe*. Paris: GREMI.

Bagnasco, A. (1977), *Le tre Italie*, Bologna, Il Mulino.

Bagnasco, A. (1988), *La costruzione sociale del mercato*, Bologna, Il Mulino.

Bagnasco, A., & Trigilia C., (1984). *Società e politica nelle aree di piccola impresa: il caso di Bassano*. Arsenale: Venise.

Bearing Point-Erding-Technopolis ITD. (2012). Rapport d'évaluation des Pôles de Compétitivité.

Becattini, G. (1979). Dal settore industriale al distretto industriale. Alcune considération sull'unità di indagine dell'economia industriale. *Rivista di Economia e Politica Industriale, 2*, 7–21.

Becattini, G. (1987). *Mercato e forze locali : il distretto industriale*, Bologna, Il mulino.

Becattini, G. (1989). « riflessioni sul distretto industriale marshalliano come conceto socio-economico » Stato e Mercato, avril 1989, pp. 111–128. (I.e. réflexions sur le district industriel marshallien comme concept socio-économique)

Behfar, S. K., Turkina, E., & Burger-Helmchen, T. (2018). Knowledge management in OSS communities: Relationship between dense and sparse network structures. *International Journal of Information Management, 38*(1), 167–174.

Béjean, M., Picard, R., & Bréda, G. (2021). Living labs, innovation collaborative et écosystèmes : le cas de l'initiative « Concept Maturity Levels » dans les Medtech. Innovations, https://doi.org/10.3917/inno.pr2.0105

Benko, G., Dunford, M., & Lipiez, A. (1996). Les districts Industriels revisités. In Pecqueur, B. (Eds.), *Dynamiques territoriales et mutations économiques*. L'Harmattan. Dynamiques territoriales et mutations économiques.

Bigelow, J. (1829). Elements of Technology. (Eds), *G. L. and W. Hilliard.*

Bottazzi, L., & Peri, G., (2003). Innovation and spillovers in regions: Evidence from European patent data. *European Economic Review, 47*(4), 687–710.

Cairncross, F. (2001). *The death of distance: How the communications revolution is changing our* (Harvard Bu).

Chabault, D. (2006). Les systèmes territoriaux de production : revue de littérature et approches théoriques d'un concept évolutif. *Cahiers de Recherche du CERMAT, 32* p., en ligne : http://cermat.iae.univ-tours.fr/IMG/pdf/Chabault-20061.pdf

Chesbrough, H. (2006). *Open innovation: The new imperative for creating and profiting from technology* (Harvard Bu).

Chesbrough, H., & Bogers, M. (2014). Explicating open innovation: Clarifying an emerging paradigm for understanding innovation. In Chesbrough, H., Vanhaverbeke, W., & West, J. (Eds.), *New frontiers in open innovation*. Oxford: Oxford University Press, Forthcoming: 3–28.

Christensen, J. L. (2001). Changes in Danish innovation policy: Responses to the challenges of a dynamic business environment.

CM International & Boston Consulting Group. (2008). L'évaluation des pôles de compétitivité 2005–2008, La documentation française, 112 pages.

Coenen, M., & Kok, R. A. W. (2014). Workplace flexibility and new product development performance : The role of telework and flexible work schedules. *European Management Journal, 32*(4), 564–576. https://doi.org/10.1016/j.emj.2013.12.003

Cooke, P. & Morgan, K. (1998). *The Associational Economy*, Oxford: Oxford University Press.

Cooke, P. (1996). Networking for Competitive Advantage. Dublin: National Economic and Social Council.

Courlet, C. (1994). Les systèmes productifs localisés, de quoi parle-t-on? *Industrie, territoire et politiques publiques,* 13–32.

Di Méo, G., & Buléon, P. (2005). *L'espace social. Lecture géographique des sociétés*. Paris : Armand Colin.

Dupouët, O., Bernela, B., & Ferru, M. (2019). Network dynamics and communities in applied biomedical research. *Journal of Innovation Economics & Management, 30*(3), 213. https://doi.org/10.3917/jie.pr1.0053

Eagar, R., Van Oene, F., Boulton, C., Roos, D., & Dekeyser, C. (2011). The future of innovation management: The next 10 years. *Prism, 1*, 21–37.

Encaoua, D. (2010). Interactions science-technologie : quelles politiques publiques ?. *Revue française d'économie, 25*(4), 75–119.

Fagerberg, J. (2004). Innovation: A guide to the literature. In *The Oxford handbook of innovation* (pp. 1–26). https://doi.org/10.1093/oxfordhb/9780199286805.003.0001

Foray, D. (2000). *L'économie de la connaissance*. Paris: Edition La Découverte & Syros.

Gilly, J. P. (1987). Espace productifs locaux, politique d'emploi des firmes et transformations du rapport salarial. In Fourcade, C. (Eds.), *Industries et régions*. Paris: Economica, pp. 45–53.

Grange, C., & Sponem, S. (2021). Les travailleurs du savoir face au bouleversement technologique. *Gestion, 1*(1), 42–49. https://doi.org/10.3917/riges.461.0042

Granstrand, O., & Holgersson, M. (2020). Innovation ecosystems: A conceptual review and a new definition. *Technovation*, 90–91(May 2019). https://doi.org/10.1016/j.technovation.2019.102098

Haudeville, B., & Le Bas, C. (2016). « L'innovation frugale, paradigme technologique naissant ou nouveau modèle d'innovation ? ». *Innovations, 3*/2016 (n° 51), 9–25.

INSEE. (2015). Activité, chômage, emploi et inactivité en 2014, Enquête emploi en continu, Insee Résultats – No 173, Paru le 28/10/2015.

Jaffe, A. B. (1989). Real effects of academic research. *American Economic Review, 79*(5), 957–970.

Krugman, P. (1991). *Trade and geography*. Cambridge: MIT Press.

Laperche, B. (2017). *Enterprise knowledge capital*. John Wiley & Sons.

Laperche, B. (2018). *Le capital savoir de l'entreprise* (Vol. 16). ISTE Group.

Laperche, B., & Lefebvre, G. (2012). The globalization of Research & Development in industrial corporations: Towards "reverse innovation": The cases of General Electric and Renault. *Journal of Innovation Economics & Management, 2*(2), 53–79. https://doi.org/10.3917/jie.010.0053

Laperche, B., Lima, M., Seuillet, E., & Trousse, B. (2019). Ecosystèmes d'innovation : regards croisés des acteurs clés (No. hal — 02418541).

Levy, M., & Jouyet, P. (2006). L'économie de l'immatériel, La croissance de demain, Rapport de la commission sur l'économie de l'immatériel du Ministère de l'Economie et des Finance de la France, Décembre 2006.

Loilier, A., & Tellier, A. (2005). Structure, fonctionnement et performance des réseaux territorialisés d'innovation : bilan et perspectives de recherche, CR 35, Ecole de Management de Normandie.

Maillat, D. (2003). Développement des systèmes territoriaux de production, compétitivité et innovation, Acte du colloque international de développement local : le développement local dans la perspective du développement humain, Campo Grande, Brésil 25–28 novembre 2003.

Maillat, D., Quevit, M., & Senn, L. (1993). Réseau d'innovation et milieux innovateurs : un pari pour le développement régional. Editions de la Division économique et sociale, Université de Neuchâtel (GREMI)/ EDES 1993.

Marshall, A. (1890). *Principes d'économie politique*. Paris: Giard et Brière, 1ere édition française, 1906.

Marshall, A. (1919). Industry and trade, Traduction française de Leduc C. (1934), Edition Marcel Giard, p. 442, Paris.

Massard, N., & Torre, A. (2004). Proximité géographique et innovation. Economie de Proximités, Hermes science, 2-7462-0855-5. ⟨hal-02833509⟩

Mongo, M. (2021). Services innovants et action publique pour dynamiser les économies territoriales : éléments d'analyse. *Technologie et Innovation, 6*(1), 1–11.

Moulaert, F., & Sekia, F. (2003). Territorial innovation models: A critical survey. *Regional Studies, 37*(3), 289–302.

Muet, P. (2006). Impacts économiques de la révolution numérique. *Revue économique, 3*(3), 347–375. https://doi.org/10.3917/reco.573.0347

OCDE. (2019). Perspectives économiques de l'OCDE, Volume 2020, Numéro, OECD Publishing.

OCDE. (2021). Perspectives de l'OCDE sur les PME et l'entrepreneuriat 2021, chapitre 4 : La crise du COVID-19 : un accélérateur de l'innovation et de l'entrepreneuriat? Paris: OECD Publishing. https://doi.org/10.1787/dbe26a97-fr

Piore, M., & Sabel, C. F. (1984). The second industrial divide: Possibilities for prosperity. *The Journal of American History, 73*, p. 355. New York: Basic Books.

Polèse, M. (1974). Le secteur tertiaire et le développement économique régional : vers un modèle opérationnel des activités motrices. *L'Actualité économique, 50*(4), octobre–décembre 1974, pp. 475–490.

Pontier, M. (2014). Télétravail indépendant ou télétravail salarié : quelles modalités de contrôle et quel degré d'autonomie. *La Revue Des Sciences de Gestion, 265*, 31–39.

Porter, M. E. (1990). *The Competitive Advantage of Nations. Free Press, New York*

Porter, M. E. (1993). *L'avantage concurrentiel des nations [1990]*. Paris: Intereditions.

Porter, M. E. (1994). The role of location in competition. *Journal of the Economics of Business, 1(1),* 35–39.

Porter, M. E. (1998). Clusters and the new economics of competition. *Harvard Business Review, 76*(6), 77–90.

Porter, M. E. (2000). Locations, clusters, and company strategy. In Clark, G. L., Feldman, M. P., et Gertler, M. S. (Eds.), *The Oxford handbook of economic geography*. Oxford: Oxford University Press, 253–274.

Porter, M. E. (2004). Building the microeconomic foundations of prosperity: Findings from the business competitiveness index'. In Porter, M. E., Schwab, K., Sala-i-Martin, X., & Lopez-Claros, A. (Eds.), *The Global Competitiveness Report 2004–2005*. New York: Palgrave Macmillan, World Economic Forum, pp. 19–50.

Radjou, N., & Prabhu, J. (2013). « *L'innovation jugaad, redevenons ingénieux* ». éditions Diateino.

Rocha, H. O. (2004). Entrepreneurship and development: The role of clusters, a literature review. *Small Business Economics, 23*(5), 363–400.

Saives, A. L. (2002). *Territoire et compétitivité de l'entreprise*. Paris: L'Harmattan.

Saives, A., & Desmarteau, R. H. (2010). Milieux, modèles d'affaires et territorialisation des entreprises : le cas de l'agroalimentaire au Québec. In Actes de la XIXème Conférence Internationale de Management Stratégique.

Santamaría, L., Jesús, M., & Rodríguez, A. (2021). Failed and successful innovations: The role of geographic proximity and international diversity of partners in technological collaboration. *Technological Forecasting & Social Change, 166*(December 2020), 1–13. https://doi.org/10.1016/j.techfore.2021.120575

Saxenian, A. (1994). *Regional Advantage: Culture and Competition in Silicon Valley and Route 128*. Cambridge, MA: Harvard University Press.

Schumpeter, J. (1939). Business cycles: A theoretical, historical, and statistical analysis of the Capitalist Process (Vol. 2). New York. New York Toronto London : McGraw-Hill Book Company, 461. Abridged, with an introduction, by Rendigs Fels

Scott, A. J. (1988). *New industrial spaces*. London: Pion

Shift Project. (2018). Lean ICT: pour une sobriété numérique.

Simon, HA. (1996). *The Sciences of the Artificial*, 3rd ed. Cambridge, MA: The MIT Press.

Soltwedel, R., & Laaser, C. (2003). Spatial impacts of the new economy: Death of distance and decline of cities? In Pethig, R. & Rauscher, M. (Eds.), *Challenges to the world economy*. Springer, pp. 151–164. Retrieved from https://doi.org/10.1007/978-3-642-19018-6_13

Storper, M. (1997). Térritoires, flows and hierarchies in the global economy. *Aussenwirtschaft, 50*(2), 265–293.

Storper, M., & Scott, A. (1988). The geographical foundations and social regulation of flexible production complexes. In Wolch, J. & Dear, M. (Eds.), *The power of geography*. London: Allen and Unwin.

Taskin, L. (2003). Les enjeux du télétravail pour l'organisation. *Reflets et Perspectives de La Vie économique, 1*, 81–94. https://doi.org/https://doi.org/10.3917/rpve.421.0081

Thiaw, C. (2013). Innovation collaborative et orientation client/marché au sein des Pôles de compétitivité : Analyse empirique des dynamiques de projets/acteurs (Cas des Réseaux d'innovation en Région PACA), Thèse en vue de l'obtention du grade de docteur ès Sciences de Gestion, Université Nice-Sophia Antipolis, le 9 Avril 2013.

Thiaw, C. (2017). Innovation collaborative, un modèle de création de processus de coévolution entre science, technologies et innovation dans les pays émergents (Cas spécifique au Sénégal), SERGe Days, 5ème édition, 27–29 Avril 2017, Saint-Louis, Sénégal.

Thiaw, C. A. L. (2018). L'innovation localisée pour le développement économique du énégal. Paris : Édition Harmattan, 2018.

Thiaw, C. A. L. (2021). Orientation marché et innovation collaborative par les interactions université-industrie. *Technologie et innovation, 6*(1). DOI: 10.21494/ISTE.OP.2021.0591.

Thiaw, C., & Aliouat, B. (2016). Entrepreneuriat en équipe et vision partagée : Le cas des pôles de compétitivité, in Paturel Robert, Levy Thierry : L'entrepreneuriat en équipe, Presses Universitaires de Provence.

Uzunidis, D. (2008). Milieux innovateur et gestation d'un entrepreneuriat innovant. *Marché et organisations, 1*(1), 119–145. https://doi.org/10.3917/maorg.006.0119

Uzunidis, D. (2010). Innovation et Proximité : Entreprises, Entrepreneurs et Milieux innovateurs. *La Revue des Sciences de Gestion, 1*(1), 13–22. https://doi.org/10.3917/rsg.241.0013

Veltz, P. (1996). *Mondialisation, villes et territoires, L'économie d'archipel.* Paris : PUF.

Wang, Y., Wang, Y., Chen, Y., & Qin, Q. (2020). Unique epidemiological and clinical features of the emerging 2019 novel coronavirus pneumonia (COVID-19) implicate special control measures. *Journal of Medical Virology, 92*(6), 568–576. https://doi.org/10.1002/jmv.25748

WORLD BANK. (2020). A global Study on Digital Capabilities https://documents1.worldbank.org/curated/en/959181623060169420/pdf/A-Global-Study-on-Digital-Capabilities.pdf

Scientific Committee

Published titles

Vol. 31 – Laurent Adatto, Camille Aouinaït, Son Thi Kim Le and Michelle Mongo (Eds.), *Innovation Ecosystems in the New Economic Era. Digital Revolution and Ecological Transition,* 2023.

Vol. 30 – Joelle Forest et Bertrand Bocquet (dir.), *Imaginer le futur à partir du passé,* 2023.

Vol. 29 – Manon Enjolras, Mauricio Camargo, Christophe Schmitt (eds.), *Innovation and Internationalization of Small and Medium Enterprises. A Crossroads Perspective*, 2022.

Vol. 28 – Samuel-Jacques Priso-Essawe, Intégration régionale « appropriée » en Afrique. Éléments juridiques d'effectivité, 2021.

Vol. 27 – Vincent Herbert (dir.), *Tourisme et Territoires. Espaces d'innovations*, 2021.

Vol. 26 – Jean-Alain Héraud et Nathalie Popiolek, *L'organisation et la valorisation de la recherche. Problématique européenne et étude comparée de la France et de l'Allemagne*, 2021.

Vol. 25 – Stéphanie Lachaud-Martin, Corinne Marache, Julie McIntyre, Mikaël Pierre (eds.), *Wine, Networks and Scales. Intermediation in the Production, Distribution and Consumption of Wine*, 2021.

Vol. 24 – Verónica González-Araujo, Roberto-Carlos Álvarez-Delgado, Ángel Sancho-Rodríguez (eds.), *Ethics in Business Communication. New Challenges in the Digital World*, 2020.

Vol. 23 – Didier Caveng, *L'éthique dans la finance. Les banques genevoises à l'épreuve des faits*, 2019.

Vol. 22 – Andre Tiran et Dimitri Uzunidis (dir.), *Libéralisme et protectionnisme*, 2019.

Vol. 21 – Dominique Desjeux, *The anthropological perspective of the world. The inductive method illustrated*, 2018.

Vol. 20 – Benoit Bernard, *Management Public. 65 schémas pour analyser et changer les organisations publiques*, 2018.

Vol. 19 – Dimitri Uzunidis (dir.), *Recherche académique et innovation. La force productive de la science*, 2018.

Vol. 18 – Jean Vercherand, *Le marché du travail. L'esprit libéral et la revanche du politique*, 2018.

Vol. 17 – Dominique Desjeux (dir.), *L'empreinte anthropologique du monde. Méthode inductive illustrée*, 2018.

Vol. 16 – Sophie Boutillier, *Entrepreneuriat et innovation*, 2017.

Vol. 15 – Arvind Ashta, *Microfinance. Battling a Wicked Problem*, 2016.

Vol. 14 – Jean Vercherand, *Microéconomie. Une approche critique : Théorie et exercices*, 2016.

Vol. 13 – Reseau de Recherche sur l'innovation, Blandine Laperche (dir.), *Géront'innovations. Trajectoires d'innovation dans une économie vieillissante*, 2016.

Vol. 12 – Societe Internationale Jean-Baptiste Say, Dimitri Uzunidis (dir.), *Et Jean-Baptiste Say… créa l'Entrepreneur*, 2015.

Vol. 11 – Faiz Gallouj, Francois Stankiewicz (dir.), *Le DRH innovateur. Management des ressources humaines et dynamiques d'innovation*, 2014.

Vol. 10 – Charlotte Fourcroy, *Services et environnement. Les enjeux énergétiques de l'innovation dans les services*, 2014.

Vol. 9 – Remy Herrera, Wim Dierckxsens, Paulo Nakatani (eds.), *Beyond the Systemic Crisis and Capital-Led Chaos. Theoretical and Applied Studies*, 2014.

Vol. 8 – Reseau de Recherche sur l'Innovation, Sophie Boutillier, Joelle Forest, Delphine Gallaud, Blandine Laperche, Corinne Tanguy, Leila Temri (dir.), *Principes d'économie de l'innovation*, 2014.

Vol. 7 – Michel Santi, *Capitalism without Conscience*, 2013.

Vol. 6 – Arnaud Diemer, Jean-Pierre Potier, Léon Walras. *Un siècle après (1910-2010)*, 2013.

Vol. 5 – Sophie Boutillier, Faridah Djellal, Dimitri Uzunidis (Reseau de Recherche sur l'Innovation) (dir.), *L'innovation. Analyser, anticiper, agir*, 2013.

Vol. 4 – Aurelie Trouve, Marielle Berriet-Solliec, Denis Lepicier (dir.), *Le développement rural en Europe. Quel avenir pour le deuxième pilier de la Politique agricole commune* ?, 2013.

Vol. 3 – Sophie Boutillier, Faridah Djellal, Faiz Gallouj, Blandine Laperche, Dimitri Uzunidis (dir.), *L'innovation verte. De la théorie aux bonnes pratiques*, 2012.

Vol. 2 – Faridah Djellal, Faiz Gallouj, *La productivité à l'épreuve des services,* 2012.

Vol. 1 – Abdelillah Hamdouch, Sophie Reboud, Corinne Tanguy (dir.), PME, *dynamiques entrepreneuriales et innovation*, 2011.

Milton Keynes UK
Ingram Content Group UK Ltd.
UKHW021525090124
435741UK00034B/316

9 782875 745248